Pañcaratna Gītā,

by Devi Mandir Publications
5950 Highway 128
Napa, CA 94558 USA
Communications: Phone and Fax 1-707-966-2802
E-Mail swamiji@shreemaa.org
Please visit us on the World Wide Web at
http://www.shreemaa.org/

 ISBN 1-877795-51-8
Library of Congress Control Number: 2001119914

Pañcaratna Gītā
Swami Satyananda Saraswati
1. Hindu Religion. 2. Worship. 3. Spirituality.
4. Philosophy. I. Saraswati, Swami Satyananda;

Saṁskṛta and Computer Layout
by Swami Adaityananda Saraswati

Table of Contents

Introduction	1
devatā praṇām	7
viṣṇu dhyānam	9
ācamana	17
saṅkalpa	21
Gītā Māhātmya	26
Dvitīya Māhātmya	33
Bhagavadgītā Nyāsa	35
Chapter 1	44
Chapter 2	57
Chapter 3	78
Chapter 4	90
Chapter 5	101
Chapter 6	109
Chapter 7	122
Chapter 8	130
Chapter 9	139
Chapter 10	149
Chapter 11	160
Chapter 12	184
Chapter 13	190
Chapter 14	200
Chapter 15	208
Chapter 16	215
Chapter 17	222
Chapter 18	230
śrīviṣṇusahasranāmastotram	251
bhīṣmastavarājaḥ	272
anusmṛtiḥ	303
gajendra mokṣa	329
jaya jagadīśa Hare	357
praṇām	361
Appendix	
viṣṇusahasranāmāvalyāḥ with translation	366
The Pronunciation of Saṁskṛta Transliteration	493

Introduction

Even to talk about the Bhagavad Gītā stimulates consciousness. To contemplate it inspires the most noble understanding. To study every syllable of every line gives rise to an experience of personal transformation. Gītā changes from an intellectual pursuit into an intuitive expression.

Words fail to pay tribute to the stimulation attained through the Gītā. That is why every sādhu in every generation should rewrite the Gītā, retranslate it into contemporary language and symbols, which are meaningful to the understanding of that culture in terms of time, place and circumstances. Let as many interpretors as possible share their understanding of the message of Gītā with as many as wish to understand. The more individuals who accept even a portion of these noble ideals into their lives, the more this creation will manifest peace and harmony.

This interpretation of the Gītā takes its key from the first word of the first verse -- dharma. We translate dharma to be the ideal of perfection. Other translations say variously: "On the field of Kuru, on the field of sacred duty," "in the holy field of Kurukṣetra," "in the place of pilgrimage at Kurukṣetra," "on the sacred soil of Kurukṣetra," and in other ways relate to a history of events that have taken place in the distant past in a distant land, rather than to a present reality which all of us are experiencing today and every day. Dharma means the ideal of perfection. Kuru means karma, action. Kṣetra means field. Striving to attain the ideal behavior in every action, the Dharmakṣetra Kurukṣetra demands that we are each fighting our own battle. This battle is continuous. It is ongoing. It is ever present. It is the same for all of us. At any time selfishness can raise its ugly head and tell us that it is not necessary to give the most or the best. The attachments of the ego can dramatically call out, "What's in it for me!"

And therefore, it is necessary to study the Bhagavad Gītā as it relates to our own personal struggle, not necessarily how Arjuna resolved his dilemma. More importantly, how am I going to solve mine.Hence a new translation. This translation strives toward the ideal. It is our aspiration to define every word, every name of every character, every attribute of every participant, in its highest idyllic sense. We may stretch the limits of the Grammarian's patience, we may step on the toes of the Historian's revelations, we may even fail to concur with sectarian theology, and even the accepted dogmas of academic philosophy, but we are seeking the highest ideal in every word we are reading.

Therefore, a new translation. We are searching for inspiration in every verse of the Gītā. Enough of the histories of yesterday. We are looking for what can be applied to today. The Mahābhārata is extremely entertaining. It is without doubt epic poetry. It conveys the history of a people, the succession of a lineage, the struggles of a family, along with being a repository of literature, theology, philosophy -- a true epic.

The Bhagavad Gītā is contained in one small part of the Mahābhārata. It comprises a mere 700 hundred verses of an epic tome 100,000 verses long. Yet it has synthesized Vedic Philosophy so succinctly that it has become the most widely translated book of Saṁskṛta literature.

The allegory as we share it tells the story of a blind king whose name literally means "Custodian of the Nation or Whose Nation Continues." Practically he plays the part of "Blind Ambition." His oldest son is named "Defender of Evil," Duryodhana, who is selfishness incarnate. Defender of Evil is constantly plotting how to deprive his cousins, the Sons of Who is Without Prejudice, Pāṇḍavas, of their share of the kingdom.

Just look at the actual etymology of some of the names of the cast of characters mentioned in the first chapter.

Commanders of the forces of Darkness:

Dṛtarāṣṭra	Custodian of the Nation or Blind Ambition
Duryodhana	Defender of Evil
Droṇa	Who injures his foes with Weapons
Bhīṣma	Who Rules Fear
Karṇa	Who listens to others, or from Kṛ Who thinks himself the Doer
Aśvatthāmā	Who has the strength of a horse, or the obstinacy of a horse

Commanders of the forces of Light:

Pāṇḍu	Brother of Dṛtarāṣṭra, Literally Who has no Color, or Who is without Prejudice
Yudiṣṭhira	Who remains committed to dharma, the Ideal of Perfection
Arjuna	Clarity of Pure Devotion
Dṛṣṭaketu	Continuity of Light
Sahadeva	Equal to the Gods
Virāṭa	Brilliantly shining
Śaibya	Son of unselfishness
Kuntibhoja	Who Enjoys Taking Away the Deficiency of Others

Even the name of Kṛṣṇa must be understood in its most divine sense.

ककार कारण देह रकार सुक्ष्म देह स्याद् ।
इषा शब्द अदिपतिः ण प्रतक्षरूप प्रकाश ॥

kakāra kāraṇa deha rakāra sukṣma deha syād
iṣā śabda adipatḥi ṇa pratakṣarūpa prakāśa
The letter ka means the Causal Body. The letter ra means the Subtle Body. The word iṣā means the Supreme Lord of All. The syllable ṇa is the illumination of the perceivable form.

कृंकार सर्व कर्म स्याद् इष शब्द चेतन्य प्रकाश ।
णः पद व्याक्ति रूप कृष्णार्थ सृष्टि परा ॥

kṛṁkāra sarva karma syād iṣa śabda cetanya prakāśa
ṇaḥ pada vyākti rūpa kṛṣṇārtha sṛiṣṭi parā
The meaning of the letter kṛṁ is the One Who Performs all Action. The word iṣa means the illumination of Consciousness. The syllable ṇa means individual form. The meaning of the word Kṛṣṇa is He Who is Beyond Creation.

कृषि शब्द धर्मक्षेत्र चास णा पद्म व्याक्ति फूल प्रकाश ।
कृष्ण सृष्टि माली कर्तव्यक् सर्व कर्म फाल प्रदाम् ॥

kṛṣi śabda dharmakṣetra cāsa
ṇā padma vyākti phūla prakāśa
kṛṣṇa sṛṣṭi mālī kartavyak sarva karma phāla pradām
The meaning of the word kṛṣi is the Cultivator of the Field of the Ideals of Perfection. The meaning of the syllable ṇā is the flowering of each and every flower. Kṛṣṇa is responsible as the Gardener of Creation, and grants the fruit of all actions.

क पदार्थ आदि कारण ऋषि शब्द ज्ञान पृथक् प्रकाश ।
णा मूलार्थ परं परा व्याक्ति कृष्ण नित्य समाष्ठि रूप ॥

ka padārtha ādi kāraṇa ṛṣi śabda jñāna pṛthak prakāśa
ṇā mūlārtha paraṁ parā vyākti kṛṣṇa nitya samāṣṭi rūpa

The meaning of the syllable ka is the First Cause. The meaning of the word ṛṣi is Who illuminates Wisdom again. The root meaning of ṇā is the individual most supreme. Kṛṣṇa is the Eternal Form of the Universe.

As you can see, the understanding of the names of the cast of characters is of paramount importance -- just who is conducting this dialogue with whom. Who are the opponents in the battle, and what is this "Kingdom" they are seeking to win? Especially throughout the discussion, Kṛṣṇa calls Arjuna by many names which describe his qualities, his attainments, and depict the epitome of respect with which a guru instructs his disciple. In return Arjuna addresses his Guru Kṛṣṇa with various epithets which convey the sense of privilege from a disciple receiving valuable instruction from the Guru he conceives to be the incarnation of the Respected Supreme Divinity of all creation.

These names and qualities are extremely valuable to an understanding of the relationship between Guru and disciple, and also add a significant dimension to the understanding of the text. For that reason they have all been translated and included in the present text, along with an identification as to whether they apply to Kṛṣṇa or Arjuna, so that the reader can be free from any confusion. The Respected Supreme Divinity, as a name of Kṛṣṇa, and Clarity of Pure Devotion, as a name of Arjuna, have been left without identification because of their repetitious use, and a complete Glossary of Names has been added as an Appendix.

The ideal of perfection is constantly evolving, changing its form according to the variety of circumstances which cause the interaction of all that lives. Bhagavad Gītā sings a Song of inspiration and conveys the greatest blessings of purity and clarity in understanding that Ideal. What is Devotion? What is Wisdom? How do the paths intertwine?

Understanding Kṛṣṇa to be the Supreme Lord of all Action, and Arjuna the Clarity of Pure Devotion struggling to manifest the ideal behavior in every action, let us tune into the dialogue which will inspire all of life to become one with the Soul of Existence.

Swami Satyananda Saraswati
Napa, California, 1997

Preface to the Third Edition

It is the year 2003. Nations are pointing weapons of mass destruction at each other, terrorists are threatening the very fabric of social normality. Zealots of every hue are proclaiming only themselves competent to guide the evolution of civilization, rogue nations headed by egotistical dictators are challenging the security of freedom loving peoples, and democracy is being relegated to an experiment in history.

The timeless battle of the Mahābhārata is ever so pertinent to the circumstances of today. It is even more incumbent upon devotees to recite the Bhagavad Gītā and to demonstrate the ideals of perfection, our dharma, as our impending battles approach.

We must define the Peace we are striving to maintain. What are its constituent elements? How much are we willing to oppress the rights of others so that we are able to maintain our own rights? Is it possible that my dedication to my own goals of perfection will preclude others from reaching their own?

This is not merely a political discussion. I am talking about spirituality. As a clergyman with a presence on five continents, I am speaking of inner strife which is common to all people, a universal principle which is keeping us from realizing our highest potential.

The enemy is within. He is inside. He is pointing his weapons at all that we hold dear: universal peace, love for all, the evolution of mankind -- nothing is sacred. He will demolish them all only to serve his interests. This ego I -- the one who says, "I know, I am different, I am special," this ego I is the culprit.

And now, the Bhagavad Gītā comes along and says, "I have been calling out to you since Vedic times! I have been trying to explain to you since thousands of years! Don't allow the ego to rule! You must subdue the ego! Only then can we ever hope for peace."

Please, my friends, devotees, well-wishers! Conquer the ego! Let us make that our battle! Direct all our attention towards the subjugation of duality, and let us realize that the One God dwells in the hearts of us all.

Swami Satyananda Saraswati
Napa, California, 2003

Introduction to the *Pañcaratna Gītā*

It is the year 2015, and we are still here. We learned that only Love will keep us grounded in the One Reality; pure, divine, unselfish love! Spiritual Love!

The five jewels have been added to the original Bhagavad Gitā: The Gita Mahatmyam, the Greatness of the Gita; Vishnusahasranam, the Thousand Names of Vishnu; Bhishmastavaraja, the King of the Spiritual Songs of Bhishma - the Powerful; Anusmriti, the Remembrance of the Most Subtle; and Gajendra Moksha, the Liberation of the King of Elephants.

Taken together this scripture is known as the Pancharatna Gita, the Gita or Song of God along with five jewels. These jewels are ornaments of the Gita.

Gita teaches us an attitude towards life, the greatness of which can only be experienced in loving devotion. Add to that a Thousand Names of Vishnu, indicative of a thousand qualities we are asked to exhibit, and then the pertinent spiritual questions: how to remember God at the time of death, what does it mean to live with the remembrance of the most subtle, how to keep focused on the good dream?

These and other issues are answered in three to four hours of spiritual discipline for sadhus who are willing to dedicate themselves to the love affair with God.

What a privilege to consecrate our actions as an offering to God. Shree Maa joins with me in sending you all the greatest blessings for a life filled with love and joy, and the privilege to live this life as a child of God.

Shree Maa and Swami Satyananda Saraswati,
Fairfield, 2015

देवता प्रणाम्
devatā praṇām

श्रीमन्महागणाधिपतये नमः

śrīmanmahāgaṇādhipataye namaḥ
We bow to the Respected Great Lord of Wisdom.

लक्ष्मीनारायणाभ्यां नमः

lakṣmīnārāyaṇābhyāṁ namaḥ
We bow to Lakṣmī and Nārāyaṇa, The Goal of all Existence and the Perceiver of all.

उमामहेश्वराभ्यां नमः

umāmaheśvarābhyāṁ namaḥ
We bow to Umā and Maheśvara, She who protects existence, and the Great Consciousness or Seer of all.

वाणीहिरण्यगर्भाभ्यां नमः

vāṇīhiraṇyagarbhābhyāṁ namaḥ
We bow to Vāṇī and Hiraṇyagarbha, Sarasvatī and Brahmā, who create the cosmic existence.

शचीपुरन्दराभ्यां नमः

śacīpurandarābhyāṁ namaḥ
We bow to Śacī and Purandara, Indra and his wife, who preside over all that is divine.

मातापितृभ्यां नमः

mātāpitṛbhyāṁ namaḥ
We bow to the Mothers and Fathers.

इष्टदेवताभ्यो नमः

iṣṭadevatābhyo namaḥ
We bow to the chosen deity of worship.

कुलदेवताभ्यो नमः

kuladevatābhyo namaḥ
We bow to the family deity of worship.

ग्रामदेवताभ्यो नमः

grāmadevatābhyo namaḥ
We bow to the village deity of worship.

वास्तुदेवताभ्यो नमः

vāstudevatābhyo namaḥ
We bow to the particular household deity of worship.

स्थानदेवताभ्यो नमः

sthānadevatābhyo namaḥ
We bow to the established deity of worship.

सर्वेभ्यो देवेभ्यो नमः

sarvebhyo devebhyo namaḥ
We bow to all the Gods.

सर्वेभ्यो ब्राह्मणेभ्यो नमः

sarvebhyo brāhmaṇebhyo namaḥ
We bow to all the Knowers of divinity.

विष्णु ध्यानम्
viṣṇu dhyānam

ॐ नारायणाय विद्महे वासुदेवाय धीमहे ।
तन्नो विष्णुः प्रचोदयात् ॥

oṁ nārāyaṇāya vidmahe vaśudevāya dhīmahe
tanno viṣṇu pracodayāt

Oṁ We meditate on the manifestation of Consciousness, we contemplate the Lord of the Earth. May that Viṣṇu grant us increase.

शान्ताकारं भुजग-शयनं पद्मनाभं सुरेशम् ।
विश्वाधारं गगन-सदृशं मेघवर्णं शुभाङ्गम् ॥

śāntākāraṁ bhujaga-śayanaṁ padmanābhaṁ sureśam
viśvādhāraṁ gagana-sadṛśaṁ meghavarṇaṁ śubhāṅgam

The Cause of Peace is lying on a snake, from whose navel sprang the lotus. He is the Lord of Gods, who supports the universe, appearing as the sky, and is dark as a cloud, with a beautiful body.

लक्ष्मीकान्तं कमलनयनं योगिभिर्ध्यान-गम्यम् ।
वन्दे विष्णुं भव-भय-हरं सर्वलोकैकनाथम् ॥

lakṣmīkāntaṁ kamalanayanaṁ yogibhirdhyāna-gamyam
vande viṣṇuṁ bhava-bhaya-haraṁ sarvalokaikanātham

The Lord of Lakṣmī, with lotus eyes, is realized by Yogis in meditation. We worship Viṣṇu, who removes the fear of existence and who is Master of the all of the worlds.

ॐ अग्निर्ज्योतिर्ज्योतिरग्निः स्वाहा ।
सूर्यो ज्योतिर्ज्योतिः सूर्यः स्वाहा ।
अग्निर्वर्चो ज्योतिर्वर्चः स्वाहा ।
सूर्यो वर्चो ज्योतिर्वर्चः स्वाहा ।
ज्योतिः सूर्यः सूर्यो ज्योतिः स्वाहा ॥

oṁ agnir jyotir jyotir agniḥ svāhā
sūryo jyotir jyotiḥ sūryaḥ svāhā
agnir varco jyotir varcaḥ svāhā
sūryo varco jyotir varcaḥ svāhā
jyotiḥ sūryaḥ sūryo jyotiḥ svāhā

oṁ The Divine Fire is the Light, and the Light is the Divine Fire; I am One with God! The Light of Wisdom is the Light, and the Light is the Light of Wisdom; I am One with God! The Divine Fire is the offering, and the Light is the Offering; I am One with God! The Light of Wisdom is the Offering, and the Light is the Light of Wisdom; I am One with God!

(Wave light)

ॐ अग्निर्ज्योती रविर्ज्योतिश्चन्द्रो ज्योतिस्तथैव च ।
ज्योतिषामुत्तमो देव दीपोऽयं प्रतिगृह्यताम् ॥
एष दीपः ॐ क्लीं विष्णवे नमः ॥

oṁ agnirjyotī ravirjyotiścandro jyotistathaiva ca
jyotiṣāmuttamo deva dīpo-yaṁ pratigṛhyatām
eṣa dīpaḥ oṁ klīṁ viṣṇave namaḥ

oṁ The Divine Fire is the Light, the Light of Wisdom is the Light, the Light of Devotion is the Light as well. The Light of the Highest Bliss, Oh God, is in the Light which we offer, the Light which we request you to accept. With the offering of Light oṁ klīṁ I bow to Viṣṇu.

(Wave incense)

ॐ वनस्पतिरसोत्पन्नो गन्धात्ययी गन्ध उत्तमः ।

आघ्रेयः सर्वदेवानां धूपोऽयं प्रतिगृह्यताम् ॥

एष धूपः ॐ क्लीं विष्णवे नमः ॥

oṁ vanaspatirasotpanno gandhātyayī gandha uttamaḥ
āghreyaḥ sarvadevānāṁ dhūpo-yaṁ pratigṛhyatām
eṣa dhūpaḥ oṁ klīṁ viṣṇave namaḥ

oṁ Spirit of the Forest, from you is produced the most excellent of scents. The scent most pleasing to all the Gods, that scent we request you to accept. With the offering of fragrant scent oṁ klīṁ I bow to Viṣṇu.

ārātrikam

ॐ चन्द्रादित्यौ च धरणी विद्युदग्निस्तथैव च ।

त्वमेव सर्वज्योतीषिं आरात्रिकं प्रतिगृह्यताम् ॥

ॐ क्लीं विष्णवे नमः आरात्रिकं समर्पयामि

oṁ candrādityau ca dharaṇī vidyudagnistathaiva ca
tvameva sarvajyotīṣiṁ ārātrikaṁ pratigṛhyatām
oṁ klīṁ viṣṇave namaḥ ārātrikaṁ samarpayāmi

All knowing as the Moon, the Sun and the Divine Fire, you alone are all light, and this light we request you to accept. With the offering of light oṁ klīṁ I bow to Viṣṇu.

ॐ पयः पृथिव्यां पय ओषधीषु

पयो दिव्यन्तरिक्षे पयो धाः ।

पयःस्वतीः प्रदिशः सन्तु मह्यम् ॥

oṁ payaḥ pṛthivyāṁ paya oṣadhīṣu
payo divyantarikṣe payo dhāḥ
payaḥsvatīḥ pradiśaḥ santu mahyam

oṁ Earth is a reservoir of nectar, all vegetation is a reservoir of nectar, the divine atmosphere is a reservoir of nectar, and also above. May all perceptions shine forth with the sweet taste of nectar for us.

ॐ अग्निर्देवता वातो देवता सूर्यो देवता चन्द्रमा देवता वसवो देवता रुद्रो देवता ऽदित्या देवता मरुतो देवता विश्वे देवा देवता बृहस्पतिर्देवतेन्द्रो देवता वरुणो देवता ॥

oṁ agnirdevatā vāto devatā sūryo devatā candramā devatā vasavo devatā rudro devatā-dityā devatā maruto devatā viśve devā devatā bṛhaspatirdevatendro devatā varuṇo devatā

oṁ The Divine Fire (Light of Purity) is the shining God, the Wind is the shining God, the Sun (Light of Wisdom) is the shining God, the Moon (Lord of Devotion) is the shining God, the Protectors of the Wealth are the shining Gods, the Relievers of Sufferings are the shining Gods, the Sons of the Light are the shining Gods; the Emancipated seers (Maruts) are the shining Gods, the Universal Shining Gods are the shining Gods, the Guru of the Gods is the shining God, the Ruler of the Gods is the shining God, the Lord of Waters is the shining God.

ॐ भूर्भुवः स्वः ।
तत् सवितुर्वरेण्यम् भर्गो देवस्य धीमहि ।
धियो यो नः प्रचोदयात् ॥

oṁ bhūr bhuvaḥ svaḥ
tat savitur vareṇyam bhargo devasya dhīmahi
dhiyo yo naḥ pracodayāt

oṁ the Infinite Beyond Conception, the gross body, the subtle body and the causal body; we meditate upon that Light of Wisdom which is the Supreme Wealth of the Gods. May it grant to us increase in our meditations.

ॐ भूः

oṁ bhūḥ
oṁ the gross body

ॐ भुवः

oṁ bhuvaḥ
oṁ the subtle body

ॐ स्वः

oṁ svaḥ
oṁ the causal body

ॐ महः

oṁ mahaḥ
oṁ the great body of existence

ॐ जनः

oṁ janaḥ
oṁ the body of knowledge

ॐ तपः

oṁ tapaḥ
oṁ the body of light

ॐ सत्यं

oṁ satyaṁ
oṁ the body of Truth

ॐ तत् सवितुर्वरेण्यम् भर्गो देवस्य धीमहि ।
धियो यो नः प्रचोदयात् ॥

oṁ tat savitur vareṇyam bhargo devasya dhīmahi
dhiyo yo naḥ pracodayāt

oṁ we meditate upon that Light of Wisdom which is the Supreme Wealth of the Gods. May it grant to us increase in our meditations.

ॐ आपो ज्योतीरसोमृतं ब्रह्म भूर्भुवस्स्वरोम् ॥

oṁ āpo jyotīrasomṛtaṁ brahma bhūrbhuvassvarom
May the divine waters luminous with the nectar of immortality of Supreme Divinity fill the earth, the atmosphere and the heavens.

ॐ मां माले महामाये सर्वशक्तिस्वरूपिणि ।
चतुर्वर्गस्त्वयि न्यस्तस्तस्मान्मे सिद्धिदा भव ॥

oṁ māṁ māle mahāmāye sarvaśaktisvarūpiṇi
catur vargas tvayi nyastas tasmān me siddhidā bhava
oṁ My Rosary, The Great Measurement of Consciousness, containing all energy within as your intrinsic nature, give to me the attainment of your Perfection, fulfilling the four objectives of life.

ॐ अविघ्नं कुरु माले त्वं गृह्णामि दक्षिणे करे ।
जपकाले च सिद्ध्यर्थं प्रसीद मम सिद्धये ॥

oṁ avighnaṁ kuru māle tvaṁ gṛhṇāmi dakṣiṇe kare
japakāle ca siddhyarthaṁ prasīda mama siddhaye
oṁ Rosary, You please remove all obstacles. I hold you in my right hand. At the time of recitation be pleased with me. Allow me to attain the Highest Perfection.

ॐ अक्षमालाधिपतये सुसिद्धिं देहि देहि
सर्वमन्त्रार्थसाधिनि साधय साधय सर्वसिद्धिं परिकल्पय
परिकल्पय मे स्वाहा ॥

oṁ akṣa mālā dhipataye susiddhiṁ dehi dehi sarva
mantrārtha sādhini sādhaya sādhaya sarva siddhiṁ
parikalpaya parikalpaya me svāhā
oṁ Rosary of rudrākṣa seeds, my Lord, give to me excellent attainment. Give to me, give to me. Illuminate the meanings of all mantras, illuminate, illuminate! Fashion me with all excellent attainments, fashion me! I am One with God!

एते गन्धपुष्पे ॐ गं गणपतये नमः

ete gandhapuṣpe oṁ gaṁ gaṇapataye namaḥ

With these scented flowers oṁ we bow to the Lord of Wisdom, Lord of the Multitudes.

एते गन्धपुष्पे ॐ आदित्यादिनवग्रहेभ्यो नमः

ete gandhapuṣpe oṁ ādityādi navagrahebhyo namaḥ

With these scented flowers oṁ we bow to the Sun, the Light of Wisdom, along with the nine planets.

एते गन्धपुष्पे ॐ शिवादिपञ्चदेवताभ्यो नमः

ete gandhapuṣpe oṁ śivādipañcadevatābhyo namaḥ

With these scented flowers oṁ we bow to Śiva, the Consciousness of Infinite Goodness, along with the five primary deities (Śiva, Śakti, Viṣṇu, Gaṇeśa, Sūrya).

एते गन्धपुष्पे ॐ इन्द्रादिदशदिक्पालेभ्यो नमः

ete gandhapuṣpe oṁ indrādi daśadikpālebhyo namaḥ

With these scented flowers oṁ we bow to Indra, the Ruler of the Pure, along with the Ten Protectors of the ten directions.

एते गन्धपुष्पे ॐ मत्स्यादिदशावतारेभ्यो नमः

ete gandhapuṣpe oṁ matsyādi daśāvatārebhyo namaḥ

With these scented flowers oṁ we bow to Viṣṇu, the Fish, along with the Ten Incarnations which He assumed.

एते गन्धपुष्पे ॐ प्रजापतये नमः

ete gandhapuṣpe oṁ prajāpataye namaḥ

With these scented flowers oṁ we bow to the Lord of All Created Beings.

एते गन्धपुष्पे ॐ नमो नारायणाय नमः

ete gandhapuṣpe oṁ namo nārāyaṇāya namaḥ
With these scented flowers oṁ we bow to the Perfect Perception of Consciousness.

एते गन्धपुष्पे ॐ सर्वेभ्यो देवेभ्यो नमः

ete gandhapuṣpe oṁ sarvebhyo devebhyo namaḥ
With these scented flowers oṁ we bow to All the Gods.

एते गन्धपुष्पे ॐ सर्वाभ्यो देवीभ्यो नमः

ete gandhapuṣpe oṁ sarvābhyo devībhyo namaḥ
With these scented flowers oṁ we bow to All the Goddesses.

एते गन्धपुष्पे ॐ श्री गुरवे नमः

ete gandhapuṣpe oṁ śrī gurave namaḥ
With these scented flowers oṁ we bow to the Guru.

एते गन्धपुष्पे ॐ ब्राह्मणेभ्यो नमः

ete gandhapuṣpe oṁ brāhmaṇebhyo namaḥ
With these scented flowers oṁ we bow to All Knowers of Wisdom.

Tie a piece of string around right middle finger or wrist.

ॐ कुशासने स्थितो ब्रह्मा कुशे चैव जनार्दनः ।
कुशे ह्याकाशवद् विष्णुः कुशासन नमोऽस्तु ते ॥

oṁ kuśāsane sthito brahmā kuśe caiva janārdanaḥ
kuśe hyākāśavad viṣṇuḥ kuśāsana namo-stu te
Brahmā is in the shining light (or kuśa grass), in the shining light resides Janārdana, the Lord of Beings. The Supreme all-pervading Consciousness, Viṣṇu, resides in the shining light. Oh Repository of the shining light, we bow down to you, the seat of kuśa grass.

आचमन

ācamana

ॐ केशवाय नमः स्वाहा

oṁ keśavāya namaḥ svāhā
We bow to the one of beautiful hair.

ॐ माधवाय नमः स्वाहा

oṁ mādhavāya namaḥ svāhā
We bow to the one who is always sweet.

ॐ गोविन्दाय नमः स्वाहा

oṁ govindāya namaḥ svāhā
We bow to He who is one-pointed light.

ॐ विष्णुः ॐ विष्णुः ॐ विष्णुः

oṁ viṣṇuḥ oṁ viṣṇuḥ oṁ viṣṇuḥ
oṁ Consciousness, oṁ Consciousness, oṁ Consciousness.

ॐ तत् विष्णोः परमं पदम् सदा पश्यन्ति सूरयः ।
दिवीव चक्षुराततम् ॥

oṁ tat viṣṇoḥ paramaṁ padam sadā paśyanti sūrayaḥ
divīva cakṣurā tatam
oṁ That Consciousness of the highest station, who always sees the Light of Wisdom, give us Divine Eyes.

ॐ तद् विप्र स पिपानोव जुविग्रन्सो सोमिन्द्रते ।
विष्णुः तत् परमं पदम् ॥

oṁ tad vipra sa pipānova juvigranso somindrate
viṣṇuḥ tat paramaṁ padam
oṁ That twice-born teacher who is always thirsty for accepting the nectar of devotion, Oh Consciousness, you are in that highest station.

ॐ अपवित्रः पवित्रो वा सर्वावस्थां गतोऽपि वा ।
यः स्मरेत् पुण्डरीकाक्षं स बाह्याभ्यन्तरः शुचिः ॥

oṁ apavitraḥ pavitro vā sarvāvasthāṁ gato-pi vā
yaḥ smaret puṇḍarīkākṣaṁ sa bāhyābhyantaraḥ śuciḥ
oṁ The Impure and the Pure reside within all objects. Who remembers the lotus-eyed Consciousness is conveyed to radiant beauty.

ॐ सर्वमङ्गलमाङ्गल्यम् वरेण्यम् वरदं शुभं ।
नारायणं नमस्कृत्य सर्वकर्माणि कारयेत् ॥

oṁ sarva maṅgala māṅgalyam
vareṇyam varadaṁ śubhaṁ
nārāyaṇaṁ namaskṛtya sarvakarmāṇi kārayet
All the Welfare of all Welfare, the highest blessing of Purity and Illumination, with the offering of respect we bow down to the Supreme Consciousness who is the actual performer of all action.

ॐ सूर्य्यश्चमेति मन्त्रस्य ब्रह्मा ऋषिः प्रकृतिश्छन्दः आपो
देवता आचमने विनियोगः ॥

oṁ sūryyaścameti mantrasya brahmā ṛṣiḥ
prakṛtiśchandaḥ āpo devatā ācamane viniyogaḥ
oṁ these are the mantras of the Light of Wisdom, the Creative Capacity is the Seer, Nature is the meter, the divine flow of waters is the deity, being applied in washing the hands and rinsing the mouth.

Draw the asana yantra with some drops of water and/or sandal paste at the front of your seat. Place a flower on the bindu in the middle.

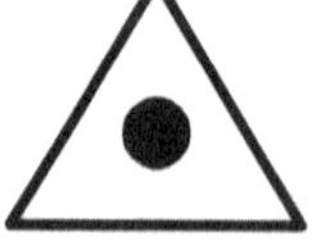

ॐ आसनस्य मन्त्रस्य मेरुपृष्ठ ऋषिः सुतलं छन्दः कूर्म्मो
देवता आसनोपवेशने विनियोगः ॥

oṁ āsanasya mantrasya merupṛṣṭha ṛṣiḥ sutalaṁ
chandaḥ kūrmmo devatā āsanopaveśane viniyogaḥ

Introducing the mantras of the Purification of the seat. The Seer is He whose back is Straight, the meter is of very beautiful form, the tortoise who supports the earth is the deity. These mantras are applied to make the seat free from obstructions.

एते गन्धपुष्पे ॐ ह्रीं आधारशक्तये कमलासनाय नमः ॥

ete gandhapuṣpe oṁ hrīṁ ādhāraśaktaye kamalāsanāya namaḥ

With these scented flowers oṁ hrīṁ we bow to the Primal Energy situated in this lotus seat.

ॐ पृथ्वि त्वया धृता लोका देवि त्वं विष्णुना धृता ।
त्वञ्च धारय मां नित्यं पवित्रं कुरु चासनम् ॥

oṁ pṛthvi tvayā dhṛtā lokā devi tvaṁ viṣṇunā dhṛtā
tvañca dhāraya māṁ nityaṁ pavitraṁ kuru cāsanam

oṁ Earth! You support the realms of the Goddess. You are supported by the Supreme Consciousness. Also bear me eternally and make pure this seat.

ॐ गुरुभ्यो नमः

oṁ gurubhyo namaḥ

oṁ I bow to the Guru.

ॐ परमगुरुभ्यो नमः

oṁ paramagurubhyo namaḥ

oṁ I bow to the Guru's Guru.

ॐ परापरगुरुभ्यो नमः

oṁ parāparagurubhyo namaḥ

oṁ I bow to the Gurus of the lineage.

ॐ परमेष्ठिगुरुभ्यो नमः

oṁ parameṣṭhigurubhyo namaḥ

oṁ I bow to the Supreme Gurus.

ॐ गं गणेशाय नमः

oṁ gaṁ gaṇeśāya namaḥ
oṁ I bow to the Lord of Wisdom.

ॐ अनन्ताय नमः

oṁ anantāya namaḥ
oṁ I bow to the Infinite One.

ॐ ऐं ह्रीं क्लीं चामुण्डायै विच्चे

oṁ aiṁ hrīṁ klīṁ cāmuṇḍāyai vicce
oṁ Creation, Circumstance, Transformation are known by Consciousness.

ॐ नमः शिवाय

oṁ namaḥ śivāya
oṁ I bow to the Consciousness of Infinite Goodness.

Clap hands 3 times and snap fingers in the ten directions (N S E W NE SW NW SE UP DOWN) repeating

ॐ क्लीं विष्णवे नमः

oṁ klīṁ viṣṇave namaḥ
oṁ klīṁ I bow to Viṣṇu.

सङ्कल्प
saṅkalpa

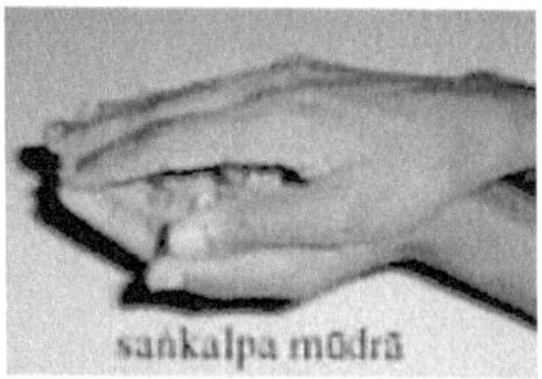

saṅkalpa mudrā

विष्णुः ॐ तत् सत्। ॐ अद्य जम्बूद्वीपे ( ) देशे ( )
प्रदेशे ( ) नगरे ( ) मन्दिरे ( ) मासे ( ) पक्षे ( ) तिथौ
( ) गोत्र श्री ( ) कृतैतत् श्रीविष्णुकामः पूजाकर्माहं
पञ्चरत्नगीता पाठामयाहम् करिष्ये ॥

viṣṇuḥ oṁ tat sat oṁ adya jambūdvīpe (Country) deśe (State) pradeśe (City) nagare (Name of house or temple) mandire (month) māse (śukla or kṛṣṇa) pakṣe (name of day) tithau (name of) gotra śrī (your name) kṛtaitat śrī viṣṇu kāmaḥ pūjā karmāhaṁ pañcaratngītā pāṭhāmyāham kariṣye

The Consciousness Which Pervades All, oṁ That is Truth. Presently, on the Planet Earth, Country of (Name), State of (Name), City of (Name), in the Temple of (Name), (Name of Month) Month, (Bright or Dark) fortnight, (Name of Day) Day, (Name of Sādhu Family), Śrī (Your Name) is performing the worship for the satisfaction of the Respected Viṣṇu by reciting Pañcaratna Gītā.

ॐ यज्जाग्रतो दूरमुदेति दैवं तदु सुप्तस्य तथैवैति।
दूरङ्गमं ज्योतिषां ज्योतिरेकं तन्मे मनः शिवसङ्कल्पमस्तु ॥

oṁ yajjāgrato dūramudeti
daivaṁ tadu suptasya tathaivaiti
dūraṅgamaṁ jyotiṣāṁ jyotirekaṁ
tanme manaḥ śiva saṅkalpamastu

May our waking consciousness replace pain and suffering with divinity as also our awareness when asleep. Far extending be our radiant aura of light, filling our minds with light. May that be the firm determination of the Consciousness of Infinite Goodness.

या गुङ्गूर्या सिनीवाली या राका या सरस्वती ।
ईन्द्राणीमह्व ऊतये वरुणानीं स्वस्तये ॥

yā guṅgūryā sinīvālī yā rākā yā sarasvatī
īndrāṇīmahva ūtaye varuṇānīṁ svastaye

May that Goddess who wears the Moon of Devotion protect the children of Devotion. May that Goddess of All-Pervading Knowledge protect us. May the Energy of the Rule of the Pure rise up. Oh Energy of Equilibrium grant us the highest prosperity.

ॐ स्वस्ति न इन्द्रो वृद्धश्रवाः स्वस्ति नः पूषा विश्ववेदाः ।
स्वस्ति नस्तार्क्ष्यो अरिष्टनेमिः स्वस्ति नो बृहस्पतिर्दधातु ॥

oṁ svasti na indro vṛddhaśravāḥ
svasti naḥ pūṣā viśvavedāḥ
svasti nastārkṣyo ariṣṭanemiḥ
svasti no bṛhaspatirdadhātu

The Ultimate Prosperity to us, Oh Rule of the Pure, who perceives all that changes; the Ultimate Prosperity to us, Searchers for Truth, Knowers of the Universe; the Ultimate Prosperity to us, Oh Divine Being of Light, keep us safe; the Ultimate Prosperity to us, Oh Spirit of All-Pervading Delight, grant that to us.

ॐ गणानां त्वा गणपतिꣳ हवामहे
प्रियाणां त्वा प्रियपतिꣳ हवामहे
निधीनां त्वा निधिपतिꣳ हवामहे वसो मम ।
आहमजानि गर्भधमा त्वमजासि गर्भधम् ॥

oṁ gaṇānāṁ tvā gaṇapati guṁ havāmahe
priyāṇāṁ tvā priyapati guṁ havāmahe
nidhīnāṁ tvā nidhipati guṁ havāmahe vaso mama
āhamajāni garbbhadhamā tvamajāsi garbbhadham

We invoke you with offerings, Oh Lord of the Multitudes; we invoke you with offerings, Oh Lord of Love; we invoke you with offerings, Oh Guardian of the Treasure. Sit within me, giving birth to the realm of the Gods within me; yes, giving birth to the realm of the Gods within me.

ॐ गणानां त्वा गणपतिꣳ हवामहे
कविं कवीनामुपमश्रवस्तमम् ।
ज्येष्ठराजं ब्रह्मणां ब्रह्मणस्पत
आ नः शृण्वन्नूतिभिः सीद सादनम् ॥

oṁ gaṇānāṁ tvā gaṇapati guṁ havāmahe
kaviṁ kavīnāmupamaśravastamam
jyeṣṭharājaṁ brahmaṇāṁ brahmaṇaspata
ā naḥ śṛṇvannūtibhiḥ sīda sādanam

We invoke you with offerings, Oh Lord of the Multitudes, Seer among Seers, of unspeakable grandeur. Oh Glorious King, Lord of the Knowers of Wisdom, come speedily hearing our supplications and graciously take your seat amidst our assembly.

ॐ अदितिर्द्यौरदितिरन्तरिक्षमदितिर्माता स पिता स
पुत्रः । विश्वे देवा अदितिः पञ्च जना
अदितिर्जातमदितिर्जनित्वम् ॥

oṁ aditir dyauraditirantarikṣamaditirmātā
sa pitā sa putraḥ
viśve devā aditiḥ pañca janā
aditirjātamaditirjanitvam

The Mother of Enlightenment pervades the heavens; the Mother of Enlightenment pervades the atmosphere; the Mother of Enlightenment pervades Mother and Father and child. All Gods of the Universe are pervaded by the Mother, the five forms of living beings, all Life. The Mother of Enlightenment, She is to be known.

ॐ त्वं स्त्रीस्त्वं पुमानसि त्वं कुमार अत वा कुमारी ।
त्वं जिर्नो वन्देन वञ्चसि त्वं जातो भवसि विश्वतोमुखः ॥

oṁ tvaṁ strīstvaṁ pumānasi
tvaṁ kumāra ata vā kumarī
tvaṁ jirno vandena vañcasi
tvaṁ jāto bhavasi viśvatomukhaḥ

You are Female, you are Male; you are a young boy, you are a young girl. You are the word of praise by which we are singing; you are all creation existing as the mouth of the universe.

ॐ अम्बेऽम्बिकेऽम्बालिके न मा नयति कश्चन ।
ससस्त्यश्वकः सुभद्रिकां काम्पीलवासिनीम् ॥

oṁ ambe-ambike-mbālike na mā nayati kaścana
sasastyaśvakaḥ subhadrikāṁ kāmpīlavāsinīm

Mother of the Perceivable Universe, Mother of the Conceivable Universe, Mother of the Universe of Intuitive Vision, lead me to that True Existence. As excellent crops (or grains) are harvested, so may I be taken to reside with the Infinite Consciousness.

ॐ शान्ता द्यौः शान्तापृथिवी शान्तमिदमुर्वन्तरिक्षम् ।
शान्ता उदन्वतिरापः शान्ताः नः शान्त्वोषधीः ॥

oṁ śāntā dyauḥ śāntā pṛthivī śāntam idamurvantarikṣam
śāntā udanvatirāpaḥ śāntāḥ naḥ śāntvoṣadhīḥ

Peace in the heavens, Peace on the earth, Peace upwards and permeating the atmosphere; Peace upwards, over, on all sides and further; Peace to us, Peace to all vegetation;

ॐ शान्तानि पूर्वरूपाणि शान्तं नोऽस्तु कृताकृतम् ।
शान्तं भूतं च भव्यं च सर्वमेव शमस्तु नः ॥

oṁ śāntāni pūrva rūpāṇi śāntaṁ no-stu kṛtākṛtam
śāntaṁ bhūtaṁ ca bhavyaṁ ca sarvameva śamastu naḥ

Peace to all that has form, Peace to all causes and effects; Peace to all existence, and to all intensities of reality including all and everything; Peace be to us.

ॐ पृथिवी शान्तिरन्तरिक्षं शान्तिर्द्यौः
शान्तिरापः शान्तिरोषधयः शान्तिः वनस्पतयः शान्तिर्विश्वे मे
देवाः शान्तिः सर्वे मे देवाः शान्तिर्ब्रह्म शान्तिरापः शान्तिः
सर्वं शान्तिरेधि शान्तिः शान्तिः सर्व शान्तिः सा मा शान्तिः
शान्तिभिः ॥

oṁ pṛthivī śāntir antarikṣaṁ śāntir dyauḥ śāntir āpaḥ śāntir oṣadhayaḥ śāntiḥ vanaspatayaḥ śāntir viśve me devāḥ śāntiḥ sarve me devāḥ śāntir brahma śāntirāpaḥ śāntiḥ sarvaṁ śāntiredhi śāntiḥ śāntiḥ sarva śāntiḥ sā mā śāntiḥ śāntibhiḥ

Let the earth be at Peace, the atmosphere be at Peace, the heavens be filled with Peace. Even further may Peace extend, Peace be to waters, Peace to all vegetation, Peace to All Gods of the Universe, Peace to All Gods within us, Peace to Creative Consciousness, Peace be to Brilliant Light, Peace to All, Peace to Everything, Peace, Peace, altogether Peace, equally Peace, by means of Peace.

ताभिः शान्तिभिः सर्वशान्तिभिः समया मोहं यदिह घोरं
यदिह क्रूरं यदिह पापं तच्छान्तं
तच्छिवं सर्वमेव समस्तु नः ॥

tābhiḥ śāntibhiḥ sarva śāntibhiḥ samayā mohaṁ yadiha ghoraṁ yadiha krūraṁ yadiha pāpaṁ tacchāntaṁ tacchivaṁ sarvameva samastu naḥ

Thus by means of Peace, altogether one with the means of Peace, Ignorance is eliminated, Violence is eradicated, Improper Conduct is eradicated, Confusion (sin) is eradicated, all that is, is at Peace, all that is perceived, each and everything, altogether for us,

ॐ शान्तिः शान्तिः शान्तिः ॥

oṁ śāntiḥ śāntiḥ śāntiḥ

oṁ Peace, Peace, Peace

ॐ श्रीपरमात्मने नमः

oṁ śrīparamātmane namaḥ
oṁ We bow to the Supreme Soul of the Universe

अथ गीतामाहात्म्यप्रारम्भः

atha gītāmāhātmyaprārambhaḥ
And Now, The Greatness of the Gītā

धरोवाच

dharovāca
Dhara said:

-1-

भगवन् परमेशान भक्तिरव्यभिचारिणी ।
प्रारब्धं भुज्यमानस्य कथं भवति हे प्रभो ॥ १ ॥

bhagavan parameśāna bhaktiravyabhicāriṇī
prārabdhaṁ bhujyamānasya kathaṁ bhavati he prabho
Oh Supreme Lord, Highest Ruler of those who move with devotion, hey Most Respected One, give us the teaching which grants understanding for future actions.

श्रीविष्णुरुवाच

śrīviṣṇuruvāca
The Respected Viṣṇu said:

-2-

प्रारब्धं भुज्यमानो हि गीताभ्यासरतः सदा ।
स मुक्तः स सुखी लोके कर्मणा नोपलिप्यते ॥ २ ॥

prārabdhaṁ bhujyamāno hi gītābhyāsarataḥ sadā
sa muktaḥ sa sukhī loke karmaṇā nopalipyate
For the understanding of future actions always practice the Gītā. He (who practices) becomes liberated, content in the world, released from the bonds of all actions.

-3-

महापापादिपापानि गीताध्यानं करोति चेत् ।
क्वचित्स्पर्शं न कुर्वन्ति नलिनीदलमम्बुवत् ॥ ३ ॥

mahāpāpādipāpāni gītādhyānaṁ karoti cet
kvacitsparśaṁ na kurvanti nalinīdalamambuvat

For he who will meditate on the Gītā with full consciousness, neither great sins will touch him, nor other confusions blossom to fruition.

-4-

गीतायाः पुस्तकं यत्र यत्र पाठः प्रवर्तते ।
तत्र सर्वाणि तीर्थानि प्रयागादीनि तत्र वै ॥ ४ ॥

gītāyāḥ pustakaṁ yatra yatra pāṭhaḥ pravartate
tatra sarvāṇi tīrthāni prayāgādīni tatra vai

Wherever is located the Gītā Book, wherever its recitation is performed, there all the places of pilgrimage are situated, there is Prayāg and other holy sites.

-5-

सर्वे देवाश्च ऋषयो योगिनः पन्नगाश्च ये ।
गोपाला गोपिका वापि नारदोद्धवपार्षदैः ।
सहायो जायते शीघ्रं यत्र गीता प्रवर्तते ॥ ५ ॥

sarve devāśca ṛṣayo yoginaḥ pannagāśca ye
gopālā gopikā vāpi nāradoddhavapārṣadaiḥ
sahāyo jāyate śīghraṁ yatra gītā pravartate

All of the Gods, ṛṣis, yogis, heavenly beings; the cow-herds and herdesses (gopis) and Nārada and others quickly manifest their help where the Gītā is recited.

-6-

यत्र गीताविचारश्च पठनं पाठनं श्रुतम् ।
तत्राहं निश्चितं पृथ्वि निवसामि सदैव हि ॥ ६ ॥

yatra gītāvicāraśca paṭhanaṁ pāṭhanaṁ śrutam
tatrāhaṁ niścitaṁ pṛthvi nivasāmi sadaiva hi

Where the Gītā is contemplated, read, recited or heard, there in that place I always reside without a doubt.

-7-

गीताश्रयेऽहं तिष्ठामि गीतामे चोत्तमं गृहम् ।
गीताज्ञानमुपाश्रित्य त्रींल्लोकान्पालयाम्यहम् ॥ ७ ॥

gītāśraye-haṁ tiṣṭhāmi gītāme cottamaṁ gṛham
gītājñānamupāśritya trīllokānpālayāmyaham

I am situated in the Gītā as my refuge, and the Gītā is my excellent home. Taking refuge in the wisdom of the Gītā, I protect the three worlds.

-8-

गीता मे परमा विद्या ब्रह्मरूपा न संशयः ।
अर्धमात्राक्षरा नित्या स्वानिर्वाच्यपदात्मिका ॥ ८ ॥

gītā me paramā vidyā brahmarūpā na saṁśayaḥ
ardhamātrākṣarā nityā svānirvācyapadātmikā

Gītā is my highest knowledge, the form of God without a doubt. The regular (contemplation) of even a half verse or a letter, (is the contemplation) of my unspeakable soul or essence.

-9-

चिदानन्देन कृष्णेन प्रोक्ता स्वमुखतोऽर्जुनम् ।
वेदत्रयी परानन्दा तत्त्वार्थज्ञानसंयुता ॥ ९ ॥

cidānandena kṛṣṇena proktā svamukhato-rjunam
vedatrayī parānandā tattvārthajñānasaṁyutā

Within is the bliss of consciousness with which Kṛṣṇa discoursed face to face with Arjuna the wisdom of the meaning of the Principles, the highest bliss of the three Vedas.

-10-

योऽष्टादश जपेन्नित्यं नरो निश्चलमानसः ।
ज्ञानसिद्धिं स लभते ततो याति परं पदम् ॥ १० ॥

yo-ṣṭādaśa japennityaṁ naro niścalamānasaḥ
jñānasiddhiṁ sa labhate tato yāti paraṁ padam

Those men who always recite these eighteen chapters without a wandering mind, earn the attainment of perfect wisdom and thence go to the highest position.

-11-

पाठेऽसमर्थः संपूर्णे ततोऽर्धं पाठमाचरेत् ।
तदा गोदानजं पुण्यं लभते नात्र संशयः ॥ ११ ॥

pāṭhe-samarthaḥ saṁpūrṇe tato-rdhaṁ pāṭhamācaret
tadā godānajaṁ puṇyaṁ labhate nātra saṁśayaḥ

If one is incapable of making the complete recitation, then one should recite a half. Thus one earns the merits of a gift of cows, of this there is no doubt.

-12-

त्रिभागं पठमानस्तु गङ्गास्नानफलं लभेत् ।
षडंशं जपमानस्तु सोमयागफलं लभेत् ॥ १२ ॥

tribhāgaṁ paṭhamānastu gaṅgāsnānaphalaṁ labhet
ṣaḍaṁśaṁ japamānastu somayāgaphalaṁ labhet

If one reads and contemplates a one third portion, one receives the fruit of a bath in the Ganges. Contemplation of a sixth portion bears the fruit of a sacrifice with Soma.

-13-

एकाध्यायं तु यो नित्यं पठते भक्तिसंयुतः ।
रुद्रलोकमवाप्नोति गणो भूत्वा वसेच्चिरम् ॥ १३ ॥

ekādhyāyaṁ tu yo nityaṁ paṭhate bhaktisaṁyutaḥ
rudralokamavāpnoti gaṇo bhūtvā vasecciram

Whoever will regularly read one chapter with devotion will attain to the Rudra Loka, the realms of Rudra, and will become a member of Rudra's entourage for all of time.

-14-

अध्यायं श्लोकपादं वा नित्यं यः पठते नरः ।
स याति नरतां यावन्मन्वन्तरं वसुन्धरे ॥ १४ ॥

adhyāyaṁ ślokapādaṁ vā nityaṁ yaḥ paṭhate naraḥ
sa yāti naratāṁ yāvanmanvantaraṁ vasundhare

Whoever will regularly read the words, verses or chapters, will become one with humanity so long as the earth may exist.

-15-

गीतायाः श्लोकदशकं सप्त पञ्च चतुष्टयम् ।
द्वौ त्रीनेकं तदर्धं वा श्लोकानां यः पठेन्नरः ॥ १५ ॥

gītāyāḥ ślokadaśakaṁ sapta pañca catuṣṭayam
dvau trīnekaṁ tadardhaṁ vā ślokānāṁ yaḥ paṭhennaraḥ

Those men who will read the verses of the Gītā, ten verses, seven verses, five verses, four verses, two, three or one, or even one half a verse,

-16-

चन्द्रलोकमवाप्नोति वर्षाणामयुतं ध्रुवम् ।
गीतापाठसमायुक्तो मृतो मानुषतां व्रजेत् ॥ १६ ॥

candralokamavāpnoti varṣāṇāmayutaṁ dhruvam
gītāpāṭhasamāyukto mṛto mānuṣatāṁ vrajet

will attain to the realm of the moon for ten million years of Dhruva (the eternally young sage). Human beings united in the recitation of Gītā avert death.

-17-

गीताभ्यासं पुनः कृत्वा लभते मुक्तिमुत्तमाम् ।
गीतेत्युच्चारसंयुक्तो म्रियमाणो गतिं लभेत् ॥ १७ ॥

gītābhyāsaṁ punaḥ kṛtvā labhate muktimuttamām
gītetyuccārasaṁyukto mriyamāṇo gatiṁ labhet

Again, those who practice the Gītā attain the most excellent liberation. Those who are united in the pronunciation of the Gītā, attain the dissolution of the substance of all thought.

-18-

गीतार्थश्रवणासक्तो महापापयुतोऽपि वा ।
वैकुण्ठं समवाप्नोति विष्णुना सह मोदते ॥ १८ ॥

gītārthaśravaṇāsakto mahāpāpayuto-pi vā
vaikuṇṭhaṁ samavāpnoti viṣṇunā saha modate

Who can listen to the meaning of the Gītā is protected from great sins. He attains to the abode of Viṣṇu, Vaikuṇṭha, and Viṣṇu is pleased with him.

-19-

गीतार्थं ध्यायते नित्यं कृत्वा कर्माणि भूरिशः ।

जीवन्मुक्तः सविज्ञेयो देहान्ते परमं पदम् ॥ १९ ॥

gītārthaṁ dhyāyate nityaṁ kṛtvā karmāṇi bhūriśaḥ
jīvanmuktaḥ savijñeyo dehānte paramaṁ padam

Who regularly meditates on the meaning of the Gītā, and performs his actions in accordance (with its teachings), is known as "Liberated while Living," and at the end of his earthly body attains the highest position.

-20-

गीतामाश्रित्य बहवो भूभुजो जनकादयः ।

निर्धूतकल्मषा लोके गीता याताः परं पदम् ॥ २० ॥

gītāmāśritya bahavo bhūbhujo janakādayaḥ
nirdhūtakalmaṣā loke gītā yātāḥ paraṁ padam

Who takes refuge in the Gītā becomes a progenitor of abundance in the universe. He will expel all impurities from the world and advance to the highest position of Gītā.

-21-

गीतायाः पठनं कृत्वा माहात्म्यं नैव यः पठेत् ।

वृथा पाठो भवेत्तस्य श्रम एव ह्युदाहृतः ॥ २१ ॥

gītāyāḥ paṭhanaṁ kṛtvā
māhātmyaṁ naiva yaḥ paṭhet
vṛthā pāṭho bhavettasya śrama eva hyudāhṛtaḥ

Who reads the Gītā, but without reading this "Glory of the Gītā," the recitation has an obstruction, and it becomes a labor in vain, with a concealment of heart or satisfaction.

-22-

एतन्माहात्म्यसंयुक्तं गीताभ्यासं करोति यः ।

स तत्फलमवाप्नोति दुर्लभां गतिमाप्नुयात् ॥ २२ ॥

etanmāhātmyasaṁyuktaṁ gītābhyāsaṁ karoti yaḥ
sa tatphalamavāpnoti durlabhāṁ gatimāpnuyāt

Whoever will perform the practice of the Gītā with this "Glory of the Gītā," will attain to that fruit which is most difficult to be attained.

सूत उवाच
sūta uvāca
Suta said:

-23-

माहात्म्यमेतद्गीताया मया प्रोक्तंसनातनम् ।
गीतान्ते च पठेद्यस्तु यदुक्तंतत्फलं लभेत् ॥ २३ ॥

māhātmyametadgītāyā mayā proktaṁsanātanam
gītānte ca paṭhedyastu yaduktaṁtatphalaṁ labhet
I have disclosed this "Glory of the Gītā." It should be read again at the end of the Gītā, and the appropriate fruits will be attained.

अथ द्वितीयमाहात्म्यम्

atha dvitīyamāhātmyam

And now, the Second Part of the Glory of the Gītā

-1-

गीताशास्त्रमिदं पुण्यं यः पठेत्प्रयतः पुमान् ।

विष्णोः पदमवाप्नोति भयशोकादिवर्जितः ॥ १ ॥

gītāśāstramidaṁ puṇyaṁ yaḥ paṭhetprayataḥ pumān
viṣṇoḥ padamavāpnoti bhayaśokādivarjitaḥ

This Gītā scripture has such merit that whoever tries to read it completely will be freed from fear and grief, etc., and will attain to Viṣṇu's highest position.

-2-

गीताध्ययनशीलस्य प्राणायामपरस्य च ।

नैव सन्ति हि पापानि पूर्वजन्मकृतानि च ॥ २ ॥

gītādhyayanaśīlasya prāṇāyāmaparasya ca
naiva santi hi pāpāni pūrvajanmakṛtāni ca

Whoever will recite the chapters of the Gītā with the method of breath control known as Prāṇāyāma, will be freed from all sins, even those committed during previous lives.

-3-

मलनिर्मोचनं पुंसां जलस्नानं दिने दिने ।

सकृद्गीताम्भसि स्नानं संसारमलनाशनम् ॥ ३ ॥

malanirmocanaṁ puṁsāṁ jalasnānaṁ dine dine
sakṛdgītāmbhasi snānaṁ saṁsāramalanāśanam

Every day one takes a bath with water to remove the dirt from the body. Whoever takes a bath by reciting the Gītā, cleanses the dirt from all existence.

-4-

गीता सुगीता कर्तव्या किमन्यैः शास्त्रविस्तरैः ।

या स्वयं पद्मनाभस्य मुखपद्माद्विनिः सृता ॥ ४ ॥

gītā sugītā kartavyā kimanyaiḥ śāstravistaraiḥ
yā svayaṁ padmanābhasya mukhapadmādviniḥ sṛtā

This excellent Gītā, what other scripture can be compared with it? From the lotus of his own navel (the Creator) came forth, from the lotus of his mouth Gītā was created.

-5-

भारतामृतसर्वस्वं विष्णोर्वक्त्राद्विनिः सृतम् ।

गीतागङ्गोदकं पीत्वा पुनर्जन्म न विद्यते ॥ ५ ॥

bhāratāmṛtasarvasvaṁ viṣṇorvaktrādviniḥ sṛtam
gītāgaṅgodakaṁ pītvā punarjanma na vidyate

All of the nectar of immortal wisdom and light was created from Viṣṇu's mouth. Who will drink from the Ganges of Gītā will not know another birth.

-6-

सर्वोपनिषदो गावो दोग्धा गोपालनन्दनः ।

पार्थो वत्सः सुधीर्भोक्ता दुग्धं गीतामृतं महत् ॥ ६ ॥

sarvopaniṣado gāvo dogdhā gopālanandanaḥ
pārtho vatsaḥ sudhīrbhoktā dugdhaṁ gītāmṛtaṁ mahat

The Blissful Protector of Cows, Gopāla, has given the cream from the cow of all the Upaniṣads. Arjuna is he who enjoys that milk, which is the greatness of the nectar of Gītā.

-7-

एकं शास्त्रं देवकीपुत्रगीतमेको देवो देवकीपुत्र एव ।

एको मन्त्रस्तस्य नामानि यानि कर्माप्येकं तस्य देवस्य सेवा

॥ ७ ॥

ekaṁ śāstraṁ devakīputra
gītameko devo devakīputra eva
eko mantrastasya nāmāni
yāni karmāpyekaṁ tasya devasya sevā

There is but one scripture from the son of Devakī, and that is the Gītā. There is one God, the son of Devakī. He is one, his mantras are many, many are his various names. Perform the service of the one God.

अथ श्रीमद्भगवद्गीताकरन्यासध्यानादि

atha śrīmadbhagavadgītākaranyāsadhyānādi

And Now, The Establishment and Meditation
of the Mantras of the Respected Bhagavad Gītā

ॐ अस्य श्रीमद्भगवद्गीतामालामन्त्रस्य
भगवान्वेदव्यास ऋषिः ॥

oṁ asya śrīmadbhagavadgītāmālāmantrasya bhagavānvedavyāsa ṛṣiḥ

Presenting the garland of mantras of the respected Bhagavad Gītā, the Divine Veda Vyāsa is the ṛṣi

अनुष्टुप्छन्दः ॥

anuṣṭupchandaḥ

anuṣṭupa is the meter (32 syllables to the verse)

श्रीकृष्णः परमात्मा देवता ॥

śrīkṛṣṇaḥ paramātmā devatā

the Supreme Soul, the respected Kṛṣṇa is the deity

अशोच्यानन्वशोचस्त्वं प्रज्ञावादांश्च भाषसे इति बीजम् ॥

aśocyānanvaśocastvaṁ prajñāvādāṁśca bhāṣase iti bījam

You speak words of wisdom, while you grieve without cause is the seed.

सर्वधर्मान्परित्यज्य मामेकं शरणं व्रज इति शक्तिः ॥

sarvadharmānparityajya māmekaṁ śaraṇaṁ vraja iti śaktiḥ

Renouncing all other ideals, take refuge in Me alone is the energy.

अहं त्वा सर्वपापेभ्यो मोक्षयिष्यामि मा शुच इति कीलकम् ॥

ahaṁ tvā sarvapāpebhyo mokṣayiṣyāmi mā śuca iti kīlakam

I will liberate you from all sin is the pin.

नैनं छिन्दन्ति शस्त्राणि नैनं दहति पावक

इत्यङ्गुष्ठाभ्यां नमः ॥

nainaṁ chindanti śastrāṇi nainaṁ dahati pāvaka ityaṅguṣṭhābhyāṁ namaḥ

Weapons cannot cut It, fire cannot burn It, is the mantra with which I bow to the thumbs.

न चैनं क्लेदयन्त्यापो न शोषयति मारुत इति

तर्जनीभ्यां नमः ॥

na cainaṁ kledayantyāpo na śoṣayati māruta iti tarjanībhyāṁ namaḥ

Water cannot wet It, wind cannot dry It is the mantra with which I bow to the forefingers.

अच्छेद्योऽयमदाह्योऽयमक्लेद्योऽशोष्य एव च इति

मध्यमाभ्यां नमः ॥

acchedyo-yamadāhyo-yamakledyo-śoṣya eva ca iti madhyamābhyāṁ namaḥ

It cannot be cut, It cannot be burnt, It cannot be wet, It cannot be dried is the mantra with which I bow to the middle fingers.

नित्यः सर्वगतः स्थाणुरचलोऽयं सनातन

इत्यानामिकाभ्यां नमः ॥

nityaḥ sarvagataḥ sthāṇuracalo-yaṁ sanātana ityānāmikābhyāṁ namaḥ

It is eternal, existent within all, consistent, immovable, for all time is the mantra with which I bow to the ring fingers.

पश्य मे पार्थ रूपाणि शतशोऽथ सहस्रश इति
कनिष्ठिकाभ्यां नमः ॥

paśya me pārtha rūpāṇi śataśo-tha sahasraśa iti kaniṣṭhikābhyāṁ namaḥ
See my hundreds and thousands of forms, Son of She Who Excels (Arjuna) is the mantra with which I bow to the baby fingers.

नानाविधानि दिव्यानि नानावर्णाकृतीनि च इति
करतलकरपृष्ठाभ्यां नमः ॥

nānāvidhāni divyāni nānāvarṇākṛtīni ca iti karatalakarapṛṣṭhābhyāṁ namaḥ
of various divine kinds, of various colors and shapes is the mantra with which I bow to the hand over hand front and back.

इति करन्यासः ॥

iti karanyāsaḥ
And that is the establishment of the mantras in the hands.

अथ हृदयादिन्यासः

atha hṛdayādinyāsaḥ

And Now the establishment of
the mantras in the heart, etc.

नैनं छिन्दन्ति शस्त्राणि नैनं दहति पावक इति

हृदयाय नमः ॥

nainaṁ chindanti śastrāṇi nainaṁ dahati pāvaka iti hṛdayāya namaḥ

Weapons cannot cut It, fire cannot burn It, is the mantra with which I bow to the heart.

न चैनं क्लेदयन्त्यापो न शोषयति मारुत इति शिरसे स्वाहा ॥

na cainaṁ kledayantyāpo na śoṣayati māruta iti śirase svāhā

Water cannot wet It, wind cannot dry It, is the mantra with which I establish in the head, I am One with God!

अच्छेद्योऽयमदाह्योऽयमक्लेद्योऽशोष्य एव च इति

शिखायै वषट् ॥

acchedyo-yamadāhyo-yamakledyo-śoṣya eva ca iti śikhāyai vaṣaṭ

It cannot be cut, It cannot be burnt, It cannot be wet, It cannot be dried is the mantra which I place on the top of the head, Purify!

नित्यः सर्वगतः स्थाणुरचलोऽयं सनातन इति

कवचाय हुम् ॥

nityaḥ sarvagataḥ sthāṇuracalo-yaṁ sanātana iti kavacāya hum

It is eternal, existent within all, consistent, immovable, for all time is the mantra with which I cross both arms as my armor.

पश्य मे पार्थ रूपाणि शतशोऽथ सहस्रश इति
नेत्रत्रयाय वौषट् ॥

paśya me pārtha rūpaṇi śataśo-tha sahasraśa iti
netratrayāya vauṣaṭ
See my hundreds and thousands of forms, Son of She Who Excels (Arjuna) is the mantra with which I purify the three eyes.

नानाविधानि दिव्यानि नानावर्णाकृतीनि च इति
अस्त्राय फट् ॥

nānāvidhāni divyāni nānāvarṇākṛtīni ca
iti astrāya phaṭ
of various divine kinds, of various colors and shapes is the mantra with which I apply the ultimate weapon of purity.

श्रीकृष्णप्रीत्यर्थे पाठे विनियोगः

śrīkṛṣṇaprītyarthe pāṭhe viniyogaḥ

The application of reciting these mantras beloved to the Respected Kṛṣṇa

-1-

ॐ पार्थाय प्रतिबोधितां भगवता नारायणेन स्वयं
व्यासेन ग्रथितां पुराणमुनिना मध्येमहाभारताम् ।
अद्वैतामृतवर्षिणीं भगवतीमष्टादशाध्यायिनीमम्ब
त्वामनुसंदधामि भगवद्गीते भवद्वेषिणीम् ॥ १ ॥

oṁ pārthāya pratibodhitāṁ bhagavatā nārāyaṇena svayaṁ
vyāsena grathitāṁ purāṇamuninā madhyemahābhāratām
advaitāmṛtavarṣiṇīṁ bhagavatīmaṣṭādaśādhyāyinīmamba
tvāmanusaṁdadhāmi bhagavadgīte bhavadveṣiṇīm

Nārāyaṇa, the manifestation of God, himself taught this divine knowledge to the Son of She Who Excels (Arjuna), while Vyāsa, the ancient sage, wrote it down in the middle of the Mahābhārata. The search through the eighteen chapters of the Bhagavad Gītā yields a rain of the nectar of non-duality upon a creation filled with the conflict of duality.

-2-

नमोऽस्तु ते व्यास विशालबुद्धे फुल्लारविन्दायतपत्रनेत्र ।
येन त्वया भारततैलपूर्णः प्रज्वालितो ज्ञानमयः प्रदीपः ॥ २ ॥

namo-stu te vyāsa viśālabuddhe
phullāravindāyatapatranetra
yena tvayā bhāratatailapūrṇaḥ
prajvālito jñānamayaḥ pradīpaḥ

I bow down to Vyāsa of great intelligence, who has eyes like the flowers of the lotus plant, by whom the oil has been supplied with which to illuminate the light of wisdom in the Land where the Light of Wisdom Always Shines, Bhārata.

-3-

प्रपन्नपारिजाताय तोत्त्रवेत्रैकपाणये ।
ज्ञानमुद्राय कृष्णाय गीतामृतदुहे नमः ॥ ३ ॥

prapannapārajātāya tottravetraikapāṇaye
jñānamudrāya kṛṣṇāya gītāmṛtaduhe namaḥ

I bow down to Kṛṣṇa, the symbol of wisdom, who has given forth the nectar of the Gītā for the pleasure of those who travel the worlds in search for knowledge.

-4-

वसुदेवसुतं देवं कंसचाणूरमर्दनम् ।
देवकीपरमानन्दं कृष्णं वन्दे जगद्गुरुम् ॥ ४ ॥

vasudevasutaṁ devaṁ kaṁsacāṇūramardanam
devakīparamānandaṁ kṛṣṇaṁ vande jagadgurum

He is God, the son of Vasudeva who killed Kaṁsa and Cāṇūra. Laud Kṛṣṇa, the Guru of the World, the supreme delight of Devakī.

-5-

भीष्मद्रोणताटा जयद्रथजला गान्धारनीलोत्पला
शल्यग्रहवती कृपेण वहनी कर्णेन वेलाकुला ।
अश्वत्थामविकर्णघोरमकरा दुर्योधनावर्तिनी सोत्तीर्णा खलु
पाण्डवै रणनदी कैवर्तकः केशवः ॥ ५ ॥

bhīṣmadroṇataṭā jayadrathajalā gāndhāranīlotpalā
śalyagrahavatī kṛpeṇa vahanī karṇena velākulā
aśvatthāmavikarṇaghoramakarā duryodhanāvartinī
sottīrṇā khalu pāṇḍavai raṇanadī kaivartakaḥ keśavaḥ

Bhīṣma and Droṇa are the banks of the river, Jayadratha is its water. Gāndhārī's sons are protecting the waters, and Śalya is a crocodile. Kṛpācārya is the flow of the river, and Karṇa is the land through which it runs. Aśvatthāma and Vikarṇa are sharks lurking in the waters and Duryodhana is a traveler in the river of battle. Keśava, the One of Beautiful Hair, is the Guide who takes the Sons of He Who is Without Prejudice across the river.

-6-

पाराशर्यवचः सरोजममलं गीतार्थगन्धोत्कटं
नानाख्यानककेसरं हरिकथासंबोधनाबोधितम् ।
लोके सज्जनषट् पदैरहरहः पेपीयमानं मुदा
भूयाद्भारतपङ्कजं कलिमलप्रध्वंसि नः श्रेयसे ॥ ६ ॥

pārāśaryavacaḥ sarojamamalaṁ gītārthagandhotkaṭaṁ
nānākhyānkakesaraṁ harikathāsaṁbodhanābodhitam
loke sajjanṣaṭ padairaharahaḥ pepīyamānaṁ mudā
bhūyādbhāratapaṅkajaṁ kalimala
pradhvaṁsi naḥ śreyase

The son of Pārāśara Ṛṣi, Veda Vyāsa, recorded the meaning of Gītā as the fragrant scent of the lotus in the Land Where the Light of Wisdom Always Shines, the knowledge of God, which is the knowledge of all knowledge to be known, and it gives to people welfare and the ultimate knowledge with which to destroy the impurities of the Age of Darkness.

-7-

मूकं करोति वाचालं पङ्गुं लङ्घयते गिरिम् ।
यत्कृपा तमहं वन्दे परमानन्दमाधवम् ॥ ७ ॥

mūkaṁ karoti vācālaṁ paṅguṁ laṅghayate girim
yatkṛpā tamahaṁ vande paramānandamādhavam

I laud the Sweet One of Supreme Bliss, by whose Grace those of diminished capacity are capable to cross.

-8-

यं ब्रह्मा वरुणेन्द्ररुद्रमरुतः स्तुन्वन्ति दिव्यैः स्तवैर्वेदैः
साङ्गपदक्रमोपनिषदैर्गायन्ति यं सामगाः ।
ध्यानावस्थिततद्गतेन मनसा पश्यन्ति यं योगिनो
यस्यान्तं न विदुः सुरसुरगण देवाय तस्मै नमः ॥ ८ ॥

yaṁ brahmā varuṇendrarudramarutaḥ
stunvanti divyaiḥ stavairvedaiḥ
sāṅgapadakramopaniṣadairgāyanti yaṁ sāmagāḥ
dhyānāvasthitatadgatena manasā paśyanti yaṁ yogino
yasyāntaṁ na viduḥ surasuragaṇa devāya tasmai namaḥ

Who Brahmā, Varuṇa, Indra, Rudra, Marutas praise with songs of divinity, and also about whom the Vedas and the Upaniṣads are sung; who yogis see in their minds when they are sitting in meditation, and whom they are constantly striving to know; I bow to Him, to that God, to the Lord of All Gods.

॥ ॐ नमो भगवते वासुदेवाय ॥

oṁ namo bhagavate vāsudevāya

oṁ I bow to the Supreme Lord of the Earth

॥ अथ श्रीमद्भगवद्गीता ॥

Atha Śrīmad Bhagavad Gītā

And Now, the Respected Bhagavad Gītā

धृतराष्ट्र उवाच

dhṛtarāṣṭra uvāca

Blind Ambition said:

-1-

धर्मक्षेत्रे कुरुक्षेत्रे समवेता युयुत्सवः ।
मामकाः पाण्डवाश्चैव किमकुर्वत संजय ॥ १ ॥

dharmakṣetre kurukṣetre samavetā yuyutsavaḥ
māmakāḥ pāṇḍavāścaiva kimakurvata saṁjaya

In the battle to manifest the ideal of perfection, in the battlefield of all action and all behavior, where my own children and the sons of He Who is without Prejudice gathered with the desire to fight, what transpired, Oh You Who are Victorious Over All?

संजय उवाच

saṁjaya uvāca

He Who is Victorious Over All said:

-2-

दृष्ट्वा तु पाण्डवानीकं व्यूढं दुर्योधनस्तदा ।
आचार्यमुपसङ्गम्य राजा वचनमब्रवीत् ॥ २ ॥

dṛṣṭvā tu pāṇḍavānīkaṁ vyūḍhaṁ duryodhanastadā
ācāryamupasaṅgamya rājā vacanamabravīt

Seeing the battle formation of the forces of Those without Prejudice, the Supreme Leader, Defender of Evil, approached the Great Teacher, Who Injures his foes with Weapons, and spoke these words:

-3-

पश्यैतां पाण्डुपुत्राणामाचार्य महतीं चमूम् ।
व्यूढां द्रुपदपुत्रेण तव शिष्येण धीमता ॥ ३ ॥

paśyaitāṁ pāṇḍuputrāṇāmācārya mahatīṁ camūm
vyūḍhāṁ drfipadaputreṇa tava śiṣyeṇa dhīmatā

Oh Great Teacher, look at the battle formation of the mighty forces of Those without Prejudice, deployed by the son of Who Stands like a Wooden Pillar, (whose name is Who attacks Impurity), and by your own disciples with excellent contemplation.

-4-

अत्र शूरा महेष्वासा भीमार्जुनसमा युधि ।
युयुधानो विराटश्च द्रुपदश्च महारथः ॥ ४ ॥

atra śūrā maheṣvāsā bhīmārjunasamā yudhi
yuyudhāno virāṭaśca drfipadaśca mahārathaḥ

There are heroic warriors equal to Who Knows no Fear and the Clarity of Pure Devotion who wield mighty bows. Defender of the Wealth (another name of Whose Nature is Truth), and Brilliantly Shining and He Who Stands like a Wooden Pillar, great warriors;

-5-

धृष्टकेतुश्चेकितानः काशिराजश्च वीर्यवान् ।
पुरुजित् कुन्तिभोजश्च शैब्यश्च नरपुङ्गवः ॥ ५ ॥

dhṛṣṭaketuścekitānaḥ kāśirājaśca vīryavān
purujit kuntibhojaśca śaibyaśca narapuṅgavaḥ

Continuity of Light and One Tone in Chanting and the King of Manifested Light are heroic warriors. Who Has Complete Victory, Who Enjoys Taking Away the Deficiency of Others and the Son of Unselfishness are the best of men.

-6-

युधामन्युश्च विक्रान्त उत्तमौजाश्च वीर्यवान् ।
सौभद्रो द्रौपदेयाश्च सर्व एव महारथाः ॥ ६ ॥

yudhāmanyuśca vikrānta uttamaujāśca vīryavān
saubhadro draupadeyāśca sarva eva mahārathāḥ

Who Conquers the Mind and Who is not Overcome and Excellent Ability are mighty heroes. The Son of the Excellent of Excellence (whose name is Whose Mind Is Directed), the Sons of the Enemy of Offenders, all are great warriors.

-7-

अस्माकं तु विशिष्टा ये तान्निबोध द्विजोत्तम ।

नायका मम सैन्यस्य संज्ञार्थं तान्ब्रवीमि ते ॥ ७ ॥

asmākaṁ tu viśiṣṭā ye tānnibodha dvijottama
nāyakā mama sainyasya saṁjñārthaṁ tānbravīmi te

Know also the principals of our side, oh excellent among the twice-born. For your knowledge I declare to you the leaders of my army.

-8-

भवान्भीष्मश्च कर्णश्च कृपश्च समितिंजयः ।

अश्वत्थामा विकर्णश्च सौमदत्तिस्तथैव च ॥ ८ ॥

bhavānbhīṣmaśca karṇaśca kṛpaśca samitiṁjayaḥ
aśvatthāmā vikarṇaśca saumadattistathaiva ca

Yourself and Who Rules Fear and Who Thinks Himself the Doer and Who Does and Gets, always victorious in battle; Who has the Obstinacy of a Horse, Who is Deaf to Evil and the Son of the Ambassador of the Nectar of Devotion;

-9-

अन्ये च बहवः शूरा मदर्थे त्यक्तजीविताः ।

नानाशस्त्रप्रहरणाः सर्वे युद्धविशारदाः ॥ ९ ॥

anye ca bahavaḥ śūrā madarthe tyaktajīvitāḥ
nānāśastrapraharaṇāḥ sarve yuddhaviśāradāḥ

and there are many other heroic warriors who will risk their lives for me, wielding various weapons, all well versed in the skills of battle.

-10-

अपर्याप्तं तदस्माकं बलं भीष्माभिरक्षितम् ।

पर्याप्तं त्विदमेतेषां बलं भीमाभिरक्षितम् ॥ १० ॥

aparyāptaṁ tadasmākaṁ balaṁ bhīṣmābhirakṣitam
paryaptaṁ tvidameteṣāṁ balaṁ bhīmābhirakṣitam

Invincible is this force of ours protected by Who Rules Fear, while their force protected by Who Knows no Fear will be easy to defeat.

-11-

अयनेषु च सर्वेषु यथाभागमवस्थिताः ।
भीष्ममेवाभिरक्षन्तु भवन्तः सर्व एव हि ॥ ११ ॥

ayaneṣu ca sarveṣu yathābhāgamavasthitāḥ
bhīṣmamevābhirakṣantu bhavantaḥ sarva eva hi

In whatever situation or wherever your position, Who Rules Fear must definitely always be protected.

-12-

तस्य संजनयन्हर्षं कुरुवृद्धः पितामहः ।
सिंहनादं विनद्योच्चैः शङ्खं दध्मौ प्रतापवान् ॥ १२ ॥

tasya saṁjanayanharṣaṁ kuruvṛddhaḥ pitāmahaḥ
siṁhanādaṁ vinadyoccaiḥ śaṅkhaṁ dadhmau pratāpavān

The elder of the Kuru family, the celebrated great grandfather, (Who Rules Fear), blew on his conch shell to make it sound loudly like a lion's roar, filling him (Defender of Evil) with delight.

-13-

ततः शङ्खाश्च भेर्यश्च पणवानकगोमुखाः ।
सहसैवाभ्यहन्यन्त स शब्दस्तुमुलोऽभवत् ॥ १३ ॥

tataḥ śaṅkhāśca bheryaśca paṇavānakagomukhāḥ
sahasaivābhyahanyanta sa śabdastumulo-bhavat

Then all at once conches, drums, cymbals and horns reverberated in a tumultuous sound.

-14-

ततः श्वेतैर्हयैर्युक्ते महति स्यन्दने स्थितौ ।
माधवः पाण्डवश्चैव दिव्यौ शङ्खौ प्रदध्मतुः ॥ १४ ॥

tataḥ śvetairhayairyukte mahati syandane sthitau
mādhavaḥ pāṇḍavaścaiva divyau śaṅkhau pradadhmatuḥ

Then, situated on a magnificent chariot attached to white horses, both Whose Sweetness is Intoxicating (Kṛṣṇa) and the son of Who is without Prejudice (Arjuna) sounded their divine conch shells.

-15-

पाञ्चजन्यं हृषीकेशो देवदत्तं धनंजयः ।
पौण्ड्रं दध्मौ महाशङ्खं भीमकर्मा वृकोदरः ॥ १५ ॥

pāñcajanyaṁ hṛṣīkeśo devadattaṁ dhanaṁjayaḥ
pauṇḍraṁ dadhmau mahāśaṅkhaṁ
bhīmakarmā vṛkodaraḥ

Of the Five Elements (was the name) of the conch which belongs to Ruler of the Senses (Kṛṣṇa), Ambassador of the Gods (was the name) of the conch of Conqueror of Wealth (Arjuna); Mark of Distinction (was the name) of the great conch of the one of fearful activities, Who Has a Voracious Appetite.

-16-

अनन्तविजयं राजा कुन्तीपुत्रो युधिष्ठिरः ।
नकुलः सहदेवश्च सुघोषमणिपुष्पकौ ॥ १६ ॥

anantavijayaṁ rājā kuntīputro yudhiṣṭhiraḥ
nakulaḥ sahadevaśca sughoṣamaṇipuṣpakau

The King, Who Remains Committed to the Ideal, the son of Who Takes Away the Deficiency of Others, (with his conch named) Infinite Victory; Who Is Free from Pain (with his conch named) Excellent Battle-cry, Equal to the Gods (with his conch named) Ornament of Jewels;

-17-

काश्यश्च परमेष्वासः शिखण्डी च महारथः ।
धृष्टद्युम्नो विराटश्च सात्यकिश्चापराजितः ॥ १७ ॥

kāśyaśca parameṣvāsaḥ śikhaṇḍī ca mahārathaḥ
dhṛṣṭadyfimno virāṭaśca sātyakiścāparājitaḥ

the Supreme King of Manifested Light, Who Dwells at the Summit, great warriors; Who attacks Impurity, Brilliantly Shining, Whose Nature is Truth, who are undefeated;

-18-

द्रुपदो द्रौपदेयाश्च सर्वशः पृथिवीपते ।
सौभद्रश्चमहाबाहुः शङ्खान्दध्मुः पृथक्पृथक् ॥ १८ ॥

drupado draupadeyāśca sarvaśaḥ pṛthivīpate
saubhadraścamahābāhuḥ śaṅkhāndadhmuḥ pṛthakpṛthak

He Who Stands like a Wooden Pillar, the sons of the Enemy of Offenders, the son of the Excellent of Excellence, with mighty arms; they all blew their conches again and again, Oh Lord of the Earth.

-19-

स घोषो धार्तराष्ट्राणां हृदयानि व्यदारयत् ।

नभश्च पृथिवीं चैव तुमुलो व्यनुनादयन् ॥ १९ ॥

sa ghoṣo dhārtarāṣṭrāṇāṁ hṛdayāni vyadārayat
nabhaśca pṛthivīṁ caiva tumulo vyanunādayan

That tumultuous sound, which echoed between heaven and earth, pierced the hearts of the supporters of Blind Ambition.

-20-

अथ व्यवस्थितान्दृष्ट्वा धार्तराष्ट्रान्कपिध्वजः ।

प्रवृत्ते शस्त्रसंपाते धनुरुद्यम्य पाण्डवः ॥ २० ॥

atha vyavasthitāndṛṣṭvā dhārtarāṣṭrānkapidhvajaḥ
pravṛtte śastrasaṁpāte dhanurudyamya pāṇḍavaḥ

Now, seeing the supporters of Blind Ambition in battle array, with their weapons at the ready to commence the fight, the son of He Who is without Prejudice (Arjuna), who had the monkey on his flag, raised his bow.

-21-

हृषीकेशं तदा वाक्यमिदमाह महीपते ।

hṛṣīkeśaṁ tadā vākyamidamāha mahīpate

Then, Oh Lord of the Earth, he spoke these words to Ruler of the Senses (Kṛṣṇa),

अर्जुन उवाच

arjuna uvāca

Clarity of Pure Devotion said:

सेनयोरुभयोर्मध्ये रथं स्थापय मेऽच्यु त ॥ २१ ॥

senayorubhayormadhye
rathaṁ sthāpaya me-cyu ta

"Oh You Who Remain Established in the Self (Kṛṣṇa), place my chariot between the two armies,

-22-

यावदेतान्निरीक्षेऽहं योद्धुकामानवस्थितान् ।
कैर्मया सह योद्धव्यमस्मिन्रणसमुद्यमे ॥ २२ ॥

yāvadetānnirīkṣe-haṁ yoddhukāmānavasthitān
kairmayā saha yoddhavyamasminraṇasamudyame

so that I may see those who are positioned with the desire for war with whom I shall require to engage in battle.

-23-

योत्स्यमानानवेक्षेऽहं य एतेऽत्र समागताः ।
धार्तराष्ट्रस्य दुर्बुद्धेर्युद्धे प्रियचिकीर्षवः ॥ २३ ॥

yotsyamānānavekṣe-haṁ ya ete-tra samāgatāḥ
dhārtarāṣṭrasya durbuddheryuddhe priyacikīrṣavaḥ

I shall see those who have assembled here for war, the supporters of the corrupted intelligence of Defender of Evil, and those who wish well to Blind Ambition.

संजय उवाच

saṁjaya uvāca

He Who is Victorious Over All said:

-24-

एवमुक्तो हृषीकेशो गुडाकेशेन भारत ।
सेनयोरुभयोर्मध्ये स्थापयित्वा रथोत्तमम् ॥ २४ ॥

evamukto hṛṣīkeśo guḍākeśena bhārata
senayorubhayormadhye sthāpayitvā rathottamam

Oh You Who Dwell in the Land Where the Light of Wisdom Always Shines, thus addressed by He Who Has Conquered Sleep (Arjuna), Ruler of the Senses (Kṛṣṇa) placed the excellent chariot between the two armies

-25-

भीष्मद्रोणप्रमुखतः सर्वेषां च महीक्षिताम् ।
उवाच पार्थ पश्यैतान् समवेतान्कुरूनिति ॥ २५ ॥

bhīṣmadroṇapramukhataḥ sarveṣāṁ ca mahīkṣitām
uvāca pārtha paśyaitān samavetānkurūniti

facing Who Rules Fear and Who injures his foes with Weapons and all the other kings, and said, "Oh Son of She Who Excels (Arjuna), see this assembly of those who will act (or the members of your family, the descendants of action).

-26-

तत्रापश्यत्स्थितान्पार्थः पितॄनथ पितामहान् ।
आचार्यान्मातुलान्भ्रातॄन्पुत्रान्पौत्रान्सखींस्तथा ॥ २६ ॥

tatrāpaśyatsthitānpārthaḥ pitṝnatha pitāmahān
ācāryānmātulānbhrātṝnputrānpautrānsakhīṁstathā

There Son of She Who Excels (Arjuna) saw fathers and grandfathers, teachers and uncles, cousins, sons, grandsons and even friends;

-27-

श्वसुरान् सुहृदश्चैव सेनयोरुभयोरपि ।
तान्समीक्ष्य स कौन्तेयः सर्वान्बन्धूनवस्थितान् ॥ २७ ॥

śvasurān suhṛdaścaiva senayorubhayorapi
tānsamīkṣya sa kaunteyaḥ sarvān bandhūnavasthitān

fathers-in-law, and well wishers were in both of the opposing armies. Seeing that (the opposing armies) were comprised of relatives, son of Who Takes Away the Deficiency of Others (Arjuna) became

-28-

कृपया परयाविष्टो विषीदन्निदमब्रवीत् ।

kṛpayā parayāviṣṭo viṣīdannidamabravīt

extremely grieved and with great sorrow spoke these words.

अर्जुन उवाच

arjuna uvāca

Clarity of Pure Devotion said:

दृष्ट्वेमं स्वजनं कृष्ण युयुत्सुं समुपस्थितम्॥ २८ ॥

dṛṣṭvemaṁ svajanaṁ kṛṣṇa yuyutsuṁ samupasthitam
Oh Lord of all Action (Kṛṣṇa), at the sight of all my relatives positioned in battle formation

-29-

सीदन्ति मम गात्राणि मुखं च परिशुष्यति ।
वेपथुश्च शरीरे मे रोमहर्षश्च जायते ॥ २९ ॥

sīdanti mama gātrāṇi mukhaṁ ca pariśuṣyati
vepathuśca śarīre me romaharṣaśca jāyate
my limbs droop, my mouth becomes dry, shivers course through my body, and my hair stands on edge.

-30-

गाण्डीवं स्रंसते हस्तात्त्वक्चैव परिदह्यते ।
न च शक्नोम्यवस्थातुं भ्रमतीव च मे मनः ॥ ३० ॥

gāṇḍīvaṁ sraṁsate hastāttvakcaiva paridahyate
na ca śaknomyavasthātuṁ bhramatīva ca me manaḥ
My bow (named) Whose Song Causes Terror slips from my hand, and my skin feels a burning sensation. My mind is filled with confusion, and I am unable to assume my position.

-31-

निमित्तानि च पश्यामि विपरीतानि केशव ।
न च श्रेयोऽनुपश्यामि हत्वा स्वजनमाहवे ॥ ३१ ॥

nimittāni ca paśyāmi viparītāni keśava
na ca śreyo-nupaśyāmi hatvā svajanamāhave
And, You Of Beautiful Hair (Kṛṣṇa), I see adverse signs (which tell that) nothing good can be obtained by killing my own family in useless war.

-32-

न काङ्क्षे विजयं कृष्ण न च राज्यं सुखानि च ।
किं नो राज्येन गोविन्द किं भोगैर्जीवितेन वा ॥ ३२ ॥

na kāṅkṣe vijayaṁ kṛṣṇa na ca rājyaṁ sukhāni ca
kiṁ no rājyena govinda kiṁ bhogairjīvitena vā

Oh Lord of all Action (Kṛṣṇa), I have no longing for victory, nor for a kingdom, nor even for happiness. Oh One of One-pointed Light (Kṛṣṇa), what is (the value) of a kingdom, of enjoyments, or even life?

-33-

येषामर्थे काङ्क्षितं नो राज्यं भोगाः सुखानि च ।

त इमेऽवस्थिता युद्धे प्राणांस्त्यक्त्वा धनानि च ॥ ३३ ॥

yeṣāmarthe kāṅkṣitaṁ no rājyaṁ bhogāḥ sukhāni ca
ta ime-vasthitā yuddhe prāṇāṁstyaktvā dhanāni ca

Those persons for whom we would desire a kingdom, enjoyments and happiness, those very persons are positioned here ready to risk their lives and treasures in battle.

-34-

आचार्याः पितरः पुत्रास्तथैव च पितामहाः ।

मातुला श्वशुराः पौत्राः श्याला सम्बन्धिनस्तथा ॥ ३४ ॥

ācāryāḥ pitaraḥ putrāstathaiva ca pitāmahāḥ
mātulā śvaśurāḥ pautrāḥ śyālā sambandhinastathā

Teachers, fathers, sons and even grandfathers; uncles, fathers-in-law, grandsons, brothers-in-law, and other relations:

-35-

एतान्न हन्तुमिच्छामि घ्नतोऽपि मधुसूदन ।

अपि त्रैलोक्यराज्यस्य हेतोः किं नु महीकृते ॥ ३५ ॥

etānna hantumicchāmi ghnato-pi madhusūdana
api trailokyarājyasya hetoḥ kiṁ nu mahīkṛte

Oh Slayer of Too Much (Kṛṣṇa), I don't desire to kill them for the kingdom of the three worlds, how then for an earthly kingdom.

-36-

निहत्य धार्तराष्ट्रान्नः का प्रीतिः स्याज्जनार्दन ।

पापमेवाश्रयेदस्मान्हत्वैतानाततायिनः ॥ ३६ ॥

nihatya dhārtarāṣṭrānnaḥ kā prītiḥ syājjanārdana
pāpamevāśrayedasmānhatvaitānātatāyinaḥ

Oh You Who are invoked by the People (Kṛṣṇa), what delight will come to us from slaying the supporters of Blind Ambition? Only sin can accrue to us for the slaying of these selfish thieves.

-37-

तस्मान्नार्हा वयं हन्तुं धार्तराष्ट्रान् स्वबान्धवान् ।
स्वजनं हि कथं हत्वा सुखिनः स्याम माधव ॥ ३७ ॥

tasmānnārha vayaṁ hantuṁ dhārtarāṣṭrān svabāndhavān
svajanaṁ hi kathaṁ hatvā sukhinaḥ syāma mādhava

Therefore, we should not kill the supporters of Blind Ambition, our own relatives. How can we be happy by destroying our own family?

-38-

यद्यप्येते न पश्यन्ति लोभोपहतचेतसः ।
कुलक्षयकृतं दोषं मित्रद्रोहे च पातकम् ॥ ३८ ॥

yadyapyete na paśyanti lobhopahatacetasaḥ
kulakṣayakṛtaṁ doṣaṁ mitradrohe ca pātakam

Greed has obscured their consciousness so that they cannot perceive the defects in the destruction of their own family, and the sin in behaving as traitors with friends.

-39-

कथं न ज्ञेयमस्माभिः पापादस्मान्निवर्तितुम् ।
कुलक्षयकृतं दोषं प्रपश्यद्भिर्जनार्दन ॥ ३९ ॥

kathaṁ na jñeyamasmābhiḥ pāpādasmānnivartitum
kulakṣayakṛtaṁ doṣaṁ prapaśyadbhirjanārdana

Why don't we who have understanding, and are able to perceive the defects, turn away from the sin of destroying our family, Oh You Who are invoked by the People (Kṛṣṇa).

-40-

कुलक्षये प्रणश्यन्ति कुलधर्माः सनातनाः ।
धर्मे नष्टे कुलं कृत्स्नमधर्मोऽभिभवत्युत ॥ ४० ॥

kulakṣaye praṇaśyanti kuladharmāḥ sanātanāḥ
dharme naṣṭe kulaṁ kṛtsnamadharmo-bhibhavatyuta

With the destruction of a family comes the loss of the ideals of the family, the manifestation of that which is Eternal. When the ideals are lost to a family, then behavior becomes contrary to the ideal.

-41-

अधर्माभिभवात्कृष्ण प्रदुष्यन्ति कुलस्त्रियः ।
स्त्रीषु दुष्टासु वार्ष्णेय जायते वर्णसङ्करः ॥ ४१ ॥

adharmābhibhavātkṛṣṇa praduṣyanti kulastriyaḥ
strīṣu duṣṭāsu vārṣṇeya jāyate varṇasaṅkaraḥ

When behavior becomes contrary to the ideal, Lord of all Action (Kṛṣṇa), there is corruption of the engendering and nurturing nature of the family. When the engendering and nurturing nature of the family becomes corrupt, Oh All Powerful, there becomes a confusion of attitudes.

-42-

सङ्करो नरकायैव कुलघ्नानां कुलस्य च ।
पतन्ति पितरो ह्येषां लुप्तपिण्डोदकक्रियाः ॥ ४२ ॥

saṅkaro narakāyaiva kulaghnānāṁ kulasya ca
patanti pitaro hyeṣāṁ luptapiṇḍodakakriyāḥ

Engendering confusion creates a hell for the family as well as for those born in the family. When ancestors are deprived of offerings of respect, everyone falls.

-43-

दोषैरेतैः कुलघ्नानां वर्णसङ्करकारकैः ।
उत्साद्यन्ते जातिधर्माः कुलधर्माश्च शाश्वताः ॥ ४३ ॥

doṣairetaiḥ kulaghnānāṁ varṇasaṅkarakārakaiḥ
utsādyante jātidharmāḥ kuladharmāśca śāśvatāḥ

With these defects in engendering confusion, the traditions of a destroyed family become extinct, along with the ideals of life and the ideals of family.

-44-

उत्सन्नकुलधर्माणां मनुष्याणां जनार्दन ।
नरकेऽनियतं वासो भवतीत्यनुशुश्रुम ॥ ४४ ॥

utsannakuladharmāṇāṁ manuṣyāṇāṁ janārdana
narake-niyataṁ vāso bhavatītyanuśuśruma

Oh You Who are invoked by the People (Kṛṣṇa), those men who are bereft of the ideals of family reside in hell for an eternity, so we have been taught.

-45-

अहो बत महत्पापं कर्तुं व्यवसिता वयम् ।
यद्राज्यसुखलोभेन हन्तुं स्वजनमुद्यताः ॥ ४५ ॥

aho bata mahatpāpaṁ kartuṁ vyavasitā vayam
yadrājyasukhalobhena hantuṁ svajanamudyatāḥ

How amazing that we could have considered to commit such a great sin of killing our own relations through greed for the pleasures of a kingdom.

-46-

यदि मामप्रतीकारमशस्त्रं शस्त्रपाणयः ।
धार्तराष्ट्रा रणे हन्युस्तन्मे क्षेमतरं भवेत् ॥ ४६ ॥

yadi māmapratīkāramaśastraṁ śastrapāṇayaḥ
dhārtarāṣṭrā raṇe hanyustanme kṣemataraṁ bhavet

If I were slain unarmed and unresisting by weapons of the supporters of Blind Ambition, that would be better for me.

संजय उवाच

saṁjaya uvāca

He Who is Victorious Over All said:

-47-

एवमुक्त्वार्जुनः संख्ये रथोपस्थ उपाविशत् ।
विसृज्य सशरं चापं शोकसंविग्नमानसः ॥ ४७ ॥

evamuktvārjunaḥ saṁkhye rathopastha upāviśat
visṛjya saśaraṁ cāpaṁ śokasaṁvignamānasaḥ

Thus Clarity of Pure Devotion spoke of his conflict, and with his mind obscured by anguish, set aside his bow and arrows, and sank into his chariot.

इति श्रीमद्भगवद्गीतासु प्रथमोऽध्यायः ॥ १ ॥

२

संजय उवाच

saṁjaya uvāca
He Who is Victorious Over All said:

-1-

तं तथा कृपयाविष्टमश्रुपूर्णाकुलेक्षणम् ।
विषीदन्तमिदं वाक्यमुवाच मधुसूदनः ॥ १ ॥

taṁ tathā kṛpayāviṣṭamaśrupūrṇākulekṣaṇam
viṣīdantamidaṁ vākyamuvāca madhusūdanaḥ
Then Slayer of Too Much (Kṛṣṇa) spoke these words to he whose eyes were filled by tears being overcome by misery and sorrow.

श्रीभगवानुवाच

śrībhagavānuvāca
The Respected Supreme Divinity said:

-2-

कुतस्त्वा कश्मलमिदं विषमे समुपस्थितम् ।
अनार्यजुष्टमस्वर्ग्यमकीर्तिकरमर्जुन ॥ २ ॥

kutastvā kaśmalamidaṁ viṣame samupasthitam
anāryajuṣṭamasvargyamakīrtikaramarjuna
Clarity of Pure Devotion, from where has such despair presented itself at such a time as this? It is not the most noble character, and it leads neither to fame nor to heaven.

-3-

क्लैब्यं मा स्म गमः पार्थ नैतत्त्वय्युपपद्यते ।
क्षुद्रं हृदयदौर्बल्यं त्यक्त्वोत्तिष्ठ परंतप ॥ ३ ॥

klaibyaṁ mā sma gamaḥ pārtha naitattvayyupapadyate
kṣudraṁ hṛdayadaurbalyaṁ tyaktvottiṣṭha paraṁtapa
Son of She Who Excels (Arjuna), do not yield to sentimentality. Do not allow such a feeling to rise in you. Renounce this lowly weakness of heart and stand up with the greatness of illumination.

अर्जुन उवाच

arjuna uvāca
Clarity of Pure Devotion said:

-4-

कथं भीष्ममहं संख्ये द्रोणं च मधुसूदन ।
इषुभिः प्रतियोत्स्यामि पूजार्हावरिसूदन ॥ ४ ॥

katharh bhīṣmamaharh saṁkhye
droṇaṁ ca madhusūdana
iṣubhiḥ pratiyotsyāmi pūjārhāvarisūdana
Slayer of Too Much (Kṛṣṇa), how shall I engage Who Rules Fear and Who injures his foes with Weapons in armed confrontation? They are both worthy of adoration, oh Destroyer of Enemies.

-5-

गुरूनहत्वा हि महानुभावान्
श्रेयो भोक्तुं भैक्ष्यमपीह लोके ।
हत्वार्थकामांस्तु गुरूनिहैव
भुञ्जीय भोगान् रुधिरप्रदिग्धान् ॥ ५ ॥

gurūnahatvā hi mahānubhāvān
śreyo bhoktfiṁ bhaikṣyamapīha loke
hatvārthakāmāṁstu gurūnihaiva
bhuñjīya bhogān rudhirapradigdhān
Rather than slaying Gurus of such great feelings, it is better to enjoy begging in this world. With the slaying of Gurus I understand that all desires and objects of enjoyment will be stained with blood.

-6-

न चैतद्विद्मः कतरन्नो गरीयो
यद्वा जयेम यदि वा नो जयेयुः ।
यानेव हत्वा न जिजीविषाम-
स्तेऽवस्थिताः प्रमुखे धार्तराष्ट्राः ॥ ६ ॥

na caitadvidmaḥ kataranno garīyo
yadvā jayema yadi vā no jayeyuḥ
yāneva hatvā na jijīviṣāma -
ste-vasthitāḥ pramukhe dhārtarāṣṭrāḥ

Even this we do not know, whether our victory or their victory is preferable, or who will win. Deployed before us are the Supporters of Blind Ambition. By killing them we do not even wish to live.

-7-

कार्पण्यदोषोपहतस्वभावः
पृच्छामि त्वां धर्मसंमूढचेताः ।
यच्छ्रेयः स्यान्निश्चितं ब्रूहि तन्मे
शिष्यस्तेऽहं शाधि मां त्वां प्रपन्नम् ॥ ७ ॥

kārpaṇyadoṣopahatasvabhāvaḥ
pṛcchāmi tvāṁ dharmasaṁmūḍhacetāḥ
yacchreyaḥ syānniścitaṁ brūhi tanme
śiṣyaste-haṁ śādhi māṁ tvāṁ prapannam

The defect of attachment is mocking my intrinsic nature. Because confusion obstructs my consciousness, I am asking you, what is the Ideal? I am your disciple who has taken refuge in you. Tell me, instruct me, of that which is best without a doubt.

-8-

न हि प्रपश्यामि ममापनुद्या-

द्यच्छोकमुच्छोषणमिन्द्रियाणाम् ।

अवाप्य भूमावसपत्नमृद्धं

राज्यं सुराणामपि चाधिपत्यम् ॥ ८ ॥

na hi prapaśyāmi mamāpanudyā -
dyacchokamucchoṣaṇamindriyāṇām
avāpya bhūmāvasapatnamṛddhaṁ
rājyaṁ surāṇāmapi cādhipatyam

For even if we obtain undisputed wealth, kingdom, or even Lordship over the Gods, I cannot see how to rid myself of this grief which saps the strength from my body.

संजय उवाच

saṁjaya uvāca

He Who is Victorious Over All said:

-9-

एवमुक्त्वा हृषीकेशं गुडाकेशः परंतप ।

न योत्स्य इति गोविन्दमुक्त्वा तूष्णीं बभूव ह ॥ ९ ॥

evamuktvā hṛṣīkeśaṁ guḍākeśaḥ paraṁtapa
na yotsya iti govindamuktvā tūṣṇīṁ babhūva ha

Having thus spoken to Controller of Senses (Kṛṣṇa), Who Has Conquered Sleep (Arjuna), of great illumination, said to He Who is One-pointed Light (Kṛṣṇa), "I will not do battle," and became silent.

-10-

तमुवाच हृषीकेशः प्रहसन्निव भारत ।

सेनयोरुभयोर्मध्ये विषीदन्तमिदं वचः ॥ १० ॥

tamuvāca hṛṣīkeśaḥ prahasanniva bhārata
senayorubhayormadhye viṣīdantamidaṁ vacaḥ

Oh Descendant of the Light of Wisdom, then in the middle between the two armies, a smiling Controller of Senses (Kṛṣṇa) said these words to he who was sorrowing.

श्रीभगवानुवाच

śrībhagavānuvāca

The Respected Supreme Divinity said:

-11-

अशोच्यानन्वशोचस्त्वं प्रज्ञावादांश्च भाषसे ।
गतासूनगतासूंश्च नानुशोचन्ति पण्डिताः ॥ ११ ॥

aśocyānanvaśocastvaṁ prajñāvādāṁśca bhāṣase
gatāsūnagatāsūṁśca nānuśocanti paṇḍitāḥ

You speak words of wisdom, while you grieve without cause. The learned grieve for neither those from whom life has fled, nor for those who yet remain alive.

-12-

न त्वेवाहं जातु नासं न त्वं नेमे जनाधिपाः ।
न चैव न भविष्यामः सर्वे वयमतः परम् ॥ १२ ॥

na tvevāhaṁ jātu nāsaṁ na tvaṁ neme janādhipāḥ
na caiva na bhaviṣyāmaḥ sarve vayamataḥ param

Never was I not, nor you, nor these rulers of men, nor shall any of us ever cease to be.

-13-

देहिनोऽस्मिन्यथा देहे कौमारं यौवनं जरा ।
तथा देहान्तरप्राप्तिर्धीरस्तत्र न मुह्यति ॥ १३ ॥

dehino-sminyathā dehe kaumāraṁ yauvanaṁ jarā
tathā dehāntaraprāptirdhīrastatra na muhyati

Just as the Wearer of the Body is present in the body in childhood and youth and old age, in the same way at the end of the body comes another acquisition. Thinkers are not mistaken about this.

-14-

मात्रास्पर्शास्तु कौन्तेय शीतोष्णसुखदुःखदाः ।
आगमापायिनोऽनित्यास्तांस्तितिक्षस्व भारत ॥ १४ ॥

mātrāsparśāstu kaunteya śītoṣṇasukhaduḥkhadāḥ
āgamāpāyino-nityāstāṁstitikṣasva bhārata

Oh Son of Who Takes Away the Deficiency of Others (Arjuna), cold, hot, pleasure, pain, merely touch. They are temporary and impermanent. Oh Descendant of the Light of Wisdom (Arjuna), be beyond them.

-15-

यं हि न व्यथयन्त्येते पुरुषं पुरषर्षभ ।
समदुःखसुखं धीरं सोऽमृतत्वाय कल्पते ॥ १५ ॥

yaṁ hi na vyathayantyete puruṣaṁ puraṣarṣabha
samaduḥkhasukhaṁ dhīraṁ so-mṛtatvāya kalpate

Oh Best of People, those people who are not tormented, who experience pain with the equanimity of pleasure, those are they whom thinkers conceive to have attained immortality.

-16-

नासतो विद्यते भावो नाभावो विद्यते सतः ।
उभयोरपि दृष्टोऽन्तस्त्वनयोस्तत्त्वदर्शिभिः ॥ १६ ॥

nāsato vidyate bhāvo nābhāvo vidyate sataḥ
ubhayorapi dṛṣṭo-ntastvanayostattvadarśibhiḥ

The untrue cannot be known to exist, nor can the true be known not to exist. The essence of both has been perceived by those who have intuitive vision of this principle.

-17-

अविनाशि तु तद्विद्धि येन सर्वमिदं ततम् ।
विनाशमव्ययस्यास्य न कश्चित्कर्तुमर्हति ॥ १७ ॥

avināśi tu tadviddhi yena sarvamidaṁ tatam
vināśamavyayasyāsya na kaścitkartumarhati

Know That of which this All is a consequence to be indestructible. No one has the capacity to destroy the Imperishable.

-18-

अन्तवन्त इमे देहा नित्यस्योक्ताः शरीरिणः ।
अनाशिनोऽप्रमेयस्य तस्माद्युध्यस्व भारत ॥ १८ ॥

antavanta ime dehā nityasyoktāḥ śarīriṇaḥ
anāśino-prameyasya tasmādyudhyasva bhārata

These bodies are perishable. Who wears the Body is eternal, undefinable, indestructible. Therefore, you should do battle, Oh Descendant of the Light of Wisdom (Arjuna).

-19-

य एनं वेत्ति हन्तारं यश्चैनं मन्यते हतम् ।
उभौ तौ न विजानीतो नायं हन्ति न हन्यते ॥ १९ ॥

ya enaṁ vetti hantāraṁ yaścainaṁ manyate hatam
ubhau tau na vijānīto nāyaṁ hanti na hanyate

They both do not know, who presumes the capacity to kill and who thinks It to be killed. It neither kills nor is It killed.

-20-

न जायते म्रियते वा कदाचि-
न्नायं भूत्वा भविता वा न भूयः ।
अजो नित्यः शाश्वतोऽयं पुराणो
न हन्यते हन्यमाने शरीरे ॥ २० ॥

na jāyate mriyate vā kadācin-
nāyaṁ bhūtvā bhavitā vā na bhūyaḥ
ajo nityaḥ śāśvato-yaṁ purāṇo
na hanyate hanyamāne śarīre

It does not take birth nor does It experience death, nor does It become only after manifestation. It is unborn, eternal, everlasting since ancient times, and It is not slain when the body is thought to die.

-21-

वेदाविनाशिनं नित्यं य एनमजमव्ययम् ।
कथं स पुरुषः पार्थ कं घातयति हन्ति कम् ॥ २१ ॥

vedāvināśinaṁ nityaṁ ya enamajamavyayam
kathaṁ sa puruṣaḥ pārtha kaṁ ghātayati hanti kam

Son of She Who Excels (Arjuna), that man who knows It as indestructible, eternal, free from decay, how can he kill and by whom can he be killed?

-22-

वासांसि जीर्णानि यथा विहाय
नवानि गृह्णाति नरोऽपराणि ।
तथा शरीराणि विहाय जीर्णा-
न्यन्यानि संयाति नवानि देही ॥ २२ ॥

vāsāṁsi jīrṇāni yathā vihāya
navāni gṛhṇāti naro-parāṇi
tathā śarīrāṇi vihāya jīrṇān-
yanyāni saṁyāti navāni dehī

As a man discards old worn out clothes and accepts other new ones, just so the Wearer of the Body discards old worn out bodies and enters into other new ones.

-23-

नैनं छिन्दन्ति शस्त्राणि नैनं दहति पावकः ।
न चैनं क्लेदयन्त्यापो न शोषयति मारुतः ॥ २३ ॥

nainaṁ chindanti śastrāṇi nainaṁ dahati pāvakaḥ
na cainaṁ kledayantyāpo na śoṣayati mārutaḥ

Weapons cannot cut It, fire cannot burn It; water cannot wet It, wind cannot dry It.

-24-

अच्छेद्योऽयमदाह्योऽयमक्लेद्योऽशोष्य एव च ।
नित्यः सर्वगतः स्थाणुरचलोऽयं सनातनः ॥ २४ ॥

acchedyo-yamadāhyo-yamakledyo-śoṣya eva ca
nityaḥ sarvagataḥ sthāṇuracalo-yaṁ sanātanaḥ

It cannot be cut, It cannot be burnt, It cannot be wet, It cannot be dried. It is eternal, existent within all, consistent, immovable, for all time.

-25-

अव्यक्तोऽयमचिन्त्योऽयमविकार्योऽयमुच्यते ।
तस्मादेवं विदित्वैनं नानुशोचितुमर्हसि ॥ २५ ॥

avyakto-yamacintyo-yamavikāryo-yamucyate
tasmādevaṁ viditvainaṁ nānuśocitumarhasi

It is said to be unmanifest, inconceivable, without change. Therefore, knowing It as such, one should not grieve.

-26-

अथ चैनं नित्यजातं नित्यं वा मन्यसे मृतम् ।
तथापि त्वं महाबाहो नैवं शोचितुमर्हसि ॥ २६ ॥

atha cainaṁ nityajātaṁ nityaṁ vā manyase mṛtam
tathāpi tvaṁ mahābāho naivaṁ śocitumarhasi

If you were to regard It as continually taking birth and continually dying, then also you should not grieve, oh you of Mighty Arms (Arjuna).

-27-

जातस्य हि ध्रुवो मृत्युर्ध्रुवं जन्म मृतस्य च ।
तस्मादपरिहार्येऽर्थे न त्वं शोचितुमर्हसि ॥ २७ ॥

jātasya hi dhruvo mṛtyurdhruvaṁ janma mṛtasya ca
tasmādaparihārye-rthe na tvaṁ śocitumarhasi

For those who take birth, death is certain, just as from death birth is certain. Therefore, you should not grieve over that which must be.

-28-

अव्यक्तादीनि भूतानि व्यक्तमध्यानि भारत ।
अव्यक्तनिधनान्येव तत्र का परिदेवना ॥ २८ ॥

avyaktādīni bhūtāni vyaktamadhyāni bhārata
avyaktanidhanānyeva tatra kā paridevanā

All beings were unmanifest before, and will become unmanifest after, oh Descendant of the Light of Wisdom (Arjuna). They are manifest only in the middle. Then why sorrow?

-29-

आश्चर्यवत्पश्यति कश्चिदेन-
माश्चर्यवद्वदति तथैव चान्यः ।
आश्चर्यवच्चैनमन्यः शृणोति
श्रुत्वाप्येनं वेद न चैव कश्चित् ॥ २९ ॥

āścaryavatpaśyati kaścidena-
māścaryavadvadati tathaiva cānyaḥ
āścaryavacainamanyaḥ śṛṇoti
śrutvāpyenaṁ veda na caiva kaścit

So very few perceive It as wonderful, and even fewer others speak of It as wonderful. Very few others hear of It as wonderful, while the majority do not understand It even having heard.

-30-

देही नित्यमवध्योऽयं देहे सर्वस्य भारत ।
तस्मात्सर्वाणि भूतानि न त्वं शोचितुमर्हसि ॥ ३० ॥

dehī nityamavadhyo-yaṁ dehe sarvasya bhārata
tasmātsarvāṇi bhūtāni na tvaṁ śocitumarhasi

Oh Descendant of the Light of Wisdom (Arjuna), the Wearer of the Body who dwells in the body is eternal and does not ever admit to death. Therefore, you should not grieve for any unmanifested existence.

-31-

स्वधर्ममपि चावेक्ष्य न विकम्पितुमर्हसि ।
धर्म्याद्धि युद्धाच्छ्रेयोऽन्यत्क्षत्रियस्य न विद्यते ॥ ३१ ॥

svadharmamapi cāvekṣya na vikampitumarhasi
dharmyāddhi yuddhācchreyo-nyat
kṣatriyasya na vidyate

Considering your own Ideal of Perfection you should not waver. For a man born to fight, fighting for the Ideal of Perfection is better than any other reason known.

-32-

यदृच्छया चोपपन्नं स्वर्गद्वारमपावृतम् ।

सुखिनः क्षत्रियाः पार्थ लभन्ते युद्धमीदृशम् ॥ ३२ ॥

yadṛcchayā copapannaṁ svargadvāramapāvṛtam
sukhinaḥ kṣatriyāḥ pārtha labhante yuddhamīdṛśam

Of its own accord the gate of heaven has opened to you, Son of She Who Excels (Arjuna). Happy are the warriors who attain to such a battle.

-33-

अथ चेत्त्वमिमं धर्म्यं संग्रामं न करिष्यसि ।

ततः स्वधर्मं कीर्तिं च हित्वा पापमवाप्स्यसि ॥ ३३ ॥

atha cettvamimaṁ dharmyaṁ saṁgrāmaṁ na kariṣyasi
tataḥ svadharmaṁ kīrtiṁ ca hitvā pāpamavāpsyasi

If you refuse to engage in this battle for the Ideal of Perfection, then you will incur the sin of destroying the fame or value of your Ideal.

-34-

अकीर्तिं चापि भूतानि कथयिष्यन्ति तेऽव्ययाम् ।

सम्भावितस्य चाकीर्तिर्मरणादति रिच्यते ॥ ३४ ॥

akīrtiṁ cāpi bhūtāni kathayiṣyanti te-vyayām
sambhāvitasya cākīrtirmaraṇādati ricyate

Beings will speak in derogation of your undying Ideal, and for the highly respected such derogation is worse than death.

-35-

भयाद्रणादुपरतं मंस्यन्ते त्वां महारथाः ।

येषां च त्वं बहुमतो भूत्वा यास्यसि लाघवम् ॥ ३५ ॥

bhayādraṇāduparataṁ maṁsyante tvāṁ mahārathāḥ
yeṣāṁ ca tvaṁ bahumato bhūtvā yāsyasi lāghavam

Great warriors may think that from fear of battle you desisted, and you who are held in high esteem will attain smallness.

-36-

अवाच्यवादांश्च बहून्वदिष्यन्ति तवाहिताः ।
निन्दन्तस्तव सामर्थ्यं ततो दुःखतरं नु किम् ॥ ३६ ॥

avācyavādāṁśca bahflnvadiṣyanti tavāhitāḥ
nindantastava sāmarthyaṁ tato duḥkhataraṁ nu kim

Your enemies will speak many unspeakable words in ridicule of your capacity. Won't this be painful?

-37-

हतो वा प्राप्स्यसि स्वर्गं जित्वा वा भोक्ष्यसे महीम् ।
तस्मादुत्तिष्ठ कौन्तेय युद्धाय कृतनिश्चयः ॥ ३७ ॥

hato vā prāpsyasi svargaṁ jitvā vā bhokṣyase mahīm
tasmāduttiṣṭha kaunteya yuddhāya kṛtaniścayaḥ

If you are killed, you attain heaven, or if you are victorious, the enjoyment of the earth. Therefore, arise, Oh Son of Who Takes Away the Deficiency of Others (Arjuna), determined to fight the war.

-38-

सुखदुःखे समे कृत्वा लाभालाभौ जयाजयौ ।
ततो युद्धाय युज्यस्व नैवं पापमवाप्स्यसि ॥ ३८ ॥

sukhaduḥkhe same kṛtvā lābhālābhau jayājayau
tato yuddhāya yujyasva naivaṁ pāpamavāpsyasi

Perceive with equanimity pleasure and pain, gain and loss, victory or defeat. Only with such preparation for war can you be free from sin.

-39-

एषा तेऽभिहिता सांख्ये बुद्धिर्योगे त्विमां शृणु ।
बुद्ध्या युक्तो यया पार्थ कर्मबन्धं प्रहास्यसि ॥ ३९ ॥

eṣā te-bhihitā sāṁkhye buddhiryoge tvimāṁ śṛṇu
buddhyā yukto yayā pārtha karmabandhaṁ prahāsyasi

This has been presented to you in the Philosophy of Sāṁkhyā, the Enumeration of the Principles, the union with the intellect. Now hear of that intelligence united with which you will be liberated from the bonds of action.

-40-

नेहाभिक्रमनाशोऽस्ति प्रत्यवायो न विद्यते ।
स्वल्पमप्यस्य धर्मस्य त्रायते महतो भयात् ॥ ४० ॥

nehābhikramanāśo-sti pratyavāyo na vidyate
svalpamapyasya dharmasya trāyate mahato bhayāt

In this way neither loss of effort nor contrary results can be known. Even striving towards this Ideal a little takes away the greatest fears.

-41-

व्यवसायात्मिका बुद्धिरेकेह कुरुनन्दन ।
बहुशाखा ह्यनन्ताश्च बुद्धयोऽव्यवसायिनाम् ॥ ४१ ॥

vyavasāyātmikā buddhirekeha kurunandana
bahuśākhā hyanantāśca buddhayo-vyavasāyinām

Oh Delight of Action (Arjuna), who has defined the goal in this way has one single mind. Scattered in infinite directions or branches are the thoughts of those whose goals are not defined.

-42-

यामिमां पुष्पितां वाचं प्रवदन्त्यविपश्चितः ।
वेदवादरताः पार्थ नान्यदस्तीति वादिनः ॥ ४२ ॥

yāmimāṁ puṣpitāṁ vācaṁ pravadantyavipaścitaḥ
vedavādaratāḥ pārtha nānyadastīti vādinaḥ

Oh Son of She Who Excels (Arjuna), there are those of obscured consciousness who utter flowery words, who are devoted to worldly knowledge, and speak of no other position.

-43-

कामात्मानः स्वर्गपरा जन्मकर्मफलप्रदाम् ।
क्रियाविशेषबहुलां भोगैश्वर्यगतिं प्रति ॥ ४३ ॥

kāmātmānaḥ svargaparā janmakarmaphalapradām
kriyāviśeṣabahfilāṁ bhogaiśvaryagatiṁ prati

Their thoughts are bound by desires for the highest heaven, and their actions give the fruit of rebirth. They perform many special acts for the supremacy of enjoyment.

-44-

भोगैश्वर्यप्रसक्तानां तयापहृतचेतसाम् ।
व्यवसायात्मिका बुद्धिः समाधौ न विधीयते ॥ ४४ ॥

bhogaiśvaryaprasaktānāṁ tayāpahṛtacetasām
vyavasāyātmikā buddhiḥ samādhau na vidhīyate

For those who have directed their intelligence to the supremacy of enjoyment as the delight of consciousness, absorption in divine consciousness is not contemplated.

-45-

त्रैगुण्यविषया वेदा निस्त्रैगुण्यो भवार्जुन ।
निर्द्वन्द्वो नित्यसत्त्वस्थो निर्योगक्षेम आत्मवान् ॥ ४५ ॥

traiguṇyaviṣayā vedā nistraiguṇyo bhavārjuna
nardvandvo nityasattvastho niryogakṣema ātmavān

Clarity of Pure Devotion, there is knowledge which contemplates the three attributes of nature, as also that by which one becomes beyond the three attributes of nature, beyond conflict, eternally established in truth, taking refuge in union with his own soul.

-46-

यावानर्थ उदपाने सर्वतः संप्लुतोदके ।
तावान्सर्वेषु वेदेषु ब्राह्मणस्य विजानतः ॥ ४६ ॥

yāvānartha udapāne sarvataḥ saṁplitodake
tāvānsarveṣu vedeṣu brāhmaṇasya vijānataḥ

As is the value of a well beside a flood of waters, just so is all (worldly) knowledge to a knowledgeable one who knows divinity.

-47-

कर्मण्येवाधिकारस्ते मा फलेषु कदाचन ।
मा कर्मफलहेतुर्भूर्मा ते सङ्गोऽस्त्वकर्मणि ॥ ४७ ॥

karmaṇyevādhikāraste mā phaleṣu kadācana
mā karmaphalaheturbhūrmā te saṅgo-stvakarmaṇi

You have authority over actions, but never over the fruits. Never let your motive be to the fruits of action, nor let your attachment cause inefficiency.

-48-

योगस्थः कुरु कर्माणि सङ्गं त्यक्त्वा धनंजय ।
सिद्ध्यसिद्ध्योः समो भूत्वा समत्वं योग उच्यते ॥ ४८ ॥

yogasthaḥ kuru karmāṇi saṅgaṁ tyaktvā dhanaṁjaya
siddhyasiddhyoḥ samo bhūtvā samatvaṁ yoga ucyate

Perform all action established in union, renouncing all attachment, Conqueror of Wealth (Arjuna). Remaining the same in success or in failure, such equilibrium is called "Yoga."

-49-

दूरेण ह्यवरं कर्म बुद्धियोगाद्धनंजय ।
बुद्धौ शरणमन्विच्छ कृपणाः फलहेतवः ॥ ४९ ॥

dūreṇa hyavaraṁ karma buddhiyogāddhanaṁjaya
buddhau śaraṇamanviccha kṛpaṇāḥ phalahetavaḥ

For inferior actions are far from union with intelligence. Conqueror of Wealth (Arjuna), seek refuge in intelligence. Miserable are those motivated by fruits.

-50-

बुद्धियुक्तो जहातीह उभे सुकृतदुष्कृते ।
तस्माद्योगाय युज्यस्व योगः कर्मसु कौशलम् ॥ ५० ॥

buddhiyukto jahātīha ubhe sukṛtaduṣkṛte
tasmādyogāya yujyasva yogaḥ karmasu kauśalam

United with intelligence one abandons both good actions and bad actions. Therefore, strive to attain union in Yoga. Yoga is efficient action.

-51-

कर्मजं बुद्धियुक्ता हि फलं त्यक्त्वा मनीषिणः ।
जन्मबन्धविनिर्मुक्ताः पदं गच्छन्त्यनामयम् ॥ ५१ ॥

karmajaṁ buddhiyuktā hi phalaṁ tyaktvā manīṣiṇaḥ
janmabandhavinirmuktāḥ padaṁ gacchantyanāmayam

Wise men who are united with intelligence renounce the fruit born of their actions and attain liberation from the bondage of birth. They go to a blissful state.

-52-

यदा ते मोहकलिलं बुद्धिर्व्यतितरिष्यति ।
तदा गन्तासि निर्वेदं श्रोतव्यस्य श्रुतस्य च ॥ ५२ ॥

yadā te mohakalilaṁ buddhirvyatitariṣyati
tadā gantāsi nirvedaṁ śrotavyasya śrutasya ca

When your intelligence will overcome being covered with ignorance, then you will attain indifference to what is heard and what will be heard.

-53-

श्रुतिविप्रतिपन्नाते यदा स्थास्यति निश्चला ।
समाधावचला बुद्धिस्तदा योगमवाप्स्यसि ॥ ५३ ॥

śrutivipratipannāte yadā sthāsyati niścalā
samādhāvacalā buddhistadā yogamavāpsyasi

When your intelligence will rest without movement, free from hearing false opinions, from mistakes or from errors, it will be fixed in pure intuitive vision. Then you will attain union in Yoga.

अर्जुन उवाच

arjuna uvāca

Clarity of Pure Devotion said:

-54-

स्थितप्रज्ञस्य का भाषा समाधिस्थस्य केशव ।
स्थितधीः किं प्रभाषेत किमासीत व्रजेत किम् ॥ ५४ ॥

sthitaprajñasya kā bhāṣā samādhisthasya keśava
sthitadhīḥ kiṁ prabhāṣeta kimāsīta vrajeta kim

Oh Embodiment of the Functions of Creation, Preservation and Transformation (Kṛṣṇa), expound upon he who is established in wisdom, who experiences pure intuitive vision, who has fixed his mind, how does such a being speak, how does he sit, how does he move?

श्रीभगवानुवाच

śrībhagavānuvāca

The Respected Supreme Divinity said:

-55-

प्रजहाति यदा कामान्सर्वान्पार्थ मनोगतान् ।
आत्मन्येवात्मना तुष्टः स्थितप्रज्ञस्तदोच्यते ॥ ५५ ॥

prajahāti yadā kāmānsarvānpārtha manogatān
ātmanyevātmanā tuṣṭaḥ sthitaprajñastadocyate

Son of She Who Excels (Arjuna), ignoring all desires born of the mind, when one remains satisfied with his own soul and his own soul alone, then he is said to be established in wisdom.

-56-

दुःखेष्वनुद्विग्नमनाः सुखेषु विगतस्पृहः ।
वीतरागभयक्रोधः स्थितधीर्मुनिरुच्यते ॥ ५६ ॥

duḥkheṣvanudvignamanāḥ sukheṣu vigataspṛhaḥ
vītarāgabhayakrodhaḥ sthitadhīrmunirucyate

Whose mind remains without obstacles when in pain, who remains free from desires when in pleasure, who is free from passion, fear and anger, is said to be the wise one who has fixed his mind.

-57-

यः सर्वत्रानभिस्नेहस्तत्तत्प्राप्य शुभाशुभम् ।
नाभिनन्दति न द्वेष्टि तस्य प्रज्ञा प्रतिष्ठिता ॥ ५७ ॥

yaḥ sarvatrānabhisnehastattatprāpya śubhāśubham
nābhinandati na dveṣṭi tasya prajñā pratiṣṭhitā

Who is equally in love with all that is, attains neither elation nor aversion to the pure and impure, such a being is established in his wisdom.

-58-

यदा संहरते चायं कूर्मोऽङ्गानीव सर्वशः ।
इन्द्रियाणीन्द्रियार्थेभ्यस्तस्य प्रज्ञा प्रतिष्ठिता ॥ ५८ ॥

yadā saṁharate cāyaṁ kfirmo-ṅgānīva sarvaśaḥ
indriyāṇīndriyārthebhyastasya prajñā pratiṣṭhitā

When he can withdraw his senses from their objects of perception, just as a tortoise withdraws his limbs, such a being is established in his wisdom.

-59-

विषया विनिवर्तन्ते निराहारस्य देहिनः ।
रसवर्जं रसोऽप्यस्य परं दृष्ट्वा निवर्तते ॥ ५९ ॥

viṣayā vinivartante nirāhārasya dehinaḥ
rasavarjaṁ raso-pyasya paraṁ dṛṣṭvā nivartate

From a Wearer of a Body who does not partake, desire itself turns away. For one who has perceived the Supreme, the experience of emotion is devoid of emotion.

-60-

यततो ह्यपि कौन्तेय पुरुषस्य विपश्चितः ।
इन्द्रियाणि प्रमाथीनि हरन्ति प्रसभं मनः ॥ ६० ॥

yatato hyapi kaunteya puruṣasya vipaścitaḥ
indriyāṇi pramāthīni haranti prasabhaṁ manaḥ

Oh Son of Who Takes Away the Deficiency of Others (Arjuna), for the senses are so strong as to harass even the wisest of men, to carry away the mind even of he who makes an effort.

-61-

तानि सर्वाणि संयम्य युक्त आसीत मत्परः ।
वशे हि यस्येन्द्रियाणि तस्य प्रज्ञा प्रतिष्ठिता ॥ ६१ ॥

tāni sarvāṇi saṁyamya yukta āsīta matparaḥ
vaśe hi yasyendriyāṇi tasya prajñā pratiṣṭhitā

Having controlled all of them, sit in union with Me, the Highest. For he who has subdued his senses becomes established in his wisdom.

-62-

ध्यायतो विषयान्पुंसः सङ्गस्तेषूपजायते ।
सङ्गात्संजायते कामः कामात्क्रोधोऽभिजायते ॥ ६२ ॥

dhyāyato viṣayānpuṁsaḥ saṅgasteṣūpajāyate
saṅgātsaṁjāyate kāmaḥ kāmātkrodho-bhijāyate

The man who meditates upon any idea cultivates attachment. From attachment comes desire, and from desire comes anger.

-63-

क्रोधाद्भवति सम्मोहः सम्मोहात्स्मृतिविभ्रमः ।
स्मृतिभ्रंशाद्बुद्धिनाशो बुद्धिनाशात्प्रणश्यति ॥ ६३ ॥

krodhādbhavati sammohaḥ sammohātsmṛtivibhramaḥ
smṛtibhraṁśādbfiddhināśo buddhināśātpraṇaśyati

From anger comes ignorance, from ignorance confusion of memory. From confusion of memory the intellect is destroyed, and when the intellect is destroyed one is lost.

-64-

रागद्वेषवियुक्तैस्तु विषयानिन्द्रियैश्चरन् ।
आत्मवश्यैर्विधेयात्मा प्रसादमधिगच्छति ॥ ६४ ॥

rāgadveṣaviyuktaistu viṣayānindriyaiścaran
ātmavaśyairvidheyātmā prasādamadhigacchati

He whose soul takes control of the various ideas wandering with the movement of the senses, that knowledgeable soul attains as a gift of offering freedom from the activities of feeling (sentiments or passions).

-65-

प्रसादे सर्वदुःखानां हानिरस्योपजायते ।
प्रसन्नचेतसो ह्याशु बुद्धिः पर्यवतिष्ठते ॥ ६५ ॥

prasāde sarvaduḥkhānāṁ hānirasyopajāyate
prasannacetaso hyāśu buddhiḥ paryavatiṣṭhate

The gift of offering gives birth to the loss of all pain, whereby the Intelligent One becomes firmly established in the delight of consciousness.

-66-

नास्ति बुद्धिरयुक्तस्य न चायुक्तस्य भावना ।
न चाभावयतः शान्तिरशान्तस्य कुतः सुखम् ॥ ६६ ॥

nāsti buddhirayuktasya na cāyuktasya bhāvanā
na cābhāvayataḥ śāntiraśāntasya kutaḥ sukham

This cannot be for one who is not united with the intellect, nor for one who is not united with an attitude of awareness. And for one without an attitude of awareness there is no peace, and for one without peace, how can there be happiness?

-67-

इन्द्रियाणां हि चरतां यन्मनोऽनु विधीयते ।
तदस्य हरति प्रज्ञां वायुर्नावमिवाम्भसि ॥ ६७ ॥

indriyāṇāṁ hi caratāṁ yanmano-nu vidhīyate
tadasya harati prajñāṁ vāyurnāvamivāmbhasi

For the movement of the senses enjoins the mind in contemplation, that takes away his wisdom as a boat is pushed across the waters by the wind.

-68-

तस्माद्यस्य महाबाहो निगृहीतानि सर्वशः ।
इन्द्रियाणीन्द्रियार्थेभ्यस्तस्य प्रज्ञा प्रतिष्ठिता ॥ ६८ ॥

tasmādyasya mahābāho nigṛhītāni sarvaśaḥ
indriyāṇīndriyārthebhyastasya prajñā pratiṣṭhitā

Therefore, One of Mighty Arms (Arjuna), he whose senses have been consistently restrained from the objects of perception, is established in wisdom.

-69-

या निशा सर्वभूतानां तस्यां जागर्ति संयमी ।
यस्यां जाग्रति भूतानि सा निशा पश्यतो मुनेः ॥ ६९ ॥

yā niśā sarvabhūtānāṁ tasyāṁ jāgarti saṁyamī
yasyāṁ jāgrati bhūtāni sā niśā paśyato muneḥ

That which all existence regards as darkness inspires wakefulness to he who practices self-control. That which inspires wakefulness to the rest of existence, the wise man perceives as darkness.

-70-

आपूर्यमाणमचलप्रतिष्ठं
समुद्रमापः प्रविशन्ति यद्वत् ।
तद्वत्कामा यं प्रविशन्ति सर्वे
स शान्तिमाप्नोति न कामकामी ॥ ७० ॥

āpūryamāṇamacalapratiṣṭhaṁ
samudramāpaḥ praviśanti yadvat
tadvatkāmā yaṁ praviśanti sarve
sa śāntimāpnoti na kāmakāmī

Just as waters enter the ocean which fills but does not overflow, just so all desires are attained for he who has attained peace, not for he who desires greater pleasure.

-71-

विहाय कामान्यः सर्वान्पुमांश्चरति निःस्पृहः ।
निर्ममो निरहङ्कारः स शान्तिमधिगच्छति ॥ ७१ ॥

vihāya kāmānyaḥ sarvānpumāṁścarati niḥspṛhaḥ
nirmamo nirahaṅkāraḥ sa śāntimadhigacchati

That man who renounces all desires and moves without desire, without attachment, without ego, he has peace.

-72-

एषा ब्राह्मी स्थितिः पार्थ नैनां प्राप्य विमुह्यति ।
स्थित्वास्यामन्तकालेऽपि ब्रह्मनिर्वाणमृच्छति ॥ ७२ ॥

eṣā brāhmī sthitiḥ pārtha
naināṁ prāpya vimuhyati
sthitvāsyāmantakāle-pi brahmanirvāṇamṛcchati

Oh Son of She Who Excels (Arjuna), this is establishment in Supreme Divinity, wherein one becomes free from delusion. Being thus established, even at the end of time, he will attain complete dissolution in Supreme Divinity.

इति श्रीमद्भगवद्गीतासु द्वितीयोऽध्यायः ॥ २ ॥

३

अर्जुन उवाच

arjuna uvāca
Clarity of Pure Devotion said:

-1-

ज्यायसी चेत्कर्मणस्ते मता बुद्धिर्जनार्दन ।
तत्किं कर्मणि घोरे मां नियोजयसि केशव ॥ १ ॥

jyāyasī cetkarmaṇaste matā buddhirjanārdana
tatkiṁ karmaṇi ghore māṁ niyojayasi keśava
You Who are Worshiped by the People (Kṛṣṇa), if you consider intelligence to be superior to action, why then do you counsel this dreadful action, Embodiment of the Functions of Creation, Preservation and Transformation (Kṛṣṇa)?

-2-

व्यामिश्रेणेव वाक्येन बुद्धिं मोहयसीव मे ।
तदेकं वद निश्चित्य येन श्रेयोऽहमाप्नुयाम् ॥ २ ॥

vyāmiśreṇeva vākyena buddhiṁ mohayasīva me
tadekaṁ vada niścitya yena śreyo-hamāpnñyām
My intellect is confused because of these conflicting statements. Tell that one thing by which without a doubt I may obtain the highest good.

श्रीभगवानुवाच

śrībhagavānuvāca
The Respected Supreme Divinity said:

-3-

लोकेऽस्मिन्द्विविधा निष्ठा पुरा प्रोक्ता मयानघ ।
ज्ञानयोगेन सांख्यानां कर्मयोगेन योगिनाम् ॥ ३ ॥

loke-smindvividhā niṣṭhā purā proktā mayānagha
jñānayogena sāṁkhyānāṁ karmayogena yoginām

Oh you without sin, in this world two paths of perfection have been elucidated by Me: union with wisdom according to the enumeration of the principles (Śāṁkhyā), and union with action are the names (or kinds) of union.

-4-

न कर्मणामनारम्भान्नैष्कर्म्यं पुरुषोऽश्नुते ।
न च संन्यसनादेव सिद्धिं समधिगच्छति ॥ ४ ॥

na karmaṇāmanārambhānnaiṣkarmyaṁ puruṣo-śnute
na ca saṁnyasanādeva siddhiṁ samadhigacchati

Man cannot attain freedom from action without undertaking actions, nor can he attain renunciation, nor perfection of complete absorption.

-5-

न हि कश्चित्क्षणमपि जातु तिष्ठत्यकर्मकृत् ।
कार्यते ह्यवशः कर्म सर्वः प्रकृतिजैर्गुणैः ॥ ५ ॥

na hi kaścitkṣaṇamapi jātu tiṣṭhatyakarmakṛt
kāryate hyavaśaḥ karma sarvaḥ prakṛtijairguṇaiḥ

Undoubtedly there is no being born who can refrain from all activity even for a moment, for all beings are required to perform action by the attributes of nature.

-6-

कर्मेन्द्रियाणि संयम्य य आस्ते मनसा स्मरन् ।
इन्द्रियार्थान्विमूढात्मा मिथ्याचारः स उच्यते ॥ ६ ॥

karmendriyāṇi saṁyamya ya āste manasā smaran
indriyārthānvimūḍhātmā mithyācāraḥ sa ucyate

Who restrains the organs of action while sitting, while the mind remembers the objects of the senses, such is called a foolish soul, a person of untrue behavior.1

-7-

यस्त्विन्द्रियाणि मनसा नियम्यारभतेऽर्जुन ।
कर्मेन्द्रियैः कर्मयोगमसक्तः स विशिष्यते ॥ ७ ॥

yastvindriyāṇi manasā niyamyārabhate-rjuna
karmendriyaiḥ karmayogamasaktaḥ sa viśiṣyate

Clarity of Pure Devotion, who has undertaken to discipline the organs of knowledge and action, has detached his mind from worldly feelings. He comes into union with action by means of the organs of action. This is superior.

-8-

नियतं कुरु कर्म त्वं कर्म ज्यायो ह्यकर्मणः ।
शरीरयात्रापि च ते न प्रसिद्ध्येदकर्मणः ॥ ८ ॥

niyataṁ kuru karma tvaṁ karma jyāyo hyakarmaṇaḥ
śarīrayātrāpi ca te na prasiddhyedakarmaṇaḥ

Perform the activities of your discipline, for action is superior to refraining from action. Even your body cannot be maintained by refraining from action.

-9-

यज्ञार्थात्कर्मणोऽन्यत्र लोकोऽयं कर्मबन्धनः ।
तदर्थं कर्म कौन्तेय मुक्तसङ्गः समाचर ॥ ९ ॥

yajñārthātkarmaṇo-nyatra loko-yaṁ karmabandhanaḥ
tadarthaṁ karma kaunteya muktasaṅgaḥ samācara

Only those actions performed for the purpose of sacrifice are efficient behaviors free from attachment, Son of Who Takes Away the Deficiency of Others (Arjuna). All other actions in this world are actions of attachment.

-10-

सहयज्ञाः प्रजाः सृष्ट्वा पुरोवाच प्रजापतिः ।
अनेन प्रसविष्यध्वमेष वोऽस्त्विष्टकामधुक् ॥ १० ॥

sahayajñāḥ prajāḥ sṛṣṭvā purovāca prajāpatiḥ
anena prasaviṣyadhvameṣa vo-stviṣṭakāmadhuk

The Lord of All Beings Born created mankind in the beginning with sacrifice and said, "By this you will attain prosperity and the fulfillment of all desires.

-11-

देवान्भावयतानेन ते देवा भावयन्तु वः ।
परस्परं भावयन्तः श्रेयः परमवाप्स्यथ ॥ ११ ॥

devānbhāvayatānena te devā bhāvayantu vaḥ
parasparaṁ bhāvayantaḥ śreyaḥ paramavāpsyatha

Through this you may deeply intuit the Gods and the Gods may deeply intuit you. Each deeply intuiting the other will bring about the highest good."

-12-

इष्टान्भोगान्हि वो देवा दास्यन्ते यज्ञभाविताः ।
तैर्दत्तानप्रदायैभ्यो यो भुङ्क्ते स्तेन एव सः ॥ १२ ॥

iṣṭānbhogānhi vo devā dāsyante yajñabhāvitāḥ
tairdattānapradāyaibhyo yo bhuṅkte stena eva saḥ

Deeply intuiting the attitude of sacrifice, the Gods will bestow the highest enjoyment. Those who enjoy the gifts from the Gods without offering to them are surely thieves.

-13-

यज्ञशिष्टाशिनः सन्तो मुच्यन्ते सर्वकिल्बिषैः ।
भुञ्जते ते त्वघं पापा ये पचन्त्यात्मकारणात् ॥ १३ ॥

yajñaśiṣṭāśinaḥ santo mucyante sarvakilbiṣaiḥ
bhuñjate te tvaghaṁ pāpā ye pacantyātmakāraṇāt

The virtuous who partake from the remains of sacrifice erase the effects of all sins. Lowly sinners cook and eat for their own selfishness.

-14-

अन्नाद्भवन्ति भूतानि पर्जन्यादन्नसंभवः ।
यज्ञाद्भवति पर्जन्यो यज्ञः कर्मसमुद्भवः ॥ १४ ॥

annādbhavanti bhūtāni parjanyādannasaṁbhavaḥ
yajñādbhavati parjanyo yajñaḥ karmasamudbhavaḥ

All existence evolves from food, and from rain does food arise. From sacrifice does rain pour forth, and sacrifice comes from disciplined action.

-15-

कर्म ब्रह्मोद्भवं विद्धि ब्रह्माक्षरसमुद्भवम् ।
तस्मात्सर्वगतं ब्रह्म नित्यं यज्ञे प्रतिष्ठितम् ॥ १५ ॥

karma brahmodbhavaṁ viddhi
brahmākṣarasamudbhavam
tasmātsarvagataṁ brahma nityaṁ yajñe pratiṣṭhitam

From Supreme Divinity has come forth knowledge of action, and from Supreme Divinity has come forth knowledge of that which is imperishable. Therefore, Supreme Divinity is always eternally established in sacrifice.

-16-

एवं प्रवर्तितं चक्रं नानुवर्तयतीह यः ।
अघायुरिन्द्रियारामो मोघं पार्थ स जीवति ॥ १६ ॥

evaṁ pravartitaṁ cakraṁ nānuvartayatīha yaḥ
aghāyurindriyārāmo moghaṁ pārtha sa jīvati

Whoever does not respect the movement of this cycle lives a useless life of attachment to the impure senses, oh Son of She Who Excels (Arjuna).

-17-

यस्त्वात्मरतिरेव स्यादात्मतृप्तश्च मानवः ।
आत्मन्येव च संतुष्टस्तस्य कार्यं न विद्यते ॥ १७ ॥

yastvātmaratireva syādātmatṛptaśca mānavaḥ
ātmanyeva ca saṁtuṣṭastasya kāryaṁ na vidyate

That man who delights in his own soul, who is contented with his own soul, and who is satisfied only with his own soul, he knows of nothing left to be done.

-18-

नैव तस्य कृतेनार्थो नाकृतेनेह कश्चन ।
न चास्य सर्वभूतेषु कश्चिदर्थव्यपाश्रयः ॥ १८ ॥

naiva tasya kṛtenārtho nākṛteneha kaścana
na cāsya sarvabhūteṣu kaścidarthavyapāśrayaḥ

For him neither is there a purpose for completed actions nor for incomplete actions, and he regards all beings of existence without selfishness.

-19-

तस्मादसक्तः सततं कार्यं कर्म समाचर ।
असक्तो ह्याचरन्कर्म परमाप्नोति पूरुषः ॥ १९ ॥

tasmādasaktaḥ satataṁ kāryaṁ karma samācara
asakto hyācarankarma paramāpnoti pūruṣaḥ

Therefore, always efficiently perform all actions without attachment, for the man who performs actions without attachment attains the Supreme.

-20-

कर्मणैव हि संसिद्धिमास्थिता जनकादयः ।
लोकसंग्रहमेवापि संपश्यन्कर्तुमर्हसि ॥ २० ॥

karmaṇaiva hi saṁsiddhimāsthitā janakādayaḥ
lokasaṁgrahamevāpi saṁpaśyankartumarhasi

For only through actions did Janaka2 and others become established in the attainment of perfection. You should act only with perception of the harmony of the world.

-21-

यद्यदाचरति श्रेष्ठस्तत्तदेवेतरो जनः ।
स यत्प्रमाणं कुरुते लोकस्तदनुवर्तते ॥ २१ ॥

yadyadācarati śreṣṭhastattadevetaro janaḥ
sa yatpramāṇaṁ kurute lokastadanuvartate

In whatever way the best of men behave, they establish an example which may be respected by other men.

-22-

न मे पार्थास्ति कर्तव्यं त्रिषु लोकेषु किंचन ।
नानवाप्तमवाप्तव्यं वर्त एव च कर्मणि ॥ २२ ॥

na me pārthāsti kartavyaṁ triṣu lokeṣu kiṁcana
nānavāptamavāptavyaṁ varta eva ca karmaṇi

Oh Son of She Who Excels (Arjuna), for Me there is no remaining obligation in the three worlds, nothing worth attaining which has not been attained. Even so, I persist in action.

-23-

यदि ह्यहं न वर्तेयं जातु कर्मण्यतन्द्रितः ।
मम वर्त्मानुवर्तन्ते मनुष्याः पार्थ सर्वशः ॥ २३ ॥

yadi hyahaṁ na varteyaṁ jātu karmaṇyatandritaḥ
mama vartmānuvartante manuṣyāḥ pārtha sarvaśaḥ

For if ever I did not persist in unwearied action, men will respect my example in all ways, Son of She Who Excels (Arjuna).

-24-

उत्सीदेयुरिमे लोका न कुर्यां कर्म चेदहम् ।
सङ्करस्य च कर्ता स्यामुपहन्यामिमाः प्रजाः ॥ २४ ॥

utsīdeyurime lokā na kuryāṁ karma cedaham
saṅkarasya ca kartā syāmupahanyāmimāḥ prajāḥ

If I do not perform action, these worlds will perish, and I will have become the cause of confusion which could destroy mankind.

-25-

सक्ताः कर्मण्यविद्वांसो यथा कुर्वन्ति भारत ।
कुर्याद्विद्वांस्तथासक्तश्चिकीर्षुर्लोकसंग्रहम् ॥ २५ ॥

saktāḥ karmaṇyavidvāṁso yathā kurvanti bhārata
kuryādvidvāṁstathāsaktaścikīrṣurlokasaṁgraham

Descendant of the Light of Wisdom (Arjuna), the ignorant act with attachment to their actions. The intelligent should act without attachment seeking the harmony of the world.

-26-

न बुद्धिभेदं जनयेदज्ञानां कर्मसङ्गिनाम् ।
जोषयेत्सर्वकर्माणि विद्वान्युक्तः समाचरन् ॥ २६ ॥

na buddhibhedaṁ janayedajñānāṁ karmasaṅginām
joṣayetsarvakarmāṇi vidvānyuktaḥ samācaran

Do not try to cause an alteration in the intelligence of the ignorant who are attached to their action. The intelligent one who is united with efficient behavior will take delight in all action.

-27-

प्रकृतेः क्रियमाणानि गुणैः कर्माणि सर्वशः ।
अहङ्कारविमूढात्मा कर्ताहमिति मन्यते ॥ २७ ॥

prakṛteḥ kriyamāṇāni guṇaiḥ karmāṇi sarvaśaḥ
ahaṅkāravimūḍhātmā kartāhamiti manyate

All actions are performed by the attributes of nature. The soul deluded by his own ego thinks his ego-self to be the doer.

-28-

तत्त्ववित्तु महाबाहो गुणकर्मविभागयोः ।
गुणा गुणेषु वर्तन्त इति मत्वा न सज्जते ॥ २८ ॥

tattvavittu mahābāho guṇakarmavibhāgayoḥ
guṇā guṇeṣu vartanta iti matvā na sajjate

Oh One of Mighty Arms (Arjuna), who Knows the Principles distinguishes the attributes of action. Understanding that the attributes of nature are revolving around each other, he remains free from attachment.

-29-

प्रकृतेर्गुणसंमूढाः सज्जन्ते गुणकर्मसु ।
तानकृत्स्नविदो मन्दान्कृत्स्नविन्न विचालयेत् ॥ २९ ॥

prakṛterguṇasaṁmūḍhāḥ sajjante guṇakarmasu
tānakṛtsnavido mandānkṛtsnavinna vicālayet

Those who are deluded by the attributes of nature remain attached to the attributes of their actions. Who acts in accordance with his knowledge, should not associate with those foolish beings who do not act according to what they know to be right.

-30-

मयि सर्वाणि कर्माणि संन्यस्याध्यात्मचेतसा ।
निराशीर्निर्ममो भूत्वा युध्यस्व विगतज्वरः ॥ ३० ॥

mayi sarvāṇi karmāṇi saṁnyasyādhyātmacetasā
nirāśīrnirmamo bhūtvā yudhyasva vigatajvaraḥ

With full renunciation, fix your consciousness in spiritual knowledge performing all actions for Me. Becoming free from desire, free from attachment, fight this disease of darkness.

-31-

ये मे मतमिदं नित्यमनुतिष्ठन्ति मानवाः ।
श्रद्धावन्तोऽनसूयन्तो मुच्यन्ते तेऽपि कर्मभिः ॥ ३१ ॥

ye me matamidaṁ nityamanutiṣṭhanti mānavāḥ
śraddhāvanto-nasūyanto mucyante te-pi karmabhiḥ

Those men who always follow this doctrine of mine with the highest faith, free from envy, they become free through action.

-32-

ये त्वेतदभ्यसूयन्तो नानुतिष्ठन्ति मे मतम् ।
सर्वज्ञानविमूढांस्तान्विद्धि नष्टानचेतसः ॥ ३२ ॥

ye tvetadabhyasūyanto nānutiṣṭhanti me matam
sarvajñānavimūḍhāṁstānviddhi naṣṭānacetasaḥ

Those who are adamant and do not follow this doctrine of mine, know that they are deluded in their lack of wisdom and lost in unconsciousness.

-33-

सदृशं चेष्टते स्वस्याः प्रकृतेर्ज्ञानवानपि ।
प्रकृतिं यान्ति भूतानि निग्रहः किं करिष्यति ॥ ३३ ॥

sadṛśaṁ ceṣṭate svasyāḥ prakṛterjñānavānapi
prakṛtiṁ yānti bhūtāni nigrahaḥ kiṁ kariṣyati

The wise man makes efforts according to his own perception, according to his own nature. All living beings follow their nature. How can they be stopped?

-34-

इन्द्रियस्येन्द्रियस्यार्थे रागद्वेषौ व्यवस्थितौ ।
तयोर्न वशमागच्छेत्तौ ह्यस्य परिपन्थिनौ ॥ ३४ ॥

indriyasyendriyasyārthe rāgadveṣau vyavasthitau
tayorna vaśamāgacchettau hyasya paripanthinau

In the relationship between the senses and the objects of perception both attraction and repulsion are situated. Avoid the influence of both of them, for they are adversaries who obstruct the way.

-35-

श्रेयान्स्वधर्मो विगुणः परधर्मात्स्वनुष्ठितात् ।
स्वधर्मे निधनं श्रेयः परधर्मो भयावहः ॥ ३५ ॥

śreyānsvadharmo viguṇaḥ paradharmātsvanuṣṭhitāt
svadharme nidhanaṁ śreyaḥ paradharmo bhayāvahaḥ

Preferable is one's own Ideal of Perfection however deficient, to another's Ideal, however well-observed. Even poverty in the pursuit of one's own Ideal is better, while another's Ideal is filled with fear.

अर्जुन उवाच

arjuna uvāca
Clarity of Pure Devotion said:

-36-

अथ केन प्रयुक्तोऽयं पापं चरति पूरुषः ।
अनिच्छन्नपि वार्ष्णेय बलादिव नियोजितः ॥ ३६ ॥

atha kena prayukto-yaṁ pāpaṁ carati pūruṣaḥ
anicchannapi vārṣṇeya balādiva niyojitaḥ
Then why does man move to unite with sin? By what force is he driven, even against his will?

श्रीभगवानुवाच

śrībhagavānuvāca
The Respected Supreme Divinity said:

-37-

काम एष क्रोधः एष रजोगुणसमुद्भवः ।
महाशनो महापाप्मा विद्ध्येनमिह वैरिणम् ॥ ३७ ॥

kāma eṣa krodhaḥ eṣa rajoguṇasamudbhavaḥ
mahāśano mahāpāpmā viddhyenamiha vairiṇam
Desire and anger arise from Nature's quality of passion. They are insatiable and terribly wicked. Know them as the enemies.

-38-

धूमेनाव्रियते वह्निर्यथादर्शो मलेन च ।
यथोल्बेनावृतो गर्भस्तथा तेनेदमावृतम् ॥ ३८ ॥

dhūmenāvriyate vahniryathādarśo malena ca
yatholbenāvṛto garbhastathā tenedamāvṛtam
As fire is covered by smoke, the highest Ideal covered by imperfection, the fetus hidden in the womb, just so is Wisdom hidden by these enemies.

-39-

आवृतं ज्ञानमेतेन ज्ञानिनो नित्यवैरिणा ।
काममरूपेण कौन्तेय दुष्पूरेणानलेन च ॥ ३९ ॥

āvṛtaṁ jñānametena jñānino nityavairiṇā
kāmarūpeṇa kaunteya duṣpūreṇānalena ca

The wisdom of the wise is hidden by these eternal enemies in the form of selfish desires which are insatiable like fire, oh Son of Who Takes Away the Deficiency of Others (Arjuna).

-40-

इन्द्रियाणि मनो बुद्धिरस्याधिष्ठानमुच्यते ।
एतैर्विमोहयत्येष ज्ञानमावृत्य देहिनम् ॥ ४० ॥

indriyāṇi mano buddhiraśyādhiṣṭhānamucyate
etairvimohayatyeṣa jñānamāvṛtya dehinam

The senses, mind and intellect are said to be their residence. Through these, the Wearer of the Body becomes deluded, and Wisdom becomes hidden.

-41-

तस्मात्त्वमिन्द्रियाण्यादौ नियम्य भरतर्षभ ।
पाप्मानं प्रजहि ह्येनं ज्ञानविज्ञाननाशनम् ॥ ४१ ॥

tasmāttvamindriyāṇyādau niyamya bharatarṣabha
pāpmānaṁ prajahi hyenaṁ jñānavijñānanāśanam

Therefore, oh Best of the Descendants of the Light of Wisdom (Arjuna), first you must control the senses, killing this evil which destroys Wisdom and the application of Wisdom.

-42-

इन्द्रियाणि पराण्याहुरिन्द्रियेभ्यः परं मनः ।
मनसस्तु परा बुद्धिर्यो बुद्धेः परतस्तु सः ॥ ४२ ॥

indriyāṇi parāṇyāhurindriyebhyaḥ paraṁ manaḥ
manasastu parā buddhiryo buddheḥ paratastu saḥ

The senses are said to be great. Greater than the senses is the mind. Greater than the mind is the intellect. Greater than the intellect is He.

-43-

एवं बुद्धेः परं बुद्ध्वा संस्तभ्यात्मानमात्मना ।
जहि शत्रुं महाबाहो कामरूपं दुरासदम् ॥ ४३ ॥

evaṁ buddheḥ paraṁ buddhvā
saṁstabhyātmānamātmanā
jahi śatruṁ mahābāho kāmarūpaṁ durāsadam

Oh One of Mighty Arms (Arjuna), knowing that which is greater than the intellect, subdue your own self by means of your own soul. Kill this enemy in the form of desire, which is so difficult to overcome.

इति श्रीमद्भगवद्गीतासु तृतीयोऽध्यायः ॥ ३ ॥

४

श्रीभगवानुवाच

śrībhagavānuvāca

The Respected Supreme Divinity said:

-1-

इमं विवस्वते योगं प्रोक्तवानहमव्ययम् ।
विवस्वान्मनवे प्राह मनुरिक्ष्वाकवेऽब्रवीत् ॥ १ ॥

imaṁ vivasvate yogaṁ proktavānahamavyayam
vivasvānmanave prāha manurikṣvākave-bravīt

I explained this eternal union to Brilliantly Shining, and Brilliantly Shining explained it to his son Protector of Mind. Protector of Mind taught it to his son Beholding Witness.

-2-

एवं परम्पराप्राप्तमिमं राजर्षयो विदुः ।
स कालेनेह महता योगो नष्टः परंतप ॥ २ ॥

evaṁ paramparāprāptamimaṁ rājarṣayo viduḥ
sa kāleneha mahatā yogo naṣṭaḥ paraṁtapa

Thus it was communicated through the generations of wise kings who knew. Because of the great passage of time this knowledge of union was lost, oh Supreme Light (Arjuna).

-3-

स एवायं मया तेऽद्य योगः प्रोक्तः पुरातनः ।
भक्तोऽसि मे सखा चेति रहस्यं ह्येतदुत्तमम् ॥ ३ ॥

sa evāyaṁ mayā te-dya yogaḥ proktaḥ purātanaḥ
bhakto-si me sakhā ceti rahasyaṁ hyetaduttamam

This is that same ancient teaching of union which I disclose to you today, this excellent secret, because you are a devotee and my friend.

अर्जुन उवाच

arjuna uvāca

Clarity of Pure Devotion said:

-4-

अपरं भवतो जन्म परं जन्म विवस्वतः ।

कथमेतद्विजानीयां त्वमादौ प्रोक्तवानिति ॥ ४ ॥

aparaṁ bhavato janma paraṁ janma vivasvataḥ
kathametadvijānīyāṁ tvamādau proktavāniti

Your birth was subsequent to that of Brilliantly Shining, and his birth was prior to yours. How shall I understand that this was taught by you from the beginning?

श्रीभगवानुवाच

śrībhagavānuvāca

The Respected Supreme Divinity said:

-5-

बहूनि मे व्यतीतानि जन्मानि तव चार्जुन ।

तान्यहं वेद सर्वाणि न त्वं वेत्थ परंतप ॥ ५ ॥

bahflni me vyatītāni janmāni tava cārjuna
tānyahaṁ veda sarvāṇi na tvaṁ vettha paraṁtapa

Many births have gone before, for both you and for Me, Clarity of Pure Devotion. I know all of them, but you have forgotten, oh One of Great Illumination.

-6-

अजोऽपि सन्नव्ययात्मा भूतानामीश्वरोऽपि सन् ।

प्रकृतिं स्वामधिष्ठाय संभवाम्यात्ममायया ॥ ६ ॥

ajo-pi sannavyayātmā bhūtānāmīśvaro-pi san
prakṛtiṁ svāmadhiṣṭhāya saṁbhavāmyātmamāyayā

This soul is never born, and never does it die. I exist as the Lord of All Existence. By controlling my nature, my soul manifests in measured (limited or perceivable) form.

-7-

यदा यदा हि धर्मस्य ग्लानिर्भवति भारत ।

अभ्युत्थानमधर्मस्य तदात्मानं सृजाम्यहम् ॥ ७ ॥

yadā yadā hi dharmasya glānirbhavati bhārata
abhyutthānamadharmasya tadātmānaṁ sṛjāmyaham

For whenever the Ideals of Perfection decline, Descendant of the Light of Wisdom (Arjuna), and there is a corresponding increase in selfish conduct, in derogation to the Ideal, then I make myself manifest.

-8-

परित्राणाय साधूनां विनाशाय च दुष्कृताम् ।
धर्मसंस्थापनार्थाय संभवामि युगे युगे ॥ ८ ॥

paritrāṇāya sādhūnāṁ vināśāya ca duṣkṛtām
dharmasaṁsthāpanārthāya saṁbhavāmi yuge yuge

For the protection of the performers of virtuous efficiency, for the destruction of evil actions, for the purpose of establishing the Ideal of Perfection, I take birth from time to time.

-9-

जन्म कर्म च मे दिव्यमेवं यो वेत्ति तत्त्वतः ।
त्यक्त्वा देहं पुनर्जन्म नैति मामेति सोऽर्जुन ॥ ९ ॥

janma karma ca me divyamevaṁ yo vetti tattvataḥ
tyaktvā dehaṁ punarjanma naiti māmeti so-rjuna

Who understands this principle that my birth and actions are divine, upon renouncing his body does not move from birth to birth. He attains Me.

-10-

वीतरागभयक्रोधा मन्मया मामुपाश्रिताः ।
बहवो ज्ञानतपसा पूता मद्भावमागताः ॥ १० ॥

vītarāgabhayakrodhā manmayā māmupāśritāḥ
bahavo jñānatapasā pūtā madbhāvamāgatāḥ

Devoid of passion, fear and anger, with mind fully absorbed in Me, purified by the light of wisdom, many have entered into My attitude of awareness.

-11-

ये यथा मां प्रपद्यन्ते तांस्तथैव भजाम्यहम् ।
मम वर्त्मानुवर्तन्ते मनुष्याः पार्थ सर्वशः ॥ ११ ॥

ye yathā māṁ prapadyante tāṁstathaiva bhajāmyaham
mama vartmānuvartante manuṣyāḥ pārtha sarvaśaḥ

Son of She Who Excels (Arjuna), in every way which men seek Me, in that same way I come to them, for every way that men follow is My path.

-12-

काङ्क्षन्तः कर्मणां सिद्धिं यजन्त इह देवताः ।
क्षिप्रं हि मानुषे लोके सिद्धिर्भवति कर्मजा ॥ १२ ॥

kāṅkṣantaḥ karmaṇāṁ siddhiṁ yajanta iha devatāḥ
kṣipraṁ hi mānuṣe loke siddhirbhavati karmajā

In any action in which men seek the attainment of perfection, they worship the Gods. Quickly in the world of men attainment of perfection is born from action.

-13-

चातुर्वर्ण्यं मया सृष्टं गुणकर्मविभागशः ।
तस्य कर्तारमपि मां विद्ध्यकर्तारमव्ययम् ॥ १३ ॥

cāturvarṇyaṁ mayā sṛṣṭaṁ guṇakarmavibhāgaśaḥ
tasya kartāramapi māṁ viddhyakartāramavyayam

The four functions of society3 were created by Me, divided by the predominant qualities of actions. Even though action is performed by Me, know Me to be beyond action.

-14-

न मां कर्माणि लिम्पन्ति न मे कर्मफले स्पृहा ।
इति मां योऽभिजानाति कर्मभिर्न स बध्यते ॥ १४ ॥

na māṁ karmāṇi limpanti na me karmaphale spṛhā
iti māṁ yo-bhijānāti karmabhirna sa badhyate

Actions do not bind Me because I do not desire the fruits of action. Who knows Me in this way will not be bound by actions.

-15-

एवं ज्ञात्वा कृतं कर्म पूर्वैरपि मुमुक्षुभिः ।
कुरु कर्मैव तस्मात्त्वं पूर्वैः पूर्वतरं कृतम् ॥ १५ ॥

evaṁ jñātvā kṛtaṁ karma pūrvairapi mumukṣubhiḥ
kuru karmaiva tasmāttvaṁ pūrvaiḥ pūrvataraṁ kṛtam

Knowing this, liberated souls from ancient times have performed their actions. Therefore, you also should perform all actions as those of ancient times have always performed.

-16-

किं कर्म किमकर्मेति कवयोऽप्यत्र मोहिताः ।
तत्ते कर्म प्रवक्ष्यामि यज्ज्ञात्वा मोक्ष्यसेऽशुभात् ॥ १६ ॥

kiṁ karma kimakarmeti kavayo-pyatra mohitāḥ
tatte karma pravakṣyāmi yajjñātvā mokṣyase-śubhāt

What is action? What is inaction? Even inspired poets are in confusion. I shall teach you of that action, knowing which, you will be liberated from impurity.

-17-

कर्मणो ह्यपि बोद्धव्यं बोद्धव्यं च विकर्मणः ।
अकर्मणश्च बोद्धव्यं गहना कर्मणो गतिः ॥ १७ ॥

karmaṇo hyapi boddhavyaṁ boddhavyaṁ ca vikarmaṇaḥ
akarmaṇaśca boddhavyaṁ gahanā karmaṇo gatiḥ

Know what is action, and know what is inefficient action. Know also what is inaction. The path of action is difficult to discern.

-18-

कर्मण्यकर्म यः पश्येदकर्मणि च कर्म यः ।
स बुद्धिमान्मनुष्येषु स युक्तः कृत्स्नकर्मकृत् ॥ १८ ॥

karmaṇyakarma yaḥ paśyedakarmaṇi ca karma yaḥ
sa buddhimānmanuṣyeṣu sa yuktaḥ kṛtsnakarmakṛt

Who perceives inaction in action, and action in inaction, is intelligent among men. He remains in union in every action he may perform.

-19-

यस्य सर्वे समारम्भाः कामसङ्कल्पवर्जिताः ।
ज्ञानाग्निदग्धकर्माणं तमाहुः पण्डितं बुधाः ॥ १९ ॥

yasya sarve samārambhāḥ kāmasaṅkalpavarjitāḥ
jñānāgnidagdhakarmāṇaṁ tamāhuḥ paṇḍitaṁ budhāḥ

Whose all undertakings have excluded selfish desire, whose actions have been purified in the fire of wisdom, is called knowledgeable by the intelligent.

-20-

त्यक्त्वा कर्मफलासङ्गं नित्यतृप्तो निराश्रयः ।

कर्मण्यभिप्रवृत्तोऽपि नैव किञ्चित्करोति सः ॥ २० ॥

tyaktvā karmaphalāsaṅgaṁ nityatṛpto nirāśrayaḥ
karmaṇyabhipravṛtto-pi naiva kiñcitkaroti saḥ

Having renounced attachment to the fruit of his actions, even while engaged in action, he does nothing at all. He is always satisfied and he is not dependent.

-21-

निराशीर्यतचित्तात्मा त्यक्तसर्वपरिग्रहः ।

शारीरं केवलं कर्म कुर्वन्नाप्नोति किल्बिषम् ॥ २१ ॥

nirāśīryatacittātmā tyaktasarvaparigrahaḥ
śārīraṁ kevalaṁ karma kurvannāpnoti kilbiṣam

Without desires, having controlled all thought reflected by the soul, renouncing all possession, only his body performs action. He incurs no fault.

-22-

यदृच्छालाभसंतुष्टो द्वन्द्वातीतो विमत्सरः ।

समः सिद्धावसिद्धौ च कृत्वापि न निबध्यते ॥ २२ ॥

yadṛcchālābhasaṁtuṣṭo dvandvātīto vimatsaraḥ
samaḥ siddhāvasiddhau ca kṛtvāpi na nibadhyate

He who is easily satisfied, beyond all opposites, without jealousy, equally balanced in success or in failure, even when acting he is not bound.

-23-

गतसङ्गस्य मुक्तस्य ज्ञानावस्थितचेतसः ।

यज्ञायाचरतः कर्म समग्रं प्रविलीयते ॥ २३ ॥

gatasaṅgasya muktasya jñānāvasthitacetasaḥ
yajñāyācarataḥ karma samagraṁ pravilīyate

He whose consciousness resides in wisdom is liberated from all attachments. He performs all action as sacrifice, and becomes completely absorbed.

-24-

ब्रह्मार्पणं ब्रह्म हविर्ब्रह्माग्नौ ब्रह्मणा हुतम् ।
ब्रह्मैव तेन गन्तव्यं ब्रह्मकर्मसमाधिना ॥ २४ ॥

brahmārpaṇaṁ brahma havir
brahmāgnau brahmaṇā hutam
brahmaiva tena gantavyaṁ brahmakarmasamādhinā

The Supreme Divinity makes the offering; the Supreme Divinity is the offering; offered to the Supreme Divinity, in the fire of the Supreme Divinity. By seeing the Supreme Divinity in all actions, one realizes that Supreme Divinity.

-25-

दैवमेवापरे यज्ञं योगिनः पर्युपासते ।
ब्रह्माग्नावपरे यज्ञं यज्ञेनैवोपजुह्वति ॥ २५ ॥

daivamevāpare yajñaṁ yoginaḥ paryupāsate
brahmāgnāvapare yajñaṁ yajñenaivopajuhvati

Some seekers of union offer worship in sacrifice only to the Gods, while others offer sacrifice in the fire of Supreme Divinity.

-26-

श्रोत्रादीनीन्द्रियाण्यन्ये संयमाग्निषु जुह्वति ।
शब्दादीन्विषयानन्य इन्द्रियाग्निषु जुह्वति ॥ २६ ॥

śrotrādīnīndriyāṇyanye saṁyamāgniṣu juhvati
śabdādīnviṣayānanya indriyāgniṣu juhvati

Others offer hearing and other senses into the fire of self-control, while others offer sound and other objects of perception into the fire of the senses.

-27-

सर्वाणीन्द्रियकर्माणि प्राणकर्माणि चापरे ।
आत्मसंयमयोगाग्नौ जुह्वति ज्ञानदीपिते ॥ २७ ॥

sarvāṇīndriyakarmāṇi prāṇakarmāṇi cāpare
ātmasaṁyamayogāgnau juhvati jñānadīpite

Some offer all the actions of all the organs, or the actions of breath or life itself, into the fire of union with a self-controlled soul illuminated by the light of wisdom.

-28-

द्रव्ययज्ञास्तपोयज्ञा योगयज्ञास्तथापरे ।

स्वाध्यायज्ञानयज्ञाश्च यतयः संशितव्रताः ॥ २८ ॥

dravyayajñāstapoyajñā yogayajñāstathāpare
svādhyāyajñānayajñāśca yatayaḥ saṁśitavratāḥ

Some offer sacrifice with things, some sacrifice through austerities, some sacrifice through the practice of union; some sacrifice through the study of wisdom, while other souls strive through the observance of vows.

-29-

अपाने जुह्वति प्राणं प्राणेऽपानं तथापरे ।

प्राणापानगती रुद्ध्वा प्राणायामपरायणाः ॥ २९ ॥

apāne juhvati prāṇaṁ prāṇe-pānaṁ tathāpare
prāṇāpānagatī ruddhvā prāṇāyāmaparāyaṇāḥ

Some offer the out-flowing breath into the in-flowing breath and the in-flowing breath into the out-flowing breath. Controlling the method of inhalation and exhalation, they strive for control of the life force.

-30-

अपरे नियताहाराः प्राणान्प्राणेषु जुह्वति ।

सर्वेऽप्येते यज्ञविदो यज्ञक्षपितकल्मषाः ॥ ३० ॥

apare niyatāhārāḥ prāṇānprāṇeṣu juhvati
sarve-pyete yajñavido yajñakṣapitakalmaṣāḥ

Others offer the restricted intake of food, or their breath into life. All these know sacrifice, and through sacrifice become devoid of faults.

-31-

यज्ञशिष्टामृतभुजो यान्ति ब्रह्म सनातनम् ।

नायं लोकोऽस्त्ययज्ञस्य कुतोऽन्यः कुरुसत्तम ॥ ३१ ॥

yajñaśiṣṭāmṛtabhujo yānti brahma sanātanam
nāyaṁ loko-styayajñasya kuto-nyaḥ kurusattama

Those who enjoy the nectar which remains from sacrifice attain the eternal Supreme Divinity. How can one be in this world if he does not sacrifice, oh Best among the Performers of Action (Arjuna)?

-32-

एवं बहुविधा यज्ञा वितता ब्रह्मणो मुखे ।
कर्मजान्विद्धि तान्सर्वानेवं ज्ञात्वा विमोक्ष्यसे ॥ ३२ ॥

evaṁ bahuvidhā yajñā vitatā brahmaṇo mukhe
karmajānviddhi tānsarvānevaṁ jñātvā vimokṣyase

Many ways of sacrifice have been expounded through the mouths of the knowledgeable. Know them all to be born from action, and this wisdom will set you free.

-33-

श्रेयान्द्रव्यमयाद्यज्ञाज्ज्ञानयज्ञः परंतप ।
सर्वं कर्माखिलं पार्थ ज्ञाने परिसमाप्यते ॥ ३३ ॥

śreyāndravyamayādyajñājjñānayajñaḥ paraṁtapa
sarvaṁ karmākhilaṁ pārtha jñāne parisamāpyate

Better than the sacrifice with things is the sacrifice with wisdom, oh Supremely Illuminated One (Arjuna). Son of She Who Excels (Arjuna), all actions without exception culminate in wisdom.

-34-

तद्विद्धि प्रणिपातेन परिप्रश्नेन सेवया ।
उपदेक्ष्यन्ति ते ज्ञानं ज्ञानिनस्तत्त्वदर्शिनः ॥ ३४ ॥

tadviddhi praṇipātena paripraśnena sevayā
upadekṣyanti te jñānaṁ jñāninastattvadarśinaḥ

The wise ones who have seen this principle can teach you wisdom. Bow to them, serve them, and ask this knowledge.

-35-

यज्ज्ञात्वा न पुनर्मोहमेवं यास्यसि पाण्डव ।
येन भूतान्यशेषेण द्रक्ष्यस्यात्मन्यथो मयि ॥ ३५ ॥

yajjñātvā na punarmohamevaṁ yāsyasi pāṇḍava
yena bhūtānyaśeṣeṇa drakṣyasyātmanyatho mayi

Oh Son of He Who is without Prejudice (Arjuna), knowing this you will no longer be subjected to confusion. By this you will see infinite existence in your own soul, and then your own soul in Me.

-36-

अपि चेदसि पापेभ्यः सर्वेभ्यः पापकृत्तमः ।

सर्वं ज्ञानप्लवेनैव वृजिनं संतरिष्यसि ॥ ३६ ॥

api cedasi pāpebhyaḥ sarvebhyaḥ pāpakṛttamaḥ
sarvaṁ jñānaplavenaiva vṛjinaṁ saṁtariṣyasi

Even if you were a person who committed great evil amongst all sinners, you can surely cross the ocean of evil by the raft of wisdom.

-37-

यथैधांसि समिद्धोऽग्निर्भस्मसात्कुरुतेऽर्जुन ।

ज्ञानाग्निः सर्वकर्माणि भस्मसात्कुरुते तथा ॥ ३७ ॥

yathaidhāṁsi samiddho-gnirbhasmasātkurute-rjuna
jñānāgniḥ sarvakarmāṇi bhasmasātkurute tathā

As the sacred fire turns all offerings to ashes, Clarity of Pure Devotion, so the fire of wisdom turns all actions to ashes.

-38-

न हि ज्ञानेन सदृशं पवित्रमिह विद्यते ।

तत्स्वयं योगसंसिद्धः कालेनात्मनि विन्दति ॥ ३८ ॥

na hi jñānena sadṛśaṁ pavitramiha vidyate
tatsvayaṁ yogasaṁsiddhaḥ kālenātmani vindati

For there is nothing that can be known or perceived to be more pure than wisdom. That one must learn for himself through the timely attainment of perfection of union with his own soul.

-39-

श्रद्धावाँल्लभते ज्ञानं तत्परः संयतेन्द्रियः ।

ज्ञानं लब्ध्वा परां शान्तिमचिरेणाधिगच्छति ॥ ३९ ॥

śraddhāvāṁllabhate jñānaṁ tatparaḥ saṁyatendriyaḥ
jñānaṁ labdhvā parāṁ śāntimacireṇādhigacchati

Having obtained strength of faith in the highest wisdom, one controls his senses. Having attained wisdom, he quickly attains to the highest peace.

-40-

अज्ञश्चाश्रद्दधानश्च संशयात्मा विनश्यति ।

नायं लोकोऽस्ति न परो न सुखं संशयात्मनः ॥ ४० ॥

ajñaścāśraddadhānaśca saṁśayātmā vinaśyati
nāyaṁ loko-sti na paro na sukhaṁ saṁśayātmanaḥ

The ignorant lack faith, and doubts destroy (or torment) the soul. For the soul in doubt neither this world has comfort, nor the higher worlds.

-41-

योगसंन्यस्तकर्माणं ज्ञानसंछिन्नसंशयम् ।

आत्मवन्तं न कर्माणि निबध्नन्ति धनंजय ॥ ४१ ॥

yogasaṁnyastakarmāṇaṁ jñānasaṁchinnasaṁśayam
ātmavantaṁ na karmāṇi nibadhnanti dhanaṁjaya

Conqueror of Wealth (Arjuna), who has renounced all action in divine union, who has cut all doubts to pieces by wisdom, who is master of his own soul, he is not bound by action.

-42-

तस्मादज्ञानसंभूतं हृत्स्थं ज्ञानासिनात्मनः ।

छित्त्वैनं संशयं योगमातिष्ठोत्तिष्ठ भारत ॥ ४२ ॥

tasmādajñānasaṁbhūtaṁ hṛtsthaṁ jñānāsinātmanaḥ
chittvainaṁ saṁśayaṁ yogamātiṣṭhottiṣṭha bhārata

Therefore, oh Descendant of the Light of Wisdom (Arjuna), let your soul take the sword of wisdom, and cut to pieces the doubts of your heart born of ignorance. Rise and become established in the perfection of union.

इति श्रीमद्भगवद्गीतासु चतुर्थोऽध्यायः ॥ ४ ॥

५

अर्जुन उवाच

arjuna uvāca
Clarity of Pure Devotion said:

-1-

संन्यासं कर्मणां कृष्ण पुनर्योगं च शंससि ।
यच्छ्रेय एतयोरेकं तन्मे ब्रूहि सुनिश्चितम् ॥ १ ॥

saṁnyāsaṁ karmaṇāṁ kṛṣṇa punaryogaṁ ca śaṁsasi
yacchreya etayorekaṁ tanme brūhi suniścitam

Doer of All (Kṛṣṇa), you praise union through establishment in truth and renunciation, and again union through action. Of the two tell me which is definitely better.

श्रीभगवानुवाच

śrībhagavānuvāca
The Respected Supreme Divinity said:

-2-

संन्यासः कर्मयोगश्च निःश्रेयसकरावुभौ ।
तयोस्तु कर्मसंन्यासात्कर्मयोगो विशिष्यते ॥ २ ॥

saṁnyāsaḥ karmayogaśca niḥśreyasakarāvubhau
tayostu karmasaṁnyāsātkarmayogo viśiṣyate

Union through establishment in truth and renunciation and union through action are both conducive to the highest good. But of the two, union through action is superior.

-3-

ज्ञेयः स नित्यसंन्यासी यो न द्वेष्टि न काङ्क्षति ।
निर्द्वन्द्वो हि महाबाहो सुखं बन्धात्प्रमुच्यते ॥ ३ ॥

jñeyaḥ sa nityasaṁnyāsī yo na dveṣṭhi na kāṅkṣati
nirdvandvo hi mahābāho sukhaṁ bandhātpramucyate

Oh One of Mighty Arms (Arjuna), the one who maintains neither desires for nor desires against, is free from conflict, and is known as someone who is eternally established in truth and renunciation. His happiness lies in freedom from bondage.

-4-

सांख्ययोगौ पृथग्बालाः प्रवदन्ति न पण्डिताः ।
एकमप्यास्थितः सम्यगुभयोर्विन्दते फलम् ॥ ४ ॥

**sāṁkhyayogau pṛthagbālāḥ pravadanti na paṇḍitāḥ
ekamapyāsthitaḥ samyagubhayorvindate phalam**

Only those without understanding declare the path of the Enumeration of Principles to be different from the Path of Union, not the knowledgeable. Firmly established in either path, one attains to the fruit of both.

-5-

यत्सांख्यैः प्राप्यते स्थानं तद्योगैरपि गम्यते ।
एकं सांख्यं च योगं च यः पश्यति स पश्यति ॥ ५ ॥

**yatsāṁkhyaiḥ prāpyate sthānaṁ tadyogairapi gamyate
ekaṁ sāṁkhyaṁ ca yogaṁ ca yaḥ paśyati sa paśyati**

That position (realization) attained by the practitioners of the path of the Enumeration of Principles, is also reached by practitioners of the Path of Union. Who sees that the path of the Enumeration of Principles and the Path of Union are one and the same, he truly sees, (he really understands).

-6-

संन्यासस्तु महाबाहो दुःखमाप्तुमयोगतः ।
योगयुक्तो मुनिर्ब्रह्म नचिरेणाधिगच्छति ॥ ६ ॥

**saṁnyāsastu mahābāho duḥkhamāptumayogataḥ
yogayukto munirbrahma nacireṇādhigacchati**

Oh One of Mighty Arms (Arjuna), establishment in truth and renunciation is impossible to attain without union. United in union, a wise man reaches Supreme Divinity in a short time.

-7-

योगयुक्तो विशुद्धात्मा विजितात्मा जितेन्द्रियः ।
सर्वभूतात्मभूतात्मा कुर्वन्नपि न लिप्यते ॥ ७ ॥

**yogayukto viśuddhātmā vijitātmā jitendriyaḥ
sarvabhūtātmabhūtātmā kurvannapi na lipyate**

United in union, with a purified soul, master of his soul, he has control of his senses. Recognizing his soul as the soul of all existence, even performing action, he remains unattached.

-8-

नैव किंचित्करोमीति युक्तो मन्येत तत्त्ववित्।

पश्यञ्शृण्वन्स्पृशञ्जिघ्रन्नश्नन्गच्छन्स्वपञ्श्वसन् ॥ ८ ॥

naiva kiṁcitkaromīti yukto manyeta tattvavit
paśyañśṛṇvanspṛśañjighrannaśnangacchansvapañśvasan

The man of union, who knows the principles, thinks "I am doing nothing" (or I am not the doer). Even while seeing, hearing, moving, touching, smelling, eating, drinking, moving, sleeping, breathing,

-9-

प्रलपन्विसृजन्गृह्णन्नुन्मिषन्निमिषन्नपि ।

इन्द्रियाणीन्द्रियार्थेषु वर्तन्त इति धारयन् ॥ ९ ॥

pralapanvisṛjangṛhṇannunmiṣannimiṣannapi
indriyāṇīndriyārtheṣu vartanta iti dhārayan
speaking, attending the calls of nature, grasping, opening and closing the eyes, he contemplates that the senses are moving among the objects of sense.

-10-

ब्रह्मण्याधाय कर्माणि सङ्गं त्यक्त्वा करोति यः ।

लिप्यते न स पापेन पद्मपत्रमिवाम्भसा ॥ १० ॥

brahmaṇyādhāya karmāṇi saṅgaṁ tyaktvā karoti yaḥ
lipyate na sa pāpena padmapatramivāmbhasā

He who performs all actions as an offering to Supreme Divinity renouncing all attachment, remains free from sin as water does not remain upon the lotus leaf.

-11-

कायेन मनसा बुद्ध्या केवलैरिन्द्रियैरपि ।

योगिनः कर्म कुर्वन्ति सङ्गं त्यक्त्वात्मशुद्धये ॥ ११ ॥

kāyena manasā buddhyā kevalairindriyairapi
yoginaḥ karma kurvanti saṅgaṁ tyaktvātmaśuddhaye

Men of union, renouncing all attachment, perform all action with a pure soul. Only body, mind, intellect, and organs of knowledge and action work, free from the feeling of mine.

-12-

युक्तः कर्मफलं त्यक्त्वा शान्तिमाप्नोति नैष्ठिकीम् ।
अयुक्तः कामकारेण फले सक्तो निबध्यते ॥ १२ ॥

yuktaḥ karmaphalaṁ tyaktvā śāntimāpnoti naiṣṭhikīm
ayuktaḥ kāmakāreṇa phale sakto nibadhyate

Renouncing the fruits of action, the man of union attains peace, not the man of desires. He who is not in union, motivated by selfish desires, becomes bound by attachment to results.

-13-

सर्वकर्माणि मनसा संन्यस्यास्ते सुखं वशी ।
नवद्वारे पुरे देही नैव कुर्वन्न कारयन् ॥ १३ ॥

sarvakarmāṇi manasā saṁnyasyāste sukhaṁ vaśī
navadvāre pure dehī naiva kurvanna kārayan

He who is self-controlled rests in comfort, renouncing the contemplations of all actions. The Wearer of the Body who dwells in the City of Nine Gates neither acts nor causes others to act.

-14-

न कर्तृत्वं न कर्माणि लोकस्य सृजति प्रभुः ।
न कर्मफलसंयोगं स्वभावस्तु प्रवर्तते ॥ १४ ॥

na kartṛtvaṁ na karmāṇi lokasya sṛjati prabhuḥ
na karmaphalasaṁyogaṁ svabhāvastu pravartate

The Lord creates neither the actors nor the actions, nor even union with the fruits of actions. Rather, the essential nature of individual beings evolves (according to its nature).

-15-

नादत्ते कस्यचित्पापं न चैव सुकृतं विभुः ।
अज्ञानेनावृतं ज्ञानं तेन मुह्यन्ति जन्तवः ॥ १५ ॥

nādatte kasyacitpāpaṁ na caiva sukṛtaṁ vibhuḥ
ajñānenāvṛtaṁ jñānaṁ tena muhyanti jantavaḥ

The Omnipresent Lord does not accept the sins of anyone nor their acts of excellence. Wisdom and ignorance continually revolve around each other. Therefore, living beings become foolish.

-16-

ज्ञानेन तु तदज्ञानं येषां नाशितमात्मनः ।
तेषामादित्यवज्ज्ञानं प्रकाशयति तत्परम् ॥ १६ ॥

jñānena tu tadajñānaṁ yeṣāṁ nāśitamātmanaḥ
teṣāmādityavajjñānaṁ prakāśayati tatparam

But for those souls whose ignorance has been destroyed by wisdom, their wisdom illuminates the Supreme like the radiance of the light of the sun.

-17-

तद्बुद्धयस्तदात्मानस्तन्निष्ठास्तत्परायणाः ।
गच्छन्त्यपुनरावृत्तिं ज्ञाननिर्धूतकल्मषाः ॥ १७ ॥

tadbuddhayastadātmānastanniṣṭhāstatparāyaṇāḥ
gacchantyapunarāvṛttiṁ jñānanirdhūtakalmaṣāḥ

Those for whom the intellect contemplates only That, the soul is absorbed in That, bear loyalty only to That, have That as their ultimate goal; they go and again do not return. Wisdom has made them void of defects.

-18-

विद्याविनयसंपन्ने ब्राह्मणे गवि हस्तिनि ।
शुनि चैव श्वपाके च पण्डिताः समदर्शिनः ॥ १८ ॥

vidyāvinayasaṁpanne brāhmaṇe gavi hastini
śuni caiva śvapāke ca paṇḍitāḥ samadarśinaḥ

Knowledge endows one with humility. The learned perceive with equanimity one who knows wisdom, a cow, an elephant, a dog, or a man of low status.

-19-

इहैव तैर्जितः सर्गो येषां साम्ये स्थितं मनः ।
निर्दोषं हि समं ब्रह्म तस्माद् ब्रह्मणि ते स्थिताः ॥ १९ ॥

ihaiva tairjitaḥ sargo yeṣāṁ sāmye sthitaṁ manaḥ
nirdoṣaṁ hi samaṁ brahma tasmād brahmaṇi te sthitāḥ

Even here, creation is conquered by them whose minds are established in equanimity. For Supreme Divinity allows no faults and is always the same. Therefore, they are established in Supreme Divinity.

-20-

न प्रहृष्येत्प्रियं प्राप्य नोद्विजेत्प्राप्य चाप्रियम् ।
स्थिरबुद्धिरसंमूढो ब्रह्मविद् ब्रह्मणि स्थितः ॥ २० ॥

na prahṛṣyetpriyaṁ prāpya nodvijetprāpya cāpriyam
sthirabuddhirasaṁmūḍho brahmavid brahmaṇi sthitaḥ

Neither will he rejoice upon obtaining that which is desirable, nor will he be perturbed upon obtaining the undesirable. Fixed in intelligence unencumbered by foolishness, one who knows Supreme Divinity is established in Supreme Divinity.

-21-

बाह्यस्पर्शेष्वसक्तात्मा विन्दत्यात्मनि यत्सुखम् ।
स ब्रह्मयोगयुक्तात्मा सुखमक्षयमश्नुते ॥ २१ ॥

bāhyasparśeṣvasaktātmā vindatyātmani yatsukham
sa brahmayogayuktātmā sukhamakṣayamaśnute

With his soul unattached to the contacts with the external, happiness is found in the Soul Itself. He has united his soul in the union with Supreme Divinity, and enjoys infinite happiness.

-22-

ये हि संस्पर्शजा भोगा दुःखयोनय एव ते ।
आद्यन्तवन्तः कौन्तेय न तेषु रमते बुधः ॥ २२ ॥

ye hi saṁsparśajā bhogā duḥkhayonaya eva te
ādyantavantaḥ kaunteya na teṣu ramate budhaḥ

For those pleasures born from external contacts are certainly the womb of sorrows. Oh Son of Who Takes Away the Deficiency of Others (Arjuna), the intelligent will not rejoice in that which has a beginning and an end.

-23-

शक्नोतीहैव यः सोढुं प्राक्शरीरविमोक्षणात् ।
कामक्रोधोद्भवं वेगं स युक्तः स सुखी नरः ॥ २३ ॥

śaknotīhaiva yaḥ soḍhuṁ prākśarīravimokṣaṇāt
kāmakrodhodbhavaṁ vegaṁ sa yuktaḥ sa sukhī naraḥ

That man who is able to bear patiently the agitation born of desire and anger even here, before being liberated from the body, he is in union, he is happy.

-24-

योऽन्तःसुखोऽन्तरारामस्तथान्तर्ज्योतिरेव यः ।
स योगी ब्रह्मनिर्वाणं ब्रह्मभूतोऽधिगच्छति ॥ २४ ॥

yo-ntaḥsukho-ntarārāmastathāntarjyotireva yaḥ
sa yogī brahmanirvāṇaṁ brahmabhūto-dhigacchati

Who has happiness within, who has tranquility within, who is in union with the light within, he alone is a man in union with the Infinite Supreme Bliss, and attains to Oneness with the Supreme Divinity.

-25-

लभन्ते ब्रह्मनिर्वाणमृषयः क्षीणकल्मषाः ।
छिन्नद्वैधा यतात्मानः सर्वभूतहिते रताः ॥ २५ ॥

labhante brahmanirvāṇamṛṣayaḥ kṣīṇakalmaṣāḥ
chinnadvaidhā yatātmānaḥ sarvabhūtahite ratāḥ

Having attained to Oneness with the Supreme Divinity, the seers of divinity have destroyed their defects. Controlling their own selves, they cut through duality. They delight in the welfare of all beings.

-26-

कामक्रोधवियुक्तानां यतीनां यतचेतसाम् ।
अभितो ब्रह्मनिर्वाणं वर्तते विदितात्मनाम् ॥ २६ ॥

kāmakrodhaviyuktānāṁ yatīnāṁ yatacetasām
abhito brahmanirvāṇaṁ vartate viditātmanām

Those self-controlled beings who have controlled their consciousness are free from anger and desire. The soul established in wisdom on all sides (in every way) exists in Oneness with the Supreme Divinity.

-27-

स्पर्शान्कृत्वा बहिर्बाह्यांश्चक्षुश्चैवान्तरे भ्रुवोः ।
प्राणापानौ समौ कृत्वा नासाभ्यन्तरचारिणौ ॥ २७ ॥

sparśānkṛtvā bahirbāhyāṁścakṣuścaivāntare bhruvoḥ
prāṇāpānau samau kṛtvā nāsābhyantaracāriṇau

Withdrawing contacts from all externals, and fixing the gaze within between the two eyebrows, making the incoming breath equal to the outflowing breath moving through the nostrils,

-28-

यतेन्द्रियमनोबुद्धिर्मुनिर्मोक्षपरायणः ।
विगतेच्छाभयक्रोधो यः सदा मुक्त एव सः ॥ २८ ॥

yatendriyamanobuddhirmunirmokṣaparāyaṇaḥ
vigatecchābhayakrodho yaḥ sadā mukta eva saḥ

controlling the senses, mind and intellect, the goal of the wise is liberation. Without desire, fear or anger, he alone is certainly free.

-29-

भोक्तारं यज्ञतपसां सर्वलोकमहेश्वरम् ।
सुहृदं सर्वभूतानां ज्ञात्वा मां शान्तिमृच्छति ॥ २९ ॥

bhoktāraṁ yajñatapasāṁ sarvalokamaheśvaram
suhṛdaṁ sarvabhūtānāṁ jñātvā māṁ śāntimṛcchati

By knowing Me as the Enjoyer of sacrifices and purifying austerities, and as the Great Supreme Lord of all the worlds, as the friend of all existence, he attains peace.

इति श्रीमद्भगवद्गीतासु पञ्चमोऽध्यायः ॥ ५ ॥

६

श्रीभगवानुवाच

śrībhagavānuvāca

The Respected Supreme Divinity said:

-1-

अनाश्रितः कर्मफलं कार्यं कर्म करोति यः ।
स संन्यासी च योगी च न निरग्निर्न चाक्रियः ॥ १ ॥

anāśritaḥ karmaphalaṁ kāryaṁ karma karoti yaḥ
sa saṁnyāsī ca yogī ca na niragnirna cākriyaḥ

Who performs all actions without dependency on the fruits or effects of action, he is established in truth and renunciation and is a man of union, not he who is without fire or without action.

-2-

यं संन्यासमिति प्राहुर्योगं तं विद्धि पाण्डव ।
न ह्यसंन्यस्तसङ्कल्पो योगी भवति कश्चन ॥ २ ॥

yaṁ saṁnyāsamiti prāhuryogaṁ taṁ viddhi pāṇḍava
na hyasaṁnyastasaṅkalpo yogī bhavati kaścana

Oh Son of He Who is without Prejudice (Arjuna), know that which is called union is the same as being established in truth and renunciation; for no one becomes a man of union without renouncing personal desires.

-3-

आरुरुक्षोर्मुनेर्योगं कर्म कारणमुच्यते ।
योगारूढस्य तस्यैव शमः कारणमुच्यते ॥ ३ ॥

ārurukṣormuneryogaṁ karma kāraṇamucyate
yogārūḍhasya tasyaiva śamaḥ kāraṇamucyate

Action is said to be the cause for the wise man who is striving to union. Peace and freedom from external objects is the method of reaching to union.

-4-

यदा हि नेन्द्रियार्थेषु न कर्मस्वनुषज्जते ।
सर्वसङ्कल्पसंन्यासी योगारूढस्तदोच्यते ॥ ४ ॥

yadā hi nendriyārtheṣu na karmasvanuṣajjate
sarvasaṅkalpasaṁnyāsī yogārūḍhastadocyate

Then one is said to have reached to union. When in all desires he is established in truth and renunciation, he remains without attachment to the objects of sense in all actions.

-5-

उद्धरेदात्मनात्मानं नात्मानमवसादयेत् ।
आत्मैव ह्यात्मनो बन्धुरात्मैव रिपुरात्मनः ॥ ५ ॥

uddharedātmanātmānaṁ nātmānamavasādayet
ātmaiva hyātmano bandhurātmaiva ripurātmanaḥ

Let the soul be raised by the soul, and do not let the soul be lowered. Only the soul is the friend of the soul, only the soul is the enemy of the soul.

-6-

बन्धुरात्मात्मनस्तस्य येनात्मैवात्मना जितः ।
अनात्मनस्तु शत्रुत्वे वर्तेतात्मैव शत्रुवत् ॥ ६ ॥

bandhurātmātmanastasya yenātmaivātmanā jitaḥ
anātmanastu śatrutve vartetātmaiva śatruvat

For he who has conquered his soul by his soul, he has actually made his soul a friend to his soul. But for he whose soul is in the position of an enemy, he treats his soul as an enemy.

-7-

जितात्मनः प्रशान्तस्य परमात्मा समाहितः ।
शीतोष्णसुखदुःखेषु तथा मानापमानयोः ॥ ७ ॥

jitātmanaḥ praśāntasya paramātmā samāhitaḥ
śītoṣṇasukhaduḥkheṣu tathā mānāpamānayoḥ

Who has conquered his soul has the peace of the Supreme Soul, maintaining equilibrium while experiencing cold or hot, pleasure or pain, honor or insult.

-8-

ज्ञानविज्ञानतृप्तात्मा कूटस्थो विजितेन्द्रियः ।
युक्त इत्युच्यते योगी समलोष्टाश्मकाञ्चनः ॥ ८ ॥

**jñānavijñānatṛptātmā kūṭastho vijitendriyaḥ
yukta ityucyate yogī samaloṣṭāśmakāñcanaḥ**

That soul who has conquered his senses, who remains fixed in the delight of knowledge and wisdom, who is in harmony, who regards earth, stone or gold as of equal value, he is said to be a man of union.

-9-

सुहृन्मित्रार्युदासीनमध्यस्थद्वेष्यबन्धुषु ।
साधुष्वपि च पापेषु समबुद्धिर्विशिष्यते ॥ ९ ॥

**suhṛnmitrāryudāsīnamadhyasthadveṣyabandhuṣu
sādhuṣvapi ca pāpeṣu samabuddhirviśiṣyate**

He excels, who from a good heart, without any selfish interest, regards friends, enemies and those in between, the contemptible and the beloved, the virtuous and the sinful, with equality of intelligence.

-10-

योगी युञ्जीत सततमात्मानं रहसि स्थितः ।
एकाकी यतचित्तात्मा निराशीरपरिग्रहः ॥ १० ॥

**yogī yuñjīta satatamātmānaṁ rahasi sthitaḥ
ekākī yatacittātmā nirāśīraparigrahaḥ**

A man of union should always remain in secretive communion with his own soul, in Oneness, controlling the awareness of his soul, without desire, greed or jealousy.

-11-

शुचौ देशे प्रतिष्ठाप्य स्थिरमासनमात्मनः ।
नात्युच्छ्रितं नातिनीचं चैलाजिनकुशोत्तरम् ॥ ११ ॥

**śucau deśe pratiṣṭhāpya sthiramāsanamātmanaḥ
nātyucchritaṁ nātinīcaṁ cailājinakuśottaram**

Such an individual should establish his seat for meditation in a clean place, neither too high nor too low, covered by cloth, deer skin or kuśa grass.

-12-

तत्रैकाग्रं मनः कृत्वा यतचित्तेन्द्रियक्रियः ।

उपविश्यासने युञ्ज्याद्योगमात्मविशुद्धये ॥ १२ ॥

tatraikāgraṁ manaḥ kṛtvā yatacittendriyakriyaḥ
upaviśyāsane yuñjyādyogamātmaviśuddhaye

Being seated there on the meditation seat, he should make his mind one-pointed, control the awareness of the functions of sense, and commune in the union with the purity of his own soul.

-13-

समं कायशिरोग्रीवं धारयन्नचलं स्थिरः ।

संप्रेक्ष्य नासिकाग्रं स्वं दिशश्चानवलोकयन् ॥ १३ ॥

samaṁ kāyaśirogrīvaṁ dhārayannacalaṁ sthiraḥ
saṁprekṣya nāsikāgraṁ svaṁ diśaścānavalokayan

Still, without movement, he should hold his body, head and neck in equipoise. Staring at the tip of his nose, he should not look in other directions.

-14-

प्रशान्तात्मा विगतभीर्ब्रह्मचारिव्रते स्थितः ।

मनः संयम्य मच्चित्तो युक्त आसीत मत्परः ॥ १४ ॥

praśāntātmā vigatabhīrbrahmacārivrate sthitaḥ
manaḥ saṁyamya maccitto yukta āsīta matparaḥ

Fixed in the vow to move towards God, without fear, with peace in his soul, controlling his mind, with awareness on Me, he should undertake to unite with Me, the Supreme.

-15-

युञ्जन्नेवं सदात्मानं योगी नियतमानसः ।

शान्तिं निर्वाणपरमां मत्संस्थामधिगच्छति ॥ १५ ॥

yuñjannevaṁ sadātmānaṁ yogī niyatamānasaḥ
śāntiṁ nirvāṇaparamāṁ matsaṁsthāmadhigacchati

Thus the man of union controls his mind and is always in union with his own soul. Established in Me, he attains the peace and ecstasy of the ultimate equilibrium.

-16-

नात्यश्नतस्तु योगोऽस्ति न चैकान्तमनश्नतः ।
न चाति स्वप्नशीलस्य जाग्रतो नैव चार्जुन ॥ १६ ॥

nātyaśnatastu yogo-sti na caikāntamanaśnataḥ
na cāti svapnaśīlasya jāgrato naiva cārjuna

Clarity of Pure Devotion, union is not for one who eats excessively, nor for one who does not eat sufficiently. Neither is it for one who sleeps too much, nor for one who does not sleep enough.

-17-

युक्ताहारविहारस्य युक्तचेष्टस्य कर्मसु ।
युक्तस्वप्नावबोधस्य योगो भवति दुःखहा ॥ १७ ॥

yuktāhāravihārasya yuktaceṣṭasya karmasu
yuktasvapnāvabodhasya yogo bhavati duḥkhahā

The man of union is in union in his consumption and his abstinence, in union with efforts of all actions, in union with his dreams and with his knowledge, and this union destroys all pain.

-18-

यदा विनियतं चित्तमात्मन्येवावतिष्ठते ।
निःस्पृहः सर्वकामेभ्यो युक्त इत्युच्यते तदा ॥ १८ ॥

yadā viniyataṁ cittamātmanyevāvatiṣṭhate
niḥspṛhaḥ sarvakāmebhyo yukta ityucyate tadā

When the objects of consciousness are fully controlled and the soul rests without the touch of desire, then one is said to be in union.

-19-

यथा दीपो निवातस्थो नेङ्गते सोपमा स्मृता ।
योगिनो यतचित्तस्य युञ्जतो योगमात्मनः ॥ १९ ॥

yathā dīpo nivātastho neṅgate sopamā smṛtā
yogino yatacittasya yuñjato yogamātmanaḥ

The soul who practices union, who has controlled the objects of consciousness in union, is compared to a still flame without flicker in a place with no wind.

-20-

यत्रोपरमते चित्तं निरुद्धं योगसेवया ।

यत्र चैवात्मनात्मानं पश्यन्नात्मनि तुष्यति ॥ २० ॥

yatroparamate cittaṁ niruddhaṁ yogasevayā
yatra caivātmanātmānaṁ paśyannātmani tuṣyati

When by the practice of union the objects of consciousness are restrained and the mind ceases from motion, and when the soul is perceived by the soul, the soul is satisfied.

-21-

सुखमात्यन्तिकं यत्तद्बुद्धि ग्राह्यमतीन्द्रियम् ।

वेत्ति यत्र न चैवायं स्थितश्चलति तत्त्वतः ॥ २१ ॥

sukhamātyantikaṁ yattadbuddhi grāhyamatīndriyam
vetti yatra na caivāyaṁ sthitaścalati tattvataḥ

He knows that universal happiness beyond the senses and beyond that which can be understood by the intellect, established in which he does not move from the true state.

-22-

यं लब्ध्वा चापरं लाभं मन्यते नाधिकं ततः ।

यस्मिन्स्थितो न दुःखेन गुरुणापि विचाल्यते ॥ २२ ॥

yaṁ labdhvā cāparaṁ lābhaṁ manyate nādhikaṁ tataḥ
yasminsthito na duḥkhena guruṇāpi vicālyate

Having gained that, he thinks there can be no greater gain. Being established in that, he remains unmoved even by the greatest pains.

-23-

तं विद्याद्दुःखसंयोगवियोगं योगसंज्ञितम् ।

स निश्चयेन योक्तव्यो योगोऽनिर्विण्णचेतसा ॥ २३ ॥

taṁ vidyādduḥkhasaṁyogaviyogaṁ yogasaṁjñitam
sa niścayena yoktavyo yogo-nirviṇṇacetasā

Let the disassociation from the union with pain be known as Yoga -- union. This union should be practiced with firm determination and unwavering consciousness

-24-

सङ्कल्पप्रभवान्कामांस्त्यक्त्वा सर्वानशेषतः ।
मनसैवेन्द्रियग्रामं विनियम्य समन्ततः ॥ २४ ॥

saṅkalpaprabhavānkāmāṁstyaktvā sarvānaśeṣataḥ
manasaivendriyagrāmaṁ viniyamya samantataḥ

by renouncing all of the determinations born of endless desires, and even controlling all of the organs of knowledge and action from all sides.

-25-

शनैः शनैरुपरमेद्बुद्ध्या धृतिगृहीतया ।
आत्मसंस्थं मनः कृत्वा न किंचिदपि चिन्तयेत् ॥ २५ ॥

śanaiḥ śanairuparamedbuddhyā dhṛtigṛhītayā
ātmasaṁsthaṁ manaḥ kṛtvā na kiṁcidapi cintayet

With the intellect held securely, gently let the mind cease from motion. Make the mind reside in the soul and do not allow other thoughts.

-26-

यतो यतो निश्चरति मनश्चञ्चलमस्थिरम् ।
ततस्ततो नियम्यैतदात्मन्येव वशं नयेत् ॥ २६ ॥

yato yato niścarati manaścañcalamasthiram
tatastato niyamyaitadātmanyeva vaśaṁ nayet

No matter what causes the restless unsteady mind to roam, let him restrain it from that. He will bring it under control in the soul alone.

-27-

प्रशान्तमनसं ह्येनं योगिनं सुखमुत्तमम् ।
उपैति शान्तरजसं ब्रह्मभूतमकल्मषम् ॥ २७ ॥

praśāntamanasaṁ hyenaṁ yoginaṁ sukhamuttamam
upaiti śāntarajasaṁ brahmabhūtamakalmaṣam

For the man of union comes the ultimate happiness, for he has peace in his mind, his passions are at peace, he is without iniquity and has verily become the Supreme Divinity.

-28-

युञ्जन्नेवं सदात्मानं योगी विगतकल्मषः ।
सुखेन ब्रह्मसंस्पर्शमत्यन्तं सुखमश्नुते ॥ २८ ॥

yuñjannevaṁ sadātmānaṁ yogī vigatakalmaṣaḥ
sukhena brahmasaṁsparśamatyantaṁ sukhamaśnute

The soul who always practices this becomes a man of union free from iniquity. Easily he touches Supreme Divinity and enjoys infinite happiness.

-29-

सर्वभूतस्थमात्मानं सर्वभूतानि चात्मनि ।
ईक्षते योगयुक्तात्मा सर्वत्र समदर्शनः ॥ २९ ॥

sarvabhūtasthamātmānaṁ sarvabhūtāni cātmani
īkṣate yogayuktātmā sarvatra samadarśanaḥ

He sees his soul residing in all beings, and all beings in his soul. The soul who is united in union sees everything everywhere in equilibrium.

-30-

यो मां पश्यति सर्वत्र सर्वं च मयि पश्यति ।
तस्याहं न प्रणश्यामि स च मे न प्रणश्यति ॥ ३० ॥

yo māṁ paśyati sarvatra sarvaṁ ca mayi paśyati
tasyāhaṁ na praṇaśyāmi sa ca me na praṇaśyati

He who sees Me everywhere in all and sees all everywhere in Me, to him I never become lost nor is he ever lost to Me.

-31-

सर्वभूतस्थितं यो मां भजत्येकत्वमास्थितः ।
सर्वथा वर्तमानोऽपि स योगी मयि वर्तते ॥ ३१ ॥

sarvabhūtasthitaṁ yo māṁ bhajatyekatvamāsthitaḥ
sarvathā vartamāno-pi sa yogī mayi vartate

He who is established in Oneness and worships Me residing in all beings in every circumstance, he dwells with Me. He lives in union with Me.

-32-

आत्मौपम्येन सर्वत्र समं पश्यति योऽर्जुन ।
सुखं वा यदि वा दुःखं स योगी परमो मतः ॥ ३२ ॥

ātmaupamyena sarvatra samaṁ paśyati yo-rjuna
sukhaṁ vā yadi vā duḥkhaṁ sa yogī paramo mataḥ

Clarity of Pure Devotion, he who perceives equilibrium everywhere just as in his own soul, he is the same in pleasure as in pain. He is regarded as a man of supreme union.

अर्जुन उवाच

arjuna uvāca

Clarity of Pure Devotion said:

-33-

योऽयं योगस्त्वया प्रोक्तः साम्येन मधुसूदन ।
एतस्याहं न पश्यामि चञ्चलत्वात्स्थितिं स्थिराम् ॥ ३३ ॥

yo-yaṁ yogastvayā proktaḥ sāmyena madhusūdana
etasyāhaṁ na paśyāmi cañcalatvātsthitiṁ sthirām

Oh Slayer of Too Much (Kṛṣṇa), I do not perceive any substance of stillness for this union of equilibrium which you are teaching. All existence is restless.

-34-

चञ्चलं हि मनः कृष्ण प्रमाथि बलवद्दृढम् ।
तस्याहं निग्रहं मन्ये वायोरिव सुदुष्करम् ॥ ३४ ॥

cañcalaṁ hi manaḥ kṛṣṇa pramāthi balavaddṛḍham
tasyāhaṁ nigrahaṁ manye vāyoriva suduṣkaram

Oh Doer of All (Kṛṣṇa), the mind is verily restless, turbulent, strong and stubborn. To gain mastery of the mind is as difficult as to control the wind.

श्रीभगवानुवाच

śrībhagavānuvāca

The Respected Supreme Divinity said:

-35-

असंशयं महाबाहो मनो दुर्निग्रहं चलम् ।
अभ्यासेन तु कौन्तेय वैराग्येण च गृह्यते ॥ ३५ ॥

asaṁśayaṁ mahābāho mano durnigrahaṁ calam
abhyāsena tu kaunteya vairāgyeṇa ca gṛhyate

Oh One of Mighty Arms (Arjuna), without a doubt the movement of the mind is difficult to control. But, oh Son of Who Takes Away the Deficiency of Others (Arjuna), by practicing freedom from attachment it can be controlled.

-36-

असंयतात्मना योगो दुष्प्राप इति मे मतिः ।
वश्यात्मना तु यतता शक्योऽवाप्तुमुपायतः ॥ ३६ ॥

asaṁyatātmanā yogo duṣprāpa iti me matiḥ
vaśyātmanā tu yatatā śakyo-vāptumupāyataḥ

I agree that union is impossible of attainment by a soul who has not self-control. But it is possible for the self-controlled soul who strives to attain it by proper means.

अर्जुन उवाच

arjuna uvāca

Clarity of Pure Devotion said:

-37-

अयतिः श्रद्धयोपेतो योगाच्चलितमानसः ।
अप्राप्य योगसंसिद्धिं कां गतिं कृष्ण गच्छति ॥ ३७ ॥

ayatiḥ śraddhayopeto yogāccalitamānasaḥ
aprāpya yogasaṁsiddhiṁ kāṁ gatiṁ kṛṣṇa gacchati

If one has faith, yet cannot control his mind which wanders away from perfection in union, what end does he meet, oh Doer of All (Kṛṣṇa)?

\- 38 -

कच्चिन्नोभयविभ्रष्टश्छिन्नाभ्रमिव नश्यति।
अप्रतिष्ठो महाबाहो विमूढो ब्रह्मणः पथि॥ ३८॥

kaccinnobhayavibhraṣṭaśchinnābhramiva naśyati
apratiṣṭho mahābāho vimūḍho brahmaṇaḥ pathi

Is it not that fallen from both paths (the path of union and the path of devotion) without the support of either, he perishes like a torn cloud, oh One of Mighty Arms (Kṛṣṇa), a seeker of truth deluded in the path?

\- 39 -

एतन्मे संशयं कृष्ण छेत्तुमर्हस्यशेषतः।
त्वदन्यः संशयस्यास्य छेत्ता न ह्युपपद्यते॥ ३९॥

etanme saṁśayaṁ kṛṣṇa chettumarhasyaśeṣataḥ
tvadanyaḥ saṁśayasyāsya chettā na hyupapadyate

You ought to completely dispel my doubts, Doer of All (Kṛṣṇa), for there is no other more capable to dispel them than you.

श्रीभगवानुवाच

śrībhagavānuvāca

The Respected Supreme Divinity said:

\- 40 -

पार्थ नैवेह नामुत्र विनाशस्तस्य विद्यते।
न हि कल्याणकृत्कश्चिद्दुर्गतिं तात गच्छति॥ ४०॥

pārtha naiveha nāmutra vināśastasya vidyate
na hi kalyāṇakṛtkaściddurgatiṁ tāta gacchati

Son of She Who Excels (Arjuna), neither does he find destruction here nor in the next world. My son, for anyone who performs meritorious actions does not find a bad result.

\- 41 -

प्राप्य पुण्यकृतां लोकानुषित्वा शाश्वतीः समाः।
शुचीनां श्रीमतां गेहे योगभ्रष्टोऽभिजायते॥ ४१॥

prāpya puṇyakṛtāṁ lokānuṣitvā śāśvatīḥ samāḥ
śucīnāṁ śrīmatāṁ gehe yogabhraṣṭo-bhijāyate

Having attained to the worlds of those who performed meritorious conduct, and having dwelt there for a season of eternity, one fallen from union will be born in the house of the pure and respected.

-42-

अथवा योगिनामेव कुले भवति धीमताम् ।

एतद्धि दुर्लभतरं लोके जन्म यदीदृशम् ॥ ४२ ॥

athavā yogināmeva kule bhavati dhīmatām
etaddhi durlabhataraṁ loke janma yadīdṛśam

Or he may be born in a family of wise practitioners of union. To attain a birth like this in this world is very difficult.

-43-

तत्र तं बुद्धिसंयोगं लभते पौर्वदेहिकम् ।

यतते च ततो भूयः संसिद्धौ कुरुनन्दन ॥ ४३ ॥

tatra taṁ buddhisaṁyogaṁ labhate paurvadehikam
yatate ca tato bhūyaḥ saṁsiddhau kurunandana

There he obtains the complete union with the intelligence of his former body, and he makes ever greater efforts to attain perfection, oh Son of Action (Arjuna).

-44-

पूर्वाभ्यासेन तेनैव ह्रियते ह्यवशोऽपि सः ।

जिज्ञासुरपि योगस्य शब्दब्रह्मातिवर्तते ॥ ४४ ॥

pūrvābhyāsena tenaiva hriyate hyavaśo-pi saḥ
jijñāsurapi yogasya śabdabrahmātivartate

He is verily helpless but to continue his former practice. Even he who asks about the practice of union moves beyond talking about God.

-45-

प्रयत्नाद्यतमानस्तु योगी संशुद्धकिल्बिषः ।

अनेक जन्मसंसिद्धस्ततो याति परां गतिम् ॥ ४५ ॥

prayatnādyatamānastu yogī saṁśuddhakilbiṣaḥ
aneka janmasaṁsiddhastato yāti parāṁ gatim

The man of union who strives with great sincerity through many births completely purifies all impurities and then reaches the highest station.

-46-

तपस्विभ्योऽधिको योगी ज्ञानिभ्योऽपि मतोऽधिकः ।

कर्मिभ्यश्चाधिको योगी तस्माद्योगी भवार्जुन ॥ ४६ ॥

tapasvibhyo-dhiko yogī jñānibhyo-pi mato-dhikaḥ
karmibhyaścādhiko yogī tasmāyogī bhavārjuna

The man of union has a superior attainment to the performer of purifying austerities. Even he is thought superior to men of knowledge. Again he is superior to the performers of action. Therefore, oh Clarity of Pure Devotion, be a man of union.

-47-

योगिनामपि सर्वेषां मद्गतेनान्तरात्मना ।

श्रद्धावान्भजते यो मां स मे युक्ततमो मतः ॥ ४७ ॥

yogināmapi sarveṣāṁ madgatenāntarātmanā
śraddhāvānbhajate yo māṁ sa me yuktatamo mataḥ

Of all men of union, he who worships Me with such faith that his inner being is merged in Me, I think him to be the most attentive.

इति श्रीमद्भगवद्गीतासु षष्ठोऽध्यायः ॥ ६ ॥

७

श्रीभगवानुवाच

śrībhagavānuvāca

The Respected Supreme Divinity said:

-1-

मय्यासक्तमनाः पार्थ योगं युञ्जन्मदाश्रयः ।
असंशयं समग्रं मां यथा ज्ञास्यसि तच्छृणु ॥ १ ॥

mayyāsaktamanāḥ pārtha yogaṁ yuñjanmadāśrayaḥ
asaṁśayaṁ samagraṁ māṁ yathā jñāsyasi tacchṛṇu

Listen, oh Son of She Who Excels (Arjuna), as to how you will know Me completely beyond a doubt, by taking refuge in Me through the practice of union with your mind centered on Me.

-2-

ज्ञानं तेऽहं सविज्ञानमिदं वक्ष्याम्यशेषतः ।
यज्ज्ञात्वा नेह भूयोऽन्यज्ज्ञातव्यमवशिष्यते ॥ २ ॥

jñānaṁ te-haṁ savijñānamidaṁ vakṣyāmyaśeṣataḥ
yajjñātvā neha bhūyo-nyajjñātavyamavaśiṣyate

I shall teach you that unending knowledge and wisdom, which, when understood, nothing more remains to be understood.

-3-

मनुष्याणां सहस्रेषु कश्चिद्यतति सिद्धये ।
यततामपि सिद्धानां कश्चिन्मां वेत्ति तत्त्वतः ॥ ३ ॥

manuṣyāṇāṁ sahasreṣu kaścidyatati siddhaye
yatatāmapi siddhānāṁ kaścinmāṁ vetti tattvataḥ

Among thousands of men, few strive for perfection, and even among those who strive, few know My reality.

-4-

भूमिरापोऽनलो वायुः खं मनो बुद्धिरेव च ।
अहङ्कार इतीयं मे भिन्ना प्रकृतिरष्टधा ॥ ४ ॥

bhūmirāpo-nalo vāyuḥ khaṁ mano buddhireva ca
ahaṅkāra itīyaṁ me bhinnā prakṛtiraṣṭadhā

Earth, water, fire, air, either, mind, intellect and ego are the eight divisions of My nature.

-5-

अपरेयमितस्त्वन्यां प्रकृतिं विद्धि मे पराम् ।

जीवभूतां महाबाहो ययेदं धार्यते जगत् ॥ ५ ॥

apareyamitastvanyāṁ prakṛtiṁ viddhi me parām
jīvabhūtāṁ mahābāho yayedaṁ dhāryate jagat

This is My lower nature, but different from it know My higher existence of Life, by which the perceivable universe is supported, oh One of Mighty Arms (Arjuna).

-6-

एतद्योनीनि भूतानि सर्वाणीत्युपधारय ।

अहं कृत्स्नस्य जगतः प्रभवः प्रलयस्तथा ॥ ६ ॥

etadyonīni bhūtāni sarvāṇītyupadhāraya
ahaṁ kṛtsnasya jagataḥ prabhavaḥ pralayastathā

Know this to be the womb of all beings. I am the origin of the entire perceivable universe as also the terminus as well.

-7-

मत्तः परतरं नान्यत्किञ्चिदस्ति धनंजय ।

मयि सर्वमिदं प्रोतं सूत्रे मणिगणा इव ॥ ७ ॥

mattaḥ parataraṁ nānyatkiñcidasti dhanaṁjaya
mayi sarvamidaṁ protaṁ sūtre maṇigaṇā iva

No one is higher than Me, Conqueror of Wealth (Arjuna), nothing greater. All this is bound by Me as a necklace of gems by a string.

-8-

रसोऽहमप्सु कौन्तेय प्रभास्मि शशिसूर्ययोः ।

प्रणवः सर्ववेदेषु शब्दः खे पौरुषं नृषु ॥ ८ ॥

raso-hamapsu kaunteya prabhāsmi śaśisūryayoḥ
praṇavaḥ sarvavedeṣu śabdaḥ khe pauruṣaṁ nṛṣu

I am the taste of water, oh Son of Who Takes Away the Deficiency of Others (Arjuna), the lustre of the moon and the sun. I am the sound of Oṁ in the Vedas. I am the perfect nature of men.

-9-

पुण्यो गन्धः पृथिव्यां च तेजश्चास्मि विभावसौ ।
जीवनं सर्वभूतेषु तपश्चास्मि तपस्विषु ॥ ९ ॥

puṇyo gandhaḥ pṛthivyāṁ ca tejaścāsmi vibhāvasau
jīvanaṁ sarvabhūteṣu tapaścāsmi tapasviṣu

I am the pure smell of the earth, and the light of the fire. I am the life of all existence, and the purifying austerities of the performers of austerities.

-10-

बीजं मां सर्वभूतानां विद्धि पार्थ सनातनम् ।
बुद्धिर्बुद्धिमतामस्मि तेजस्तेजस्विनामहम् ॥ १० ॥

bījaṁ māṁ sarvabhūtānāṁ viddhi pārtha sanātanam
buddhirbuddhimatāmasmi tejastejasvināmaham

I am the seed of all beings. Know Me, Son of She Who Excels (Arjuna), as eternal. I am the intelligence of the intelligent, the light of all illumination.

-11-

बलं बलवतां चाहं कामरागविवर्जितम् ।
धर्माविरुद्धो भूतेषु कामोऽस्मि भरतर्षभ ॥ ११ ॥

balaṁ balavatāṁ cāhaṁ kāmarāgavivarjitam
dharmāviruddho bhūteṣu kāmo-smi bharatarṣabha

I am the strength of the strong, without desire or passion. I am the desires in beings which do not conflict with the ideal, oh Lord of the Descendants of the Light of Wisdom (Arjuna).

-12-

ये चैव सात्त्विका भावा राजसास्तामसाश्च ये ।
मत्त एवेति तान्विद्धि न त्वहं तेषु ते मयि ॥ १२ ॥

ye caiva sāttvikā bhāvā rājasāstāmasāśca ye
matta eveti tānviddhi na tvahaṁ teṣu te mayi

And all beings which have an attitude of sattva, raja or tamas, know that they came from Me. But I am not in them4, they are in Me.

-13-

त्रिभिर्गुणमयैर्भावैरेभिः सर्वमिदं जगत् ।
मोहितं नाभिजानाति मामेभ्यः परमव्ययम् ॥ १३ ॥

tribhirguṇamayairbhāvairebhiḥ sarvamidaṁ jagat
mohitaṁ nābhijānāti māmebhyaḥ paramavyayam

This entire perceivable universe is deluded by the attitudes of these three qualities and they don't know Me who am beyond, without change.

-14-

दैवी ह्येषा गुणमयी मम माया दुरत्यया ।
मामेव ये प्रपद्यन्ते मायामेतां तरन्ति ते ॥ १४ ॥

daivī hyeṣā guṇamayī mama māyā duratyayā
māmeva ye prapadyante māyāmetāṁ taranti te

It is really difficult to move beyond this illusion manifest by these divine qualities. Only those who take refuge in Me can move beyond the illusion.

-15-

न मां दुष्कृतिनो मूढाः प्रपद्यन्ते नराधमाः ।
माययापहृतज्ञाना आसुरं भावमाश्रिताः ॥ १५ ॥

na māṁ duṣkṛtino mūḍhāḥ prapadyante narādhamāḥ
māyayāpahṛtajñānā āsuraṁ bhāvamāśritāḥ

Those fools who perform evil and do not take refuge in Me are the lowest of men. Illusion deprives them of wisdom and they take refuge in the attitudes of duality.

-16-

चतुर्विधा भजन्ते मां जनाः सुकृतिनोऽर्जुन ।
आर्तो जिज्ञासुरर्थार्थी ज्ञानी च भरतर्षभ ॥ १६ ॥

caturvidhā bhajante māṁ janāḥ sukṛtino-rjuna
ārto jijñāsurarthārthī jñānī ca bharatarṣabha

Clarity of Pure Devotion, four kinds of people worship Me who perform good actions: one who is in distress, one who desires knowledge, one who desires wealth, and one who is wise, oh Seer among the Descendants of the Light of Wisdom (Arjuna).

-17-

तेषां ज्ञानी नित्ययुक्त एकभक्तिर्विशिष्यते ।
प्रियो हि ज्ञानिनोऽत्यर्थमहं स च मम प्रियः ॥ १७ ॥

teṣāṁ jñānī nityayukta ekabhaktirviśiṣyate
priyo hi jñānino-tyarthamahaṁ sa ca mama priyaḥ

Of them, the wise who are eternally united with devotion in Oneness are most excellent. For I am especially beloved to the wise as he is beloved to Me.

-18-

उदाराः सर्व एवैते ज्ञानी त्वात्मैव मे मतम् ।
आस्थितः स हि युक्तात्मा मामेवानुत्तमां गतिम् ॥ १८ ॥

udārāḥ sarva evaite jñānī tvātmaiva me matam
āsthitaḥ sa hi yuktātmā māmevānuttamāṁ gatim

All of these are surely noble, but the wise has his soul fixed in thoughts of Me. For he has united his soul in Me as the supreme refuge.

-19-

बहूनां जन्मनामन्ते ज्ञानवान्मां प्रपद्यते ।
वासुदेवः सर्वमिति स महात्मा सुदुर्लभः ॥ १९ ॥

bahūnāṁ janmanāmante jñānavānmāṁ prapadyate
vāsudevaḥ sarvamiti sa mahātmā sudurlabhaḥ

At the end of many births the man of wisdom enters Me. God is all of this. Such a great soul is hard to find and hard to become.

-20-

कामैस्तैस्तैर्हृतज्ञानाः प्रपद्यन्तेऽन्यदेवताः ।
तं तं नियममास्थाय प्रकृत्या नियताः स्वया ॥ २० ॥

kāmaistaistairhṛtajñānāḥ prapadyante-nyadevatāḥ
taṁ taṁ niyamamāsthāya prakṛtyā niyatāḥ svayā

Those whose wisdom has been clouded by various desires enter other divinities. Having followed various disciplines, they are led by their own nature.

-21-

योयो यां यां तनुं भक्तः श्रद्धयार्चितुमिच्छति ।
तस्य तस्याचलां श्रद्धां तामेव विदधाम्यहम् ॥ २१ ॥

yo yo yāṁ yāṁ tanuṁ bhaktaḥ śraddhayārcitumicchati
tasya tasyācalāṁ śraddhāṁ tāmeva vidadhāmyaham

Whatever a devotee desires to offer with faith to which ever form he chooses, to him I grant immovable faith.

-22-

स तया श्रद्धया युक्तस्तस्याराधनमीहते ।
लभते च ततः कामान्मयैव विहितान्हि तान् ॥ २२ ॥

sa tayā śraddhayā yuktastasyārādhanamīhate
labhate ca tataḥ kāmānmayaiva vihitānhi tān

United with that faith he engages in the satisfaction of that form, and from that form he attains fulfillment of the desire, which surely has been proclaimed by Me.

-23-

अन्तवत्तु फलं तेषां तद्भवत्यल्पमेधसाम् ।
देवान्देवयजो यान्ति मद्भक्ता यान्ति मामपि ॥ २३ ॥

antavattu phalaṁ teṣāṁ tadbhavatyalpamedhasām
devāndevayajo yānti madbhaktā yānti māmapi

But finite are the fruits of those with small intelligence. Those who sacrifice to the Gods go to the Gods. My devotees also come to Me.

-24-

अव्यक्तं व्यक्तिमापन्नं मन्यन्ते मामबुद्धयः ।
परं भावमजानन्तो ममाव्ययमनुत्तमम् ॥ २४ ॥

avyaktaṁ vyaktimāpannaṁ manyante māmabuddhayaḥ
paraṁ bhāvamajānanto mamāvyayamanuttamam

The unknowing think of Me as having come into manifestation from the unmanifest. They do not know my Supreme Attitude as immutable and most excellent.

-25-

नाहं प्रकाशः सर्वस्य योगमायासमावृतः ।

मूढोऽयं नाभिजानाति लोको मामजमव्ययम् ॥ २५ ॥

nāhaṁ prakāśaḥ sarvasya yogamāyāsamāvṛtaḥ
mūḍho-yaṁ nābhijānāti loko māmajamavyayam

I alone am the Illuminator of this All, of the Measurement of Consciousness in union and all its modifications. Deluded by all this, people do not know Me, the unborn and unchanging.

-26-

वेदाहं समतीतानि वर्तमानानि चार्जुन ।

भविष्याणि च भूतानि मां तु वेद न कश्चन ॥ २६ ॥

vedāhaṁ samatītāni vartamānāni cārjuna
bhaviṣyāṇi ca bhūtāni māṁ tu veda na kaścana

I know the past and the present, Clarity of Pure Devotion, the future and all beings born. But no one knows Me.

-27-

इच्छाद्वेषसमुत्थेन द्वन्द्वमोहेन भारत ।

सर्वभूतानि संमोहं सर्गे यान्ति परंतप ॥ २७ ॥

icchādveṣasamutthena dvandvamohena bhārata
sarvabhūtāni saṁmohaṁ sarge yānti paraṁtapa

From the ignorance which arises from attraction and repulsion, oh Descendant of the Light of Wisdom (Arjuna), all beings born are controlled by ignorance from this birth, oh Supreme Light (Arjuna).

-28-

येषां त्वन्तगतं पापं जनानं पुण्यकर्मणाम् ।

ते द्वन्द्वमोहनिर्मुक्ता भजन्ते मां दृढव्रताः ॥ २८ ॥

yeṣāṁ tvantagataṁ pāpaṁ jnānaṁ puṇyakarmaṇām
te dvandvamohanirmuktā bhajante māṁ dṛḍhavratāḥ

Men whose sins have ended through meritorious actions are liberated from the ignorance of opposites. They constantly sing to Me with intense vows.

-29-

जरामरणमोक्षाय मामाश्रित्य यतन्ति ये ।

ते ब्रह्म तद्विदुः कृत्स्नमध्यात्मं कर्म चाखिलम् ॥ २९ ॥

jarāmaraṇamokṣāya māmāśritya yatanti ye
te brahma tadviduḥ kṛtsnamadhyātmaṁ karma cākhilam

Those who make efforts to take refuge in Me are liberated in old age and death. They know that whole Supreme Divinity and the entirety of spiritual knowledge.

-30-

साधिभूताधिदैवं मां साधियज्ञं च ये विदुः ।

प्रयाणकालेऽपि च मां ते विदुर्युक्तचेतसः ॥ ३० ॥

sādhibhūtādhidaivaṁ māṁ sādhiyajñaṁ ca ye viduḥ
prayāṇakāle-pi ca māṁ te viduryuktacetasaḥ

Those who know Me as the Primary Existence, as the Highest Divinity and as the Ultimate Sacrifice, even at the time of leaving, they know Me united with consciousness.

इति श्रीमद्भगवद्गीतासु सप्तमोऽध्यायः ॥ ७ ॥

८

अर्जुन उवाच

arjuna uvāca

Clarity of Pure Devotion said:

-1-

किं तद्ब्रह्म किमध्यात्मं किं कर्म पुरुषोत्तम ।
अधिभूतं च किं प्रोक्तमधिदैवं किमुच्यते ॥ १ ॥

kiṁ tadbrahma kimadhyātmaṁ kiṁ karma puruṣottama
adhibhūtaṁ ca kiṁ proktamadhidaivaṁ kimucyate

What is that Supreme Divinity? What is the Ultimate Spirituality? Oh Most Excellent Among Men (Kṛṣṇa), what is action, and what is said to be the essence of manifested existence, and what is called the essence of divinity?

-2-

अधियज्ञः कथं कोऽत्र देहेऽस्मिन्मधुसूदन ।
प्रयाणकाले च कथं ज्ञेयोऽसि नियतात्मभिः ॥ २ ॥

adhiyajñaḥ kathaṁ ko-tra dehe-sminmadhusūdana
prayāṇakāle ca kathaṁ jñeyo-si niyatātmabhiḥ

Who performs the Supreme Sacrifice in this body and how is it performed, Slayer of Too Much (Kṛṣṇa)? How are You to be known at the time of transformation by those who have controlled themselves?

श्रीभगवानुवाच

śrībhagavānuvāca

The Respected Supreme Lord said:

-3-

अक्षरं ब्रह्म परमं स्वभावोऽध्यात्ममुच्यते ।
भूतभावोद्भवकरो विसर्गः कर्मसंज्ञितः ॥ ३ ॥

akṣaraṁ brahma paramaṁ svabhāvo-dhyātmamucyate
bhūtabhāvodbhavakaro visargaḥ karmasaṁjñitaḥ

The Supreme Divinity is the Ultimate Imperishable, whose intrinsic nature is said to be spirituality. The offering which generates the attitudes of existence is known as action.

-4-

अधिभूतं क्षरो भावः पुरुषश्चाधिदैवतम् ।
अधियज्ञोऽहमेवात्र देहे देहभृतां वर ॥ ४ ॥

adhibhūtaṁ kṣaro bhāvaḥ puruṣaścādhidaivatam
adhiyajño-hamevātra dehe dehabhṛtāṁ vara

The existence which constantly transforms is the essence of manifested being, and the fully perfect unchanging soul is the essence of divinity. I alone am the Supreme Sacrificer here in the body, oh you who are best among those who have bodies.

-5-

अन्तकाले च मामेव स्मरन्मुक्त्वा कलेवरम् ।
यः प्रयाति स मद्भावं याति नास्त्यत्र संशयः ॥ ५ ॥

antakāle ca māmeva smaranmuktvā kalevaram
yaḥ prayāti sa madbhāvaṁ yāti nāstyatra saṁśayaḥ

And he who is liberated from the body at the time of death remembering Me alone, he goes and attains My Being without a doubt.

-6-

यं यं वापि स्मरन्भावं त्यजत्यन्ते कलेवरम् ।
तं तमेवैति कौन्तेय सदा तद्भावभावितः ॥ ६ ॥

yaṁ yaṁ vāpi smaranbhāvaṁ tyajatyante kalevaram
taṁ tamevaiti kaunteya sadā tadbhāvabhāvitaḥ

Whatever attitude or existence one remembers when one renounces the body in the end, oh Son of Who Takes Away the Deficiency of Others (Arjuna), that alone does he become, always thinking of that.

-7-

तस्मात्सर्वेषु कालेषु मामनुस्मर युध्य च ।
मय्यर्पितमनोबुद्धिर्मामेवैष्यस्यसंशयम् ॥ ७ ॥

tasmātsarveṣu kāleṣu māmanusmara yudhya ca
mayyarpitamanobuddhirmāmevaiṣyasyasaṁśayam

Therefore, in all times and in all confrontations remember Me. Offering your mind and intellect to Me, you will come to Me without a doubt.

-8-

अभ्यासयोगयुक्तेन चेतसा नान्यगामिना ।

परमं पुरुषं दिव्यं याति पार्थानुचिन्तयन् ॥ ८ ॥

abhyāsayogayuktena cetasā nānyagāminā
paramaṁ puruṣaṁ divyaṁ yāti pārthānucintayan

United in the practice of yoga or union, with consciousness not moving to any other perception, deeply contemplating the Supreme Divine Perfect Consciousness, Son of She Who Excels (Arjuna), he attains.

-9-

कविं पुराणमनुशासितार-

मणोरणीयांसमनुस्मरेद्यः ।

सर्वस्य धातारमचिन्त्यरूप-

मादित्यवर्णं तमसः परस्तात् ॥ ९ ॥

kaviṁ purāṇamanuśāsitāra-
maṇoraṇīyāṁsamanusmaredyaḥ
sarvasya dhātāramacintyarūpa-
mādityavarṇaṁ tamasaḥ parastāt

Who remembers the ancient poet, the Ruler, who is smaller than an atom, Supporter of All, of inconceivable form, of the color of the sun, beyond all darkness;

-10-

प्रयाणकाले मनसाचलेन
भक्त्या युक्तो योगबलेन चैव ।
भ्रुवोर्मध्ये प्राणमावेश्य सम्यक्
स तं परं पुरुषमुपैति दिव्यम् ॥ १० ॥

prayāṇkāle manasācalena
bhaktyā yukto yogabalena caiva
bhruvormadhye prāṇamāveśya samyak
sa taṁ paraṁ puruṣamupaiti divyam

at the time of death, with a still mind filled with devotion, and by the strength of union having the life force concentrated in the middle between the eyebrows, he completely attains the divine Supreme Perfect Consciousness.

-11-

यदक्षरं वेदविदो वदन्ति
विशन्ति यद्यतयो वीतरागाः ।
यदिच्छन्तो ब्रह्मचर्यं चरन्ति
तत्ते पदं संग्रहेण प्रवक्ष्ये ॥ ११ ॥

yadakṣaraṁ vedavido vadanti
viśanti yadyatayo vītarāgāḥ
yadicchanto brahmacaryaṁ caranti
tatte padaṁ saṁgraheṇa pravakṣye

Those who know wisdom call That the Imperishable. Those who are self-controlled and free from attachment enter it. Desiring That they practice moving in Godliness. That goal I shall briefly describe to you.

-12-

सर्वद्वाराणि संयम्य मनो हृदि निरुध्य च ।
मूर्ध्न्याधायात्मनः प्राणमास्थितो योगधारणाम् ॥ १२ ॥

sarvadvārāṇi saṁyamya mano hṛdi nirudhya ca
mūrdhnyādhāyātmanaḥ prāṇamāsthito yogadhāraṇām

Having controlled all of the doors to the body, having restrained the mind within the heart, having placed the life force in the highest summit, the soul is established in the union of contemplation.

-13-

ओमित्येकाक्षरं ब्रह्म व्याहरन्मामनुस्मरन् ।

यः प्रयाति त्यजन्देहं स याति परमां गतिम् ॥ १३ ॥

omityekākṣaraṁ brahma vyāharanmāmanusmaran
yaḥ prayāti tyajandehaṁ sa yāti paramāṁ gatim

Who says Oṁ, the one syllabled Supreme Divinity, remembering Me as he departs renouncing the body, he attains the supreme goal.

-14-

अनन्यचेताः सततं यो मां स्मरति नित्यशः ।

तस्याहं सुलभः पार्थ नित्ययुक्तस्य योगिनः ॥ १४ ॥

ananyacetāḥ satataṁ yo māṁ smarati nityaśaḥ
tasyāhaṁ sulabhaḥ pārtha nityayuktasya yoginaḥ

He who always remembers Me with consciousness absorbed, for him, Son of She Who Excels (Arjuna), I am easily attainable, for the yogi who is always in union.

-15-

मामुपेत्य पुनर्जन्म दुःखालयमशाश्वतम् ।

नाप्नुवन्ति महात्मानः संसिद्धिं परमां गताः ॥ १५ ॥

māmupetya punarjanma duḥkhālayamaśāśvatam
nāpnuvanti mahātmānaḥ saṁsiddhiṁ paramāṁ gatāḥ

Having attained to Me, the great souls who have reached the highest perfection do not take birth again in the place of transitory pain.

-16-

आब्रह्मभुवनाल्लोकाः पुनरावर्तिनोऽर्जुन ।

मामुपेत्य तु कौन्तेय पुनर्जन्म न विद्यते ॥ १६ ॥

ābrahmabhuvanāllokāḥ punarāvartino-rjuna
māmupetya tu kaunteya punarjanma na vidyate

All the worlds, Clarity of Pure Devotion, even the world of Supreme Divinity, return again. But having attained to Me, oh Son of Who Takes Away the Deficiency of Others (Arjuna), another birth is not known.5

-17-

सहस्रयुगपर्यन्तमहर्यद्‌ब्रह्मणो विदुः ।
रात्रिं युगसहस्रान्तां तेऽहोरात्रविदो जनाः ॥ १७ ॥

sahasrayugaparyantamaharyadbrahmaṇo viduḥ
rātriṁ yugasahasrāntāṁ te-horātravido janāḥ

Those people who know the day of the Supreme to be a thousand ages, and the night of the Supreme to end in a thousand ages, they are those who know day and night.

-18-

अव्यक्ताद्व्यक्तयः सर्वाः प्रभवन्त्यहरागमे ।
रात्र्यागमे प्रलीयन्ते तत्रैवाव्यक्तसंज्ञके ॥ १८ ॥

avyaktādvyaktayaḥ sarvāḥ prabhavantyaharāgame
rātryāgame pralīyante tatraivāvyaktasaṁjñake

When day comes, all manifest from the unmanifest, and when night comes all dissolve in that which is known as the unmanifest.

-19-

भूतग्रामः स एवायं भूत्वा भूत्वा प्रलीयते ।
रात्र्यागमेऽवशः पार्थ प्रभवत्यहरागमे ॥ १९ ॥

bhūtagrāmaḥ sa evāyaṁ bhūtvā bhūtvā pralīyate
rātryāgame-vaśaḥ pārtha prabhavatyaharāgame

This village of existence manifests again and again. Helplessly they dissolve at the coming of night and manifest at the coming of day, Son of She Who Excels (Arjuna).

-20-

परस्तस्मात्तु भावोऽन्योऽव्यक्तोऽव्यक्तात्सनातनः ।
यः स सर्वेषु भूतेषु नश्यत्सु न विनश्यति ॥ २० ॥

parastasmāttu bhāvo-nyo-vyakto-vyaktātsanātanaḥ
yaḥ sa sarveṣu bhūteṣu naśyatsu na vinaśyati

But superior to that unmanifest is another existence which is the eternal unmanifest in all beings, which is not destroyed when beings perish.

-21-

अव्यक्तोऽक्षर इत्युक्तस्तमाहुः परमां गतिम् ।
यं प्राप्य न निवर्तन्ते तद्धाम परमं मम ॥ २१ ॥

avyakto-kṣara ityuktastamāhuḥ paramāṁ gatim
yaṁ prāpya na nivartante taddhāma paramaṁ mama

This unmanifest is called Imperishable, said to be the Highest Goal. Those who attain It do not return. That is My supreme place.

-22-

पुरुषः स परः पार्थ भक्त्या लभ्यस्त्वनन्यया ।
यस्यान्तः स्थानि भूतानि येन सर्वमिदं ततम् ॥ २२ ॥

puruṣaḥ sa paraḥ pārtha bhaktyā labhyastvananyayā
yasyāntaḥ sthāni bhūtāni yena sarvamidaṁ tatam

That Supreme Full Consciousness, who resides in all beings, by whom this all is pervaded, is attained by totally focused devotion, Son of She Who Excels (Arjuna).

-23-

यत्र काले त्वनावृत्तिमावृत्तिं चैव योगिनः ।
प्रयाता यान्ति तं कालं वक्ष्यामि भरतर्षभ ॥ २३ ॥

yatra kāle tvanāvṛttimāvṛttiṁ caiva yoginaḥ
prayātā yānti taṁ kālaṁ vakṣyāmi bharatarṣabha

I explain to you the times of departure in which yogis will return and in which they will not return, oh Supreme Among Descendants of the Light of Wisdom (Arjuna).

-24-

अग्निर्ज्योतिरहः शुक्लः षण्मासा उत्तरायणम् ।
तत्र प्रयाता गच्छन्ति ब्रह्म ब्रह्मविदो जनाः ॥ २४ ॥

agnirjyotirahaḥ śuklaḥ ṣaṇmāsā uttarāyaṇam
tatra prayātā gacchanti brahma brahmavido janāḥ

People who know the Supreme Divinity go to the Supreme Divinity if they depart at the time of fire, light, day time, the bright lunar fortnight, the six months while the sun is in the northern hemisphere.

-25-

धूमो रात्रिस्तथा कृष्णः षण्मासा दक्षिणायनम् ।
तत्र चान्द्रमसं ज्योतिर्योगी प्राप्य निवर्तते ॥ २५ ॥

dhūmo rātristathā kṛṣṇaḥ ṣaṇmāsā dakṣiṇāyanam
tatra cāndramasaṁ jyotiryogī prāpya nivartate

At the time of smoke, night, the dark lunar fortnight, such yogi attains the light of the moon and returns.

-26-

शुक्लकृष्णे गती ह्येते जगतः शाश्वते मते ।
एकया यात्यनावृत्तिमन्यययावर्तते पुनः ॥ २६ ॥

śuklakṛṣṇe gatī hyete jagataḥ śāśvate mate
ekayā yātyanāvṛttimanyayayāvartate punaḥ

Light and dark are considered to be the ways of the manifested world. By one an individual goes without return, by the other he returns again.

-27-

नैते सृती पार्थ जानन्योगी मुह्यति कश्चन ।
तस्मात्सर्वेषु कालेषु योगयुक्तो भवार्जुन ॥ २७ ॥

naite sṛtī pārtha jānanyogī muhyati kaścana
tasmātsarveṣu kāleṣu yogayukto bhavārjuna

Any yogi not knowing these ways, Son of She Who Excels (Arjuna), is in the delusion of ignorance. Therefore be united in union at all times, Clarity of Pure Devotion.

-28-

वेदेषु यज्ञेषु तपःसु चैव
दानेषु यत्पुण्यफलं प्रदिष्टम् ।
अत्येति तत्सर्वमिदं विदित्वा
योगी परं स्थानमुपैति चाद्यम् ॥ २८ ॥

vedeṣu yajñeṣu tapaḥsu caiva
dāneṣu yatpuṇyaphalaṁ pradiṣṭam
atyeti tatsarvamidaṁ viditvā
yogī paraṁ sthānamupaiti cādyam

Whatever meritorious fruits have been proclaimed in the Vedas, in sacrifices, in purifying austerities, and in charitable gifts, all of that is surpassed by the yogi who knows the Supreme and attains to the foremost place.

इति श्रीमद्भगवद्गीतासु अष्टमोऽध्यायः ॥ ८ ॥

९

श्रीभगवानुवाच
śrībhagavānuvāca
The Respected Supreme Divinity said:

-1-

इदं तु ते गुह्यतमं प्रवक्ष्याम्यनसूयवे ।
ज्ञानं विज्ञानसहितं यज्ज्ञात्वा मोक्ष्यसेऽशुभात् ॥ १ ॥

idaṁ tu te guhyatamaṁ pravakṣyāmyanasūyave
jñānaṁ vijñānasahitaṁ yajjñātvā mokṣyase-śubhāt
I shall tell you this profound secret because you are free from envy. Knowing this wisdom and knowledge, you will be free from impurity.

-2-

राजविद्या राजगुह्यं पवित्रमिदमुत्तमम् ।
प्रत्यक्षावगमं धर्म्यं सुसुखं कर्तुमव्ययम् ॥ २ ॥

rājavidyā rājaguhyaṁ pavitramidamuttamam
pratyakṣāvagamaṁ dharmyaṁ
susukhaṁ kartumavyayam
The supreme knowledge is a supreme secret and conveys excellent purity. It is empirically verifiable, in accordance with the imperishable ideal of perfection, and is easily performed.

-3-

अश्रद्दधानाः पुरुषा धर्मस्यास्य परंतप ।
अप्राप्य मां निवर्तन्ते मृत्युसंसारवर्त्मनि ॥ ३ ॥

aśraddadhānāḥ puruṣā dharmasyāsya paraṁtapa
aprāpya māṁ nivartante mṛtyusaṁsāravartmani
Oh Supreme Light (Arjuna), men without faith in the ideal of perfection return to the ways of the mortal world of objects and relationships without attaining Me.

-4-

मया ततमिदं सर्वं जगदव्यक्तमूर्तिना ।
मत्स्थानि सर्वभूतानि न चाहं तेष्ववस्थितः ॥ ४ ॥

mayā tatamidaṁ sarvaṁ jagadavyaktamūrtinā
matsthāni sarvabhūtāni na cāhaṁ teṣvavasthitaḥ

All of this perceivable world is pervaded by Me in the image of the unmanifest. All beings reside in Me, but I am not in them.

-5-

न च मत्स्थानि भूतानि पश्य मे योगमैश्वरम् ।
भूतभृन्न च भूतस्थो ममात्मा भूतभावनः ॥ ५ ॥

na ca matsthāni bhūtāni paśya me yogamaiśvaram
bhūtabhṛnna ca bhūtastho mamātmā bhūtabhāvanaḥ

One cannot see all the beings residing in Me. This is My imperishable union. My soul fills all beings, dwells in all beings, is the existence of all beings.

-6-

यथाकाशस्थितो नित्यं वायुः सर्वत्रगो महान् ।
तथा सर्वाणि भूतानि मत्स्थानीत्युपधारय ॥ ६ ॥

yathākāśasthito nityaṁ vāyuḥ sarvatrago mahān
tathā sarvāṇi bhūtāni matsthānītyupadhāraya

Just as the great wind which moves everywhere always resides in the ether, know that all beings are situated in Me.

-7-

सर्वभूतानि कौन्तेय प्रकृतिं यान्ति मामिकाम् ।
कल्पक्षये पुनस्तानि कल्पादौ विसृजाम्यहम् ॥ ७ ॥

sarvabhūtāni kaunteya prakṛtiṁ yānti māmikām
kalpakṣaye punastāni kalpādau visṛjāmyaham

All beings go to My nature at the end of an age of time, oh Son of Who Takes Away the Deficiency of Others (Arjuna), and at the beginning of another age I create them again.

-8-

प्रकृतिं स्वामवष्टभ्य विसृजामि पुनः पुनः ।

भूतग्राममिमं कृत्स्नमवशं प्रकृतेर्वशात् ॥ ८ ॥

prakṛtiṁ svāmavaṣṭabhya visṛjāmi punaḥ punaḥ
bhūtagrāmamimaṁ kṛtsnamavaśaṁ prakṛtervaśāt

Again and again I create this village of beings resting upon my own nature. All are helpless because of the force of Nature.

-9-

न च मां तानि कर्माणि निबध्नन्ति धनंजय ।

उदासीनवदासीनमसक्तं तेषु कर्मसु ॥ ९ ॥

na ca māṁ tāni karmāṇi nibadhnanti dhanaṁjaya
udāsīnavadāsīnamasaktaṁ teṣu karmasu

And these actions do not bind Me, Conqueror of Wealth (Arjuna). As a servant of circumstances I sit without attachment in these actions.

-10-

मयाध्यक्षेण प्रकृतिः सूयते सचराचरम् ।

हेतुनानेन कौन्तेय जगद्विपरिवर्तते ॥ १० ॥

mayādhyakṣeṇa prakṛtiḥ sūyate sacarācaram
hetunānena kaunteya jagadviparivartate

Under My leadership, Nature produces that which moves and that which does not move, and by this cause, oh Son of Who Takes Away the Deficiency of Others (Arjuna), the perceivable world revolves.

-11-

अवजानन्ति मां मूढा मानुषीं तनुमाश्रितम् ।

परं भावमजानन्तो मम भूतमहेश्वरम् ॥ ११ ॥

avajānanti māṁ mūḍhā mānuṣīṁ tanumāśritam
paraṁ bhāvamajānanto mama bhūtamaheśvaram

Fools disrespect Me because I have taken refuge in a human body. They do not know My supreme attitude as the Supreme Lord of all Beings.

-12-

मोघाशा मोघकर्माणो मोघज्ञाना विचेतसः ।

राक्षसीमासुरीं चैव प्रकृतिं मोहिनीं श्रिताः ॥ १२ ॥

moghāśā moghakarmāṇo moghajñānā vicetasaḥ
rākṣasīmāsurīṁ caiva prakṛtiṁ mohinīṁ śritāḥ

These inimical forces of selfish duality are possessed of an ignorant nature. Useless are their hopes, useless are their actions, useless is their knowledge, for they remain unconscious.

-13-

महात्मानस्तु मां पार्थ दैवीं प्रकृतिमाश्रिताः ।

भजन्त्यनन्यमनसो ज्ञात्वा भूतादिमव्ययम् ॥ १३ ॥

mahātmānastu māṁ pārtha daivīṁ prakṛtimāśritāḥ
bhajantyananyamanaso jñātvā bhūtādimavyayam

But the great souls, having taken refuge in divine nature, worship Me without any other thought, Son of She Who Excels (Arjuna). They know Me as the imperishable Supreme of all beings.

-14-

सततं कीर्तयन्तो मां यतन्तश्च दृढव्रताः ।

नमस्यन्तश्च मां भक्त्या नित्ययुक्ता उपासते ॥ १४ ॥

satataṁ kīrtayanto māṁ yatantaśca dṛḍhavratāḥ
namasyantaśca māṁ bhaktyā nityayuktā upāsate

They worship Me eternally united with devotion, always singing of Me and making efforts in sincere vows of worship, offering their respect.

-15-

ज्ञानयज्ञेन चाप्यन्ये यजन्तो मामुपासते ।

एकत्वेन पृथक्त्वेन बहुधा विश्वतोमुखम् ॥ १५ ॥

jñānayajñena cāpyanye yajanto māmupāsate
ekatvena pṛthaktvena bahudhā viśvatomukham

Others offer the sacrifice of wisdom. Some worship Me as One, others as many, in various ways, the mouth of the universe6.

-16-

अहं क्रतुरहं यज्ञः स्वधाहमहमौषधम् ।
मन्त्रोऽहमहमेवाज्यमहमग्निरहं हुतम् ॥ १६ ॥

ahaṁ kraturahaṁ yajñaḥ svadhāhamahamauṣadham
mantro-hamahamevājyamahamagniraham̐ hutam

I am the sacred rite, I am the fire sacrifice. I am Svadhā, the word of praise by which the ancestors are pleased, I am sacred plants and herbs. I am the mantra and I am the ghee. I am the fire and I am the offering.

-17-

पिताहमस्य जगतो माता धाता पितामहः ।
वेद्यं पवित्रमोङ्कार ऋक्साम यजुरेव च ॥ १७ ॥

pitāhamasya jagato mātā dhātā pitāmahaḥ
vedyaṁ pavitramoṅkāra ṛksāma yajureva ca

I am the father of the perceivable world, mother, creator, grandfather. I am to be known, the pure one, the Ṛg, Sāma, and Yajūr Vedas.

-18-

गतिर्भर्ता प्रभुः साक्षी निवासः शरणं सुहृत् ।
प्रभवः प्रलयः स्थानं निधानं बीजमव्ययम् ॥ १८ ॥

gatirbhartā prabhuḥ sākṣī nivāsaḥ śaraṇaṁ suhṛt
prabhavaḥ pralayaḥ sthānaṁ nidhānaṁ bījamavyayam

I am the refuge, the protector, the Lord, the witness, the residence, the shelter, the excellent friend; the origin, the terminus, the place, the treasure house, the seed, the Imperishable.

-19-

तपाम्यहमहं वर्षं निगृह्णाम्युत्सृजामि च ।
अमृतं चैव मृत्युश्च सदसच्चाहमर्जुन ॥ १९ ॥

tapāmyahamahaṁ varṣaṁ nigṛhṇāmyutsṛjāmi ca
amṛtaṁ caiva mṛtyuśca sadasaccāhamarjuna

I give heat, and withhold and pour forth the rains. I give immortality and I give death. I am true existence, and I am non-existence, Clarity of Pure Devotion.

-20-

त्रैविद्या मां सोमपाः पूतपापा
यज्ञैरिष्ट्वा स्वर्गतिं प्रार्थयन्ते ।
ते पुण्यमासाद्य सुरेन्द्रलोक-
मश्नन्ति दिव्यान्दिवि देवभोगान् ॥ २० ॥

**traividyā māṁ somapāḥ pūtapāpā
yajñairiṣṭvā svargatiṁ prārthayante
te puṇyāmāsādya surendrāloka-
maśnanti divyāndivi devabhogān**

Those who drink the nectar of devotion, who are free from sin, offer sacrifice and worship to Me with three kinds of knowledge. They pray to move to heaven. With merit they reach the world of the Lord of the Gods, and enjoy divine delight in the world of divine light.

-21-

ते तं भुक्त्वा स्वर्गलोकं विशालं
क्षीणे पुण्ये मर्त्यलोकं विशन्ति ।
एवं त्रयीधर्ममनुप्रपन्ना
गतागतं कामकामा लभन्ते ॥ २१ ॥

**te taṁ bhuktvā svargalokaṁ viśālaṁ
kṣīṇe puṇye martyalokaṁ viśanti
evaṁ trayīdharmamanuprapannā
gatāgataṁ kāmakāmā labhante**

Having enjoyed the immeasurable worlds of heaven, the merits become depleted and they return to the world of mortals. Thus they attain the three fold ideal of perfection, coming and going in conformity with the desires they desire.

-22-

अनन्याश्चिन्तयन्तो मां ये जनाः पर्युपासते ।
तेषां नित्याभियुक्तानां योगक्षेमं वहाम्यहम् ॥ २२ ॥

ananyāścintayanto māṁ ye janāḥ paryupāsate
teṣāṁ nityābhiyuktānāṁ yogakṣemaṁ vahāmyaham

I am the vehicle for those men who worship Me without any other thought, who are eternally united residing in union.

-23-

येऽप्यन्यदेवता भक्ता यजन्ते श्रद्धयान्विताः ।
तेऽपि मामेव कौन्तेय यजन्त्यविधिपूर्वकम् ॥ २३ ॥

ye-pyanyadevatā bhaktā yajante śraddhayānvitāḥ
te-pi māmeva kaunteya yajantyavidhipūrvakam

Even those devotees who worship other Gods with faith, they also worship only Me. Oh Son of Who Takes Away the Deficiency of Others (Arjuna), even without a system.

-24-

अहं हि सर्वयज्ञानां भोक्ता च प्रभुरेव च ।
न तु मामभिजानन्ति तत्त्वेनातश्च्यवन्ति ते ॥ २४ ॥

ahaṁ hi sarvayajñānāṁ bhoktā ca prabhureva ca
na tu māmabhijānanti tattvenātaścyavanti te

For I alone am the Enjoyer of all sacrifices and the Lord. But they do not know Me in reality. Hence they fall.

-25-

यान्ति देवव्रता देवान्पितृन्यान्ति पितृव्रताः ।
भूतानि यान्ति भूतेज्या यान्तिमद्याजिनोऽपि माम् ॥ २५ ॥

yānti devavratā devānpitṝnyānti pitṛvratāḥ
bhūtāni yānti bhūtejyā yānti madyājino-pi mām

Those who observe vows for the Gods go to the Gods. Those who observe vows to the ancestors go to the ancestors. Those who worship all beings go to all beings. My worshipers also come to Me.

-26-

पत्रं पुष्पं फलं तोयं यो मे भक्त्या प्रयच्छति ।
तदहं भक्त्युपहृतमश्नामि प्रयतात्मनः ॥ २६ ॥

patraṁ puṣpaṁ phalaṁ toyaṁ
yo me bhaktyā prayacchati
tadahaṁ bhaktyupahṛtamaśnāmi prayatātmanaḥ

Whoever offers Me even a leaf, a flower, a fruit or some water with devotion, I accept that offering of devotion from the soul who makes effort.

-27-

यत्करोषि यदश्नासि यज्जुहोषि ददासि यत् ।
यत्तपस्यसि कौन्तेय तत्कुरुष्व मदर्पणम् ॥ २७ ॥

yatkaroṣi yadaśnāsi yajjuhoṣi dadāsi yat
yattapasyasi kaunteya tatkuruṣva madarpaṇam

Whatever you do, whatever you eat, whatever you offer in sacrifice, whatever you give, whatever austerity you perform, oh Son of Who Takes Away the Deficiency of Others (Arjuna), do that as an offering to Me.

-28-

शुभाशुभफलैरेवं मोक्ष्यसे कर्मबन्धनैः ।
संन्यासयोगयुक्तात्मा विमुक्तो मामुपैष्यसि ॥ २८ ॥

śubhāśubhaphalairevaṁ mokṣyase karmabandhanaiḥ
saṁnyāsayogayuktātmā vimukto māmupaiṣyasi

Thus you will be liberated from the bondage to actions with their pure and impure fruits. The soul which is united in the union with renunciation is liberated and comes to Me.

-29-

समोऽहं सर्वभूतेषु न मे द्वेष्योऽस्ति न प्रियः ।
ये भजन्ति तु मां भक्त्या मयि ते तेषु चाप्यहम् ॥ २९ ॥

samo-haṁ sarvabhūteṣu na me dveṣyo-sti na priyaḥ
ye bhajanti tu māṁ bhaktyā mayi te teṣu cāpyaham

I am the same within all beings. Neither have I any enemy, nor is anyone especially beloved. But those who worship Me with devotion, they are in Me, and I am in them.

-30-

अपि चेत्सुदुराचारो भजते मामनन्यभाक् ।
साधुरेव स मन्तव्यः सम्यग्व्यवसितो हि सः ॥ ३० ॥

api cetsudurācāro bhajate māmananyabhāk
sādhureva sa mantavyaḥ samyagvyavasito hi saḥ

Even if a person of very bad behavior worships Me without various thoughts, certainly he should be regarded as efficient, for he has created the proper circumstances.

-31-

क्षिप्रं भवति धर्मात्मा शश्वच्छान्तिं निगच्छति ।
कौन्तेय प्रति जानीहि न मे भक्तः प्रणश्यति ॥ ३१ ॥

kṣipraṁ bhavati dharmātmā śaśvacchāntiṁ nigacchati
kaunteya prati jānīhi na me bhaktaḥ praṇaśyati

Soon he becomes an ideal soul and attains to eternal peace, oh Son of Who Takes Away the Deficiency of Others (Arjuna). A devotee who knows Me is never destroyed.

-32-

मां हि पार्थ व्यपाश्रित्य येऽपि स्युः पापयोनयः ।
स्त्रियो वैश्यास्तथा शूद्रास्तेऽपि यान्ति परां गतिम् ॥ ३२ ॥

māṁ hi pārtha vyapāśritya ye-pi syuḥ pāpayonayaḥ
striyo vaiśyāstathā śūdrāste-pi yānti parāṁ gatim

For those who take refuge in Me, even if they took birth in a sinful womb, or as women, as business people or as laborers, all attain the supreme refuge.

-33-

किं पुनर्ब्राह्मणाः पुण्या भक्ता राजर्षयस्तथा ।
अनित्यमसुखं लोकमिमं प्राप्य भजस्व माम् ॥ ३३ ॥

kiṁ punarbrāhmaṇāḥ puṇyā bhaktā rājarṣayastathā
anityamasukhaṁ lokamimaṁ prāpya bhajasva mām

How much more those meritorious souls who know divinity and the devoted supreme sages who worship Me having attained this transient world without pleasure.

-34-

मन्मना भव मद्भक्तो मद्याजीमां नमस्कुरु ।
मामेवैष्यसि युक्त्वैवमात्मानं मत्परायणः ॥ ३४ ॥

manmanā bhava madbhakto madyājīmāṁ namaskuru
māmevaiṣyasi yuktvaivamātmānaṁ matparāyaṇaḥ

Think of Me, be devoted to Me, sacrifice to Me, offer respect to Me. Having united your soul with Me, come to Me as the Supreme Goal.

इति श्रीमद्भगवद्गीतासु नवमोऽध्यायः ॥ ९ ॥

१०

श्रीभगवानुवाच

śrībhagavānuvāca

The Respected Supreme Divinity said:

-1-

भूय एव महाबाहो शृणु मे परमं वचः ।

यत्तेऽहं प्रीयमाणाय वक्ष्यामि हितकाम्यया ॥ १ ॥

bhūya eva mahābāho śṛṇu me paramaṁ vacaḥ
yatte-haṁ prīyamāṇāya vakṣyāmi hitakāmyayā

Again listen to My supreme words, oh One of Mighty Arms (Arjuna), which I speak to you because of My love and desire for your welfare.

-2-

न मे विदुः सुरगणाः प्रभवं न महर्षयः ।

अहमादिर्हि देवानां महर्षीणां च सर्वशः ॥ २ ॥

na me viduḥ suragaṇāḥ prabhavaṁ na maharṣayaḥ
ahamādirhi devānāṁ maharṣīṇāṁ ca sarvaśaḥ

My beginning is not known by the multitude of Gods nor by the great sages, for I am before all Gods and all great sages.

-3-

यो मामजमनादिं च वेत्ति लोकमहेश्वरम् ।

असंमूढः स मर्त्येषु सर्वपापैः प्रमुच्यते ॥ ३ ॥

yo māmajamanādiṁ ca vetti lokamaheśvaram
asaṁmūḍhaḥ sa martyeṣu sarvapāpaiḥ pramucyate

Who knows Me as without birth, without beginning, the Great Supreme of all worlds, he is without foolishness among mortals and all his sins have been expunged.

-4-

बुद्धिर्ज्ञानमसंमोहः क्षमा सत्यं दमः शमः ।

सुखं दुःखं भवोऽभावो भयं चाभयमेव च ॥ ४ ॥

buddhirjñānamasaṁmohaḥ kṣamā satyaṁ damaḥ śamaḥ
sukhaṁ duḥkhaṁ bhavo-bhāvo bhayaṁ cābhayameva ca

Intelligence, wisdom, freedom from ignorance, forgiveness, truth, self-control, peace; pleasure, pain, generation, dissolution, fear and freedom from fear;

-5-

अहिंसा समता तुष्टिस्तपो दानं यशोऽयशः ।
भवन्ति भावा भूतानां मत्त एव पृथग्विधाः ॥ ५ ॥

ahiṁsā samatā tuṣṭistapo dānaṁ yaśo-yaśaḥ
bhavanti bhāvā bhūtānāṁ matta eva pṛthagvidhāḥ

causing harm to no one, equanimity, satisfaction, austerities, giving, welfare, and notoriety: from Me alone these different attitudes arise.

-6-

महर्षयः सप्त पूर्वे चत्वारो मनवस्तथा ।
मद्भावा मानसा जाता येषां लोक इमाः प्रजाः ॥ ६ ॥

maharṣayaḥ sapta pūrve catvāro manavastathā
madbhāvā mānasā jātā yeṣāṁ loka imāḥ prajāḥ

The seven great sages of ancient times as also the four Manus7 arose from the mind of My existence, and from them all the beings born in all the worlds.

-7-

एतां विभूतिं योगं च मम यो वेत्ति तत्त्वतः ।
सोऽविकम्पेन योगेन युज्यते नात्र संशयः ॥ ७ ॥

etāṁ vibhūtiṁ yogaṁ ca mama yo vetti tattvataḥ
so-vikampena yogena yujyate nātra saṁśayaḥ

Who knows the principles of these manifestations of union with Me, becomes immovable from union without a doubt.

-8-

अहं सर्वस्य प्रभवो मत्तः सर्वं प्रवर्तते ।
इति मत्वा भजन्ते मां बुधा भावसमन्विताः ॥ ८ ॥

ahaṁ sarvasya prabhavo mattaḥ sarvaṁ pravartate
iti matvā bhajante māṁ budhā bhāvasamanvitāḥ

I am before the being of all. From Me all has issued forth. The wise who worship Me with this understanding remain always in the same attitude.

-9-

मच्चित्ता मद्गतप्राणा बोधयन्तः परस्परम् ।
कथयन्तश्च मां नित्यं तुष्यन्ति च रमन्ति च ॥ ९ ॥

maccittā madgataprāṇā bodhayantaḥ parasparam
kathayantaśca māṁ nityaṁ tuṣyanti ca ramanti ca

Their consciousness is absorbed in Me, their life force moves in Me, they know the Higher than the Highest. Always they speak of Me. They are satisfied and filled with delight.

-10-

तेषां सततयुक्तानां भजतां प्रीतिपूर्वकम् ।
ददामि बुद्धियोगं तं येन मामुपयान्ति ते ॥ १० ॥

teṣāṁ satatayuktānāṁ bhajatāṁ prītipūrvakam
dadāmi buddhiyogaṁ taṁ yena māmupayānti te

I give union with intelligence to those who are always united in worship with full love, by means of which they find the attainment of Me.

-11-

तेषामेवानुकम्पार्थमहमज्ञानजं तमः ।
नाशयाम्यात्मभावस्थो ज्ञानदीपेन भास्वता ॥ ११ ॥

teṣāmevānukampārthamahamajñānajaṁ tamaḥ
nāśayāmyātmabhāvastho jñānadīpena bhāsvatā

It is only because of My compassion for them that I destroy the darkness born of ignorance situated within the attitudes of the soul by means of the luminous light of wisdom.

अर्जुन उवाच

arjuna uvāca

Clarity of Pure Devotion said:

-12-

परं ब्रह्म परं धाम पवित्रं परमं भवान् ।
पुरुषं शाश्वतं दिव्यमादिदेवमजं विभुम् ॥ १२ ॥

paraṁ brahma paraṁ dhāma pavitraṁ paramaṁ bhavān
puruṣaṁ śāśvataṁ divyamādidevamajaṁ vibhum

You are the Supreme Divinity, the supreme place, the supreme purity. You are the eternal, perfect consciousness, divinity, first among Gods, unborn and omnipresent.

-13-

आहुस्त्वामृषयः सर्वे देवर्षिर्नारदस्तथा ।

असितो देवलो व्यासः स्वयं चैव ब्रवीषि मे ॥ १३ ॥

āhustvāmṛṣayaḥ sarve devarṣirnāradastathā
asito devalo vyāsaḥ svayaṁ caiva bravīṣi me

All the seers have spoken of you, also the seers among the Gods, Nārada, Asīta, Devala and Veda Vyāsa. And even you yourself say this to me.

-14-

सर्वमेतदृतं मन्ये यन्मां वदसि केशव ।

न हि ते भगवन्व्यक्तिं विदुर्देवा न दानवाः ॥ १४ ॥

sarvametadṛtaṁ manye yanmāṁ vadasi keśava
na hi te bhagavanvyaktiṁ vidurdevā na dānavāḥ

I regard all you are saying to Me as the imperishable truth, Embodiment of the Functions of Creation, Preservation and Transformation (Kṛṣṇa). For neither the forces of divinity nor the forces of duality know you in your supreme manifestation.

-15-

स्वयमेवात्मनात्मानं वेत्थ त्वं पुरुषोत्तम ।

भूतभावन भूतेश देवदेव जगत्पते ॥ १५ ॥

svayamevātmanātmānaṁ vettha tvaṁ puruṣottama
bhūtabhāvana bhūteśa devadeva jagatpate

Only your soul knows your own soul, Excellent Perfect Consciousness, the attitude of all being, the Lord of all beings, God of Gods, Lord of the perceivable universe.

-16-

वक्तुमर्हस्यशेषेण दिव्या ह्यात्मविभूतयः ।

याभिर्विभूतिभिर्लोकानिमांस्त्वं व्याप्य तिष्ठसि ॥ १६ ॥

vaktumarhasyaśeṣeṇa divyā hyātmavibhūtayaḥ
yābhirvibhūtibhirlokānimāṁstvaṁ vyāpya tiṣṭhasi

You should tell completely of the divine manifestations of your soul, by which manifestations these worlds exist pervaded by you.

-17-

कथं विद्यामहं योगिंस्त्वां सदा परिचिन्तयन् ।

केषु केषु च भावेषु चिन्त्योऽसि भगवन्मया ॥ १७ ॥

kathaṁ vidyāmahaṁ yogiṁstvāṁ sadā paricintayan
keṣu keṣu ca bhāveṣu cintyo-si bhagavanmayā

Tell me this knowledge, oh Man of Union, so that I can always think of you. In which various attitudes are you to be thought of by me, oh Supreme Divinity?

-18-

विस्तरेणात्मनो योगं विभूतिं च जनार्दन ।

भूयः कथय तृप्तिर्हि शृण्वतो नास्ति मेऽमृतम् ॥ १८ ॥

vistareṇātmano yogaṁ vibhūtiṁ ca janārdana
bhūyaḥ kathaya tṛptirhi śṛṇvato nāsti me-mṛtam

Again, tell the details of the manifestations of the soul in union, Who is Worshiped by the People (Kṛṣṇa), for I am not yet satiated from listening to the nectar of your words.

श्रीभगवानुवाच

śrībhagavānuvāca

The Respected Supreme Divinity said:

-19-

हन्त ते कथयिष्यामि दिव्या ह्यात्मविभूतयः ।

प्राधान्यतः कुरुश्रेष्ठ नास्त्यन्तो विस्तरस्य मे ॥ १९ ॥

hanta te kathayiṣyāmi divyā hyātmavibhūtayaḥ
prādhānyataḥ kuruśreṣṭha nāstyanto vistarasya me

Now I shall tell you of the predominant manifestations of My soul, oh Best of Those Who Act (Arjuna). There is no end to the details of me.

-20-

अहमात्मा गुडाकेश सर्वभूताशयस्थितः ।
अहमादिश्च मध्यं च भूतानामन्त एव च ॥ २० ॥

ahamātmā guḍākeśa sarvabhūtāśayasthitaḥ
ahamādiśca madhyaṁ ca bhūtānāmanta eva ca

I am the soul which resides within all beings, Who Has Conquered Sleep (Arjuna). I am before, in the middle and also at the end of all beings.

-21-

आदित्यानामहं विष्णुर्ज्योतिषां रविरंशुमान् ।
मरीचिर्मरुतामस्मि नक्षत्राणामहं शशी ॥ २१ ॥

ādityānāmahaṁ viṣṇurjyotiṣāṁ raviraṁśumān
marīcirmarutāmasmi nakṣatrāṇāmahaṁ śaśī

Among the children of non-duality I am Viṣṇu, He who pervades the Universe. Among lights I am the radiant sun. Among the shining ones I am a particle of light, and among the stars I am the Moon.

-22-

वेदानां सामवेदोऽस्मि देवानामस्मि वासवः ।
इन्द्रियाणां मनश्चास्मि भूतानामस्मि चेतना ॥ २२ ॥

vedānāṁ sāmavedo-smi devānāmasmi vāsavaḥ
indriyāṇāṁ manaścāmi bhūtānāmasmi cetanā

Among the Vedas I am the Wisdom of Song, among the Gods I am the one who controls, Indra. Among the organs and senses I am the mind, and among all beings I am consciousness.

-23-

रुद्राणां शङ्करश्चास्मि वित्तेशो यक्षरक्षसाम् ।
वसूनां पावकश्चास्मि मेरुः शिखरिणामहम् ॥ २३ ॥

rudrāṇāṁ śaṅkaraścāsmi vitteśo yakṣarakṣasām
vasūnāṁ pāvakaścāsmi meruḥ śikhariṇāmaham

Among the Relievers of Sufferings I am the Cause of Peace. Among those who long for material things I am the Lord of Wealth. Among the shining Gods I am Fire, and among all summits I am Mount Meru.

-24-

पुरोधसां च मुख्यं मां विद्धि पार्थ बृहस्पतिम् ।
सेनानीनामहं स्कन्दः सरसामस्मि सागरः ॥ २४ ॥

purodhasāṁ ca mukhyaṁ māṁ viddhi pārtha bṛhaspatim
senānīnāmahaṁ skandaḥ sarasāmasmi sāgaraḥ

Among gurus know Me to be the Chief, Bṛhaspati. Among leaders of armies I am Skanda, the son of Śiva. Among bodies of water I am the ocean.

-25-

महर्षीणां भृगुरहं गिरामस्म्येकमक्षरम् ।
यज्ञानां जपयज्ञोऽस्मि स्थावराणां हिमालयः ॥ २५ ॥

maharṣīṇāṁ bhṛguraham girāmasmyekamakṣaram
yajñānāṁ japayajño-smi sthāvarāṇāṁ himālayaḥ

Among great sages I am Bṛgu, among speech I am the one letter Oṁ. Among sacrifices I am the sacrifice of continuous repetition, and among the immovable I am the Himalayas.

-26-

अश्वत्थः सर्ववृक्षाणां देवर्षीणां च नारदः ।
गन्धर्वाणां चित्ररथः सिद्धानां कपिलो मुनिः ॥ २६ ॥

aśvatthaḥ sarvavṛkṣāṇāṁ devarṣīṇāṁ ca nāradaḥ
gandharvāṇāṁ citrarathaḥ siddhānāṁ kapilo muniḥ

Among all trees I am the holy fig tree, and among divine sages I am Nārada. Among celestial musicians I am Citraratha, the guru of all musicians, and among those who have attained perfection I am Kapila the wise.

-27-

उच्चैःश्रवसमश्वानां विद्धि माममृतोद्भवम् ।
ऐरावतं गजेन्द्राणां नराणां च नराधिपम् ॥ २७ ॥

uccaiḥśravasamaśvānāṁ viddhi māmamṛtodbhavam
airāvataṁ gajendrāṇāṁ narāṇāṁ ca narādhipam

Among horses know Me as Ucchaiśravas, the horse of wisdom who was born from nectar. Among elephants I am the King of elephants, Airavata, and among men I am the King.

-28-

आयुधानामहं वज्रं धेनूनामस्मि कामधुक् ।
प्रजनश्चास्मि कन्दर्पः सर्पाणामस्मि वासुकिः ॥ २८ ॥

āyudhānāmahaṁ vajraṁ dhenūnāmasmi kāmadhuk
prajanaścāsmi kandarpaḥ sarpāṇāmasmi vāsukiḥ

Among vital energies I am the thunderbolt, among cows the one who satiates desire. Among those who beget offspring I am the God of Love, and among snakes I am Vāsuki the Lord.

-29-

अनन्तश्चास्मि नागानां वरुणो यादसामहम् ।
पितॄणामर्यमा चास्मि यमः संयमतामहम् ॥ २९ ॥

anantaścāsmi nāgānāṁ varuṇo yādasāmaham
pitṝṇāmaryamā cāsmi yamaḥ saṁyamatāmaham

Among cobras I am Ananta, and among beings of the water I am Varuṇa. Among ancestors I am One Purified by knowledge, and among all who control I am Yama the Lord of Death.

-30-

प्रह्लादश्चास्मि दैत्यानां कालः कलयतामहम् ।
मृगाणां च मृगेन्द्रोऽहं वैनतेयश्च पक्षिणाम् ॥ ३० ॥

prahlādaścāsmi daityānāṁ kālaḥ kalayatāmaham
mṛgāṇāṁ ca mṛgendro-haṁ vainateyaśca pakṣiṇām

Among the beings of duality I am Prahlāda, the pure devotee. Among those who count I am time. Among deer I am the Lord of deer, among birds I am Vainateya, a name of Gaḍuda.

-31-

पवनः पवतामस्मि रामः शस्त्रभृतामहम् ।
झषाणां मकरश्चास्मि स्रोतसामस्मि जाह्नवी ॥ ३१ ॥

pavanaḥ pavatāmasmi rāmaḥ śastrabhṛtāmaham
jhaṣāṇāṁ makaraścāsmi srotasāmasmi jāhnavī

Among those who purify I am the wind, among those who hold weapons I am Rāma. Among fish I am Makara, the shark, and among those that flow I am Jāhnavī, the Ganges.

-32-

सर्गाणामादिरन्तश्च मध्यं चैवाहमर्जुन ।

अध्यात्मविद्या विद्यानां वादः प्रवदतामहम् ॥ ३२ ॥

sargāṇāmādirantaśca madhyaṁ caivāhamarjuna
adhyātmavidyā vidyānāṁ vādaḥ pravadatāmaham

Among created beings I am the beginning, the middle and the end, Clarity of Pure Devotion; among knowledge, knowledge of the soul; among expressions, speech.

-33-

अक्षराणामकारोऽस्मि द्वंद्वः सामासिकस्य च ।

अहमेवाक्षयः कालो धाताहं विश्वतोमुखः ॥ ३३ ॥

akṣarāṇāmakāro-smi dvaṁdvaḥ sāmāsikasya ca
ahamevākṣayaḥ kālo dhātāhaṁ viśvatomukhaḥ

Among letters I am the letter A, and in the competition for extreme brevity I am even imperishable time. Among those who support I am the Mouth of the Universe.

-34-

मृत्युः सर्वहरश्चाहमुद्भवश्च भविष्यताम् ।

कीर्तिः श्रीर्वाक्च नारीणां स्मृतिर्मेधा धृतिः क्षमा ॥ ३४ ॥

mṛtyuḥ sarvaharaścāhamudbhavaśca bhaviṣyatām
kīrtiḥ śrīrvākca nārīṇāṁ smṛtirmedhā dhṛtiḥ kṣamā

Among all who take away I am death, and among those who generate I am the future. Among women I am Fame, Respect, Vibrations, Recollection, Loving Intellect, Constancy, Forgiveness.

-35-

बृहत्साम तथा साम्नां गायत्री छन्दसामहम् ।

मासानां मार्गशीर्षोऽहमृतूनां कुसुमाकरः ॥ ३५ ॥

bṛhatsāma tathā sāmnāṁ gāyatrī chandasāmaham
māsānāṁ mārgaśīrṣo-hamṛtūnāṁ kusumākaraḥ

Among songs I am the great song of the Vedas, among meters I am Gāyatrī, 24 syllables to the verse. Among months I am November, and among seasons I am Spring.

-36-

द्यूतं छलयतामस्मि तेजस्तेजस्विनामहम् ।
जयोऽस्मि व्यवसायोऽस्मि सत्त्वं सत्त्ववतामहम् ॥ ३६ ॥

dyūtaṁ chalayatāmasmi tejastejasvināmaham
jayo-smi vyavasāyo-smi sattvaṁ sattvavatāmaham

I am the fraud of the deceitful, I am the light of those who are luminous. I am the victory of those who produce effort, and I am the truth of the truthful.

-37-

वृष्णीनां वासुदेवोऽस्मि पाण्डवानां धनंजयः ।
मुनीनामप्यहं व्यासः कवीनामुशना कविः ॥ ३७ ॥

vṛṣṇīnāṁ vāsudevo-smi pāṇḍavānāṁ dhanaṁjayaḥ
munīnāmapyahaṁ vyāsaḥ kavīnāmuśanā kaviḥ

Among the Vṛṣṇis I am Vāsudeva, and among the sons of He Who is without Prejudice I am Conqueror of Wealth (Arjuna). Among the wise I am Veda Vyāsa, and among inspired poets I am Uśana, a name of Śukrācārya.

-38-

दण्डो दमयतामस्मि नीतिरस्मि जिगीषताम् ।
मौनं चैवास्मि गुह्यानां ज्ञानं ज्ञानवतामहम् ॥ ३८ ॥

daṇḍo damayatāmasmi nītirasmi jigīṣatām
maunaṁ caivāsmi guhyānāṁ jñānaṁ jñānavatāmaham

Among those who maintain control I am punishment. Among those who desire victory I am diplomacy. Among the secret I am silence, among the wise I am wisdom.

-39-

यच्चापि सर्वभूतानां बीजं तदहमर्जुन ।
न तदस्ति विना यत्स्यान्मया भूतं चराचरम् ॥ ३९ ॥

yaccāpi sarvabhūtānāṁ bījaṁ tadahamarjuna
na tadasti vinā yatsyānmayā bhūtaṁ carācaram

Whatever be the seed of all beings, Clarity of Pure Devotion, whether moving or unmoving, there is no being which may exist without Me.

-40-

नान्तोऽस्ति मम दिव्यानां विभूतीनां परंतप ।
एष तूद्देशतः प्रोक्तो विभूतेर्विस्तरो मया ॥ ४० ॥

nānto-sti mama divyānāṁ vibhūtīnāṁ paraṁtapa
eṣa tūddeśataḥ prokto vibhūtervistaro mayā

There is no end to the manifestations of My divinity, Supreme Light (Arjuna). Thus has been spoken this brief explanation of the details of My manifestations.

-41-

यद्यद्विभूतिमत्सत्त्वं श्रीमदूर्जितमेव वा ।
तत्तदेवावगच्छ त्वं मम तेजोंऽशसंभवम् ॥ ४१ ॥

yadyadvibhūtimatsattvaṁ śrīmadūrjitameva vā
tattadevāvagaccha tvaṁ mama tejoṁ-śasaṁbhavam

Whatever manifestation of truth, whether respect or propriety or other, know that to have emanated from a small portion of My light.

-42-

अथवा बहुनैतेन किं ज्ञातेन तवार्जुन ।
विष्टभ्याहमिदं कृत्स्नमेकांशेन स्थितो जगत् ॥ ४२ ॥

athavā bahunaitena kiṁ jñātena tavārjuna
viṣṭabhyāhamidaṁ kṛtsnamekāṁśena sthito jagat

But why should all this be known, Clarity of Pure Devotion. I exist supporting all this perceivable universe by only one small part of Myself.

इति श्रीमद्भगवद्गीतासु दशमोऽध्यायः ॥ १० ॥

११

अर्जुन उवाच
arjuna uvāca
Clarity of Pure Devotion said:

-1-

मदनुग्रहाय परमं गुह्यमध्यात्मसंज्ञितम् ।
यत्त्वयोक्तं वचस्तेन मोहोऽयं विगतो मम ॥ १ ॥

madanugrahāya paramaṁ guhyamadhyātmasaṁjñitam
yattvayoktaṁ vacastena moho-yaṁ vigato mama
My ignorance has been dispelled by these words containing the highest secret spiritual knowledge, which you spoke because of your compassion to me.

-2-

भवाप्ययौ हि भूतानां श्रुतौ विस्तरशो मया ।
त्वत्तः कमलपत्राक्ष माहात्म्यमपि चाव्ययम् ॥ २ ॥

bhavāpyayau hi bhūtānāṁ śrutau vistaraśo mayā
tvattaḥ kamalapatrākṣa māhātmyamapi cāvyayam
You have let me hear the details of the birth and dissolution of all existence, oh Lotus Eyed, as well as about your immeasurable greatness.

-3-

एवमेतद्यथात्थ त्वमात्मानं परमेश्वर ।
द्रष्टुमिच्छामि ते रूपमैश्वरं पुरुषोत्तम ॥ ३ ॥

evametadyathāttha tvamātmānaṁ parameśvara
draṣṭumicchāmi te rūpamaiśvaraṁ puruṣottama
Even as you have declared, just so is your being, oh Supreme Lord. I desire to see your imperishable form, oh Excellent Complete Consciousness (Kṛṣṇa).

-4-

मन्यसे यदि तच्छक्यं मया द्रष्टुमिति प्रभो ।

योगेश्वर ततो मे त्वं दर्शयात्मानमव्ययम् ॥ ४ ॥

manyase yadi tacchakyaṁ mayā draṣṭumiti prabho
yogeśvara tato me tvaṁ darśayātmānamavyayam

If you think that it is possible for it to be seen by me, oh Lord, then Lord of Union (Kṛṣṇa), show your imperishable soul to me.

श्रीभगवानुवाच

śrībhagavānuvāca

The Respected Supreme Divinity said:

-5-

पश्य मे पार्थ रूपाणि शतशोऽथ सहस्रशः ।

नानाविधानि दिव्यानि नानावर्णाकृतीनि च ॥ ५ ॥

paśya me pārtha rūpāṇi śataśo-tha sahasraśaḥ
nānāvidhāni divyāni nānāvarṇākṛtīni ca

See my hundreds and thousands of forms, Son of She Who Excels (Arjuna), of various divine kinds, of various colors and shapes.

-6-

पश्यादित्यान्वसून्रुद्रानश्विनौ मरुतस्तथा ।

बहून्यदृष्टपूर्वाणि पश्याश्चर्याणि भारत ॥ ६ ॥

paśyādityānvasūnrudrānaśvinau marutastathā
bahūnyadṛṣṭapūrvāṇi paśyāścaryāṇi bhārata

See the Sons of the Light, the Lords of Wealth, the Relievers of Suffering, the Lords of Pure Desire, Those who Purify. See also many imperceptible things and wonders of old, Descendant of the Light of Wisdom (Arjuna).

-7-

इहैकस्थं जगत्कृत्स्नं पश्याद्य सचराचरम् ।

मम देहे गुडाकेश यच्चान्यद्द्रष्टुमिच्छसि ॥ ७ ॥

ihaikasthaṁ jagatkṛtsnaṁ paśyādya sacarācaram
mama dehe guḍākeśa yaccānyaddraṣṭumicchasi

Now see the entire perceivable world with that which moves and that which moves not united into one in My body, Who Has Conquered Sleep (Arjuna), and any other thing that you wish to see.

-8-

न तु मां शक्यसे द्रष्टुमनेनैव स्वचक्षुषा ।
दिव्यं ददामि ते चक्षुः पश्य मे योगमैश्वरम् ॥ ८ ॥

na tu māṁ śakyase draṣṭumanenaiva svacakṣuṣā
divyaṁ dadāmi te cakṣuḥ paśya me yogamaiśvaraṁ

But you cannot see Me with your own worldly eyes. I give you divine eyes. See My Imperishable Union.

संजय उवाच

saṁjaya uvāca

He Who is Victorious Over All said:

-9-

एवमुक्त्वा ततो राजन्महायोगेश्वरो हरिः ।
दर्शयामास पार्थाय परमं रूपमैश्वरम् ॥ ९ ॥

evamuktvā tato rājanmahāyogeśvaro hariḥ
darśayāmāsa pārthāya paramaṁ rūpamaiśvaram

Having thus spoken, oh King, the Great Lord of Union, Remover of Duality, showed His Supreme Imperishable form to Son of She Who Excels (Arjuna).

-10-

अनेकवक्त्रनयनमनेकाद्भुतदर्शनम् ।
अनेकदिव्याभरणं दिव्यानेकोद्यतायुधम् ॥ १० ॥

anekavaktranayanamanekādbhutadarśanam
anekadivyābharaṇaṁ divyānekodyatāyudham

(He showed) uncountable faces and eyes, uncountable marvelous things to be seen, uncountable divine ornaments, uncountable divine weapons at the ready.

-11-

दिव्यमाल्याम्बरधरं दिव्यगन्धानुलेपनम् ।
सर्वाश्चर्यमयं देवमनन्तं विश्वतोमुखम् ॥ ११ ॥

divyamālyāmbaradharaṁ divyagandhānulepanam
sarvāścaryamayaṁ devamanantaṁ viśvatomukham

He wore a divine garland of flowers and cloth, and emitted divine fragrance, the God who is the manifestation of all that is wonderful, the infinite face of the universe.

-12-

दिवि सूर्यसहस्रस्य भवेद्युगपदुत्थिता ।
यदि भाः सदृशी सा स्याद्भासस्तस्य महात्मनः ॥ १२ ॥

divi sūryasahasrasya bhavedyugapadutthitā
yadi bhāḥ sadṛśī sā syādbhāsastasya mahātmanaḥ

If the light of a thousand rising suns were to unite in the sky, that light would not compare to the light of that great soul.

-13-

तत्रैकस्थं जगत्कृत्स्नं प्रविभक्तमनेकधा ।
अपश्यद्देवदेवस्य शरीरे पाण्डवस्तदा ॥ १३ ॥

tatraikasthaṁ jagatkṛtsnaṁ pravibhaktamanekadhā
apaśyaddevadevasya śarīre pāṇḍavastadā

There the son of He Who is without Prejudice (Arjuna) saw the many divisions of the entire universe residing in one, the body of the God of Gods.

-14-

ततः स विस्मयाविष्टो हृष्टरोमा धनंजयः ।
प्रणम्य शिरसा देवं कृताञ्जलिरभाषत ॥ १४ ॥

tataḥ sa vismayāviṣṭo hṛṣṭaromā dhanaṁjayaḥ
praṇamya śirasā devaṁ kṛtāñjalirabhāṣata

Then Conqueror of Wealth (Arjuna) was filled with amazement, his hairs standing on edge, with hands folded and clasped in prayer and head bowed with respect, spoke to the Lord.

अर्जुन उवाच

arjuna uvāca

Clarity of Pure Devotion said:

-15-

पश्यामि देवांस्तव देव देहे
सर्वांस्तथा भूतविशेषसंघान्।
ब्रह्माणमीशं कमलासनस्थ-
मृषींश्च सर्वानुरगांश्च दिव्यान्॥ १५॥

paśyāmi devāṁstava deva dehe
sarvāṁstathā bhūtaviśeṣasaṁghān
brahmāṇamīśaṁ kamalāsanastha-
mṛṣīṁśca sarvānuragāṁśca divyān

I see in your body, oh God, all of the Gods, and also the multitude of all individual beings. The Lord Creative Consciousness seated on a lotus, the sages and all divine serpents representing energies of existence.

-16-

अनेकबाहूदरवक्त्रनेत्रं
पश्यामि त्वां सर्वतोऽनन्तरूपम्।
नान्तं न मध्यं न पुनस्तवादिं
पश्यामि विश्वेश्वर विश्वरूप॥ १६॥

anekabāhūdaravaktranetraṁ
paśyāmi tvāṁ sarvato-nantarūpam
nāntaṁ na madhyaṁ na punastavādiṁ
paśyāmi viśveśvara viśvarūpa

I see you with infinite forms on all sides, with countless arms, faces and eyes. I see no beginning, no middle and again no end, Lord of the Universe, of universal form.

-17-

किरीटिनं गदिनं चक्रिणं च
तेजोराशिं सर्वतो दीप्तिमन्तम् ।
पश्यामि त्वां दुर्निरीक्ष्यं समन्ता-
द्दीप्तानलार्कद्युतिमप्रमेयम् ॥ १७ ॥

kirīṭinaṁ gadinaṁ cakriṇaṁ ca
tejorāśiṁ sarvato dīptimantam
paśyāmi tvāṁ durnirīkṣyaṁ samantād-
dīptānalārkadyutimaprameyam

I see you with a crown, a club, a discus and a massive light shining everywhere, which is difficult to look at as it is an immeasurable light, blazing like the sun or like fire.

-18-

त्वमक्षरं परमं वेदितव्यं
त्वमस्य विश्वस्य परं निधानम् ।
त्वमव्ययः शाश्वतधर्मगोप्ता
सनातनस्त्वं पुरषो मतो मे ॥ १८ ॥

tvamakṣaraṁ paramaṁ veditavyaṁ
tvamaśya viśvasya paraṁ nidhānam
tvamavyayaḥ śāśvatadharmagoptā
sanātanastvaṁ puraṣo mato me

You are the imperishable Supreme to be known. You are the treasure of the universe. You are the infinite protector of the eternal ideal of perfection, and I regard you as the eternal full and perfect Conscious Being.

-19-

अनादिमध्यान्तमनन्तवीर्य-
मनन्तबाहुं शशिसूर्यनेत्रम् ।
पश्यामि त्वां दीप्तहुताशवक्त्रं
स्वतेजसा विश्वमिदं तपन्तम् ॥ १९ ॥

anādimadhyāntamanantavīrya-
manantabāhuṁ śaśisūryanetram
paśyāmi tvāṁ dīptahutāśavaktraṁ
śvatejasā viśvamidaṁ tapantam

I see you without beginning, middle or end, with infinite strength and infinite arms; the moon and the sun are your eyes. The light of fire is in your face. With your light you illuminate this universe.

-20-

द्यावापृथिव्योरिदमन्तरं हि
व्याप्तं त्वयैकेन दिशश्च सर्वाः ।
दृष्ट्वाद्भुतं रूपमुग्रं तवेदं
लोकत्रयं प्रव्यथितं महात्मन् ॥ २० ॥

dyāvāpṛthivyoridamantaraṁ hi
vyāptaṁ tvayaikena diśaśca sarvāḥ
dṛṣṭvādbhutaṁ rūpamugraṁ tavedaṁ
lokatrayaṁ pravyathitaṁ mahātman

Heaven, earth and the atmosphere are pervaded by you alone, as well as all the directions. Seeing this wonderful and terrible form, the three worlds tremble in fear, oh Great Soul.

-21-

अमी हि त्वां सुरसंघा विशन्ति
केचिद्भीताः प्राञ्जलयो गृणन्ति ।
स्वस्तीत्युक्त्वा महर्षिसिद्धसंघाः
स्तुवन्ति त्वां स्तुतिभिः पुष्कलाभिः ॥ २१ ॥

amī hi tvāṁ surasaṁghā viśanti
kecidbhītāḥ prāñjalayo gṛṇanti
svastītyuktvā maharṣisiddhasaṁghāḥ
stuvanti tvāṁ stutibhiḥ puṣkalābhiḥ

Verily the multitude of Gods enter into you. Some with palms joined in emotion accept your blessings. The multitude of sages and Beings of Perfect Attainment praise you with complete hymns.

-22-

रुद्रादित्या वसवो ये च साध्या
विश्वेऽश्विनौ मरुतश्चोष्मपाश्च ।
गन्धर्वयक्षासुरसिद्धसंघा
वीक्षन्ते त्वां विस्मिताश्चैव सर्वे ॥ २२ ॥

rudrādityā vasavo ye ca sādhyā
viśve-śvinau marutaścoṣmapāśca
gandharvayakṣāsurasiddhasaṁghā
vīkṣante tvāṁ vismitāścaiva sarve

The Relievers of Suffering, the Sons of the Light, the Lords of Wealth, the Pure Ones, the Universal Deities, those Who Long with Pure Desire, the Shining Ones, the ancestors, celestial singers, Those Who Protect Wealth, the forces of Duality and Beings of Perfect Attainment all are looking at you with astonishment.

-23-

रूपं महत्ते बहुवक्त्रनेत्रं

महाबाहो बहुबाहूरुपादम् ।

बहूदरं बहुदंष्ट्राकरालं

दृष्ट्वा लोकाः प्रव्यथितास्तथाहम् ॥ २३ ॥

rūpaṁ mahatte bahuvaktranetraṁ
mahābāho bahubāhūrupādam
bahūdaraṁ bahudaṁṣṭrākarālaṁ
dṛṣṭvā lokāḥ pravyathitāstathāham

Seeing your immense form with many faces, eyes, arms, thighs, feet, stomachs, oh One of Mighty Arms (Kṛṣṇa), with many fearful teeth, all beings in the world are terrified as I am also.

-24-

नभःस्पृशं दीप्तमनेकवर्णं

व्यात्ताननं दीप्तविशालनेत्रम् ।

दृष्ट्वा हि त्वां प्रव्यथितान्तरात्मा

धृतिं न विन्दामि शमं च विष्णो ॥ २४ ॥

nabhaḥspṛśaṁ dīptamanekavarṇaṁ
vyāttānanaṁ dīptaviśālanetram
dṛṣṭvā hi tvāṁ pravyathitāntarātmā
dhṛtiṁ na vindāmi śamaṁ ca viṣṇo

Seeing your light of many colors touching the atmosphere, your open mouth, your immense eyes filled with light, my inner self is filled with fear. Oh Viṣṇu, Who Pervades the Universe, I find neither courage nor peace.

-25-

दंष्ट्राकरालानि च ते मुखानि
दृष्ट्वैव कालानलसंनिभानि ।
दिशो न जाने न लभे च शर्म
प्रसीद देवेश जगन्निवास ॥ २५ ॥

daṁṣṭrākarālāni ca te mukhāni
dṛṣṭvaiva kālānalasaṁnibhāni
diśo na jāne na labhe ca śarma
prasīda deveśa jagannivāsa

Seeing your terrifying mouth gleaming in all directions like the fire at the time of dissolution, I can neither know nor attain happiness. Oh Lord of all the Gods, Residence of the Universe, be pleased.

-26-

अमी च त्वां धृतराष्ट्रस्य पुत्राः
सर्वे सहैवावनिपालसंघैः ।
भीष्मो द्रोणः सूतपुत्रस्तथासौ
सहास्मदीयैरपि योधमुख्यैः ॥ २६ ॥

amī ca tvāṁ dhṛtarāṣṭrasya putrāḥ
sarve sahaivāvanipālasaṁghaiḥ
bhīṣmo droṇaḥ sūtaputrastathāsau
sahāsmadīyairapi yodhamukhyaiḥ

In you are all the sons of Blind Ambition, and even the multitude of kings of this earth; Who Rules Fear, Who injures his foes with Weapons, the son of the charioteer, Who thinks himself the Doer, and also our own warrior chiefs.

-27-

वक्त्राणि ते त्वरमाणा विशन्ति
दंष्ट्राकरालानि भयानकानि ।
केचिद्विलग्ना दशनान्तरेषु
संदृश्यन्ते चूर्णितैरुत्तमाङ्गैः ॥ २७ ॥

vaktrāṇi te tvaramāṇā viśanti
daṁṣṭrākarālāni bhayānakāni
kecidvilagnā daśanāntareṣu
saṁdṛśyante cūrṇitairuttamāṅgaiḥ

With haste they enter through those terrible teeth into your fearful mouth. Some are found stuck between the teeth where their excellent bodies are crushed.

-28-

यथा नदीनां वहवोऽम्बुवेगाः
समुद्रमेवाभिमुखा द्रवन्ति ।
तथा तवामी नरलोकवीरा
विशन्ति वक्त्राण्यभिविज्वलन्ति ॥ २८ ॥

yathā nadīnāṁ vahavo-mbuvegāḥ
samudramevābhimukhā dravanti
tathā tavāmī naralokavīrā
viśanti vaktrāṇyabhivijvalanti

Just as the waters of many rivers flow to the sea, so these heroes of the world of men enter your radiant mouth.

-29-

यथा प्रदीप्तं ज्वलनं पतंगा
विशन्ति नाशाय समृद्धवेगाः ।
तथैव नाशाय विशन्ति लोका-
स्तवापि वक्त्राणि समृद्धवेगाः ॥ २९ ॥

yathā pradīptaṁ jvalanaṁ pataṁgā
viśanti nāśāya samṛddhavegāḥ
tathaiva nāśāya viśanti lokā-
stavāpi vaktrāṇi samṛddhavegāḥ

Just as moths enter the luminous fire to their immediate destruction, just so living beings enter your mouth to be destroyed immediately.

-30-

लेलिह्यसे ग्रसमानः समन्ता-
ल्लोकान्समग्रान्वदनैर्ज्वलद्भिः ।
तेजोभिरापूर्य जगत्समग्रं
भासस्तवोग्राः प्रतपन्ति विष्णो ॥ ३० ॥

lelihyase grasamānaḥ samantā-
llokānsamagrānvadanairjvaladbhiḥ
tejobhirāpūrya jagatsamagraṁ
bhāsastavogrāḥ pratapanti viṣṇo

The fierce rays and radiant light like fire from your face permeates, scorches and devours the worlds, oh Viṣṇu, Who Pervades the Universe.

-31-

आख्याहि मे को भवानुग्ररूपो
नमोऽस्तु ते देववर प्रसीद ।
विज्ञातुमिच्छामि भवन्तमाद्यं
न हि प्रजानामि तव प्रवृत्तिम् ॥ ३१ ॥

ākhyāhi me ko bhavānugrarūpo
namo-stu te devavara prasīda
vijñātumicchāmi bhavantamādyaṁ
na hi prajānāmi tava pravṛttim

Tell me who you are displaying this frightening form. I bow to you, oh God who grants boons. Be pleased. I wish to know you, Foremost. Indeed, I do not know the evolution of your nature.

श्रीभगवानुवाच

śrībhagavānuvāca

The Respected Supreme Divinity said:

-32-

कालोऽस्मि लोकक्षयकृत्प्रवृद्धो
लोकान्समाहर्तुमिह प्रवृत्तः ।
ऋतेऽपि त्वां न भविष्यन्ति सर्वे
येऽवस्थिताः प्रत्यनीकेषु योधाः ॥ ३२ ॥

kālo-smi lokakṣayakṛtpravṛddho
lokānsamāhartumiha pravṛttaḥ
ṛte-pi tvāṁ na bhaviṣyanti sarve
ye-vasthitāḥ pratyanīkeṣu yodhāḥ

I am mighty Time, which makes the worlds perish. Here I am engaged in the process of destruction, and even without you, all these warriors stationed in opposing armies will not live.

-33-

तस्मात्त्वमुत्तिष्ठ यशो लभस्व

जित्वा शत्रून् भुङ्क्ष्व राज्यं समृद्धम् ।

मयैवैते निहताः पूर्वमेव

निमित्तमात्रं भव सव्यसाचिन् ॥ ३३ ॥

tasmāttvamuttiṣṭha yaśo labhasva
jitvā śatrūn bhuṅkṣva rājyaṁ samṛddham
mayaivaite nihatāḥ pūrvameva
nimittamātraṁ bhava savyasācin

Therefore, rise and gain welfare. Completely conquering enemies who have already been slain by Me, enjoy the kingdom, oh You Who Can Shoot with Either Hand (Arjuna). Only you be My instrument.

-34-

द्रोणं च भीष्मं च जयद्रथं च

कर्णं तथान्यानपि योधवीरान् ।

मया हतांस्त्वं जहि मा व्यथिष्ठा

युध्यस्व जेतासि रणे सपत्नान् ॥ ३४ ॥

droṇaṁ ca bhīṣmaṁ ca jayadrathaṁ ca
karṇaṁ tathānyānapi yodhavīrān
mayā hatāṁstvaṁ jahi mā vyathiṣṭhā
yudhyasva jetāsi raṇe sapatnān

Kill Who injures his foes with Weapons, Who Rules Fear, the Conveyance of Victory, and Who thinks himself the Doer, also other brave warriors already doomed to death. Be not distressed. Fight and you will conquer the enemies in battle.

संजय उवाच

saṁjaya uvāca

He Who is Victorious Over All said:

-35-

एतच्छ्रुत्वा वचनं केशवस्य
कृताञ्जलिर्वेपमानः किरीटी ।
नमस्कृत्वा भूय एवाह कृष्णं
सगद्गदं भीतभीतः प्रणम्य ॥ ३५ ॥

etacchrutvā vacanaṁ keśavasya
kṛtāñjalirvepamānaḥ kirīṭī
namaskṛtvā bhūya evāha kṛṣṇaṁ
sagadgadaṁ bhītabhītaḥ praṇamya

Having heard the words of Embodiment of the Functions of Creation, Preservation and Transformation (Kṛṣṇa), the blessed one (Arjuna) trembled bowing down to Doer of All (Kṛṣṇa), and having bowed, spoke in a voice choked with overwhelming emotion.

अर्जुन उवाच

arjuna uvāca

Clarity of Pure Devotion said:

-36-

स्थाने हृषीकेश तव प्रकीर्त्या
जगत्प्रहृष्यत्यनुरज्यते च ।
रक्षांसि भीतानि दिशो द्रवन्ति
सर्वे नमस्यन्ति च सिद्धसंघाः ॥ ३६ ॥

sthāne hṛṣīkeśa tava prakīrtyā
jagatprahṛṣyatyanurajyate ca
rakṣāṁsi bhītāni diśo dravanti
sarve namasyanti ca siddhasaṁghāḥ

It is appropriate, Ruler of the Senses (Kṛṣṇa), that the world is delighted and rejoices in your praise. Demons fly in all directions in fear, and those of attainment bow.

-37-

कस्माच्च ते न नमेरन्महात्मन्
गरीयसे ब्रह्मणोऽप्यादिकर्त्रे ।
अनन्त देवेश जगन्निवास
त्वमक्षरं सदसत्तत्परं यत् ॥ ३७ ॥

kasmāca te na nameranmahātman
garīyase brahmaṇo-pyādikartre
ananta deveśa jagannivāsa
tvamakṣaraṁ sadasattatparaṁ yat

And why should they not bow to you, oh Great Soul, the Greatest, Supreme Divinity, Primary Doer, Infinite, Supreme of Gods, Residence of the world, Imperishable; that Supreme which is both True Being and non-being.

-38-

त्वमादिदेवः पुरुषः पुराण-
स्त्वमस्य विश्वस्य परं निधानम् ।
वेत्तासि वेद्यं च परं च धाम
त्वया ततं विश्वमनन्तरूप ॥ ३८ ॥

tvamādidevaḥ puruṣaḥ purāṇa-
stvamasya viśvasya paraṁ nidhānam
vettāsi vedyaṁ ca paraṁ ca dhāma
tvayā tataṁ viśvamanantarūpa

You are the Foremost God, the ancient full complete consciousness, the supreme refuge of this universe; the One who knows, the object of knowledge and the supreme place. The universe is pervaded by you, Infinite Form.

-39-

वायुर्यमोऽग्निर्वरुणः शशाङ्कः
प्रजापतिस्त्वं प्रपितामहश्च ।
नमो नमस्तेऽस्तु सहस्रकृत्वः
पुनश्च भूयोऽपि नमो नमस्ते ॥ ३९ ॥

vāyuryamo-gnirvaruṇaḥ śaśāṅkaḥ
prajāpatistvaṁ prapitāmahaśca
namo namaste-stu sahasrakṛtvaḥ
punaśca bhūyo-pi namo namaste

You are the Lord of Wind, the Lord of Death, Lord of Fire, Lord of Water, the Moon, Creator of Beings, and great grand-father of existence. I bow and bow to you again, thousands of times, and again and again. I bow to you, I bow to you.

-40-

नमः पुरस्तादथ पृष्ठतस्ते
नमोऽस्तु ते सर्वत एव सर्व ।
अनन्तवीर्यामितविक्रमस्त्वं
सर्वं समाप्नोषि ततोऽसि सर्वः ॥ ४० ॥

namaḥ purastādatha pṛṣṭhataste
namo-stu te sarvata eva sarva
anantavīryāmitavikramastvaṁ
sarvaṁ samāpnoṣi tato-si sarvaḥ

I bow to the front of you, I bow to the back of you, I bow to every side of you. Infinite in courage and great in capacity, you exist in all and you are all.

-41-

सखेति मत्वा प्रसभं यदुक्तं
हे कृष्ण हे यादव हे सखेति ।
अजानता महिमानं तवेदं
मया प्रमादात्प्रणयेन वापि ॥ ४१ ॥

sakheti matvā prasabhaṁ yaduktaṁ
he kṛṣṇa he yādava he sakheti
ajānatā mahimānaṁ tavedaṁ
mayā pramādātpraṇayena vāpi

Presumptuously regarding you as a friend, I called, "Hey Kṛṣṇa! Hey Member of the Tribe of Yadu! Hey Friend!" Incognizant of your greatness, because of carelessness, or even because of love,

-42-

यच्चावहासार्थमसत्कृतोऽसि
विहारशय्यासनभोजनेषु ।
एकोऽथवाप्यच्युत तत्समक्षं
तत्क्षामये त्वामहमप्रमेयम् ॥ ४२ ॥

yaccāvahāsārthamasatkṛto-si
vihāraśayyāsanabhojaneṣu
eko-thavāpyacyuta tatsamakṣaṁ
tatkṣāmaye tvāmahamaprameyam

whatever disrespect I offered while playing, lying down, sitting up or eating, alone or while in company, oh Imperishable, oh Immeasurable One, I implore you to forgive.

-43-

पितासि लोकस्य चराचरस्य
त्वमस्य पूज्यश्च गुरुर्गरीयान् ।
न त्वत्समोऽस्त्यभ्यधिकः कृतोऽन्यो
लोकत्रयेऽप्यप्रतिमप्रभाव ॥ ४३ ॥

pitāsi lokasya carācarasya
tvamasya pūjyaśca gururgarīyān
na tvatsamo-styabhyadhikaḥ kṛto-nyo
lokatraye-pyapratimaprabhāva

You are the Father of the world which moves and does not move, the highly respected Guru. There is no other in the three worlds who surpasses your greatness, none equal to you, oh Luminous Light without a second.

-44-

तस्मात्प्रणम्य प्रणिधाय कायं
प्रसादये त्वामहमीशमीड्यम् ।
पितेव पुत्रस्य सखेव सख्युः
प्रियः प्रियायार्हसि देव सोढुम् ॥ ४४ ॥

tasmātpraṇamya praṇidhāya kāyaṁ
prasādaye tvāmahamīśamīḍyam
piteva putrasya sakheva sakhyuḥ
priyaḥ priyāyārhasi deva soḍhum

Therefore, desiring your blessing I have bent my body bowing to the adorable Lord. Forgive me, oh Lord, like a father to a son, like a friend to a friend, like a lover to the beloved.

-45-

अदृष्टपूर्वं हृषितोऽस्मि दृष्ट्वा
भयेन च प्रव्यथितं मनो मे ।
तदेव मे दर्शय देव रूपं
प्रसीद देवेश जगन्निवास ॥ ४५ ॥

adṛṣṭapūrvaṁ hṛṣito-smi dṛṣṭvā
bhayena ca pravyathitaṁ mano me
tadeva me darśaya deva rūpaṁ
prasīda deveśa jagannivāsa

I am filled with delight having seen that which was not seen before, but my mind is distressed with fear. Oh Supreme among the Gods, be pleased and show me only that form, oh Residence of the Universe.

-46-

किरीटिनं गदिनं चक्रहस्त-
मिच्छामि त्वां द्रष्टुमहं तथैव ।
तेनैव रूपेण चथुर्भुजेन
सहस्रबाहो भव विश्वमूर्ते ॥ ४६ ॥

kirīṭinaṁ gadinaṁ cakrahasta-
micchāmi tvāṁ draṣṭumahaṁ tathaiva
tenaiva rūpeṇa cathurbhujena
sahasrabāho bhava viśvamūrte

I desire to see you even as before in that same form wearing a crown with four arms, holding a club and discus, oh Image of the Universe with a thousand arms.

श्रीभगवानुवाच

śrībhagavānuvāca

The Respected Supreme Divinity said:

-47-

मया प्रसन्नेन तवार्जुनेदं
रूपं परं दर्शितमात्मयोगात्।
तेजोमयं विश्वमनन्तमाद्यं
यन्मे त्वदन्येन न दृष्टपूर्वम्॥ ४७॥

mayā prasannena tavārjunedaṁ
rūpaṁ paraṁ darśitamātmayogāt
tejomayaṁ viśvamanantamādyaṁ
yanme tvadanyena na dṛṣṭapūrvam

Clarity of Pure Devotion, from My contentment in My union with My own soul, this Supreme Form, full of light, has been revealed to you: universal, infinite, foremost; which was not seen by any other before.

-48-

न वेदयज्ञाध्ययनैर्न दानै-
र्न च क्रियाभिर्न तपोभिरुग्रैः।
एवंरूपः शक्य अहं नृलोके
द्रष्टुं त्वदन्येन कुरुप्रवीर॥ ४८॥

na vedayajñādhyayanairna dānair-
na ca kriyābhirna tapobhirugraiḥ
evaṁrūpaḥ śakya ahaṁ nṛloke
draṣṭuṁ tvadanyena kurupravīra

Not by Vedic sacrifices, not by sacred study, not by the actions of severe purifying austerities, is it possible to see Me in the world of men by any other than you, oh Hero of the family of those who act.

-49-

मा ते व्यथा मा च विमूढभावो
दृष्ट्वा रूपं घोरमीदृङ्ममेदम् ।
व्यपेतभीः प्रीतमनाः पुनस्त्वं
तदेव मे रूपमिदं प्रपश्य ॥ ४९ ॥

mā te vyathā mā ca vimūḍhabhāvo
dṛṣṭvā rūpaṁ ghoramīdṛṅmamedam
vyapetabhīḥ prītamanāḥ punastvaṁ
tadeva me rūpamidaṁ prapaśya

Do not be afraid or of confused attitude having seen My terrible form. Abandon all fear and with a delighted mind again behold My form.

संजय उवाच

saṁjaya uvāca

He Who is Victorious Over All said:

-50-

इत्यर्जुनं वासुदेवस्तथोक्त्वा
स्वकं रूपं दर्शयामास भूयः ।
आश्वासयामास च भीतमेनं
भूत्वा पुनः सौम्यवपुर्महात्मा ॥ ५० ॥

ityarjunaṁ vāsudevastathoktvā
svakaṁ rūpaṁ darśayāmāsa bhūyaḥ
āśvāsayāmāsa ca bhītamenaṁ
bhūtvā punaḥ saumyavapurmahātmā

Having thus spoken to Clarity of Pure Devotion, Lord of the Earth (Kṛṣṇa) showed His own form again. Having again become of the mild form, the great soul encouraged him who had been afraid.

अर्जुन उवाच

arjuna uvāca

Clarity of Pure Devotion said:

-51-

दृष्ट्वेदं मानुषं रूपं तव सौम्यं जनार्दन ।
इदानीमस्मि संवृत्तः सचेताः प्रकृतिं गतः ॥ ५१ ॥

dṛṣṭvedaṁ mānuṣaṁ rūpaṁ tava saumyaṁ janārdana
idānīmasmi saṁvṛttaḥ sacetāḥ prakṛtiṁ gataḥ
Having seen this your mild human form, Who is Worshiped by the People (Kṛṣṇa), now I am composed with consciousness restored to its nature.

श्रीभगवानुवाच

śrībhagavānuvāca
The Respected Supreme Divinity said:

-52-

सुदुर्दर्शमिदं रूपं दृष्टवानसि यन्मम ।
देवा अप्यस्य रूपस्य नित्यं दर्शनकाङ्क्षिणः ॥ ५२ ॥

sudurdarśamidaṁ rūpaṁ dṛṣṭavānasi yanmama
devā apyasya rūpasya nityaṁ darśanakāṅkṣiṇaḥ
It is very hard to see this form as you have seen. Even the Gods desire to see this My eternal form.

-53-

नाहं वेदैर्न तपसा न दानेन न चेज्यया ।
शक्य एवंविधो द्रष्टुं दृष्टवानसि मां यथा ॥ ५३ ॥

nāhaṁ vedairna tapasā na dānena na cejyayā
śakya evaṁvidho draṣṭuṁ dṛṣṭavānasi māṁ yathā
Not by the Vedas, nor by purifying austerities, not by gifts nor by sacrifices is it possible to see Me as you have seen.

-54-

भक्त्या त्वनन्यया शक्य अहमेवंविधोऽर्जुन ।

ज्ञातुं द्रष्टुं च तत्त्वेन प्रवेष्टुं च परंतप ॥ ५४ ॥

bhaktyā tvananyayā śakya ahamevaṁvidho-rjuna
jñātuṁ draṣṭuṁ ca tattvena praveṣṭuṁ ca paraṁtapa

But only by unswerving devotion is it possible to actually see this form, to know it and to enter into it, Clarity of Pure Devotion, Supreme Light.

-55-

मत्कर्मकृन्मत्परमो मद्भक्तः सङ्गवर्जितः ।

निर्वैरः सर्वभूतेषु यः स मामेति पाण्डव ॥ ५५ ॥

matkarmakṛnmatparamo madbhaktaḥ saṅgavarjitaḥ
nirvairaḥ sarvabhūteṣu yaḥ sa māmeti pāṇḍava

Who does My actions, who is devoted to Me as the Supreme, who relies on no other, who has no enmity in all existence, he comes to Me, oh Son of He Who is without Prejudice (Arjuna).

इति श्रीमद्भगवद्गीतासु एकादशोऽध्यायः ॥ ११ ॥

१२

अर्जुन उवाच

arjuna uvāca
Clarity of Pure Devotion said:

-1-

एवं सततयुक्ता ये भक्तास्त्वां पर्युपासते ।
ये चाप्यक्षरमव्यक्तं तेषां के योगवित्तमाः ॥ १ ॥

evaṁ satatayuktā ye bhaktāstvāṁ paryupāsate
ye cāpyakṣaramavyaktaṁ teṣāṁ ke yogavittamāḥ
Those devotees who are always united in worship of you, and also those who regard the Imperishable Unmanifest, of these which union is most excellent?

श्रीभगवानुवाच

śrībhagavānuvāca
The Respected Supreme Divinity said:

-2-

मय्यावेश्य मनो ये मां नित्ययुक्ता उपासते ।
श्रद्धया परयोपेतास्ते मे युक्ततमा मताः ॥ २ ॥

mayyāveśya mano ye māṁ nityayuktā upāsate
śraddhayā parayopetāste me yuktatamā matāḥ
Those whose minds have Me with certainty, who are always united with Me, who worship Me with supreme faith, I regard as having attained to excellent union.

-3-

ये त्वक्षरमनिर्देश्यमव्यक्तं पर्युपासते ।
सर्वत्रगमचिन्त्यं च कूटस्थमचलं ध्रुवम् ॥ ३ ॥

ye tvakṣaramanirdeśyamavyaktaṁ paryupāsate
sarvatragamacintyaṁ ca kūṭasthamacalaṁ dhruvam
But some worship the Imperishable, not confined to space, unmanifest, omnipresent, unthinkable, unchanging, immovable, eternal.

-4-

संनियम्येन्द्रियग्रामं सर्वत्र समबुद्धयः ।
ते प्राप्नुवन्ति मामेव सर्वभूतहिते रताः ॥ ४ ॥

saṁniyamyendriyagrāmaṁ sarvatra samabuddhayaḥ
te prāpnuvanti māmeva sarvabhūtahite ratāḥ

Equally controlling all the senses, with equal intelligence everywhere, they rejoice in the welfare of all beings and obtain Me.

-5-

क्लेशोऽधिकतरस्तेषामव्यक्तासक्तचेतसाम् ।
अव्यक्ता हि गतिर्दुःखं देहवद्भिरवाप्यते ॥ ५ ॥

kleśo-dhikatarasteṣāmavyaktāsaktacetasām
avyaktā hi gatirduḥkhaṁ dehavadbhiravāpyate

The effort of those whose consciousness strives to recognize the unmanifest is greater, for it is difficult for those with bodies to reach the goal of the Unmanifest.

-6-

ये तु सर्वाणि कर्माणि मयि संन्यस्य मत्पराः ।
अनन्येनैव योगेन मां ध्यायन्त उपासते ॥ ६ ॥

ye tu sarvāṇi karmāṇi mayi saṁnyasya matparāḥ
ananyenaiva yogena māṁ dhyāyanta upāsate

But those who are fixed in union and meditate upon Me as the Supreme with unswerving mind, and regarding Me renounce attachment to all actions, they worship Me.

-7-

तेषामहं समुद्धर्ता मृत्युसंसारसागरात् ।
भवामि नचिरात्पार्थ मय्यावेशितचेतसाम् ॥ ७ ॥

teṣāmahaṁ samuddhartā mṛtyusaṁsārasāgarāt
bhavāmi nacirātpārtha mayyāveśitacetasām

For those whose consciousness is fixed upon Me, soon I become the saviour from the attachments to the ocean of objects and relationships of the mortal world.

-8-

मय्येव मन आधत्स्व मयि बुद्धिं निवेशय ।
निवसिष्यसि मय्येव अत ऊर्ध्वं न संशयः ॥ ८ ॥

mayyeva mana ādhatsva mayi buddhiṁ niveśaya
nivasiṣyasi mayyeva ata ūrdhvaṁ na saṁśayaḥ

Fix your mind only on Me, let your intellect reside only in Me, and you will dwell only in Me without a doubt.

-9-

अथ चित्तं समाधातुं न शक्नोषि मयि स्थिरम् ।
अभ्यासयोगेन ततो मामिच्छाप्तुं धनंजय ॥ ९ ॥

atha cittaṁ samādhātuṁ na śaknoṣi mayi sthiram
abhyāsayogena tato māmicchāptuṁ dhanaṁjaya

If you are unable to maintain the absorption of your consciousness in Me, then wish to reach Me by the practice of union, Conqueror of Wealth (Arjuna).

-10-

अभ्यासेऽप्यसमर्थोऽसि मत्कर्मपरमो भव ।
मदर्थमपि कर्माणि कुर्वन्सिद्धिमवाप्स्यसि ॥ १० ॥

abhyāse-pyasamartho-si matkarmaparamo bhava
madarthamapi karmāṇi kurvansiddhimavāpsyasi

If you are incapable of practice, then do actions for Me. By performing actions for Me you will attain perfection.

-11-

अथैतदप्यशक्तोऽसि कर्तुं मद्योगमाश्रितः ।
सर्वकर्मफलत्यागं ततः कुरु यतात्मवान् ॥ ११ ॥

athaitadapyaśakto-si kartuṁ madyogamāśritaḥ
sarvakarmaphalatyāgaṁ tataḥ kuru yatātmavān

If you are not able to do this, then take refuge in union with Me, control your own self, and renounce the fruits of all actions.

-12-

श्रेयो हि ज्ञानमभ्यासाज्ज्ञानाद्ध्यानं विशिष्यते ।

ध्यानात्कर्मफलत्यागस्त्यागाच्छान्तिरनन्तरम् ॥ १२ ॥

śreyo hi jñānamabhyāsājjñānāddhyānaṁ viśiṣyate
dhyānātkarmaphalatyāgastyāgācchāntiranantaram

Indeed better than practice is wisdom, better than wisdom is meditation, and renunciation of the fruit of action excels even meditation, for from renunciation comes immediate Peace.

-13-

अद्वेष्टा सर्वभूतानां मैत्रः करुण एव च ।

निर्ममो निरहङ्कारः समदुःखसुखः क्षमी ॥ 13॥

adveṣṭā sarvabhūtānāṁ maitraḥ karuṇa eva ca
nirmamo nirahaṅkāraḥ samaduḥkhasukhaḥ kṣamī

Without enmity among all existence, friendly, compassionate, without attachment or egotism, the same in pain or pleasure, patient;

-14-

संतुष्टः सततं योगी यतात्मा दृढनिश्चयः ।

मय्यर्पितमनोबुद्धिर्यो मद्भक्तः स मे प्रियः ॥ १४ ॥

saṁtuṣṭaḥ satataṁ yogī yatātmā dṛḍhaniścayaḥ
mayyarpitamanobuddhiryo madbhaktaḥ sa me priyaḥ

the being of union is always satisfied, has controlled his or her own self, has firm confidence, such a one is My devotee and is beloved by Me.

-15-

यस्मान्नोद्विजते लोको लोकान्नोद्विजते च यः ।

हर्षामर्षभयोद्वेगैर्मुक्तो यः स च मे प्रियः ॥ १५ ॥

yasmānnodvijate loko lokānnodvijate ca yaḥ
harṣāmarṣabhayodvegairmukto yaḥ sa ca me priyaḥ

From whom the world experiences no enmity, and who experiences no enmity from the world, who is liberated from joy, envy, fear and anxiety, such a one is beloved by Me.

-16-

अनपेक्षः शुचिर्दक्ष उदासीनो गतव्यथः ।
सर्वारम्भपरित्यागी यो मद्भक्तः स मे प्रियः ॥ १६ ॥

anapekṣaḥ śucirdakṣa udāsīno gatavyathaḥ
sarvārambhaparityāgī yo madbhaktaḥ sa me priyaḥ

Who is free from expectations, pure, efficient, the servant of circumstances, untroubled, who has renounced all undertakings, such a one is My devotee and is beloved by Me.

-17-

यो न हृष्यति न द्वेष्टि न शोचति न काङ्क्षति ।
शुभाशुभपरित्यागी भक्तिमान्यः स मे प्रियः ॥ १७ ॥

yo na hṛṣyati na dveṣṭi na śocati na kāṅkṣati
śubhāśubhaparityāgī bhaktimānyaḥ sa me priyaḥ

Who has neither attraction nor repulsion, neither joy nor sorrow, who has renounced both purity and impurity, such a one is My devotee and is beloved by Me.

-18-

समः शत्रौ च मित्रे च तथा मानापमानयोः ।
शीतोष्णसुखदुःखेषु समः सङ्गविवर्जितः ॥ १८ ॥

samaḥ śatrau ca mitre ca tathā mānāpamānayoḥ
śītoṣṇasukhaduḥkheṣu samaḥ saṅgavivarjitaḥ

Who remains the same to foe and friend, in honor or disgrace, in cold and hot, pleasure and pain, who is free from attachment;

-19-

तुल्यनिन्दास्तुतिर्मौनी संतुष्टो येन केनचित् ।
अनिकेतः स्थिरमतिर्भक्तिमान्मे प्रियो नरः ॥ १९ ॥

tulyanindāstutirmaunī saṁtuṣṭo yena kenacit
aniketaḥ sthiramatirbhaktimānme priyo naraḥ

to whom blame or praise are equal, who is silent and satisfied with everything, whose home is everywhere, whose mind is steady, who is full of devotion to Me, that man is beloved by Me.

-20-

ये तु धर्म्यामृतमिदं यथोक्तं पर्युपासते ।
श्रद्दधाना मत्परमा भक्तास्तेऽतीव मे प्रियाः ॥ २० ॥

ye tu dharmyāmṛtamidaṁ yathoktaṁ paryupāsate
śraddadhānā matparamā bhaktāste-tīva me priyāḥ

Indeed they who observe this immortal ideal of perfection with full faith as has been declared, regarding Me as Supreme, those devotees are extremely beloved by Me.

इति श्रीमद्भगवद्गीतासु द्वादशोऽध्यायः ॥ १२ ॥

१३

अर्जुन उवाच
arjuna uvāca
Clarity of Pure Devotion said:

प्रकृतिं पुरुषश्चैव क्षेत्रं क्षेत्रज्ञमेव च ।
एतद्वेदितुमिच्छामि ज्ञानं ज्ञेयञ्च केशव ॥
prakṛtiṁ puruṣaścaiva kṣetraṁ kṣetrajñameva ca
etadveditumicchāmi jñānaṁ jñeyañca keśava
0.8 I wish to know Nature and Consciousness, the field and the One who Knows the Field, wisdom and what should be known, oh Embodiment of the Functions of Creation, Preservation and Transformation (Kṛṣṇa).

श्रीभगवानुवाच
śrībhagavānuvāca
The Respected Supreme Divinity said:

-1-

इदं शरीरं कौन्तेय क्षेत्रमित्यमिधीयते ।
एतद्यो वेत्ति तं प्राहुः क्षेत्रज्ञ इति तद्विदः ॥ १ ॥
idaṁ śarīraṁ kaunteya kṣetramityamidhīyate
etadyo vetti taṁ prāhuḥ kṣetrajña iti tadvidaḥ
This body is known as the field, oh Son of Who Takes Away the Deficiency of Others (Arjuna). Who knows this is called One who Knows the Field by those who know.

-2-

क्षेत्रज्ञं चापि मां विद्धि सर्वक्षेत्रेषु भारत ।
क्षेत्रक्षेत्रज्ञयोर्ज्ञानं यत्तज्ज्ञानं मतं मम ॥ २ ॥
kṣetrajñaṁ cāpi māṁ viddhi sarvakṣetreṣu bhārata
kṣetrakṣetrajñayorjñānaṁ yattajjñānaṁ mataṁ mama
Know Me as the One who Knows all Fields, oh Descendant of the Light of Wisdom (Arjuna). The Wisdom of the Field and of the One who Knows the Field in My opinion constitute Wisdom.

-3-

तत्क्षेत्रं यच्च यादृक्च यद्विकारि यतश्च यत् ।
स च यो यत्प्रभावश्च तत्समासेन मेशृणु ॥ ३ ॥

tatkṣetraṁ yacca yādṛkca yadvikāri yataśca yat
sa ca yo yatprabhāvaśca tatsamāsena meśṛṇu

Hear from Me briefly what is the field, where it is, what it is like, and how it changes, what is its illumination.

-4-

ऋषिभिर्बहुधा गीतं छन्दोभिर्विविधैः पृथक् ।
ब्रह्मसूत्रपदैश्चैव हेतुमद्भिर्विनिश्चितैः ॥ ४ ॥

ṛṣibhirbahudhā gītaṁ chandobhirvividhaiḥ pṛthak
brahmasūtrapadaiścaiva hetumadbhirviniścitaiḥ

This has been sung in many ways by sages, in various meters, and even in distinctive words full of decisive reasoning, outlining the knowledge of Supreme Divinity.

-5-

महाभूतान्यहङ्कारो बुद्धिरव्यक्तमेव च ।
इन्द्रियाणि दशैकं च पञ्च चेन्द्रियगोचराः ॥ ५ ॥

mahābhūtānyahaṅkāro buddhiravyaktameva ca
indriyāṇi daśaikaṁ ca pañca cendriyagocarāḥ

The great elements, ego, intellect, the Unmanifested, the ten senses, the One, the objects of perception,

-6-

इच्छा द्वेषः सुखं दुःखं संघातश्चेतना धृतिः ।
एतत्क्षेत्रं समासेन सविकारमुदाहृतम् ॥ ६ ॥

icchā dveṣaḥ sukhaṁ duḥkhaṁ saṁghātaścetanā dhṛtiḥ
etatkṣetraṁ samāsena savikāramudāhṛtam

desire, repulsion, pleasure, pain, the aggregate of all consciousness, consistency: this is a brief description of the manifestation of the field.

-7-

अमानित्वमदम्भित्वमहिंसा क्षान्तिरार्जवम् ।
आचार्योपासनं शौचं स्थैर्यमात्मविनिग्रहः ॥ ७ ॥

amānitvamadambhitvamahiṁsā kṣāntirārjavam
ācāryopāsanaṁ śaucaṁ sthairyamātmavinigrahaḥ

Humility, modesty, causing harm to none, patience, the purification of knowledge, worship of the teacher, purity, consistency, self-control;

-8-

इन्द्रियार्थेषु वैराग्यमनहङ्कार एव च ।
जन्ममृत्युजराव्याधिदुःखदोषानुदर्शनम् ॥ ८ ॥

indriyārtheṣu vairāgyamanahaṅkāra eva ca
janmamṛtyujarāvyādhiduḥkhadoṣānudarśanam

no attachment to the objects of perception, no egotism, perception of the limitations in birth, death, old age, maladies and pain;

-9-

असक्तिरनभिष्वङ्गः पुत्रदारगृहादिषु ।
नित्यं च समचित्तत्वमिष्टानिष्टोपपत्तिषु ॥ ९ ॥

asaktiranabhiṣvaṅgaḥ putradāragṛhādiṣu
nityaṁ ca samacittatvamiṣṭāniṣṭopapattiṣu

no attachment or identification with the body, children, spouse or home, constant equanimity of consciousness, even on the attainment of the desirable and the undesirable;

-10-

मयि चानन्ययोगेन भक्तिरव्यभिचारिणी ।
विविक्तदेशसेवित्वमरतिर्जनसंसदि ॥ १० ॥

mayi cānyanyayogena bhaktiravyabhicāriṇī
viviktadeśasevitvamaratirjanasaṁsadi

consistent union with Me, unswerving devotion, visiting quiet and peaceful places, distaste for the society of men;

-11-

अध्यात्मज्ञाननित्यत्वं तत्त्वज्ञानार्थदर्शनम् ।
एतज्ज्ञानमिति प्रोक्तमज्ञानं यदतोऽन्यथा ॥ ११ ॥

adhyātmajñānanityatvaṁ tattvajñānārthadarśanam
etajjñānamiti proktamajñānaṁ yadato-nyathā

always residing in spiritual wisdom, perceiving all objects with the wisdom of the principles, this is proclaimed as Wisdom, and all that is opposed is ignorance.

-12-

ज्ञेयं यत्तत्प्रवक्ष्यामि यज्ज्ञात्वामृतमश्नुते ।
अनादिमत्परं ब्रह्म न सत्तन्नासदुच्यते ॥ १२ ॥

jñeyaṁ yattatpravakṣyāmi yajjñātvāmṛtamaśnute
anādimatparaṁ brahma na sattannāsaducyate

I explain that which should be known, knowing which one attains to the nectar of immortality, the Supreme Divinity without beginning, which is said to be true being and non-being.

-13-

सर्वतःपाणिपादं तत्सर्वतोऽक्षिशिरोमुखम् ।
सर्वतःश्रुतिमल्लोके सर्वमावृत्य तिष्ठति ॥ १३ ॥

sarvataḥpāṇipādaṁ tatsarvato-kṣiśiromukham
sarvataḥśrutimalloke sarvamāvṛtya tiṣṭhati

It exists encompassing all, with hands and feet everywhere, with eyes, head and mouth everywhere, and ears in all the worlds.

-14-

सर्वेन्द्रियगुणाभासं सर्वेन्द्रियविवर्जितम् ।
असक्तं सर्वभृच्चैव निर्गुणं गुणभोक्तृ च ॥ १४ ॥

sarvendriyaguṇābhāsaṁ sarvendriyavivarjitam
asaktaṁ sarvabhṛccaiva nirguṇaṁ guṇabhoktṛ ca

Radiating light because of the qualities of the senses, supporting all prohibition of attachment to the senses, totally without quality, such is the Experiencer of all qualities.

-15-

बहिरन्तश्च भूतानामचरं चरमेव च ।

सूक्ष्मत्वात्तदविज्ञेयं दूरस्थं चान्तिके च तत् ॥ १५ ॥

bahirantaśca bhūtānāmacaraṁ carameva ca
sūkṣmatvāttadavijñeyaṁ dūrasthaṁ cāntike ca tat

It is outside and inside of all beings, whether they move or move not, and because it is so subtle, it is unknowable. It is far and it is near.

-16-

अविभक्तं च भूतेषु विभक्तमिव च स्थितम् ।

भूतभर्तृ च तज्ज्ञेयं ग्रसिष्णु प्रभविष्णु च ॥ १६ ॥

avibhaktaṁ ca bhūteṣu vibhaktamiva ca sthitam
bhūtabhartṛ ca tajjñeyaṁ grasiṣṇu prabhaviṣṇu ca

It is undivided in beings, yet appears as if divided. It exists as the supporter of all beings born, and should be known because of generating and dissolving.

-17-

ज्योतिषामपि तज्ज्योतिस्तमसः परमुच्यते ।

ज्ञानं ज्ञेयं ज्ञानगम्यं हृदि सर्वस्य विष्ठितम् ॥ १७ ॥

jyotiṣāmapi tajjyotistamasaḥ paramucyate
jñānaṁ jñeyaṁ jñānagamyaṁ hṛdi sarvasya viṣṭhitam

The Light of all lights, it is said to be beyond darkness, wisdom, the wisdom which should be known, the goal of wisdom, situated in the hearts of all.

-18-

इति क्षेत्रं तथा ज्ञानं ज्ञेयं चोक्तं समासतः ।

मद्भक्त एतद्विज्ञाय मद्भावायोपपद्यते ॥ १८ ॥

iti kṣetraṁ tathā jñānaṁ jñeyaṁ coktaṁ samāsataḥ
madbhakta etadvijñāya madbhāvāyopapadyate

Thus the field, wisdom, and what should be known have been briefly explained. My devotee who knows this enters into My being.

-19-

प्रकृतिं पुरुषं चैव विद्ध्यनादी उभावपि ।
विकारांश्च गुणांश्चैव विद्धि प्रकृतिसम्भवान् ॥ १९ ॥

prakṛtiṁ puruṣaṁ caiva viddhyanādī ubhāvapi
vikārāṁśca guṇāṁścaiva viddhi prakṛtisambhavān

Know that both Nature9 and Perfect Consciousness are without beginning, and all changes in any quality arise from Nature.

-20-

कार्यकरणकर्तृत्वे हेतुः प्रकृतिरुच्यते ।
पुरुषः सुखदुःखानां भोक्तृत्वे हेतुरुच्यते ॥ २० ॥

kāryakaraṇakartṛtve hetuḥ prakṛtirucyate
puruṣaḥ sukhaduḥkhānāṁ bhoktṛtve heturucyate

Nature is said to be the cause of the actions of cause and effect. Perfect consciousness is said to be the cause of the experience of pleasure and pain.

-21-

पुरुषः प्रकृतिस्थो हि भुंक्ते प्रकृतिजान्गुणान् ।
कारणं गुणसङ्गोऽस्य सदसद्योनिजन्मसु ॥ २१ ॥

puruṣaḥ prakṛtistho hi bhuṁkte prakṛtijānguṇān
kāraṇaṁ guṇasaṅgo-sya sadasadyonijanmasu

Indeed Perfect Consciousness situated within Nature experiences the qualities born of Nature. Attachment to qualities is the cause of birth in true or evil wombs.

-22-

उपद्रष्टानुमन्ता च भर्ता भोक्ता महेश्वरः ।
परमात्मेति चाप्युक्तो देहेऽस्मिन्पुरुषः परः ॥ २२ ॥

upadraṣṭānumantā ca bhartā bhoktā maheśvaraḥ
paramātmeti cāpyukto dehe-sminpuruṣaḥ paraḥ

The Silent Witness in the body is also called the One who allows, the One who supports, the One who enjoys, the Great Seer of All, Supreme Soul, and the Supreme, Perfect Consciousness.

-23-

य एवं वेत्ति पुरुषं प्रकृतिं च गुणैः सह ।
सर्वथा वर्तमानोऽपि न स भुयोऽभिजायते ॥ २३ ॥

ya evaṁ vetti puruṣaṁ prakṛtiṁ ca guṇaiḥ saha
sarvathā vartamāno-pi na sa bhuyo-bhijāyate

Who thus knows Perfect Consciousness and Nature with their complete expression of qualities, they will not be born to the present circumstance again.

-24-

ध्यानेनात्मनि पश्यन्ति केचिदात्मानमात्मना ।
अन्ये सांख्येन योगेन कर्मयोगेन चापरे ॥ २४ ॥

dhyānenātmani paśyanti kecidātmānamātmanā
anye sāṁkhyena yogena karmayogena cāpare

By meditation some perceive the soul in its own self, some perceive the soul by their own selves, others perceive by union with the enumeration of principles, and others by union with action.

-25-

अन्ये त्वेवमजानन्तः श्रुत्वान्येभ्य उपासते ।
तेऽपि चातितरन्त्येव मृत्युं श्रुतिपरायणाः ॥ २५ ॥

anye tvevamajānantaḥ śrutvānyebhya upāsate
te-pi cātitarantyeva mṛtyuṁ śrutiparāyaṇāḥ

Still others, themselves not knowing, but having heard from others, cross beyond death by regarding what they have heard as supreme truth.

-26-

यावत्संजायते किंचित्सत्त्वं स्थावरजङ्गमम् ।
क्षेत्रक्षेत्रज्ञसंयोगात्तद्विद्धि भरतर्षभ ॥ २६ ॥

yāvatsaṁjāyate kiṁcitsattvaṁ sthāvarajaṅgamam
kṣetrakṣetrajñasaṁyogāttadviddhi bharatarṣabha

Whatever is born to true existence, whether moving or unmoving, results from the union of the field with the One who Knows the Field, Nature and Consciousness, oh best of Descendants of the Light of Wisdom (Arjuna).

-27-

समं सर्वेषु भूतेषु तिष्ठन्तं परमेश्वरम् ।
विनश्यत्स्वविनश्यन्तं यः पश्यति स पश्यति ॥ २७ ॥

samaṁ sarveṣu bhūteṣu tiṣṭhantaṁ parameśvaram
vinaśyatsvavinaśyantaṁ yaḥ paśyati sa paśyati

He sees equally the Supreme Divinity established in all beings, the Imperishable who sees the perishable.

-28-

समं पश्यन्हि सर्वत्र समवस्थितमीश्वरम् ।
न हिनस्त्यात्मनात्मानं ततो याति परां गतिम् ॥ २८ ॥

samaṁ paśyanhi sarvatra samavasthitamīśvaram
na hinastyātmanātmānaṁ tato yāti parāṁ gatim

Seeing the Supreme Consciousness dwelling equally everywhere, he does not despise himself, but goes to the supreme goal.

-29-

प्रकृत्यैव च कर्माणि क्रियमाणानि सर्वशः ।
यः पश्यति तथात्मानमकर्तारं स पश्यति ॥ २९ ॥

prakṛtyaiva ca karmāṇi kriyamāṇāni sarvaśaḥ
yaḥ paśyati tathātmānamakartāraṁ sa paśyati

He sees that only Nature performs all actions, and the soul who sees is without action.

-30-

यदा भूतपृथग्भावमेकस्थमनुपश्यति ।
तत एव च विस्तारं ब्रह्म संपद्यते तदा ॥ ३० ॥

yadā bhūtapṛthagbhāvamekasthamanupaśyati
tata eva ca vistāraṁ brahma saṁpadyate tadā

When he perceives the various varieties of existence established in the One, and from that One alone this all has come, then he becomes the Supreme Divinity.

-31-

अनादित्वान्निर्गुणत्वात्परमात्मायमव्ययः ।
शरीरस्थोऽपि कौन्तेय न करोति न लिप्यते ॥ ३१ ॥

anāditvānnirguṇatvātparamātmāyamavyayaḥ
śarīrastho-pi kaunteya na karoti na lipyate

Without a beginning, without qualities, this Supreme Soul is Imperishable. Though situated in a body, it neither acts nor is imposed upon, oh Son of Who Takes Away the Deficiency of Others (Arjuna).

-32-

यथा सर्वगतं सौक्ष्म्यादाकाशं नोपलिप्यते ।
सर्वत्रावस्थितो देहे तथात्मा नोपलिप्यते ॥ ३२ ॥

yathā sarvagataṁ saukṣmyādākāśaṁ nopalipyate
sarvatrāvasthito dehe tathātmā nopalipyate

The all-pervading ether is so subtle that it is not imposed upon. So also the Soul, situated everywhere throughout the body, is not imposed upon.

-33-

यथा प्रकशयत्येकः कृत्स्नं लोकमिमं रविः ।
क्षेत्रं क्षेत्री तथा कृत्स्नं प्रकाशयति भारत ॥ ३३ ॥

yathā prakaśayatyekaḥ kṛtsnaṁ lokamimaṁ raviḥ
kṣetraṁ kṣetrī tathā kṛtsnaṁ prakāśayati bhārata

Just as one sun illuminates the entire world, so the Lord of the Field illuminates the entire field, oh Descendant of the Light of Wisdom (Arjuna).

-34-

क्षेत्रक्षेत्रज्ञयोरेवमन्तरं ज्ञानचक्षुषा ।
भूतप्रकृतिमोक्षं च ये विदुर्यान्ति ते परम् ॥ ३४ ॥

kṣetrakṣetrajñayorevamantaraṁ jñānacakṣuṣā
bhūtaprakṛtimokṣaṁ ca ye viduryānti te param

Those who know the distinctions between the field and the One who Knows the Field, seeing through the eye of wisdom, are freed from the nature of existence and they go to the Supreme.

इति श्रीमद्भगवद्गीतासु त्रयोदशोऽध्यायः ॥ १३ ॥

१४

श्रीभगवानुवाच

śrībhagavānuvāca

The Respected Supreme Divinity said:

-1-

परं भूयः प्रवक्ष्यामि ज्ञानानां ज्ञानमुत्तमम् ।
यज्ज्ञात्वा मुनयः सर्वे परां सिद्धिमितो गताः ॥ १ ॥

paraṁ bhūyaḥ pravakṣyāmi jñānānāṁ jñānamuttamam
yajjñātvā munayaḥ sarve parāṁ siddhimito gatāḥ

Again I shall explain the supreme wisdom excellent among all knowledge, knowing which all men of wisdom have attained to supreme perfection.

-2-

इदं ज्ञानमुपाश्रित्य मम साधर्म्यमागताः ।
सर्गेऽपि नोपजायन्ते प्रलये न व्यथन्ति च ॥ २ ॥

idaṁ jñānamupāśritya mama sādharmyamāgatāḥ
sarge-pi nopajāyante pralaye na vyathanti ca

By taking refuge in this wisdom, one attains unity with Me. Neither are they born in creation, nor disturbed in dissolution.

-3-

मम योनिर्महद्ब्रह्म तस्मिन्गर्भं दधाम्यहम् ।
संभवः सर्वभूतानां ततो भवति भारत ॥ ३ ॥

mama yonirmahadbrahma
tasmingarbhaṁ dadhāmyaham
saṁbhavaḥ sarvabhūtānāṁ tato bhavati bhārata

My womb is the Vast Divinity of all Matter, in which I establish the embryo of the birth of all beings, and hence comes birth, oh Descendant of the Light of Wisdom (Arjuna).

-4-

सर्वयोनिषु कौन्तेय मूर्तयः संभवन्ति याः ।
तासां ब्रह्म महद्योनिरहं बीजप्रदः पिता ॥ ४ ॥

sarvayoniṣu kaunteya mūrtayaḥ sambhavanti yāḥ
tāsāṁ brahma mahadyonirahaṁ bījapradaḥ pitā

Oh Son of Who Takes Away the Deficiency of Others (Arjuna), for all forms which take birth in all wombs, the Vast Divinity of all Matter is the womb, and I am the Father who establishes the seed.

-5-

सत्त्वं रजस्तम इति गुणाः प्रकृतिसंभवाः ।
निबध्नन्ति महाबाहो देहे देहिनमव्ययम् ॥ ५ ॥

sattvaṁ rajastama iti guṇāḥ prakṛtisaṁbhavāḥ
nibadhnanti mahābāho dehe dehinamavyayam

Attentiveness, Desire for Activity and Inattentiveness10 are the qualities born of Nature. Oh One of Mighty Arms (Arjuna), they bind the indestructible Wearer of the Body in all bodies.

-6-

तत्र सत्त्वं निर्मलत्वात् प्रकाशकमनामयम् ।
सुखसङ्गेन बध्नाति ज्ञानसङ्गेन चानघ ॥ ६ ॥

tatra sattvaṁ nirmalatvāt prakāśakamanāmayam
sukhasaṅgena badhnāti jñānasaṅgena cānagha

Of these, Attentiveness is pure illumination. Oh one without sin, it binds in attachment to health, pleasure and wisdom.

-7-

रजो रागात्मकं विद्धि तृष्णासङ्गसमुद्भवम् ।
तन्निबध्नाति कौन्तेय कर्मसङ्गेन देहिनम् ॥ ७ ॥

rajo rāgātmakaṁ viddhi tṛṣṇāsaṅgasamudbhavam
tannibadhnāti kaunteya karmasaṅgena dehinam

Know Desire for Activity to be of the nature of passion, which gives birth to desire and attachment. Oh Son of Who Takes Away the Deficiency of Others (Arjuna), it binds the Wearer of the Body by attachment to action.

-8-

तमस्त्वज्ञानजं विद्धि मोहनं सर्वदेहिनाम् ।
प्रमादालस्यनिद्राभिस्तन्निबध्नाति भारत ॥ ८ ॥

tamastvajñānajaṁ viddhi mohanaṁ sarvadehinām
pramādālasyanidrābhistannibadhnāti bhārata

Know Inattentiveness is born from lack of wisdom, which deludes all embodied beings by binding them with excessive sleep, lack of awareness, and lack of activity , oh Descendant of the Light of Wisdom (Arjuna).

-9-

सत्त्वं सुखे संजयति रजः कर्मणि भारत ।
ज्ञानमावृत्य तु तमः प्रमादे सञ्जयत्युत ॥ ९ ॥

sattvaṁ sukhe saṁjayati rajaḥ karmaṇi bhārata
jñānamāvṛtya tu tamaḥ pramāde sañjayatyuta

Attentiveness causes attachment to pleasure, Desire for Activity to action, oh Descendant of the Light of Wisdom (Arjuna). Inattentiveness causes attachment to lack of awareness by hiding wisdom.

-10-

रजस्तमश्चाभिभूय सत्त्वं भवति भारत ।
रजः सत्त्वं तमश्चैव तमः सत्त्वं रजस्तथा ॥ १० ॥

rajastamaścābhibhūya sattvaṁ bhavati bhārata
rajaḥ sattvaṁ tamaścaiva tamaḥ sattvaṁ rajastathā

Attentiveness is predominant when it overcomes Desire for Activity and Inattentiveness; Desire for Activity over Attentiveness and Inattentiveness; Inattentiveness over Attentiveness and Desire for Activity.

-11-

सर्वद्वारेषु देहेऽस्मिन्प्रकाश उपजायते ।
ज्ञानं यदा तदा विद्याद्विवृद्धं सत्त्वमित्युत ॥ ११ ॥

sarvadvāreṣu dehe-sminprakāśa upajāyate
jñānaṁ yadā tadā vidyādvivṛddhaṁ sattvamityuta

When the Light of Wisdom shines through every door in this body, it is known that Attentiveness is the predominant quality.

-12-

लोभः प्रवृत्तिरारम्भः कर्मणामशमः स्पृहा ।
रजस्येतानि जायन्ते विवृद्धे भरतर्षभ ॥ १२ ॥

lobhaḥ pravṛttirārambhaḥ karmaṇāmaśamaḥ spṛhā
rajasyetāni jāyante vivṛddhe bharatarṣabha

Desire, commencement of evolutionary activities, restlessness, and longing arise when Desire for Activity is the predominant quality, oh Best of the Descendants of the Light of Wisdom (Arjuna).

-13-

अप्रकाशोऽप्रवृत्तिश्च प्रमादो मोह एव च ।
तमस्येतानि जायन्ते विवृद्धे कुरुनन्दन ॥ १३ ॥

aprakāśo-pravṛttiśca pramādo moha eva ca
tamasyetāni jāyante vivṛddhe kurunandana

Lack of illumination, lack of evolutionary activities, lack of awareness, and even ignorance arise when Inattentiveness becomes predominant, oh Delight of the Family of those who Act (Arjuna).

-14-

यदा सत्त्वे प्रवृद्धे तु प्रलयं याति देहभृत् ।
तदोत्तमविदां लोकानमलान्प्रतिपद्यते ॥ १४ ॥

yadā sattve pravṛddhe tu pralayaṁ yāti dehabhṛt
tadottamavidāṁ lokānamalānpratipadyate

When the Wearer of the Body leaves the body while Attentiveness is predominant, then he attains to the pure worlds of those who know the highest.

-15-

रजसि प्रलयं गत्वा कर्मसङ्गिषु जायते ।
तथा प्रलीनस्तमसि मूढयोनिषु जायते ॥ १५ ॥

rajasi pralayaṁ gatvā karmasaṅgiṣu jāyate
tathā pralīnastamasi mūḍhayoniṣu jāyate

Leaving the body while the quality of Desire for Activity is predominant, he is born again among those attached to action, and leaving the body during Inattentiveness, he is born in a womb of the foolish.

-16-

कर्मणः सुकृतस्याहुः सात्त्विकं निर्मलं फलम् ।
रजसस्तु फलं दुःखमज्ञानं तमसः फलम् ॥ १६ ॥

karmaṇaḥ sukṛtasyāhuḥ sāttvikaṁ nirmalaṁ phalam
rajasastu phalaṁ duḥkhamajñānaṁ tamasaḥ phalam

They say that the fruits of the actions of Attentiveness are pure and good, but the fruits of the actions of Desire for Activity are pain. Ignorance is the fruit of the actions of Inattentiveness.

-17-

सत्त्वात्संजायते ज्ञानं रजसो लोभ एव च ।
प्रमादमोहौ तमसो भवतोऽज्ञानमेव च ॥ १७ ॥

sattvātsaṁjāyate jñānaṁ rajaso lobha eva ca
pramādamohau tamaso bhavato-jñānameva ca

From Attentiveness arises Wisdom, from Desire for Activity arises desire, and from Inattentiveness arises lack of awareness and even ignorance.

-18-

ऊर्ध्वं गच्छन्ति सत्त्वस्था मध्ये तिष्ठन्ति राजसाः ।
जघन्यगुणवृत्तिस्था अधो गच्छन्ति तामसाः ॥ १८ ॥

ūrdhvaṁ gacchanti sattvasthā madhye tiṣṭhanti rājasāḥ
jaghanyaguṇavṛttisthā adho gacchanti tāmasāḥ

Those established in Attentiveness go upwards, those established in Desire for Activity remain in the middle, and those who remain in the lowest quality Inattentiveness, go downwards.

-19-

नान्यं गुणेभ्यः कर्तारं यदा द्रष्टानुपश्यति ।
गुणेभ्यश्च परं वेत्ति मद्भावं सोऽधिगच्छति ॥ १९ ॥

nānyaṁ guṇebhyaḥ kartāraṁ yadā draṣṭānupaśyati
guṇebhyaśca paraṁ vetti madbhāvaṁ so-dhigacchati

When the One who Sees perceives no other actor than the qualities of nature, and knows the Supreme beyond the qualities of nature, then he attains to My attitude.

-20-

गुणानेतानतीत्य त्रीन्देही देहसमुद्भवान् ।
जन्ममृत्युजरादुःखैर्विमुक्तोऽमृतमश्नुते ॥ २० ॥

guṇānetānatītya trīndehī dehasamudbhavān
janmamṛtyujarāduḥkhairvimukto-mṛtamaśnute
The Wearer of the Body who moves beyond these three qualities of nature from which the body has evolved, is liberated in birth, death, old age, pain, and attains to the nectar of immortality.

अर्जुन उवाच

arjuna uvāca
Clarity of Pure Devotion said:

-21-

कैर्लिङ्गैस्त्रीन्गुणानेतानतीतो भवति प्रभो ।
किमाचारः कथं चैतांस्त्रीन्गुणानतिवर्तते ॥ २१ ॥

kairliṅgaistrīnguṇānetānatīto bhavati prabho
kimācāraḥ kathaṁ caitāṁstrīnguṇānativartate
What are the signs of distinction of an individual who has gone beyond the three qualities? Oh Lord, what is his conduct? How does he go beyond?

श्रीभगवानुवाच

śrībhagavānuvāca
The Respected Supreme Divinity said:

-22-

प्रकाशं च प्रवृत्तिं च मोहमेव च पाण्डव ।
न द्वेष्टि संप्रवृत्तानि न निवृत्तानि काङ्क्षति ॥ २२ ॥

prakāśaṁ ca pravṛttiṁ ca mohameva ca pāṇḍava
na dveṣṭi saṁpravṛttāni na nivṛttāni kāṅkṣati
Oh Son of He Who is without Prejudice, he has no enmity with illumination, activity or ignorance when they are predominant, nor any desire for them when they are absent.

-23-

उदासीनवदासीनो गुणैर्यो न विचाल्यते ।
गुणा वर्तन्त इत्येव योऽवतिष्ठति नेङ्गते ॥ २३ ॥

udāsīnavadāsīno guṇairyo na vicālyate
guṇā vartanta ityeva yo-vatiṣṭhati neṅgate

He sits like a servant of circumstances, unmoved by the qualities, even as he sees the qualities operate, yet he does not move from his established place.

-24-

समदुःखसुखः स्वस्थः समलोष्टाश्मकाञ्चनः ।
तुल्यप्रियाप्रियो धीरस्तुल्यनिन्दात्मसंस्तुतिः ॥ २४ ॥

samaduḥkhasukhaḥ svasthaḥ samaloṣṭāśmakāñcanaḥ
tulyapriyāpriyo dhīrastulyanindātmasaṁstutiḥ

He is established in his own self, equal in pain and pleasure, regarding dirt, stones and gold equally, equal behavior to beloved people and non-beloved, consistent, equal in blame or praise.

-25-

मानापमानयोस्तुल्यस्तुल्यो मित्रारिपक्षयोः ।
सर्वारम्भपरित्यागी गुणातीतः स उच्यते ॥ २५ ॥

mānāpamānayostulyastulyo mitrāripakṣayoḥ
sarvārambhaparityāgī guṇātītaḥ sa ucyate

He is the same whether honored or dishonored, the same to friends or enemies, having renounced all activities, he is said to have moved beyond the qualities of nature.

-26-

मां च योऽव्यभिचारेण भक्तियोगेन सेवते ।
स गुणान्समतीत्यैतान्ब्रह्मभूयाय कल्पते ॥ २६ ॥

māṁ ca yo-vyabhicāreṇa bhaktiyogena sevate
sa guṇānsamatītyaitānbrahmabhūyāya kalpate

He serves Me continually united in devotion, moves beyond these qualities of nature and becomes qualified to unite with the Supreme Divinity.

-27-

ब्रह्मणो हि प्रतिष्ठाहममृतस्याव्ययस्य च ।
शाश्वतस्य च धर्मस्य सुखस्यैकान्तिकस्य च ॥ २७ ॥

brahmaṇo hi pratiṣṭhāhamamṛtasyāvyayasya ca
śāśvatasya ca dharmasya sukhasyaikāntikasya ca

Indeed, I am the Supreme Divinity, wherein is established the nectar of immortality, the unchanging, everlasting, absolute pleasure of the Ideal of Perfection.

इति श्रीमद्भगवद्गीतासु चतुर्दशोऽध्यायः ॥ १४ ॥

१८

श्रीभगवानुवाच

śrībhagavānuvāca

The Respected Supreme Divinity said:

-1-

ऊर्ध्वमूलमधःशाखमश्वत्थं प्राहुरव्ययम् ।
छन्दांसि यस्य पर्णानि यस्तं वेद स वेदवित् ॥ १ ॥

ūrdvamūlamadhaḥśākhamaśvatthaṁ prāhuravyayam
chandāṁsi yasya parṇāni yastaṁ veda sa vedavit

They speak of a Banyan tree with is roots above. Its leaves are the indestructible meters of Saṁskṛt. Who knows this, knows wisdom.

-2-

अधश्चोर्ध्वं प्रसृतास्तस्य शाखा
गुणप्रवृद्धा विषयप्रवालाः ।
अधश्च मूलान्यनुसंततानि
कर्मानुबन्धीनि मनुष्यलोके ॥ २ ॥

adhaścordhvaṁ prasṛtāstasya śākhā
guṇapravṛddhā viṣayapravālāḥ
adhaśca mūlānyanusaṁtatāni
karmānubandhīni manuṣyaloke

Below and above its branches are spread, nourished by the qualities. Opinions are its buds below, and its roots stretch forth giving rise to action in the world of men.

-3-

न रूपमस्येह तथोपलभ्यते

नान्तो न चादिर्न च संप्रतिष्ठा ।

अश्वत्थमेनं सुविरूढमूल-

मसङ्गशस्त्रेण दृढेन छित्त्वा ॥ ३ ॥

na rūpamasyeha tathopalabhyate
nānto na cādirna ca saṁpratiṣṭhā
aśvatthamenaṁ suvirūḍhamūla-
masaṅgaśastreṇa dṛḍhena chittvā

Its form is not perceived here, as it has no beginning nor end nor base. Cut down this strong rooted Banyan tree with the weapon of non-attachment.

-4-

ततः पदं तत्परिमार्गितव्यं

यस्मिन्गता न निवर्तन्ति भूयः ।

तमेव चाद्यं पुरुषं प्रपद्ये

यतः प्रवृत्तिः प्रसृता पुराणी ॥ ४ ॥

tataḥ padaṁ tatparimārgitavyaṁ
yasmingatā na nivartanti bhūyaḥ
tameva cādyaṁ puruṣaṁ prapadye
yataḥ pravṛttiḥ prasṛtā purāṇī

Then that goal should be pursued from where you will not return again. Even I seek refuge in that ancient Perfect Consciousness from which the activities of evolution originally streamed forth.

-5-

निर्मानमोहा जितसङ्गदोषा
अध्यात्मनित्या विनिवृत्तकामाः ।
द्वन्द्वैर्विमुक्ताः सुखदुःखसंज्ञै-
र्गच्छन्त्यमूढाः पदमव्ययं तत् ॥ ५ ॥

nirmānamohā jitasaṅgadoṣā
adhyātmanityā vinivṛttakāmāḥ
dvandvairvimuktāḥ sukhaduḥkhasaṁjñair-
gacchantyamūḍhāḥ padamavyayaṁ tat

Liberated by purifying ignorance, by conquering the faults of attachment, by eternally contemplating the spirit, with unchanging desires among opposing alternatives, from attachment to pleasure and pain, those who are free from delusion reach that imperishable goal.

-6-

न तद्भासयते सूर्यो न शशाङ्को न पावकः ।
यद्गत्वा न निवर्तन्ते तद्धाम परमं मम ॥ ६ ॥

na tadbhāsayate sūryo na śaśāṅko na pāvakaḥ
yadgatvā na nivartante taddhāma paramaṁ mama

The Sun does not illuminate That, nor the Moon nor Fire. Having gone to My supreme residence they do not return.

-7-

ममैवांशो जीवलोके जीवभूतः सनातनः ।
मनःषष्ठानीन्द्रियाणि प्रकृतिस्थानि कर्षति ॥ ७ ॥

mamaivāṁśo jīvaloke jīvabhūtaḥ sanātanaḥ
manaḥṣaṣṭhānīndriyāṇi prakṛtisthāni karṣati

Only a small portion of My eternal self residing in nature attracts the existence of an individual life in the manifested world, with senses and mind known as the sixth sense.

-8-

शरीरं यदवाप्नोति यच्चाप्युत्क्रामतीश्वरः ।
गृहीत्वैतानि संयाति वायुर्गन्धानिवाशयात् ॥ ८ ॥

śarīraṁ yadavāpnoti yaccāpyutkrāmatīśvaraḥ
gṛhītvaitāni saṁyāti vāyurgandhānivāśayāt

When the Great Ruler of All obtains a body, and when he leaves it as well, he accepts these with the same lack of attachment as does the wind in carrying scents from those who emit scents.

-9-

श्रोत्रं चक्षुः स्पर्शनं च रसनं घ्राणमेव च ।
अधिष्ठाय मनश्चायं विषयानुपसेवते ॥ ९ ॥

śrotraṁ cakṣuḥ sparśanaṁ ca rasanaṁ ghrāṇameva ca
adhiṣṭhāya manaścāyaṁ viṣayānupasevate

He experiences various ideas because he presides over the ears, eyes, skin, taste and scent, and also over the mind.

-10-

उत्क्रामन्तं स्थितं वापि भुञ्जानं वा गुणान्वितम् ।
विमूढा नानुपश्यन्ति पश्यन्ति ज्ञानचक्षुषः ॥ १० ॥

utkrāmantaṁ sthitaṁ vāpi bhuñjānaṁ vā guṇānvitam
vimūḍhā nānupaśyanti paśyanti jñānacakṣuṣaḥ

Those who are foolishly united with qualities do not see the one who goes or stays, or who enjoys, only those who perceive through the eyes of wisdom.

-11-

यतन्तो योगिनश्चैनं पश्यन्त्यात्मन्यवस्थितम् ।
यतन्तोऽप्यकृतात्मानो नैनं पश्यन्त्यचेतसः ॥ ११ ॥

yatanto yoginaścainaṁ paśyantyātmanyavasthitam
yatanto-pyakṛtātmāno nainaṁ paśyantyacetasaḥ

The beings of union who strive see this situated in the soul. Those who strive who have not yet purified their souls, who are not fully conscious, do not see this.

-12-

यदादित्यगतं तेजो जगद्भासयतेऽखिलम् ।

यच्चन्द्रमसि यच्चाग्नौ तत्तेजो विद्धि मामकम् ॥ १२ ॥

yadādityagataṁ tejo jagadbhāsayate-khilam
yaccandramasi yaccāgnau tattejo viddhi māmakam

The light which comes from the Sun illuminates the entire world; so also the light of the Moon and the light of Fire. Know that light as Mine.

-13-

गामाविश्य च भूतानि धारयाम्यहमोजसा ।

पुष्णामि चौषधीः सर्वाः सोमो भूत्वा रसात्मकः ॥ १३ ॥

gāmāviśya ca bhūtāni dhārayāmyahamojasā
puṣṇāmi cauṣadhīḥ sarvāḥ somo bhūtvā rasātmakaḥ

Permeating the earth, I support all beings and by My subtle energy in vegetation I nourish all. Having become the Moon, I raise the waters.

-14-

अहं वैश्वानरो भूत्वा प्राणिनां देहमाश्रितः ।

प्राणापानसमायुक्तः पचाम्यन्नं चतुर्विधम् ॥ १४ ॥

ahaṁ vaiśvānaro bhūtvā prāṇināṁ dehamāśritaḥ
prāṇāpānasamāyuktaḥ pacāmyannaṁ caturvidham

Having taken refuge in the body of living beings as the Universal Being of Light, united with the inflowing breath and the outflowing breath, I digest the four kinds of food.

-15-

सर्वस्य चाहं हृदि संनिविष्टो
मत्तः स्मृतिर्ज्ञानमपोहनं च ।
वेदैश्च सर्वैरहमेव वेद्यो
वेदान्तकृद्वेदविदेव चाहम् ॥ १५ ॥

sarvasya cāhaṁ hṛdi saṁniviṣṭo
mattaḥ smṛtirjñānamapohanaṁ ca
vedaiśca sarvarahameva vedyo
vedāntakṛdvedavideva cāham

And I am situated in the hearts of all. From Me have come memory and Wisdom and their absence. I am all that can be known, all that should be known, the author of all that is known, and the One who Knows all as well.

-16-

द्वाविमौ पुरुषौ लोके क्षरश्चाक्षर एव च ।
क्षरः सर्वाणि भूतानि कूटस्थोऽक्षर उच्यते ॥ १६ ॥

dvāvimau puruṣau loke kṣaraścākṣara eva ca
kṣaraḥ sarvāṇi bhūtāni kūṭastho-kṣara ucyate

There are two aspects of Perfect Consciousness in the world: the perishable and the Imperishable. The perishable resides in all manifested beings, and the Imperishable is called Beyond Change.

-17-

उत्तमः पुरुषस्त्वन्यः परमात्मेत्युदाहृतः ।
यो लोकत्रयमाविश्य बिभर्त्यव्यय ईश्वरः ॥ १७ ॥

uttamaḥ puruṣastvanyaḥ paramātmetyudāhṛtaḥ
yo lokatrayamāviśya bibhartyavyaya īśvaraḥ

But another name is used for the most excellent Perfect Consciousness, Supreme Soul, who is called the Ruler of All, who pervades and sustains the three worlds.

-18-

यस्मात्क्षरमतीतोऽहमक्षरादपि चोत्तमः ।
अतोऽस्मि लोके वेदे च प्रथितः पुरुषोत्तमः ॥ १८ ॥

yaśmātkṣaramatīto-hamakṣarādapi cottamaḥ
ato-smi loke vede ca prathitaḥ puruṣottamaḥ

I am the most excellent Imperishable beyond the perishable. Therefore, I am known in all Wisdom as the excellent Perfect Consciousness.

-19-

यो मामेवमसंमूढो जानाति पुरुषोत्तमम् ।
स सर्वविद्भजति मां सर्वभावेन भारत ॥ १९ ॥

yo māmevamasaṁmūḍho jānāti puruṣottamam
sa sarvavidbhajati māṁ sarvabhāvena bhārata

He who is free from delusion and knows Me as the all-knowing excellent Perfect Consciousness, he worships Me with his complete attitude, oh Descendant of the Light of Wisdom (Arjuna).

-20-

इति गुह्यतमं शास्त्रमिदमुक्तं मयानघ ।
एतद्बुद्ध्वा बुद्धिमान्स्यात्कृतकृत्यश्च भारत ॥ २० ॥

iti guhyatamaṁ śāstramidamuktaṁ mayānagha
etadbuddhvā buddhimānsyātkṛtakṛtyaśca bhārata

Thus this most secret science has been explained by Me, oh Sinless One. Knowing this, the intelligent one has accomplished all effects, oh Descendant of the Light of Wisdom (Arjuna).

इति श्रीमद्भगवद्गीतासु पञ्चदशोऽध्यायः ॥ १५ ॥

१६

श्रीभगवानुवाच

srībhagavānuvāca

The Respected Supreme Divinity said:

-1-

अभयं सत्त्वसंशुद्धिर्ज्ञानयोगव्यवस्थितिः ।

दानं दमश्च यज्ञश्च स्वाध्यायस्तप आर्जवम् ॥ १ ॥

abhayaṁ sattvasaṁśuddhirjñānayogavyavasthitiḥ
dānaṁ damaśca yajñaśca svādhyāyastapa ārjavam

Having no fear, being pure and true, being established in wisdom and union, being a giver, having self-control, performing sacred fire ceremonies, study of the scriptures, purifying austerities, the purification of knowledge;

-2-

अहिंसा सत्यमक्रोधस्त्यागः शान्तिरपैशुनम् ।

दया भूतेष्वलोलुप्त्वं मार्दवं ह्रीरचापलम् ॥ २ ॥

ahiṁsā satyamakrodhastyāgaḥ śāntirapaiśunam
dayā bhūteṣvaloluptvaṁ mārdavaṁ hrīracāpalam

causing harm to none, truthful, without anger, renunciation, peacefulness, without deceit, compassionate to all beings, without desire, gentle, modest, without fickleness;

-3-

तेजः क्षमा धृतिः शौचमद्रोहो नातिमानिता ।

भवन्ति संपदं दैवीमभिजातस्य भारत ॥ ३ ॥

tejaḥ kṣamā dhṛtiḥ śaucamadroho nātimānitā
bhavanti saṁpadaṁ daivīmabhijātasya bhārata

light, patience, constancy, purity, no enmity, absence of pride, belong to those who are born to divine qualities, oh Descendant of the Light of Wisdom (Arjuna).

-4-

दम्भो दर्पोऽभिमानश्च क्रोधः पारुष्यमेव च ।
अज्ञानं चाभिजातस्य पार्थ संपदमासुरीम् ॥ ४ ॥

dambho darpo-bhimānaśca krodhaḥ pāruṣyameva ca
ajñānaṁ cābhijātasya pārtha saṁpadamāsurīm

Hypocrisy, arrogance, self-conceit, anger, irritation, and even ignorance, are the characteristics which belong to those born to the qualities of the forces of division.

-5-

दैवी संपद्विमोक्षाय निबन्धायासुरी मता ।
मा शुचः संपदं दैवीमभिजातोऽसि पाण्डव ॥ ५ ॥

daivī saṁpadvimokṣāya nibandhāyāsurī matā
mā śucaḥ saṁpadaṁ daivīmabhijāto-si pāṇḍava

Divine qualities are for liberation, the qualities of the forces of division are for bondage. Do not sorrow, Son of She Who Excels (Arjuna), for you are born with divine qualities.

-6-

द्वौ भूतसर्गौ लोकेऽस्मिन्दैव आसुर एव च ।
दैवो विस्तरशः प्रोक्त आसुरं पार्थ मे शृणु ॥ ६ ॥

dvau bhūtasargau loke-smindaiva āsura eva ca
daivo vistaraśaḥ prokta āsuraṁ pārtha me śṛṇu

There are two kinds of beings in this world, the forces of divinity and the forces of division. The divine forces have been explained at length. Hear from Me about the forces of division.

-7-

प्रवृत्तिं च निवृत्तिं च जना न विदुरासुराः ।
न शौचं नापि चाचारो न सत्यं तेषु विद्यते ॥ ७ ॥

pravṛttiṁ ca nivṛttiṁ ca janā na vidurāsurāḥ
na śaucaṁ nāpi cācāro na satyaṁ teṣu vidyate

Men of the forces of division do not know actions of evolution nor involution, neither purity nor good behavior nor truth.

-8-

असत्यमप्रतिष्ठं ते जगदाहुरनीश्वरम् ।
अपरस्परसंभूतं किमन्यत्कामहैतुकम् ॥ ८ ॥

asatyamapratiṣṭhaṁ te jagadāhuranīśvaram
aparasparasaṁbhūtaṁ kimanyatkāmahaitukam

They say, "The world is born from mutual union for the purpose of satisfying desires. There is no God, no truth, no morality."

-9-

एतां दृष्टिमवष्टभ्य नष्टात्मानोऽल्पबुद्धयः ।
प्रभवन्त्युग्रकर्माणः क्षयाय जगतोऽहिताः ॥ ९ ॥

etāṁ dṛṣṭimavaṣṭabhya naṣṭātmāno-lpabuddhayaḥ
prabhavantyugrakarmāṇaḥ kṣayāya jagato-hitāḥ

Established in this view, these impure souls of little intellect become enemies of the world performing fierce actions for destruction.

-10-

काममाश्रित्य दुष्पूरं दम्भमानमदान्विताः ।
मोहाद्गृहीत्वासद्ग्राहान्प्रवर्तन्तेऽशुचिव्रताः ॥ १० ॥

kāmamāśritya duṣpūraṁ dambhamānamadānvitāḥ
mohādgṛhītvāsadgrāhānpravartante-śucivratāḥ

Maintaining insatiable desires, full of hypocrisy, pride and arrogance, accepting untruth and evil because of ignorance, they work with impure motives.

-11-

चिन्तामपरिमेयां च प्रलयान्तामुपाश्रिताः ।
कामोपभोगपरमा एतावदिति निश्चिताः ॥ ११ ॥

cintāmaparimeyāṁ ca pralayāntāmupāśritāḥ
kāmopabhogaparamā etāvaditi niścitāḥ

Having immeasurable concerns which only end in dissolution, they take refuge in the enjoyment of desires as the highest, and feel sure that is all.

-12-

आशापाशशतैर्बद्धाः कामक्रोधपरायणाः ।

ईहन्ते कामभोगार्थमन्यायेनार्थसंचयान् ॥ १२ ॥

āśāpāśaśatairbaddhāḥ kāmakrodhaparāyaṇāḥ
īhante kāmabhogārthamanyāyenārthasaṁcayān

Bound by a net of hundreds of hopes pursuing desire and anger, they strive for enjoyment of the objects of desire, and by any inappropriate means to obtain their objectives.

-13-

इदमद्य मया लब्धमिमं प्राप्स्ये मनोरथम् ।

इदमस्तीदमपि मे भविष्यति पुनर्धनम् ॥ १३ ॥

idamadya mayā labdhamimaṁ prāpsye manoratham
idamastīdamapi me bhaviṣyati punardhanam

"Today this has been gained by me. That desire will be mine in the future. Again, this wealth will belong to me."

-14-

असौ मया हतः शत्रुर्हनिष्ये चापरानपि ।

ईश्वरोऽहमहं भोगी सिद्धोऽहं बलवान्सुखी ॥ १४ ॥

asau mayā hataḥ śatrurhaniṣye cāparānapi
iśvaro-hamahaṁ bhogī siddho-haṁ balavānsukhī

"That enemy has been slain by me, and I shall slay others in the future. I am a lord, the enjoyer, perfect, powerful and happy."

-15-

आढ्योऽभिजनवानस्मि कोऽन्योऽस्ति सदृशो मया ।

यक्ष्ये दास्यामि मोदिष्य इत्यज्ञानविमोहिताः ॥ १५ ॥

āḍhyo-bhijanavānasmi ko-nyo-sti sadṛśo mayā
yakṣye dāsyāmi modiṣya ityajñānavimohitāḥ

"I am wealthy and have a good birth. Who else is equal to me? I will perform religious sacrifices. I will be a giver, I will rejoice." Thus deluded by ignorance

-16-

अनेकचित्तविभ्रान्ता मोहजालसमावृताः ।

प्रसक्ताः कामभोगेषु पतन्ति नरकेऽशुचौ ॥ १६ ॥

anekacittavibhrāntā mohajālasamāvṛtāḥ
prasaktāḥ kāmabhogeṣu patanti narake-śucau
with many confused perceptions entangled in the traps of ignorance, able only to pursue the enjoyment of desires, they fall into an impure hell of confusion.

-17-

आत्मसंभाविताः स्तब्धा धनमानमदान्विताः ।

यजन्ते नामयज्ञैस्ते दम्भेनाविधिपूर्वकम् ॥ १७ ॥

ātmasaṁbhāvitāḥ stabdhā dhanamānamadānvitāḥ
yajante nāmayajñaiste dambhenāvidhipūrvakam
Filled with self-conceit, stubborn, intoxicated with the pride of wealth, ostentatiously they perform religious sacrifices in name without observing the ancient procedures.

-18-

अहङ्कारं बलं दर्पं कामं क्रोधं च संश्रिताः ।

मामात्मपरदेहेषु प्रद्विषन्तोऽभ्यसूयकाः ॥ १८ ॥

ahaṅkāraṁ balaṁ darpaṁ kāmaṁ krodhaṁ ca saṁśritāḥ
māmātmaparadeheṣu pradviṣanto-bhyasūyakāḥ
Taking refuge in egotism, strength, haughtiness, desires and anger, these malicious people oppose Me as the soul of all bodies.

-19-

तानहं द्विषतः क्रूरान्संसारेषु नराधमान् ।

क्षिपाम्यजस्रमशुभानासुरीष्वेव योनिषु ॥ १९ ॥

tānahaṁ dviṣataḥ krflrānsaṁsāreṣu narādhamān
kṣipāmyajasramaśubhānāsurīṣveva yoniṣu
I throw those cruel enemies, lowest among men, in the ocean of objects and relationships for an eternity, in the impure wombs of the forces of division.

-20-

आसुरीं योनिमापन्ना मूढा जन्मनि जन्मनि ।
मामप्राप्यैव कौन्तेय ततो यान्त्यधमां गतिम् ॥ २० ॥

āsurīṁ yonimāpannā mūḍhā janmani janmani
māmaprāpyaiva kaunteya tato yāntyadhamāṁ gatim

Those deluded forces of division entering the womb in birth after birth do not attain Me, oh Son of Who Takes Away the Deficiency of Others (Arjuna). Even still, they fall into a condition lower than that.

-21-

त्रिविधं नरकस्येदं द्वारं नाशनमात्मनः ।
कामः क्रोधस्तथा लोभस्तस्मादेतत्त्रयं त्यजेत् ॥ २१ ॥

trividhaṁ narakasyedaṁ dvāraṁ nāśanamātmanaḥ
kāmaḥ krodhastathā lobhastasmādetattrayaṁ tyajet

The door to the hell of confusion, where the soul is destroyed, is of three parts: desire, anger and greed. Therefore, one should abandon these three.

-22-

एतैर्विमुक्तः कौन्तेय तमोद्वारैस्त्रिभिर्नरः ।
आचरत्यात्मनः श्रेयस्ततो याति परां गतिम् ॥ २२ ॥

etairvimuktaḥ kaunteya tamodvāraistribhirnaraḥ
ācaratyātmanaḥ śreyastato yāti parāṁ gatim

The man who is liberated from these three doors to darkness, oh Son of Who Takes Away the Deficiency of Others (Arjuna), practices what is good for his own soul and goes to the supreme goal.

-23-

यः शास्त्रविधिमुत्सृज्य वर्तते कामकारतः ।
न स सिद्धिमवाप्नोति न सुखं न परां गतिम् ॥ २३ ॥

yaḥ śāstravidhimutsṛjya vartate kāmakārataḥ
na sa siddhimavāpnoti na sukhaṁ na parāṁ gatim

He who neglects the procedures of the scriptures and acts to fulfill his desires, does not attain perfection or pleasure or the supreme goal.

-24-

तस्माच्छास्त्रं प्रमाणं ते कार्याकार्यव्यवस्थितौ ।
ज्ञात्वा शास्त्रविधानोक्तं कर्म कर्तुमिहार्हसि ॥ २४ ॥

tasmācchāstraṁ pramāṇaṁ te kāryākāryavyavasthitau
jñātvā śāstravidhānoktaṁ karma kartumihārhasi

Therefore, let the scriptures be your proof in determining the good effects and bad effects from actions, and knowing what is said in the scriptures, you should perform action here.

इति श्रीमद्भगवद्गीतासु षोडशोऽध्यायः ॥ १६ ॥

१७

अर्जुन उवाच

arjuna uvāca
Clarity of Pure Devotion said:

-1-

येशास्त्रविधिमुत्सृज्य यजन्ते श्रद्धयान्विताः ।
तेषां निष्ठा तु का कृष्ण सत्त्वमाहो रजस्तमः ॥ १ ॥

yeśāstravidhimutsṛjya yajante śraddhayānvitāḥ
teṣāṁ niṣṭhā tu kā kṛṣṇa sattvamāho rajastamaḥ

Those who neglect the procedures of the scriptures, and yet perform worship endowed with faith, infused with loyalty and sincerity, is it sattva, rajaḥ or tamaḥ, light, desire or darkness?

श्रीभगवानुवाच

śrībhagavānuvāca
The Respected Supreme Divinity said:

-2-

त्रिविधा भवति श्रद्धा देहिनां सा स्वभावजा ।
सात्त्विकी राजसी चैव तामसी चेति तां शृणु ॥ २ ॥

trividhā bhavati śraddhā dehināṁ sā svabhāvajā
sāttvikī rājasī caiva tāmasī ceti tāṁ śṛṇu

The intrinsic nature of faith for those who wear bodies is of three kinds: of light, desire or darkness. Listen.

-3-

सत्त्वानुरूपा सर्वस्य श्रद्धा भवति भारत ।
श्रद्धामयोऽयं पुरुषो यो यच्छ्रद्धः स एव सः ॥ ३ ॥

sattvānurūpā sarvasya śraddhā bhavati bhārata
śraddhāmayo-yaṁ puruṣo yo yacchraddhaḥ sa eva saḥ

Faith is the form of the true being of all, oh Descendant of the Light of Wisdom (Arjuna). Man consists of his faith. He is what he believes in.

-4-

यजन्ते सात्त्विका देवान्यक्षरक्षांसि राजसाः ।

प्रेतान्भूतगणांश्चान्ये यजन्ते तामसा जनाः ॥ ४ ॥

yajante sāttvikā devānyakṣarakṣāṁsi rājasāḥ
pretānbhūtagaṇāṁścānye yajante tāmasā janāḥ

The men of light worship the shining ones, Gods; the men of desires worship the Lords of Wealth and those who pursue selfishness; the people of darkness worship disembodied spirits and the multitude of others.

-5-

अशास्त्रविहितं घोरं तप्यन्ते ये तपो जनाः ।

दम्भाहङ्कारसंयुक्ताः कामरागबलान्विताः ॥ ५ ॥

aśāstravihitaṁ ghoraṁ tapyante ye tapo janāḥ
dambhāhaṅkārasaṁyuktāḥ kāmarāgabalānvitāḥ

Men who perform not in accordance with the procedures of the scriptures, united with hypocrisy and egotism, are attached by the strength of their desires.

-6-

कर्षयन्तः शरीरस्थं भूतग्राममचेतसः ।

मां चैवान्तःशरीरस्थं तान्विद्ध्यासुरनिश्चयान् ॥ ६ ॥

karṣayantaḥ śarīrasthaṁ bhūtagrāmamacetasaḥ
māṁ caivāntaḥśarīrasthaṁ tānviddhyāsuraniścayān

Even those people who torture the elements of their body, unconscious of Me, know that their objective is a force of division.

-7-

आहारस्त्वपि सर्वस्य त्रिविधो भवति प्रियः ।

यज्ञस्तपस्तथा दानं तेषां भेदमिमं शृणु ॥ ७ ॥

āhārastvapi sarvasya trividho bhavati priyaḥ
yajñastapastathā dānaṁ teṣāṁ bhedamimaṁ śṛṇu

The food of all, the sacrifice, the austerity, the giving, are also of three kinds. Listen to their distinctions.

-8-

आयुः सत्त्वबलारोग्यसुखप्रीतिविवर्धनाः ।
रस्याः स्निग्धाः स्थिरा हृद्या आहाराः सात्त्विकप्रियाः ॥ ८ ॥

āyuḥ sattvabalārogyasukhaprītivivardhanāḥ
rasyāḥ snigdhāḥ sthirā hṛdyā āhārāḥ sāttvikapriyāḥ

Pure people will love food which is tasty, mild, substantial and agreeable, and is conducive to life, purity, strength, freedom from disease, and gives pleasure.

-9-

कट्वम्ललवणात्युष्णतीक्ष्णरूक्षविदाहिनः ।
आहारा राजसस्येष्टा दुःखशोकामयप्रदाः ॥ ९ ॥

kaṭvamlalavaṇātyuṣṇatīkṣṇarūkṣavidāhinaḥ
āhārā rājasasyeṣṭā duḥkhaśokāmayapradāḥ

Those of the quality of desire prefer foods which are bitter, sour, salty, too hot, pungent, dry, burning, which produce pain, grief and poor health.

-10-

यातयामं गतरसं पूति पर्युषितं च यत् ।
उच्छिष्टमपि चामेध्यं भोजनं तामसप्रियम् ॥ १० ॥

yātayāmaṁ gatarasaṁ pūti paryuṣitaṁ ca yat
ucchiṣṭamapi cāmedhyaṁ bhojanaṁ tāmasapriyam

Beings of darkness like food which is stale, without taste, putrid or rotten, which is left over and is impure.

-11-

अफलाकाङ्क्षिभिर्यज्ञो विधिदृष्टो य इज्यते ।
यष्टव्यमेवेति मनः समाधाय स सात्त्विकः ॥ ११ ॥

aphalākāṅkṣibhiryajño vidhidṛṣṭo ya ijyate
yaṣṭavyameveti manaḥ samādhāya sa sāttvikaḥ

The sacrifice which is offered without a desire for fruit, observing scriptural procedures, with the mind concentrated in the offering, that is an offering of Light.

-12-

अभिसंधाय तु फलं दम्भार्थमपि चैव यत्।

इज्यते भरतश्रेष्ठ तं यज्ञं विद्धि राजसम्॥ १२॥

abhisaṁdhāya tu phalaṁ dambhārthamapi caiva yat
ijyate bharataśreṣṭha taṁ yajñaṁ viddhi rājasam

Oh Best of Descendants of the Light of Wisdom (Arjuna), that sacrifice which is offered seeking for fruit, or even for the purpose of ostentation, know that to be of the quality of desire.

-13-

विधिहीनमसृष्टान्नं मन्त्रहीनमदक्षिणम्।

श्रद्धाविरहितं यज्ञं तामसं परिचक्षते॥ १३॥

vidhihīnamasṛṣṭānnaṁ mantrahīnamadakṣiṇam
śraddhāvirahitaṁ yajñaṁ tāmasaṁ paricakṣate

That sacrifice is said to be of the quality of darkness which is performed without scriptural procedure, without distribution of food, without mantras, without gifts of appreciation and which is devoid of faith.

-14-

देवद्विजगुरुप्राज्ञपूजनं शौचमार्जवम्।

ब्रह्मचर्यमहिंसा च शारीरं तप उच्यते॥ १४॥

devadvijaguruprājñapūjanaṁ śaucamārjavam
brahmacaryamahiṁsā ca śārīraṁ tapa ucyate

The worship of the Gods, twice-born knowers of wisdom, the Guru and the wise; purity, the purification of knowledge, moving continuously with God, causing injury to no embodied being: these are called spiritual austerities.

-15-

अनुद्वेगकरं वाक्यं सत्यं प्रियहितं च यत्।

स्वाध्यायाभ्यसनं चैव वाङ्मयं तप उच्यते॥ १५॥

anudvegakaraṁ vākyaṁ satyaṁ priyahitaṁ ca yat
svādhyāyābhyasanaṁ caiva vāṅmayaṁ tapa ucyate

Speech which does not cause excitement, which is truthful, pleasant and beneficial, which reflects the practice of an individual's course of study is called the austerity of speech.

-16-

मनः प्रसादः सौम्यत्वं मौनमात्मविनिग्रहः ।

भावसंशुद्धिरित्येतत्तपो मानसमुच्यते ॥ १६ ॥

manaḥ prasādaḥ saumyatvaṁ maunamātmavinigrahaḥ
bhāvasaṁśuddhirityetattapo mānasamucyate

A consecrated mind, gentleness, silence, belonging to your own soul, a completely pure attitude, this is called austerity of the mind.

-17-

श्रद्धया परया तप्तं तपस्तत्त्रिविधं नरैः ।

अफलाकाङ्क्षिभिर्युक्तैः सात्त्विकं परिचक्षते ॥ १७ ॥

śraddhayā parayā taptaṁ tapastattrividhaṁ naraiḥ
aphalākāṅkṣibhiryuktaiḥ sāttvikaṁ paricakṣate

The three kinds of austerities11 practiced by men with the highest faith without desire for fruit are said to be in union with Light.

-18-

सत्कारमानपूजार्थं तपो दम्भेन चैव यत् ।

क्रियते तदिह प्रोक्तं राजसं चलमध्रुवम् ॥ १८ ॥

satkāramānapūjārthaṁ tapo dambhena caiva yat
kriyate tadiha proktaṁ rājasaṁ calamadhruvam

The austerity which is practiced with ostentation, for the purpose of attaining respect, honor or reverence, which is inconsistent and transitory, that is called the quality of desire.

-19-

मूढग्राहेणात्मनो यत्पीडया क्रियते तपः ।

परस्योत्सादनार्थं वा तत्तामसमुदाहृतम् ॥ १९ ॥

mūḍhagrāheṇātmano yatpīḍayā kriyate tapaḥ
parasyotsādanārthaṁ vā tattāmasamudāhṛtam

That austerity which is practiced with a foolish idea, even torturing one's own soul, for the purpose of causing injury to others, that is declared as the quality of darkness.

-20-

दातव्यमिति यद्दानं दीयतेऽनुपकारिणे ।

देशे काले च पात्रे च तद्दानं सात्त्विकं स्मृतम् ॥ २० ॥

dātavyamiti yaddānaṁ dīyate-nupakāriṇe
deśe kāle ca pātre ca taddānaṁ sāttvikaṁ smṛtam

That gift which is given to a worthy recipient, at the right place, at the right time, because of the privilege of giving without expectation of return, is remembered as the quality of Light.

-21-

यत्तु प्रत्युपकारार्थं फलमुद्दिश्य वा पुनः ।

दीयते च परिक्लिष्टं तद्दानं राजसं स्मृतम् ॥ २१ ॥

yattu pratyupakārārthaṁ phalamuddiśya vā punaḥ
dīyate ca parikliṣṭaṁ taddānaṁ rājasaṁ smṛtam

That gift which is given reluctantly with a specific motivation and an expectation to receive some fruit again in return, that gift is remembered as of the quality of desire.

-22-

अदेशकाले यद्दानमपात्रेभ्यश्च दीयते ।

असत्कृतमवज्ञातं तत्तामसमुदाहृतम् ॥ २२ ॥

adeśakāle yaddānamapātrebhyaśca dīyate
asatkṛtamavajñātaṁ tattāmasamudāhṛtam

That gift given to unworthy recipients, without respect, at the wrong place and the wrong time, with insult, is declared to be of the quality of darkness.

-23-

ॐ तत्सदिति निर्देशो ब्रह्मणस्त्रिविधः स्मृतः ।

ब्राह्मणास्तेन वेदाश्च यज्ञाश्च विहिताः पुरा ॥ २३ ॥

oṁ tatsaditi nirdeśo brahmaṇastrividhaḥ smṛtaḥ
brāhmaṇāstena vedāśca yajñāśca vihitāḥ purā

"Oṁ tat sat, The Infinite Beyond Conception, Oṁ that is truth," is the three syllabled declaration remembering Supreme Divinity. By that utterance those who know Supreme Divinity, Supreme Wisdom and sacrifice were originally created.

-24-

तस्मादोमित्युदाहृत्य यज्ञदानतपः क्रियाः ।
प्रवर्तन्ते विधानोक्ताः सततं ब्रह्मवादिनाम् ॥ २४ ॥

tasmādomityudāhṛtya yajñadānatapaḥ kriyāḥ
pravartante vidhānoktāḥ satataṁ brahmavādinām

Therefore, those who speak of divinity always begin all acts of sacrifice, giving and austerity saying, "Oṁ," as spoken of in the scriptures.

-25-

तदित्यनभिसंधाय फलं यज्ञतपःक्रियाः ।
दानक्रियाश्च विविधाःक्रियन्ते मोक्षकाङ्क्षिभिः ॥ २५ ॥

tadityanabhisaṁdhāya phalaṁ yajñatapaḥkriyāḥ
dānakriyāśca vividhāḥ kriyante mokṣakāṅkṣibhiḥ

Those who desire liberation perform various acts of sacrifice and austerity and acts of giving without coveting fruit while saying, "Tat."

-26-

सद्भावे साधुभावे च सदित्येतत्प्रयुज्यते ।
प्रशस्ते कर्मणि तथा सच्छब्दः पार्थ युज्यते ॥ २६ ॥

sadbhāve sādhubhāve ca sadityetatprayujyate
praśaste karmaṇi tathā sacchabdaḥ pārtha yujyate

The word, "Sat" is used, Son of She Who Excels (Arjuna), in the attitude of truth, in the attitude of pure efficiency, and is also used for auspicious actions.

-27-

यज्ञे तपसि दाने च स्थितिः सदिति चोच्यते ।
कर्म चैव तदर्थीयं सदित्येवाभिधीयते ॥ २७ ॥

yajñe tapasi dāne ca sthitiḥ saditi cocyate
karma caiva tadarthīyaṁ sadityevābhidhīyate

"Sat" is also proclaimed in connection with consistency in sacrifice, austerity or giving, and also in actions for that purpose.

-28-

अश्रद्धया हुतं दत्तं तपस्तप्तं कृतं च यत्।
असदित्युच्यते पार्थ न च तत्प्रेत्य नो इह ॥ २८ ॥

aśraddhayā hutaṁ dattaṁ tapastaptaṁ kṛtaṁ ca yat
asadityucyate pārtha na ca tatpretya no iha

Whatever austerity is practiced or performed or offered or given without faith, is called "Asat," untrue, unreal, without value here or in the future.

इति श्रीमद्भगवद्गीतासु सप्तदशोऽध्यायः ॥ १७ ॥

१८

अर्जुन उवाच

arjuna uvāca
Clarity of Pure Devotion said:

-1-

संन्यासस्य महाबाहो तत्त्वमिच्छामि वेदितुम् ।
त्यागस्य च हृषीकेश पृथक्केशिनिषूदन ॥ १ ॥

saṁnyāsasya mahābāho tattvamicchāmi veditum
tyāgasya ca hṛṣīkeśa pṛthakkeśiniṣūdana
Oh One of Mighty Arms (Kṛṣṇa), I wish to know the principles and distinctions of the establishment of truth within, and of renunciation, oh Ruler of the Senses (Kṛṣṇa), Slayer of the Demon of Entanglement.

श्रीभगवानुवाच

śrībhagavānuvāca
The Respected Supreme Divinity said:

-2-

काम्यानां कर्मणां न्यासं संन्यासं कवयो विदुः ।
सर्वकर्मफलत्यागं प्राहुस्त्यागं विचक्षणाः ॥ २ ॥

kāmyānāṁ karmaṇāṁ nyāsaṁ saṁnyāsaṁ kavayo viduḥ
sarvakarmaphalatyāgaṁ prāhustyāgaṁ vicakṣaṇāḥ
The establishment within of all actions which contain desire, is known by inspired poets as the establishment of truth within, while the renunciation of the fruits of all actions is declared as renunciation.

-3-

त्याज्यं दोषवदित्येके कर्म प्राहुर्मनीषिणः ।
यज्ञदानतपः कर्म न त्याज्यमिति चापरे ॥ ३ ॥

tyājyaṁ doṣavadityeke karma prāhurmanīṣiṇaḥ
yajñadānatapaḥ karma na tyājyamiti cāpare

Some thinkers declare that all action should be renounced because it has faults, while others proclaim that the actions of sacrifice, giving and austerity should not be renounced.

-4-

निश्चयं शृणु मे तत्र त्यागे भरतसत्तम ।

त्यागो हि पुरुषव्याघ्र त्रिविधः संप्रकीर्तितः ॥ ४ ॥

niścayaṁ śṛṇu me tatra tyāge bharatasattama
tyāgo hi puruṣavyāghra trividhaḥ saṁprakīrtitaḥ

Hear My conclusions about renunciation, oh Most True among the Descendants of the Light of Wisdom (Arjuna). Indeed three kinds of renunciation have become famous.

-5-

यज्ञदानतपः कर्म न त्याज्यं कार्यमेव तत् ।

यज्ञो दानं तपश्चैव पावनानि मनीषिणाम् ॥ ५ ॥

yajñadānatapaḥ karma na tyājyaṁ kāryameva tat
yajño dānaṁ tapaścaiva pāvanāni manīṣiṇām

The actions of sacrifice, giving and austerities should not be renounced. Indeed, sacrifice, giving and austerities have the effect of purifying beings who think.

-6-

एतान्यपि तु कर्माणि सङ्गं त्यक्त्वा फलानि च ।

कर्तव्यानीति मे पार्थ निश्चितं मतमुत्तमम् ॥ ६ ॥

etānyapi tu karmāṇi saṅgaṁ tyaktvā phalāni ca
kartavyānīti me pārtha niścitaṁ matamuttamam

But even while performing these actions, abandoning attachment to the fruit is necessary. Son of She Who Excels (Arjuna), this is certainly My excellent opinion.

-7-

नियतस्य तु संन्यासः कर्मणो नोपपद्यते ।

मोहात्तस्य परित्यागस्तामसः परिकीर्तितः ॥ ७ ॥

niyatasya tu saṁnyāsaḥ karmaṇo nopapadyate
mohāttasya parityāgastāmasaḥ parikīrtitaḥ

The renunciation of any necessary action from ignorance is inappropriate, and such neglectful abandonment is declared as coming from darkness.

-8-

दुःखमित्येव यत्कर्म कायक्लेशभयात्त्यजेत् ।
स कृत्वा राजसं त्यागं नैव त्यागफलं लभेत् ॥ ८ ॥

duḥkhamityeva yatkarma kāyakleśabhayāttyajet
sa kṛtvā rājasaṁ tyāgaṁ naiva tyāgaphalaṁ labhet

He who renounces action because of fear or pain to the body, is performing renunciation of the quality of desire, and does not even obtain the renunciation of fruit.

-9-

कार्यमित्येव यत्कर्म नियतं क्रियतेऽर्जुन ।
सङ्गं त्यक्त्वा फलं चैव स त्यागः सात्त्विको मतः ॥ ९ ॥

kāryamityeva yatkarma niyataṁ kriyate-rjuna
saṅgaṁ tyaktvā phalaṁ caiva sa tyāgaḥ sāttviko mataḥ

Actions performed to produce necessary effects, renouncing attachment to the fruits, are regarded as renunciation in Light, Clarity of Pure Devotion.

-10-

न द्वेष्ट्यकुशलं कर्म कुशले नानुषज्जते ।
त्यागी सत्त्वसमाविष्टो मेधावी छिन्नसंशयः ॥ १० ॥

na dveṣṭyakuśalaṁ karma kuśale nānuṣajjate
tyāgī sattvasamāviṣṭo medhāvī chinnasaṁśayaḥ

The intelligent one who sacrifices free from doubt with neither repulsion to disagreeable actions nor attachment to agreeable ones, is established in Light.

-11-

न हि देहभृता शक्यं त्यक्तुं कर्माण्यशेषतः ।
यस्तु कर्मफलत्यागी स त्यागीत्यभिधीयते ॥ ११ ॥

na hi dehabhṛtā śakyaṁ tyaktuṁ karmāṇyaśeṣataḥ
yastu karmaphalatyāgī sa tyāgītyabhidhīyate

It is verily not possible for a Wearer of a Body to renounce all action without end. But he who can renounce the fruit of action is called a renunciate.

-12-

अनिष्टमिष्टं मिश्रं च त्रिविधं कर्मणः फलम् ।

भवत्यत्यागिनां प्रेत्य न तु संन्यासिनां क्वचित् ॥ १२ ॥

aniṣṭamiṣṭaṁ miśraṁ ca trividhaṁ karmaṇaḥ phalam
bhavatyatyāginām̐ pretya na tu saṁnyāsinām̐ kvacit

The three kinds of fruit: desirable, undesirable and mixed, follow those who do not renounce even after death, which never accrues to one who has truth established within.

-13-

पञ्चैतानि महाबाहो कारणानि निबोध मे ।

सांख्ये कृतान्ते प्रोक्तानि सिद्धये सर्वकर्मणाम् ॥ १३ ॥

pañcaitāni mahābāho kāraṇāni nibodha me
sāṁkhye kṛtānte proktāni siddhaye sarvakarmaṇām

Oh One of Mighty Arms (Arjuna), learn from Me the five causes to attain the end of all action as spoken of in the Philosophy of the enumeration of the principles:

-14-

अधिष्ठानं तथा कर्ता करणं च पृथग्विधम् ।

विविधाश्च पृथक्चेष्टा दैवं चैवात्र पञ्चमम् ॥ १४ ॥

adhiṣṭhānaṁ tathā kartā karaṇaṁ ca pṛthagvidham
vividhāśca pṛthakceṣṭā daivaṁ caivātra pañcamam

a conducive place, the doer of action, the hands, the various different endeavors, and the presiding deity is the fifth.

-15-

शरीरवाङ्मनोभिर्यत्कर्म प्रारभते नरः ।

न्याय्यं वा विपरीतं वा पञ्चैते तस्य हेतवः ॥ १५ ॥

śarīravāṅmanobhiryatkarma prārabhate naraḥ
nyāyyaṁ vā viparītaṁ vā pañcaite tasya hetavaḥ

Whatever action a man performs with body, speech and mind, whether correct or opposite, these five are its motivation.

-16-

तत्रैवं सति कर्तारमात्मानं केवलं तु यः ।
पश्यत्यकृतबुद्धित्वान्न स पश्यति दुर्मतिः ॥ १६ ॥

tatraivaṁ sati kartāramātmānaṁ kevalaṁ tu yaḥ
paśyatyakṛtabuddhitvānna sa paśyati durmatiḥ

He who is of wrong opinion because of unripened intelligence, who sees himself alone as the doer, he does not see.

-17-

यस्य नाहंकृतो भावो बुद्धिर्यस्य न लिप्यते ।
हत्वापि स इमाँल्लोकान्न हन्ति न निबध्यते ॥ १७ ॥

yasya nāhaṁkṛto bhāvo buddhiryasya na lipyate
hatvāpi sa imāṁllokānna hanti na nibadhyate

He whose attitude is free from ego, and whose intelligence is not corrupted, even having slain these people, he does not slay, nor is he bound.

-18-

ज्ञानं ज्ञेयं परिज्ञाता त्रिविधा कर्मचोदना ।
करणं कर्म कर्तेति त्रिविधः कर्मसंग्रहः ॥ १८ ॥

jñānaṁ jñeyaṁ parijñātā trividhā karmacodanā
karaṇaṁ karma karteti trividhaḥ karmasaṁgrahaḥ

Wisdom, what can be known and the knower are the three which give rise to action. The hands, the action and the doer are the three united in action.

-19-

ज्ञानं कर्म च कर्ता च त्रिधैव गुणभेदतः ।
प्रोच्यते गुणसंख्याने यथावच्छृणु तान्यपि ॥ १९ ॥

jñānaṁ karma ca kartā ca tridhaiva guṇabhedataḥ
procyate guṇasaṁkhyāne yathāvacchṛṇu tānyapi

Wisdom, action and the actors are declared in the enumeration of qualities to be of three kinds according to the distinctions of qualities. Also listen to this.

-20-

सर्वभूतेषु येनैकं भावमव्ययमीक्षते ।
अविभक्तं विभक्तेषु तज्ज्ञानं विद्धि सात्त्विकम् ॥ २० ॥

sarvabhūteṣu yenaikaṁ bhāvamavyayamīkṣate
avibhaktaṁ vibhakteṣu tajjñānaṁ viddhi sāttvikam

Know that the wisdom by which one sees the indestructible, undivided One, in the division of all beings, is of the quality of Light.

-21-

पृथक्त्वेन तु यज्ज्ञानं नानाभावान्पृथग्विधान् ।
वेत्ति सर्वेषु भूतेषु तज्ज्ञानं विद्धि राजसम् ॥ २१ ॥

pṛthaktvena tu yajjñānaṁ nānābhāvānpṛthagvidhān
vetti sarveṣu bhūteṣu tajjñānaṁ viddhi rājasam

But the wisdom which distinguishes various attitudes as different from one another in all beings, know that wisdom is of the quality of desire.

-22-

यत्तु कृत्स्नवदेकस्मिन्कार्ये सक्तमहैतुकम् ।
अतत्त्वार्थवदल्पं च तत्तामसमुदाहृतम् ॥ २२ ॥

yattu kṛtsnavadekasminkārye saktamahaitukam
atattvārthavadalpaṁ ca tattāmasamudāhṛtam

And the attachment of one trivial effect to the total, without logic, and not in accordance with the principles, that is said to be of the quality of darkness.

-23-

नियतं सङ्गरहितमरागद्वेषतः कृतम् ।
अफलप्रेप्सुना कर्म यत्तत्सात्त्विकमुच्यते ॥ २३ ॥

niyataṁ saṅgarahitamarāgadveṣataḥ kṛtam
aphalaprepsunā karma yattatsāttvikamucyate

That action which is necessary, without attachment, free from likes and dislikes, performed without desire for the fruits, that is called of the quality of Light.

-24-

यत्तु कामेप्सुना कर्म साहङ्कारेण वा पुनः ।
क्रियते बहुलायासं तद्राजसमुदाहृतम् ॥ २४ ॥

yattu kāmepsunā karma sāhaṅkāreṇa vā punaḥ
kriyate bahulāyāsaṁ tadrājasamudāhṛtam

But again, that action performed with ego, with much effort, with many desires, is said to be of the quality of desire.

-25-

अनुबन्धं क्षयं हिंसामनवेक्ष्य च पौरुषम् ।
मोहादारभ्यते कर्म यत्तत्तामसमुच्यते ॥ २५ ॥

anubandhaṁ kṣayaṁ hiṁsāmanavekṣya ca pauruṣam
mohādārabhyate karma yattattāmasamucyate

That action which is commenced without regard to the consequences of loss or injury, ignorant of one's ability, is said to be of the quality of darkness.

-26-

मुक्तसङ्गोऽनहंवादी धृत्युत्साहसमन्वितः ।
सिद्ध्यसिद्ध्योर्निर्विकारः कर्ता सात्त्विक उच्यते ॥ २६ ॥

muktasaṅgo-nahaṁvādī dhṛtyutsāhasamanvitaḥ
siddhyasiddhyornirvikāraḥ kartā sāttvika ucyate

The doer who is free from attachment, without ego, has consistent enthusiasm, and remains unaffected in success or failure is called of the quality of Light.

-27-

रागी कर्मफलप्रेप्सुर्लुब्धो हिंसात्मकोऽशुचिः ।
हर्षशोकान्वितः कर्ता राजसः परिकीर्तितः ॥ २७ ॥

rāgī karmaphalaprepsurlubdho hiṁsātmako-śuciḥ
harṣaśokānvitaḥ kartā rājasaḥ parikīrtitaḥ

The doer who passionately desires the fruit of action, who is greedy, cruel, impure, experiencing joy and grief is called of the quality of desire.

-28-

अयुक्तः प्राकृतः स्तब्धः शठो नैष्कृतिकोऽलसः ।
विषादी दीर्घसूत्री च कर्ता तामस उच्यते ॥ २८ ॥

ayuktaḥ prākṛtaḥ stabdhaḥ śaṭho naiṣkṛtiko-lasaḥ
viṣādī dīrghasūtrī ca kartā tāmasa ucyate

The doer who is not united, vulgar, stubborn, deceitful, malicious, lazy, depressed or procrastinating is said to be of the quality of darkness.

-29-

बुद्धेर्भेदं धृतेश्चैव गुणतस्त्रिविधं शृणु ।
प्रोच्यमानमशेषेण पृथक्त्वेन धनंजय ॥ २९ ॥

buddherbhedaṁ dhṛteścaiva guṇatastrividhaṁ śṛṇu
procyamānamaśeṣeṇa pṛthaktvena dhanaṁjaya

Hear as I fully explain the three kinds of qualities which distinguish the firmness of the intellect, Conqueror of Wealth (Arjuna).

-30-

प्रवृत्तिं च निवृत्तिं च कार्याकार्ये भयाभये ।
बन्धं मोक्षं च या वेत्ति बुद्धिः सा पार्थ सात्त्विकी ॥ ३० ॥

pravṛttiṁ ca nivṛttiṁ ca kāryākārye bhayābhaye
bandhaṁ mokṣaṁ ca yā vetti buddhiḥ sā pārtha sāttvikī

That intellect which knows actions of evolution and involution, appropriate effects and inappropriate effects, fear and fearlessness, bondage and liberation, is of the quality of Light, Son of She Who Excels (Arjuna).

-31-

यया धर्ममधर्मं च कार्यं चाकार्यमेव च ।
अयथावत्प्रजानाति बुद्धिः सा पार्थ राजसी ॥ ३१ ॥

yayā dharmamadharmaṁ ca kāryaṁ cākāryameva ca
ayathāvatprajānāti buddhiḥ sā pārtha rājasī

That intellect which mistakenly understands the ideal of perfection and derogation of the ideal, appropriate effects and inappropriate effects, is of the quality of desire, Son of She Who Excels (Arjuna).

-32-

अधर्मं धर्ममिति या मन्यते तमसावृता ।
सर्वार्थान्विपरीतांश्च बुद्धिः सा पार्थ तामसी ॥ ३२ ॥

adharmaṁ dharmamiti yā manyate tamasāvṛtā
sarvārthānviparītāṁśca buddhiḥ sā pārtha tāmasī

That intellect which is encompassed by darkness and thinks the opposite about all things, even confuses actions in derogation of the ideal for the ideal of perfection, that is of the quality of darkness, Son of She Who Excels (Arjuna).

-33-

धृत्या यया धारयते मनः प्राणेन्द्रियक्रियाः ।
योगेनाव्यभिचारिण्या धृतिः सा पार्थ सात्त्विकी ॥ ३३ ॥

dhṛtyā yayā dhārayate manaḥ prāṇendriyakriyāḥ
yogenāvyabhicāriṇyā dhṛtiḥ sā pārtha sāttvikī

That firmness which restrains the actions of the mind, breath and senses in unswerving union is of the quality of Light, Son of She Who Excels (Arjuna).

-34-

यया तु धर्मकामार्थान्धृत्या धारयतेऽर्जुन ।
प्रसङ्गेन फलाकाङ्क्षी धृतिः सा पार्थ राजसी ॥ ३४ ॥

yayā tu dharmakāmārthāndhṛtyā dhārayate-rjuna
prasaṅgena phalākāṅkṣī dhṛtiḥ sā pārtha rājasī

But that firmness which holds on to the ideal of perfection, to desire and wealth, from attachment to desired fruits of action, is of the quality of desire.

-35-

यया स्वप्नं भयं शोकं विषादं मदमेव च ।
न विमुञ्चति दुर्मेधा धृतिः सा पार्थ तामसी ॥ ३५ ॥

yayā svapnaṁ bhayaṁ śokaṁ viṣādaṁ madameva ca
na vimuñcati durmedhā dhṛtiḥ sā pārtha tāmasī

That firmness by which a stupid man does not abandon dreaming, fear, grief, depression, conceit, that firmness is of the quality of darkness, Son of She Who Excels (Arjuna).

-36-

सुखं त्विदानीं त्रिविदं शृणु मे भरतर्षभ ।

अभ्यासाद्रमते यत्र दुःखान्तं च निगच्छति ॥ ३६ ॥

sukhaṁ tvidānīṁ trividaṁ śṛṇu me bharatarṣabha
abhyāsādramate yatra duḥkhāntaṁ ca nigacchati

Oh Best of the Descendants of the Light of Wisdom (Arjuna), now hear from me about the three kinds of pleasure by which one attains the end of pain by rejoicing in practices.

-37-

यत्तदग्रे विषमिव परिणामेऽमृतोपमम् ।

तत्सुखं सात्त्विकं प्रोक्तमात्मबुद्धिप्रसादजम् ॥ ३७ ॥

yattadagre viṣamiva pariṇāme-mṛtopamam
tatsukhaṁ sāttvikaṁ proktamātmabuddhiprasādajam

That pleasure which at first seems like poison, and in the end like nectar, is said to be of the quality of Light, as it is the consecration of the intellect and the soul.

-38-

विषयेन्द्रियसंयोगाद्यत्तदग्रेऽमृतोपमम् ।

परिणामे विषमिव तत्सुखं राजसं स्मृतम् ॥ ३८ ॥

viṣayendriyasaṁyogādyattadagre-mṛtopamam
pariṇāme viṣamiva tatsukhaṁ rājasaṁ smṛtam

That idea of pleasure which arises from union with the senses and seems at first like nectar and in the end like poison is remembered as of the quality of desire.

-39-

यदग्रे चानुबन्धे च सुखं मोहनमात्मनः ।

निद्रालस्यप्रमादोत्थं तत्तामसमुदाहृतम् ॥ ३९ ॥

yadagre cānubandhe ca sukhaṁ mohanamātmanaḥ
nidrālasyapramādotthaṁ tattāmasamudāhṛtam

That pleasure which deludes the soul from the beginning and subsequently arising from sleep, laziness or carelessness, is declared to be of the quality of darkness.

-40-

न तदस्ति पृथिव्यां वा दिवि देवेषु वा पुनः ।
सत्त्वं प्रकृतिजैर्मुक्तं यदेभिः स्यात्त्रिभिर्गुणैः ॥ ४० ॥

na tadasti pṛthivyāṁ vā divi deveṣu vā punaḥ
sattvaṁ prakṛtijairmuktaṁ yadebhiḥ syāttribhirguṇaiḥ

There is no existence born of nature liberated from these three qualities: not on the earth, not in the heavens, nor even among the Gods.

-41-

ब्राह्मणक्षत्रियविशां शूद्राणां च परंतप ।
कर्माणि प्रविभक्तानि स्वभावप्रभवैर्गुणैः ॥ ४१ ॥

brāhmaṇakṣatriyaviśāṁ śūdrāṇāṁ ca paraṁtapa
karmāṇi pravibhaktāni svabhāvaprabhavairguṇaiḥ

The activities of the Intelligence System, the Defense System, the Circulatory System, and the System which Nourishes and Cleanses are distinguished by their intrinsic natures born of these qualities.

-42-

शमो दमस्तपः शौचं क्षान्तिरार्जवमेव च ।
ज्ञानं विज्ञानमास्तिक्यं ब्रह्मकर्म स्वभावजम् ॥ ४२ ॥

śamo damastapaḥ śaucaṁ kṣāntirārjavameva ca
jñānaṁ vijñānamāstikyaṁ brahmakarma svabhāvajam

Peacefulness, self-control, austerity, purity, patience, the purification of knowledge, wisdom, the application of wisdom, and the continuous pursuit of self-realization are the actions natural to the Intelligence System.

-43-

शौर्यं तेजो धृतिर्दाक्ष्यं युद्धे चाप्यपलायनम् ।
दानमीश्वरभावश्च क्षात्रं कर्म स्वभावजम् ॥ ४३ ॥

śauryaṁ tejo dhṛtirdākṣyaṁ yuddhe cāpyapalāyanam
dānamīśvarabhāvaśca kṣātraṁ karma svabhāvajam

Courage, light, firmness, efficiency, not fleeing from the battle, giving, a regal attitude are the actions natural to the Defense System.

-44-

कृषिगौरक्ष्यवाणिज्यं वैश्यकर्म स्वभावजम् ।
परिचर्यात्मकं कर्म शूद्रस्यापि स्वभावजम् ॥ ४४ ॥

kṛṣigaurakṣyavāṇijyaṁ vaiśyakarma svabhāvajam
paricaryātmakaṁ karma śūdrasyāpi svabhāvajam

Cultivation, keeping cows and commerce are activities natural to the Circulatory System. Actions which serve are natural to the System which Nourishes and Cleanses.

-45-

स्वे स्वे कर्मण्यभिरतः संसिद्धिं लभते नरः ।
स्वकर्मनिरतः सिद्धिं यथा विन्दति तच्छृणु ॥ ४५ ॥

sve sve karmaṇyabhirataḥ saṁsiddhiṁ labhate naraḥ
svakarmanirataḥ siddhiṁ yathā vindati tacchṛṇu

Devoted in his own sphere of activity, a man attains perfection. Listen to how a man finds perfection engaged in his own actions.

-46-

यतः प्रवृत्तिर्भूतानां येन सर्वमिदं ततम् ।
स्वकर्मणा तमभ्यर्च्य सिद्धिं विन्दति मानवः ॥ ४६ ॥

yataḥ pravṛttirbhūtānāṁ yena sarvamidaṁ tatam
svakarmaṇā tamabhyarcya siddhiṁ vindati mānavaḥ

Man attains perfection worshiping Him from whom the evolution of beings has come, and by whom all this is pervaded. That is his own action.

-47-

श्रेयान्स्वधर्मो विगुणः परधर्मात्स्वनुष्ठितात् ।
स्वभावनियतं कर्म कुर्वन्नाप्नोति किल्बिषम् ॥ ४७ ॥

śreyānsvadharmo viguṇaḥ paradharmātsvanuṣṭhitāt
svabhāvaniyataṁ karma kurvannāpnoti kilbiṣam

Better is one's own ideal of perfection than the ideals of another. If they are performed well as is necessitated by one's own intrinsic nature, though of limited qualities, such performance of actions can cause no conflict.

-48-

सहजं कर्म कौन्तेय सदोषमपि न त्यजेत् ।
सर्वारम्भा हि दोषेण धूमेनाग्निरिवावृताः ॥ ४८ ॥

sahajaṁ karma kaunteya sadoṣamapi na tyajet
sarvārambhā hi doṣeṇa dhūmenāgnirivāvṛtāḥ

Do not renounce the actions of your birth, even though they have faults, for all undertakings have faults, like fire is encompassed by smoke.

-49-

असक्तबुद्धिः सर्वत्र जितात्मा विगतस्पृहः ।
नैष्कर्म्यसिद्धिं परमां संन्यासेनाधिगच्छति ॥ ४९ ॥

asaktabuddhiḥ sarvatra jitātmā vigataspṛhaḥ
naiṣkarmyasiddhiṁ paramāṁ saṁnyāsenādhigacchati

He whose intellect is everywhere unattached, who has conquered his soul, who has controlled desire, attains the supreme perfection of establishing "Being without Action" within.

-50-

सिद्धिं प्राप्तो यथा ब्रह्म तथाप्नोति निबोध मे ।
समासेनैव कौन्तेय निष्ठा ज्ञानस्य या परा ॥ ५० ॥

siddhiṁ prāpto yathā brahma tathāpnoti nibodha me
samāsenaiva kaunteya niṣṭhā jñānasya yā parā

Briefly learn from Me, oh Son of Who Takes Away the Deficiency of Others (Arjuna). Having attained that perception, he attains Supreme Divinity, which is the loyalty to the Highest Wisdom.

-51-

बुद्ध्या विशुद्धया युक्तो धृत्यात्मानं नियम्य च ।
शब्दादीन्विषयांस्त्यक्त्वा रागद्वेषौ व्युदस्य च ॥ ५१ ॥

buddhyā viśuddhayā yukto dhṛtyātmānaṁ niyamya ca
śabdādīnviṣayāṁstyaktvā rāgadveṣau vyudasya ca

With the intellect united in purity, firmly controlling the soul, renouncing sound and other ideas, abandon attraction and aversion.

-52-

विविक्तसेवी लघ्वाशी यतवाक्कायमानसः ।

ध्यानयोगपरो नित्यं वैराग्यं समुपाश्रितः ॥ ५२ ॥

viviktasevī laghvāśī yatavākkāyamānasaḥ
dyānayogaparo nityaṁ vairāgyaṁ samupāśritaḥ

Serving silence, with controlled diet, controlling speech, body and mind, always united in meditation, take refuge in equilibrium.

-53-

अहङ्कारं बलं दर्पं कामं क्रोधं परिग्रहम् ।

विमुच्य निर्ममः शान्तो ब्रह्मभूयाय कल्पते ॥ ५३ ॥

ahaṅkāraṁ balaṁ darpaṁ kāmaṁ krodhaṁ parigraham
vimucya nirmamaḥ śānto brahmabhūyāya kalpate

Eradicating ego, strength, arrogance, desires, anger, covetousness, possessiveness and being at peace, one can think to become One with the Supreme Divinity.

-54-

ब्रह्मभूतः प्रसन्नात्मा नशोचति न काङ्क्षति ।

समः सर्वषु भूतेषु मद्भक्तिं लभते पराम् ॥ ५४ ॥

brahmabhūtaḥ prasannātmā naśocati na kāṅkṣati
samaḥ sarvaṣu bhūteṣu madbhaktiṁ labhate parām

Who has become One with the Supreme Divinity loves the soul, does not grieve nor desire. He is the same to all beings, and he attains supreme devotion to Me.

-55-

भक्त्या मामभिजानाति यावान्यश्चास्मि तत्त्वतः ।

ततो मां तत्त्वतो ज्ञात्वा विशते तदनन्तरम् ॥ ५५ ॥

bhaktyā māmabhijānāti yāvānyaścāsmi tattvataḥ
tato māṁ tattvato jñātvā viśate tadanantaram

By devotion he knows the principles what I am and who I am. Having known the infinite principles, he enters Me.

-56-

सर्वकर्माण्यपि सदा कुर्वाणो मद्व्यपाश्रयः ।
मत्प्रसादादवाप्नोति शाश्वतं पदमव्ययम् ॥ ५६ ॥

sarvakarmāṇyapi sadā kurvāṇo madvyapāśrayaḥ
matprasādādavāpnoti śāśvataṁ padamavyayam

By always taking refuge in Me, he performs all actions. By My consecration he attains the eternal, indestructible goal.

-57-

चेतसा सर्वकर्माणि मयि संन्यस्य मत्परः ।
बुद्धियोगमुपाश्रित्य मच्चित्तः सततं भव ॥ ५७ ॥

cetasā sarvakarmāṇi mayi saṁnyasya matparaḥ
buddhiyogamupāśritya maccittaḥ satataṁ bhava

Establishing your consciousness in Me during all actions, unite in My supreme intelligence. Always take refuge in the consciousness of Me.

-58-

मच्चित्तः सर्वदुर्गाणि मत्प्रसादात्तरिष्यसि ।
अथ चेत्त्वमहङ्कारान्न श्रोष्यसि विनङ्क्ष्यसि ॥ ५८ ॥

maccittaḥ sarvadurgāṇi matprasādāttariṣyasi
atha cettvamahaṅkārānna śroṣyasi vinaṅkṣyasi

Absorbing consciousness in Me, you will cross over all confusion as My consecration. Now, if from egotism you will not hear, you will suffer.

-59-

यदहङ्कारमाश्रित्य न योत्स्य इति मन्यसे ।
मिथ्यैष व्यवसायस्ते प्रकृतिस्त्वां नियोक्ष्यति ॥ ५९ ॥

yadahaṅkāramāsritya na yotsya iti manyase
mithyaiṣa vyavasāyaste prakṛtistvāṁ niyokṣyati

This ideal is untrue if you egotistically think you will not fight. Your nature will compel you.

-60-

स्वभावजेन कौन्तेय निबद्धः स्वेन कर्मणा ।
कर्तुं नेच्छसि यन्मोहात्करिष्यस्यवशोऽपि तत् ॥ ६० ॥

**svabhāvajena kaunteya nibaddhaḥ svena karmaṇā
kartuṁ necchasi yanmohātkariṣyasyavaśo-pi tat**

Oh Son of Who Takes Away the Deficiency of Others (Arjuna), bound by your own intrinsic nature to perform actions, that which from ignorance you wish not to do, you will be helpless but to do just that.

-61-

ईश्वरः सर्वभूतानां हृद्देशेऽर्जुन तिष्ठति ।
भ्रामयन्सर्वभूतानि यन्त्रारूढानि मायया ॥ ६१ ॥

**īśvaraḥ sarvabhūtānāṁ hṛddeśe-rjuna tiṣṭhati
bhrāmayansarvabhūtāni yantrārūḍhāni māyayā**

Clarity of Pure Devotion, the Seer of All is established in the regions of the heart in all beings, causing all beings to move in the Illusion as if riding on a conveyance.

-62-

तमेव शरणं गच्छ सर्वभावेन भारत ।
तत्प्रसादात्परां शान्तिं स्थानं प्राप्स्यसि शाश्वतम् ॥ ६२ ॥

**tameva śaraṇaṁ gaccha sarvabhāvena bhārata
tatprasādātparāṁ śāntiṁ sthānaṁ prāpsyasi śāśvatam**

Take refuge in Him with your complete attitude, oh Descendant of the Light of Wisdom (Arjuna). By that consecration you will attain the eternal residence of supreme peace.

-63-

इति ते ज्ञानमाख्यातं गुह्याद्गुह्यतरं मया ।
विमृश्यैतदशेषेण यथेच्छसि तथा कुरु ॥ ६३ ॥

**iti te jñānamākhyātaṁ guhyādguhyataraṁ mayā
vimṛśyaitadaśeṣeṇa yathecchasi tathā kuru**

Thus, the most esoteric of all secret wisdom has been explained by Me to you. Fully contemplating this, act as you choose.

-64-

सर्वगुह्यतमं भूयः शृणु मे परमं वचः ।
इष्टोऽसि मे दृढमिति ततो वक्ष्यामि ते हितम् ॥ ६४ ॥

sarvaguhyatamaṁ bhūyaḥ śṛṇu me paramaṁ vacaḥ
iṣṭo-si me dṛḍhamiti tato vakṣyāmi te hitam

Again listen to the most secret of My supreme words. You are firmly loved by Me, and therefore, I speak for your welfare.

-65-

मन्मना भव मद्भक्तो मद्याजी मां नमस्कुरु ।
मामेवैष्यसि सत्यं ते प्रतिजाने प्रियोऽसि मे ॥ ६५ ॥

manmanā bhava madbhakto madyājī māṁ namaskuru
māmevaiṣyasi satyaṁ te pratijāne priyo-si me

Be with your mind in Me; be devoted to Me; bow with respect to me; in truth, you will come to me. This is My promise to you, for you are My beloved.

-66-

सर्वधर्मान्परित्यज्य मामेकं शरणं व्रज ।
अहं त्वा सर्वपापेभ्यो मोक्षयिष्यामि मा शुचः ॥ ६६ ॥

sarvadharmānparityajya māmekaṁ śaraṇaṁ vraja
ahaṁ tvā sarvapāpebhyo mokṣayiṣyāmi mā śucaḥ

Renouncing all other ideals, take refuge in Me alone. I will liberate you from all sin.

-67-

इदं ते नातपस्काय नाभक्ताय कदाचन ।
न चाशुश्रूषवे वाच्यं न च मां योऽभ्यसूयति ॥ ६७ ॥

idaṁ te nātapaskāya nābhaktāya kadācana
na cāśuśrūṣave vācyaṁ na ca māṁ yo-bhyasūyati

You should not explain this to those who practice no austerity, no devotion, and not ever to those who desire not to listen, or to one who disrespects Me.

-68-

य इमं परमं गुह्यं मद्भक्तेष्वभिधास्यति ।

भक्तिं मयि परां कृत्वा मामेवैष्यत्यसंशयः ॥ ६८ ॥

ya imaṁ paramaṁ guhyaṁ madbhakteṣvabhidhāsyati
bhaktiṁ mayi parāṁ kṛtvā māmevaiṣyatyasaṁśayaḥ

Who will explain this supreme secret of devotion to My devotees, will without a doubt come to Me, even becoming supreme with Me.

-69-

न च तस्मान्मनुष्येषु कश्चिन्मे प्रियकृत्तमः ।

भविता न च मे तस्मादन्यः प्रियतरो भुवि ॥ ६९ ॥

na ca tatmānmanuṣyeṣu kaścinme priyakṛttamaḥ
bhavitā na ca me tasmādanyaḥ priyataro bhuvi

On the entire earth there is no other that is more dear to Me, than he who performs excellent acts of love for Me.

-70-

अध्येष्यते च य इमं धर्म्यं संवादमावयोः ।

ज्ञानयज्ञेन तेनाहमिष्टः स्यामिति मे मतिः ॥ ७० ॥

adhyeṣyate ca ya imaṁ dharmyaṁ saṁvādamāvayoḥ
jñānayajñena tenāhamiṣṭaḥ syāmiti me matiḥ

For those who will study this discussion about the ideals of perfection, I will regard that I am desired, and have been lovingly worshiped by the sacrifice of wisdom.

-71-

श्रद्धावाननसूयश्च शृणुयादपि यो नरः ।

सोऽपि मुक्तः शुभाँल्लोकान्प्राप्नुयात्पुण्यकर्मणाम् ॥ ७१ ॥

śraddhāvānanasūyaśca śṛṇuyādapi yo naraḥ
so-pi muktaḥ śubhāṁllokānprāpnuyātpuṇyakarmaṇām

The man who is full of faith and free from malice who hears this, will attain the happiness of meritorious actions in the world as well as liberation.

-72-

कच्चिदेतच्छ्रुतं पार्थ त्वयैकाग्रेण चेतसा ।
कच्चिदज्ञानसंमोहः प्रनष्टस्ते धनंजय ॥ ७२ ॥

kaccidetacchrutaṁ pārtha tvayaikāgreṇa cetasā
kaccidajñānasaṁmohaḥ pranaṣṭaste dhanaṁjaya
Son of She Who Excels (Arjuna), did you hear this with focused consciousness, and has your ignorance of delusion been destroyed, Conqueror of Wealth (Arjuna)?

अर्जुन उवाच

arjuna uvāca
Clarity of Pure Devotion said:

-73-

नष्टो मोहः स्मृतिर्लब्धा त्वत्प्रसादान्मयाच्युत ।
स्थितोऽस्मि गतसंदेहः करिष्ये वचनं तव ॥ ७३ ॥

naṣṭo mohaḥ smṛtirlabdhā tvatprasādānmayācyuta
sthito-smi gatasaṁdehaḥ kariṣye vacanaṁ tava
My ignorance has been destroyed, my memory has been returned to me by your consecration, oh Imperishable. I have been firmly freed from doubts. I will perform as you say.

संजय उवाच

saṁjaya uvāca
He Who is Victorious Over All said:

-74-

इत्यहं वासुदेवस्य पार्थस्य च महात्मनः ।
संवादमिममश्रौषमद्भुतं रोमहर्षणम् ॥ ७४ ॥

ityahaṁ vāsudevasya pārthasya ca mahātmanaḥ
saṁvādamimamaśrauṣamadbhutaṁ romaharṣaṇam
Thus I heard this wonderful discussion between the great souls Lord of the Earth (Kṛṣṇa) and Son of She Who Excels (Arjuna), which excites my skin.

-75-

व्यासप्रसादाच्छ्रुतवानेतद्गुह्यमहं परम् ।
योगं योगेश्वरात्कृष्णात्साक्षात्कथयतः स्वयम् ॥ ७८ ॥

vyāsaprasādācchrutavānetadguhyamahaṁ param
yogaṁ yogeśvarātkṛṣṇātsākṣātkathayataḥ svayam

By the consecration of Vyāsa, I have heard this supreme secret of union directly from the Lord of Union, Doer of All (Kṛṣṇa), speaking himself.

-76-

राजन्संस्मृत्य संस्मृत्य संवादमिममद्भुतम् ।
केशवार्जुनयोः पुण्यं हृष्यामि च मुहुर्मुहुः ॥ ७६ ॥

rājansaṁsmṛtya saṁsmṛtya saṁvādamimamadbhutam
keśavārjunayoḥ puṇyaṁ hṛṣyāmi ca muhurmuhuḥ

Oh King, again and again I rejoice in the merits of remembering again and again this wonderful discussion between Embodiment of the Functions of Creation, Preservation and Transformation (Kṛṣṇa) and Clarity of Pure Devotion (Arjuna).

-77-

तच्च संस्मृत्य संस्मृत्य रूपमत्यद्भुतं हरेः ।
विस्मयो मे महान्राजन्हृष्यामि च पुनः पुनः ॥ ७७ ॥

tacca saṁsmṛtya saṁsmṛtya rūpamatyadbhutaṁ hareḥ
vismayo me mahānrājanhṛṣyāmi ca punaḥ punaḥ

Oh King, it is a great wonder to me that remembering again and again the most wonderful form of Remover of Duality (Kṛṣṇa), again and again I rejoice!

-78-

यत्र योगेश्वरः कृष्णो यत्र पार्थो धनुर्धरः ।
तत्र श्रीर्विजयो भूतिर्ध्रुवा नीतिर्मतिर्मम ॥ ७८ ॥

yatra yogeśvaraḥ kṛṣṇo yatra pārtho dhanurdharaḥ
tatra śrīrvijayo bhūtirdhruvā nītirmatirmama

Wherever is the Supreme Lord of Union, the Doer of All (Kṛṣṇa), wherever is Son of She Who Excels (Arjuna), Who wields the Bow, there will be respect, victory, happiness, consistency and wise counsel. This is My understanding.

ॐ तत् सत् ॐ

oṁ tat sat oṁ

इति श्रीमद्भगवद्गीतासु अष्टादशोऽध्यायः ॥ १८ ॥
श्रीमद्भगवद्गीता समाप्ता ॥

॥ श्रीविष्णुसहस्रनामस्तोत्रम् ॥
॥ śrīviṣṇusahasranāmastotram ॥

विश्वं विष्णुर्वषट्कारो भूतभव्यभवत्प्रभुः ।
भूतकृद्भूतभृद्भावो भूतात्मा भूतभावनः ॥ १ ॥
**viśvaṁ viṣṇurvaṣaṭkāro bhūtabhavyabhavatprabhuḥ ।
bhūtakṛdbhūtabhṛdbhāvo bhūtātmā bhūtabhāvanaḥ ॥ 1 ॥**

पूतात्मा परमात्मा च मुक्तानां परमा गतिः ।
अव्ययः पुरुषः साक्षी क्षेत्रज्ञोऽक्षर एव च ॥ २ ॥
**pūtātmā paramātmā ca muktānāṁ paramā gatiḥ ।
avyayaḥ puruṣaḥ sākṣī kṣetrajño-kṣara eva ca ॥ 2 ॥**

योगो योगविदां नेता प्रधानपुरुषेश्वरः ।
नारसिंहवपुः श्रीमान् केशवः पुरुषोत्तमः ॥ ३ ॥
**yogo yogavidāṁ netā pradhānapuruṣeśvaraḥ ।
nārasiṁhavapuḥ śrīmān keśavaḥ puruṣottamaḥ ॥ 3 ॥**

सर्वः शर्वः शिवः स्थाणुर्भूतादिर्निधिरव्ययः ।
सम्भवो भावनो भर्ता प्रभवः प्रभुरीश्वरः ॥ ४ ॥
**sarvaḥ śarvaḥ śivaḥ sthāṇurbhūtādirnidhiravyayaḥ ।
sambhavo bhāvano bhartā prabhavaḥ prabhurīśvaraḥ
॥ 4 ॥**

स्वयम्भूः शम्भुरादित्यः पुष्कराक्षो महास्वनः ।
अनादिनिधनो धाता विधाता धातुरुत्तमः ॥ ५ ॥
**svayambhūḥ śambhurādityaḥ puṣkarākṣo mahāsvanaḥ ।
anādinidhano dhātā vidhātā dhāturuttamaḥ ॥ 5 ॥**

अप्रमेयो हृषीकेशः पद्मनाभोऽमरप्रभुः ।
विश्वकर्मा मनुस्त्वष्टा स्थविष्ठः स्थविरो ध्रुवः ॥ ६ ॥

**aprameyo hṛṣīkeśaḥ padmanābho-maraprabhuḥ |
viśvakarmā manustvaṣṭā sthaviṣṭhaḥ sthaviro dhruvaḥ ‖ 6 ‖**

अग्राह्यः शाश्वतः कृष्णो लोहिताक्षः प्रतर्दनः ।
प्रभूतस्त्रिककुब्धाम पवित्रं मङ्गलं परम् ॥ ७ ॥

**agrāhyaḥ śāśvataḥ kṛṣṇo lohitākṣaḥ pratardanaḥ |
prabhūtastrikakubdhāma pavitraṁ maṅgalaṁ param ‖ 7 ‖**

ईशानः प्राणदः प्राणो ज्येष्ठः श्रेष्ठः प्रजापतिः ।
हिरण्यगर्भो भूगर्भो माधवो मधुसूदनः ॥ ८ ॥

**īśānaḥ prāṇadaḥ prāṇo jyeṣṭhaḥ śreṣṭhaḥ prajāpatiḥ |
hiraṇyagarbho bhūgarbho mādhavo madhusūdanaḥ ‖ 8 ‖**

ईश्वरो विक्रमी धन्वी मेधावी विक्रमः क्रमः ।
अनुत्तमो दुराधर्षः कृतज्ञः कृतिरात्मवान् ॥ ९ ॥

**īśvaro vikramī dhanvī medhāvī vikramaḥ kramaḥ |
anuttamo durādharṣaḥ kṛtajñaḥ kṛtirātmavān ‖ 9 ‖**

सुरेशः शरणं शर्म विश्वरेताः प्रजाभवः ।
अहः संवत्सरो व्यालः प्रत्ययः सर्वदर्शनः ॥ १० ॥

**sureśaḥ śaraṇaṁ śarma viśvaretāḥ prajābhavaḥ |
ahaḥ saṁvatsaro vyālaḥ pratyayaḥ sarvadarśanaḥ ‖ 10 ‖**

अजः सर्वेश्वरः सिद्धः सिद्धिः सर्वादिरच्युतः ।
वृषाकपिरमेयात्मा सर्वयोगविनिःसृतः ॥ ११ ॥

**ajaḥ sarveśvaraḥ siddhaḥ siddhiḥ sarvādiracyutaḥ |
vṛṣākapirameyātmā sarvayogaviniḥsṛtaḥ || 11 ||**

वसुर्वसुमनाः सत्यः समात्माऽसम्मितः समः ।
अमोघः पुण्डरीकाक्षो वृषकर्मा वृषाकृतिः ॥ १२ ॥

**vasurvasumanāḥ satyaḥ samātmā-sammitaḥ samaḥ |
amoghaḥ puṇḍarīkākṣo vṛṣakarmā vṛṣākṛtiḥ || 12 ||**

रुद्रो बहुशिरा बभ्रुर्विश्वयोनिः शुचिश्रवाः ।
अमृतः शाश्वत स्थाणुर्वरारोहो महातपाः ॥ १३ ॥

**rudro bahuśirā babhrurviśvayoniḥ śuciśravāḥ |
amṛtaḥ śāśvata sthāṇurvarāroho mahātapāḥ || 13 ||**

सर्वगः सर्वविद्भानुर्विष्वक्सेनो जनार्दनः ।
वेदो वेदविदव्यङ्गो वेदाङ्गो वेदवित् कविः ॥ १४ ॥

**sarvagaḥ sarvavidbhānurviṣvakseno janārdanaḥ |
vedo vedavidavyaṅgo vedāṅgo vedavit kaviḥ || 14 ||**

लोकाध्यक्षः सुराध्यक्षो धर्माध्यक्षः कृताकृतः ।
चतुरात्मा चतुर्व्यूहश्चतुर्दंष्ट्रश्चतुर्भुजः ॥ १५ ॥

**lokādhyakṣaḥ surādhyakṣo dharmādhyakṣaḥ kṛtākṛtaḥ |
caturātmā caturvyūhaścaturdaṁṣṭraścaturbhujaḥ || 15 ||**

भ्राजिष्णुर्भोजनं भोक्ता सहिष्णुर्जगदादिजः ।
अनघो विजयो जेता विश्वयोनिः पुनर्वसुः ॥ १६ ॥

**bhrājiṣṇurbhojanaṁ bhoktā sahiṣṇurjagadādijaḥ |
anagho vijayo jetā viśvayoniḥ punarvasuḥ || 16 ||**

उपेन्द्रो वामनः प्रांशुरमोघः शुचिरूर्जितः ।
अतीन्द्रः सङ्ग्रहः सर्गो धृतात्मा नियमो यमः ॥ १७ ॥

**upendro vāmanaḥ prāṁśuramoghaḥ śucirūrjitaḥ |
atīndraḥ saṅgrahaḥ sargo dhṛtātmā niyamo yamaḥ
|| 17 ||**

वेद्यो वैद्यः सदायोगी वीरहा माधवो मधुः ।
अतीन्द्रियो महामायो महोत्साहो महाबलः ॥ १८ ॥

**vedyo vaidyaḥ sadāyogī vīrahā mādhavo madhuḥ |
atīndriyo mahāmāyo mahotsāho mahābalaḥ || 18 ||**

महाबुद्धिर्महावीर्यो महाशक्तिर्महाद्युतिः ।
अनिर्देश्यवपुः श्रीमानमेयात्मा महाद्रिधृक् ॥ १९ ॥

**mahābuddhirmahāvīryo mahāśaktirmahādyutiḥ |
anirdeśyavapuḥ śrīmānameyātmā mahādridhṛk || 19 ||**

महेष्वासो महीभर्ता श्रीनिवासः सतां गतिः ।
अनिरुद्धः सुरानन्दो गोविन्दो गोविदां पतिः ॥ २० ॥

**maheṣvāso mahībhartā śrīnivāsaḥ satāṁ gatiḥ |
aniruddhaḥ surānando govindo govidāṁ patiḥ || 20 ||**

मरीचिर्दमनो हंसः सुपर्णो भुजगोत्तमः ।
हिरण्यनाभः सुतपाः पद्मनाभः प्रजापतिः ॥ २१ ॥

**marīcirdamano haṁsaḥ suparṇo bhujagottamaḥ |
hiraṇyanābhaḥ sutapāḥ padmanābhaḥ prajāpatiḥ || 21 ||**

अमृत्युः सर्वदृक् सिंहः सन्धाता सन्धिमान् स्थिरः ।
अजो दुर्मर्षणः शास्ता विश्रुतात्मा सुरारिहा ॥ २२ ॥
amṛtyuḥ sarvadṛk siṁhaḥ sandhātā sandhimān sthiraḥ |
ajo durmarṣaṇaḥ śāstā viśrutātmā surārihā || 22 ||

गुरुर्गुरुतमो धाम सत्यः सत्यपराक्रमः ।
निमिषोऽनिमिषः स्रग्वी वाचस्पतिरुदारधीः ॥ २३ ॥
gururgurutamo dhāma satyaḥ satyaparākramaḥ |
nimiṣo-nimiṣaḥ sragvī vācaspatirudāradhīḥ || 23 ||

अग्रणीर्ग्रामणीः श्रीमान् न्यायो नेता समीरणः ।
सहस्रमूर्धा विश्वात्मा सहस्राक्षः सहस्रपात् ॥ २४ ॥
agraṇīrgrāmaṇīḥ śrīmān nyāyo netā samīraṇaḥ |
sahasramūrdhā viśvātmā sahasrākṣaḥ sahasrapāt || 24 ||

आवर्तनो निवृत्तात्मा संवृतः सम्प्रमर्दनः ।
अहः संवर्तको वह्निरनिलो धरणीधरः ॥ २५ ॥
āvartano nivṛttātmā saṁvṛtaḥ sampramardanaḥ |
ahaḥ saṁvartako vahniranilo dharaṇīdharaḥ || 25 ||

सुप्रसादः प्रसन्नात्मा विश्वधृग्विश्वभुग्विभुः ।
सत्कर्ता सत्कृतः साधुर्जह्नुर्नारायणो नरः ॥ २६ ॥
suprasādaḥ prasannātmā viśvadhṛgviśvabhugvibhuḥ |
satkartā satkṛtaḥ sādhurjahnurnārāyaṇo naraḥ || 26 ||

असङ्ख्येयोऽप्रमेयात्मा विशिष्टः शिष्टकृच्छुचिः ।
सिद्धार्थः सिद्धसङ्कल्पः सिद्धिदः सिद्धिसाधनः ॥ २७ ॥

asaṅkhyeyo-prameyātmā viśiṣṭaḥ śiṣṭakṛcchuciḥ |
siddhārthaḥ siddhasaṅkalpaḥ siddhidaḥ siddhisādhanaḥ
|| 27 ||

वृषाही वृषभो विष्णुर्वृषपर्वा वृषोदरः ।
वर्धनो वर्धमानश्च विविक्तः श्रुतिसागरः ॥ २८ ॥

vṛṣāhī vṛṣabho viṣṇurvṛṣaparvā vṛṣodaraḥ |
vardhano vardhamānaśca viviktaḥ śrutisāgaraḥ || 28 ||

सुभुजो दुर्धरो वाग्मी महेन्द्रो वसुदो वसुः ।
नैकरूपो बृहद्रूपः शिपिविष्टः प्रकाशनः ॥ २९ ॥

subhujo durdharo vāgmī mahendro vasudo vasuḥ |
naikarūpo bṛhadrūpaḥ śipiviṣṭaḥ prakāśanaḥ || 29 ||

ओजस्तेजोद्युतिधरः प्रकाशात्मा प्रतापनः ।
ऋद्धः स्पष्टाक्षरो मन्त्रश्चन्द्रांशुर्भास्करद्युतिः ॥ ३० ॥

ojastejodyutidharaḥ prakāśātmā pratāpanaḥ |
ṛddhaḥ spaṣṭākṣaro mantraścandrāṁśurbhāskaradyutiḥ
|| 30 ||

अमृतांशूद्भवो भानुः शशबिन्दुः सुरेश्वरः ।
औषधं जगतः सेतुः सत्यधर्मपराक्रमः ॥ ३१ ॥

amṛtāṁśūdbhavo bhānuḥ śaśabinduḥ sureśvaraḥ |
auṣadhaṁ jagataḥ setuḥ satyadharmaparākramaḥ
|| 31 ||

भूतभव्यभवन्नाथः पवनः पावनोऽनलः ।
कामहा कामकृत्कान्तः कामः कामप्रदः प्रभुः ॥ ३२ ॥
bhūtabhavyabhavannāthaḥ pavanaḥ pāvano-nalaḥ |
kāmahā kāmakṛtkāntaḥ kāmaḥ kāmapradaḥ prabhuḥ
|| 32 ||

युगादिकृद्युगावर्तो नैकमायो महाशनः ।
अदृश्यो व्यक्तरूपश्च सहस्रजिदनन्तजित् ॥ ३३ ॥
yugādikṛdyugāvarto naikamāyo mahāśanaḥ |
adṛśyo vyaktarūpaśca sahasrajidanantajit || 33 ||

इष्टोऽविशिष्टः शिष्टेष्टः शिखण्डी नहुषो वृषः ।
क्रोधहा क्रोधकृत्कर्ता विश्वबाहुर्महीधरः ॥ ३४ ॥
iṣṭo-viśiṣṭaḥ śiṣṭeṣṭaḥ śikhaṇḍī nahuṣo vṛṣaḥ |
krodhahā krodhakṛtkartā viśvabāhurmahīdharaḥ || 34 ||

अच्युतः प्रथितः प्राणः प्राणदो वासवानुजः ।
अपांनिधिरधिष्ठानमप्रमत्तः प्रतिष्ठितः ॥ ३५ ॥
acyutaḥ prathitaḥ prāṇaḥ prāṇado vāsavānujaḥ |
apāṁnidhiradhiṣṭhānamapramattaḥ pratiṣṭhitaḥ || 35 ||

स्कन्दः स्कन्दधरो धुर्यो वरदो वायुवाहनः ।
वासुदेवो बृहद्भानुरादिदेवः पुरन्दरः ॥ ३६ ॥
skandaḥ skandadharo dhuryo varado vāyuvāhanaḥ |
vāsudevo bṛhadbhānurādidevaḥ purandaraḥ || 36 ||

अशोकस्तारणस्तारः शूरः शौरिर्जनेश्वरः ।
अनुकूलः शतावर्तः पद्मी पद्मनिभेक्षणः ॥ ३७ ॥
aśokastāraṇastāraḥ śūraḥ śaurirjaneśvaraḥ |
anukūlaḥ śatāvartaḥ padmī padmanibhekṣaṇaḥ || 37 ||

पद्मनाभोऽरविन्दाक्षः पद्मगर्भः शरीरभृत् ।
महर्द्धिरृद्धो वृद्धात्मा महाक्षो गरुडध्वजः ॥ ३८ ॥
padmanābho-ravindākṣaḥ padmagarbhaḥ śarīrabhṛt |
maharddhirṛddho vṛddhātmā mahākṣo garuḍadhvajaḥ || 38 ||

अतुलः शरभो भीमः समयज्ञो हविर्हरिः ।
सर्वलक्षणलक्षण्यो लक्ष्मीवान् समितिञ्जयः ॥ ३९ ॥
atulaḥ śarabho bhīmaḥ samayajño havirhariḥ |
sarvalakṣaṇalakṣaṇyo lakṣmīvān samitiñjayaḥ || 39 ||

विक्षरो रोहितो मार्गो हेतुर्दामोदरः सहः ।
महीधरो महाभागो वेगवानमिताशनः ॥ ४० ॥
vikṣaro rohito mārgo heturdāmodaraḥ sahaḥ |
mahīdharo mahābhāgo vegavānamitāśanaḥ || 40 ||

उद्भवः क्षोभणो देवः श्रीगर्भः परमेश्वरः ।
करणं कारणं कर्ता विकर्ता गहनो गुहः ॥ ४१ ॥
udbhavaḥ kṣobhaṇo devaḥ śrīgarbhaḥ parameśvaraḥ |
karaṇaṁ kāraṇaṁ kartā vikartā gahano guhaḥ || 41 ||

व्यवसायो व्यवस्थानः संस्थानः स्थानदो ध्रुवः ।
परर्द्धिः परमस्पष्टस्तुष्टः पुष्टः शुभेक्षणः ॥ ४२ ॥

**vyavasāyo vyavasthānaḥ saṁsthānaḥ sthānado dhruvaḥ |
pararddhiḥ paramaspaṣṭastuṣṭaḥ puṣṭaḥ śubhekṣaṇaḥ
|| 42 ||**

रामो विरामो विरजो मार्गो नेयो नयोऽनयः ।
वीरः शक्तिमतां श्रेष्ठो धर्मो धर्मविदुत्तमः ॥ ४३ ॥

**rāmo virāmo virajo mārgo neyo nayo-nayaḥ |
vīraḥ śaktimatāṁ śreṣṭho dharmo dharmaviduttamaḥ
|| 43 ||**

वैकुण्ठः पुरुषः प्राणः प्राणदः प्रणवः पृथुः ।
हिरण्यगर्भः शत्रुघ्नो व्याप्तो वायुरधोक्षजः ॥ ४४ ॥

**vaikuṇṭhaḥ puruṣaḥ prāṇaḥ prāṇadaḥ praṇavaḥ pṛthuḥ |
hiraṇyagarbhaḥ śatrughno vyāpto vāyuradhokṣajaḥ || 44 ||**

ऋतुः सुदर्शनः कालः परमेष्ठी परिग्रहः ।
उग्रः संवत्सरो दक्षो विश्रामो विश्वदक्षिणः ॥ ४५ ॥

**ṛtuḥ sudarśanaḥ kālaḥ parameṣṭhī parigrahaḥ |
ugraḥ saṁvatsaro dakṣo viśrāmo viśvadakṣiṇaḥ || 45 ||**

विस्तारः स्थावरस्थाणुः प्रमाणं बीजमव्ययम् ।
अर्थोऽनर्थो महाकोशो महाभोगो महाधनः ॥ ४६ ॥

**vistāraḥ sthāvarasthāṇuḥ pramāṇaṁ bījamavyayam |
artho-nartho mahākośo mahābhogo mahādhanaḥ || 46 ||**

अनिर्विण्णः स्थविष्ठोऽभूर्धर्मयूपो महामखः ।
नक्षत्रनेमिर्नक्षत्री क्षमः क्षामः समीहनः ॥ ४७ ॥
anirviṇṇaḥ sthaviṣṭho-bhūrdharmayūpo mahāmakhaḥ |
nakṣatranemirnakṣatrī kṣamaḥ kṣāmaḥ samīhanaḥ || 47 ||

यज्ञ इज्यो महेज्यश्च क्रतुः सत्रं सतां गतिः ।
सर्वदर्शी विमुक्तात्मा सर्वज्ञो ज्ञानमुत्तमम् ॥ ४८ ॥
yajña ijyo mahejyaśca kratuḥ satraṁ satāṁ gatiḥ |
sarvadarśī vimuktātmā sarvajño jñānamuttamam || 48 ||

सुव्रतः सुमुखः सूक्ष्मः सुघोषः सुखदः सुहृत् ।
मनोहरो जितक्रोधो वीरबाहुर्विदारणः ॥ ४९ ॥
suvrataḥ sumukhaḥ sūkṣmaḥ sughoṣaḥ sukhadaḥ suhṛt |
manoharo jitakrodho vīrabāhurvidāraṇaḥ || 49 ||

स्वापनः स्ववशो व्यापी नैकात्मा नैककर्मकृत् ।
वत्सरो वत्सलो वत्सी रत्नगर्भो धनेश्वरः ॥ ५० ॥
svāpanaḥ svavaśo vyāpī naikātmā naikakarmakṛt |
vatsaro vatsalo vatsī ratnagarbho dhaneśvaraḥ || 50 ||

धर्मगुब्धर्मकृद्धर्मी सदसत्क्षरमक्षरम् ।
अविज्ञाता सहस्रांशुर्विधाता कृतलक्षणः ॥ ५१ ॥
dharmagubdharmakṛddharmī sadasatkṣaramakṣaram |
avijñātā sahasrāṁśurvidhātā kṛtalakṣaṇaḥ || 51 ||

गभस्तिनेमिः सत्त्वस्थः सिंहो भूतमहेश्वरः ।
आदिदेवो महादेवो देवेशो देवभृद्गुरुः ॥ ५२ ॥
gabhastinemiḥ sattvasthaḥ siṁho bhūtamaheśvaraḥ |
ādidevo mahādevo deveśo devabhṛdguruḥ || 52 ||

उत्तरो गोपतिर्गोप्ता ज्ञानगम्यः पुरातनः ।
शरीरभूतभृद्भोक्ता कपीन्द्रो भूरिदक्षिणः ॥ ५३ ॥
uttaro gopatirgoptā jñānagamyaḥ purātanaḥ |
śarīrabhūtabhṛdbhoktā kapīndro bhūridakṣiṇaḥ || 53 ||

सोमपोऽमृतपः सोमः पुरुजित्पुरुसत्तमः ।
विनयो जयः सत्यसन्धो दाशार्हः सात्त्वताम्पतिः ॥ ५४ ॥
somapo-mṛtapaḥ somaḥ purujitpurusattamaḥ |
vinayo jayaḥ satyasandho dāśārhaḥ sāttvatāmpatiḥ || 54 ||

जीवो विनयिता साक्षी मुकुन्दोऽमितविक्रमः ।
अम्भोनिधिरनन्तात्मा महोदधिशयोऽन्तकः ॥ ५५ ॥
jīvo vinayitā sākṣī mukundo-mitavikramaḥ |
ambhonidhiranantātmā mahodadhiśayo-ntakaḥ || 55 ||

अजो महार्हः स्वाभाव्यो जितामित्रः प्रमोदनः ।
आनन्दो नन्दनो नन्दः सत्यधर्मा त्रिविक्रमः ॥ ५६ ॥
ajo mahārhaḥ svābhāvyo jitāmitraḥ pramodanaḥ |
ānando nandano nandaḥ satyadharmā trivikramaḥ || 56 ||

महर्षिः कपिलाचार्यः कृतज्ञो मेदिनीपतिः ।
त्रिपदस्त्रिदशाध्यक्षो महाशृङ्गः कृतान्तकृत् ॥ ५७ ॥
maharṣiḥ kapilācāryaḥ kṛtajño medinīpatiḥ |
tripadastridaśādhyakṣo mahāśṛṅgaḥ kṛtāntakṛt || 57 ||

महावराहो गोविन्दः सुषेणः कनकाङ्गदी ।
गुह्यो गभीरो गहनो गुप्तश्चक्रगदाधरः ॥ ५८ ॥
mahāvarāho govindaḥ suṣeṇaḥ kanakāṅgadī |
guhyo gabhīro gahano guptaścakragadādharaḥ || 58 ||

वेधाः स्वाङ्गोऽजितः कृष्णो दृढः सङ्कर्षणोऽच्युतः ।
वरुणो वारुणो वृक्षः पुष्कराक्षो महामनाः ॥ ५९ ॥

vedhāḥ svāṅgo-jitaḥ kṛṣṇo dṛḍhaḥ saṅkarṣaṇo-cyutaḥ |
varuṇo vāruṇo vṛkṣaḥ puṣkarākṣo mahāmanāḥ || 59 ||

भगवान् भगहाऽऽनन्दी वनमाली हलायुधः ।
आदित्यो ज्योतिरादित्यः सहिष्णुर्गतिसत्तमः ॥ ६० ॥

bhagavān bhagahā--nandī vanamālī halāyudhaḥ |
ādityo jyotirādityaḥ sahiṣṇurgatisattamaḥ || 60 ||

सुधन्वा खण्डपरशुर्दारुणो द्रविणप्रदः ।
दिवःस्पृक् सर्वदृग्व्यासो वाचस्पतिरयोनिजः ॥ ६१ ॥

sudhanvā khaṇḍaparaśurdāruṇo draviṇapradaḥ |
divaḥspṛk sarvadṛgvyāso vācaspatirayonijaḥ || 61 ||

त्रिसामा सामगः साम निर्वाणं भेषजं भिषक् ।
संन्यासकृच्छमः शान्तो निष्ठा शान्तिः परायणम् ॥ ६२ ॥

trisāmā sāmagaḥ sāma nirvāṇaṁ bheṣajaṁ bhiṣak |
saṁnyāsakṛcchamaḥ śānto niṣṭhā śāntiḥ parāyaṇam
|| 62 ||

शुभाङ्गः शान्तिदः स्रष्टा कुमुदः कुवलेशयः ।
गोहितो गोपतिर्गोप्ता वृषभाक्षो वृषप्रियः ॥ ६३ ॥

śubhāṅgaḥ śāntidaḥ sraṣṭā kumudaḥ kuvaleśayaḥ |
gohito gopatirgoptā vṛṣabhākṣo vṛṣapriyaḥ || 63 ||

अनिवर्ती निवृत्तात्मा सङ्क्षेप्ता क्षेमकृच्छिवः ।
श्रीवत्सवक्षाः श्रीवासः श्रीपतिः श्रीमतांवरः ॥ ६४ ॥
anivartī nivṛttātmā saṅkṣeptā kṣemakṛcchivaḥ |
śrīvatsavakṣāḥ śrīvāsaḥ śrīpatiḥ śrīmatāṁvaraḥ || 64 ||

श्रीदः श्रीशः श्रीनिवासः श्रीनिधिः श्रीविभावनः ।
श्रीधरः श्रीकरः श्रेयः श्रीमांल्लोकत्रयाश्रयः ॥ ६५ ॥
śrīdaḥ śrīśaḥ śrīnivāsaḥ śrīnidhiḥ śrīvibhāvanaḥ |
śrīdharaḥ śrīkaraḥ śreyaḥ śrīmāṁllokatrayāśrayaḥ || 65 ||

स्वक्षः स्वङ्गः शतानन्दो नन्दिर्ज्योतिर्गणेश्वरः ।
विजितात्माऽविधेयात्मा सत्कीर्तिश्छिन्नसंशयः ॥ ६६ ॥
svakṣaḥ svaṅgaḥ śatānando nandirjyotirgaṇeśvaraḥ |
vijitātmā-vidheyātmā satkīrtiśchinnasaṁśayaḥ || 66 ||

उदीर्णः सर्वतश्चक्षुरनीशः शाश्वतस्थिरः ।
भूशयो भूषणो भूतिर्विशोकः शोकनाशनः ॥ ६७ ॥
udīrṇaḥ sarvataścakṣuranīśaḥ śāśvatasthiraḥ |
bhūśayo bhūṣaṇo bhūtirviśokaḥ śokanāśanaḥ || 67 ||

अर्चिष्मानर्चितः कुम्भो विशुद्धात्मा विशोधनः ।
अनिरुद्धोऽप्रतिरथः प्रद्युम्नोऽमितविक्रमः ॥ ६८ ॥
arciṣmānarcitaḥ kumbho viśuddhātmā viśodhanaḥ |
aniruddho-pratirathaḥ pradyumno-mitavikramaḥ || 68 ||

कालनेमिनिहा वीरः शौरिः शूरजनेश्वरः ।
त्रिलोकात्मा त्रिलोकेशः केशवः केशिहा हरिः ॥ ६९ ॥
kālaneminihā vīraḥ śauriḥ śūrajaneśvaraḥ |
trilokātmā trilokeśaḥ keśavaḥ keśihā hariḥ || 69 ||

कामदेवः कामपालः कामी कान्तः कृतागमः ।
अनिर्देश्यवपुर्विष्णुर्वीरोऽनन्तो धनञ्जयः ॥ ७० ॥

kāmadevaḥ kāmapālaḥ kāmī kāntaḥ kṛtāgamaḥ |
anirdeśyavapurviṣṇurvīro-nanto dhanañjayaḥ || 70 ||

ब्रह्मण्यो ब्रह्मकृद् ब्रह्मा ब्रह्म ब्रह्मविवर्धनः ।
ब्रह्मविद् ब्राह्मणो ब्रह्मी ब्रह्मज्ञो ब्राह्मणप्रियः ॥ ७१ ॥

brahmaṇyo brahmakṛd brahmā
brahma brahmavivardhanaḥ |
brahmavid brāhmaṇo brahmī
brahmajño brāhmaṇapriyaḥ || 71 ||

महाक्रमो महाकर्मा महातेजा महोरगः ।
महाक्रतुर्महायज्वा महायज्ञो महाहविः ॥ ७२ ॥

mahākramo mahākarmā mahātejā mahoragaḥ |
mahākraturmahāyajvā mahāyajño mahāhaviḥ || 72 ||

स्तव्यः स्तवप्रियः स्तोत्रं स्तुतिः स्तोता रणप्रियः ।
पूर्णः पूरयिता पुण्यः पुण्यकीर्तिरनामयः ॥ ७३ ॥

stavyaḥ stavapriyaḥ stotraṁ stutiḥ stotā raṇapriyaḥ |
pūrṇaḥ pūrayitā puṇyaḥ puṇyakīrtiranāmayaḥ || 73 ||

मनोजवस्तीर्थकरो वसुरेता वसुप्रदः ।
वसुप्रदो वासुदेवो वसुर्वसुमना हविः ॥ ७४ ॥

manojavastīrthakaro vasuretā vasupradaḥ |
vasuprado vāsudevo vasurvasumanā haviḥ || 74 ||

सद्गतिः सत्कृतिः सत्ता सद्भूतिः सत्परायणः ।
शूरसेनो यदुश्रेष्ठः सन्निवासः सुयामुनः ॥ ७५ ॥
sadgatiḥ satkṛtiḥ sattā sadbhūtiḥ satparāyaṇaḥ |
śūraseno yaduśreṣṭhaḥ sannivāsaḥ suyāmunaḥ || 75 ||

भूतावासो वासुदेवः सर्वासुनिलयोऽनलः ।
दर्पहा दर्पदो दृप्तो दुर्धरोऽथापराजितः ॥ ७६ ॥
bhūtāvāso vāsudevaḥ sarvāsunilayo-nalaḥ |
darpahā darpado dṛpto durdharo-thāparājitaḥ || 76 ||

विश्वमूर्तिर्महामूर्तिर्दीप्तमूर्तिरमूर्तिमान् ।
अनेकमूर्तिरव्यक्तः शतमूर्तिः शताननः ॥ ७७ ॥
viśvamūrtirmahāmūrtirdīptamūrtiramūrtimān |
anekamūrtiravyaktaḥ śatamūrtiḥ śatānanaḥ || 77 ||

एको नैकः सवः कः किं यत् तत्पदमनुत्तमम् ।
लोकबन्धुर्लोकनाथो माधवो भक्तवत्सलः ॥ ७८ ॥
eko naikaḥ savaḥ kaḥ kiṁ yat tatpadamanuttamam |
lokabandhurlokanātho mādhavo bhaktavatsalaḥ || 78 ||

सुवर्णवर्णो हेमाङ्गो वराङ्गश्चन्दनाङ्गदी ।
वीरहा विषमः शून्यो घृताशीरचलश्चलः ॥ ७९ ॥
suvarṇavarṇo hemāṅgo varāṅgaścandanāṅgadī |
vīrahā viṣamaḥ śūnyo ghṛtāśīracalaścalaḥ || 79 ||

अमानी मानदो मान्यो लोकस्वामी त्रिलोकधृक् ।
सुमेधा मेधजो धन्यः सत्यमेधा धराधरः ॥ ८० ॥
amānī mānado mānyo lokasvāmī trilokadhṛk |
sumedhā medhajo dhanyaḥ satyamedhā dharādharaḥ
|| 80 ||

तेजोवृषो द्युतिधरः सर्वशस्त्रभृतां वरः ।
प्रग्रहो निग्रहो व्यग्रो नैकश‍ृङ्गो गदाग्रजः ॥ ८१ ॥
tejovṛṣo dyutidharaḥ sarvaśastrabhṛtāṁ varaḥ |
pragraho nigraho vyagro naikaśṛṅgo gadāgrajaḥ || 81 ||

चतुर्मूर्तिश्चतुर्बाहुश्चतुर्व्यूहश्चतुर्गतिः ।
चतुरात्मा चतुर्भावश्चतुर्वेदविदेकपात् ॥ ८२ ॥
caturmūrtiścaturbāhuścaturvyūhaścaturgatiḥ |
caturātmā caturbhāvaścaturvedavidekapāt || 82 ||

समावर्तोऽनिवृत्तात्मा दुर्जयो दुरतिक्रमः ।
दुर्लभो दुर्गमो दुर्गो दुरावासो दुरारिहा ॥ ८३ ॥
samāvarto-nivṛttātmā durjayo duratikramaḥ |
durlabho durgamo durgo durāvāso durārihā || 83 ||

शुभाङ्गो लोकसारङ्गः सुतन्तुस्तन्तुवर्धनः ।
इन्द्रकर्मा महाकर्मा कृतकर्मा कृतागमः ॥ ८४ ॥
śubhāṅgo lokasāraṅgaḥ sutantustantuvardhanaḥ |
indrakarmā mahākarmā kṛtakarmā kṛtāgamaḥ || 84 ||

उद्भवः सुन्दरः सुन्दो रत्ननाभः सुलोचनः ।
अर्को वाजसनः शृङ्गी जयन्तः सर्वविज्जयी ॥ ८५ ॥
udbhavaḥ sundaraḥ sundo ratnanābhaḥ sulocanaḥ |
arko vājasanaḥ śṛṅgī jayantaḥ sarvavijjayī || 85 ||

सुवर्णबिन्दुरक्षोभ्यः सर्ववागीश्वरेश्वरः ।
महाह्रदो महागर्तो महाभूतो महानिधिः ॥ ८६ ॥
suvarṇabindurakṣobhyaḥ sarvavāgīśvareśvaraḥ |
mahāhrado mahāgarto mahābhūto mahānidhiḥ || 86 ||

कुमुदः कुन्दरः कुन्दः पर्जन्यः पावनोऽनिलः ।
अमृतांशोऽमृतवपुः सर्वज्ञः सर्वतोमुखः ॥ ८७ ॥
kumudaḥ kundaraḥ kundaḥ parjanyaḥ pāvano-nilaḥ |
amṛtāṁśo-mṛtavapuḥ sarvajñaḥ sarvatomukhaḥ || 87 ||

सुलभः सुव्रतः सिद्धः शत्रुजिच्छत्रुतापनः ।
न्यग्रोधोऽदुम्बरोऽश्वत्थश्चाणूरान्ध्रनिषूदनः ॥ ८८ ॥
sulabhaḥ suvrataḥ siddhaḥ śatrujicchatrutāpanaḥ |
nyagrodho-dumbaro-śvatthaścāṇūrāndhraniṣūdanaḥ || 88 ||

सहस्रार्चिः सप्तजिह्वः सप्तैधाः सप्तवाहनः ।
अमूर्तिरनघोऽचिन्त्यो भयकृद्भयनाशनः ॥ ८९ ॥
sahasrārciḥ saptajihvaḥ saptaidhāḥ saptavāhanaḥ |
amūrtiranagho-cintyo bhayakṛdbhayanāśanaḥ || 89 ||

अणुर्बृहत्कृशः स्थूलो गुणभृन्निर्गुणो महान् ।
अधृतः स्वधृतः स्वास्यः प्राग्वंशो वंशवर्धनः ॥ ९० ॥

**aṇurbṛhatkṛśaḥ sthūlo guṇabhṛnnirguṇo mahān |
adhṛtaḥ svadhṛtaḥ svāsyaḥ prāgvaṁśo vaṁśavardhanaḥ || 90 ||**

भारभृत् कथितो योगी योगीशः सर्वकामदः ।
आश्रमः श्रमणः क्षामः सुपर्णो वायुवाहनः ॥ ९१ ॥

**bhārabhṛt kathito yogī yogīśaḥ sarvakāmadaḥ |
āśramaḥ śramaṇaḥ kṣāmaḥ suparṇo vāyuvāhanaḥ || 91 ||**

धनुर्धरो धनुर्वेदो दण्डो दमयिता दमः ।
अपराजितः सर्वसहो नियन्ताऽनियमोऽयमः ॥ ९२ ॥

**dhanurdharo dhanurvedo daṇḍo damayitā damaḥ |
aparājitaḥ sarvasaho niyantā-niyamo-yamaḥ || 92 ||**

सत्त्ववान् सात्त्विकः सत्यः सत्यधर्मपरायणः ।
अभिप्रायः प्रियार्होऽर्हः प्रियकृत् प्रीतिवर्धनः ॥ ९३ ॥

**sattvavān sāttvikaḥ satyaḥ satyadharmaparāyaṇaḥ |
abhiprāyaḥ priyārho-rhaḥ priyakṛt prītivardhanaḥ || 93 ||**

विहायसगतिर्ज्योतिः सुरुचिर्हुतभुग्विभुः ।
रविर्विरोचनः सूर्यः सविता रविलोचनः ॥ ९४ ॥

**vihāyasagatirjyotiḥ surucirhutabhugvibhuḥ |
ravirvirocanaḥ sūryaḥ savitā ravilocanaḥ || 94 ||**

अनन्तो हुतभुग्भोक्ता सुखदो नैकजोऽग्रजः ।
अनिर्विण्णः सदामर्षी लोकाधिष्ठानमद्भुतः ॥ ९५ ॥
ananto hutabhugbhoktā sukhado naikajo-grajaḥ |
anirviṇṇaḥ sadāmarṣī lokādhiṣṭhānamadbhutaḥ || 95 ||

सनात्सनातनतमः कपिलः कपिरव्ययः ।
स्वस्तिदः स्वस्तिकृत्स्वस्ति स्वस्तिभुक्स्वस्तिदक्षिणः ॥ ९६ ॥
sanātsanātanatamaḥ kapilaḥ kapiravyayaḥ |
svastidaḥ svastikṛtsvasti svastibhuksvastidakṣiṇaḥ || 96 ||

अरौद्रः कुण्डली चक्री विक्रम्यूर्जितशासनः ।
शब्दातिगः शब्दसहः शिशिरः शर्वरीकरः ॥ ९७ ॥
araudraḥ kuṇḍalī cakrī vikramyūrjitaśāsanaḥ |
śabdātigaḥ śabdasahaḥ śiśiraḥ śarvarīkaraḥ || 97 ||

अक्रूरः पेशलो दक्षो दक्षिणः क्षमिणांवरः ।
विद्वत्तमो वीतभयः पुण्यश्रवणकीर्तनः ॥ ९८ ॥
akrūraḥ peśalo dakṣo dakṣiṇaḥ kṣamiṇāṁvaraḥ |
vidvattamo vītabhayaḥ puṇyaśravaṇakīrtanaḥ || 98 ||

उत्तारणो दुष्कृतिहा पुण्यो दुःस्वप्ननाशनः ।
वीरहा रक्षणः सन्तो जीवनः पर्यवस्थितः ॥ ९९ ॥
uttāraṇo duṣkṛtihā puṇyo duḥsvapnanāśanaḥ |
vīrahā rakṣaṇaḥ santo jīvanaḥ paryavasthitaḥ || 99 ||

अनन्तरूपोऽनन्तश्रीर्जितमन्युर्भयापहः ।
चतुरश्रो गभीरात्मा विदिशो व्यादिशो दिशः ॥ १०० ॥
anantarūpo-nantaśrīrjitamanyurbhayāpahaḥ |
caturaśro gabhīrātmā vidiśo vyādiśo diśaḥ || 100 ||

अनादिर्भूर्भुवो लक्ष्मीः सुवीरो रुचिराङ्गदः ।
जननो जनजन्मादिर्भीमो भीमपराक्रमः ॥ १०१ ॥
anādirbhūrbhuvo lakṣmīḥ suvīro rucirāṅgadaḥ |
janano janajanmādirbhīmo bhīmaparākramaḥ || 101 ||

आधारनिलयोऽधाता पुष्पहासः प्रजागरः ।
ऊर्ध्वगः सत्पथाचारः प्राणदः प्रणवः पणः ॥ १०२ ॥
ādhāranilayo-dhātā puṣpahāsaḥ prajāgaraḥ |
ūrdhvagaḥ satpathācāraḥ prāṇadaḥ praṇavaḥ paṇaḥ || 102 ||

प्रमाणं प्राणनिलयः प्राणभृत्प्राणजीवनः ।
तत्त्वं तत्त्वविदेकात्मा जन्ममृत्युजरातिगः ॥ १०३ ॥
pramāṇaṁ prāṇanilayaḥ prāṇabhṛtprāṇajīvanaḥ |
tattvaṁ tattvavidekātmā janmamṛtyujarātigaḥ || 103 ||

भूर्भुवःस्वस्तरुस्तारः सविता प्रपितामहः ।
यज्ञो यज्ञपतिर्यज्वा यज्ञाङ्गो यज्ञवाहनः ॥ १०४ ॥
bhūrbhuvaḥsvastarustāraḥ savitā prapitāmahaḥ |
yajño yajñapatiryajvā yajñāṅgo yajñavāhanaḥ || 104 ||

यज्ञभृद् यज्ञकृद् यज्ञी यज्ञभुग् यज्ञसाधनः ।
यज्ञान्तकृद् यज्ञगुह्यमन्नमन्नाद एव च ॥ १०५ ॥
yajñabhṛd yajñakṛd yajñī yajñabhug yajñasādhanaḥ |
yajñāntakṛd yajñaguhyamannamannāda eva ca || 105 ||

आत्मयोनिः स्वयञ्जातो वैखानः सामगायनः ।
देवकीनन्दनः स्रष्टा क्षितीशः पापनाशनः ॥ १०६ ॥

ātmayoniḥ svayañjāto vaikhānaḥ sāmagāyanaḥ |
devakīnandanaḥ sraṣṭā kṣitīśaḥ pāpanāśanaḥ || 106 ||

शङ्खभृन्नन्दकी चक्री शार्ङ्गधन्वा गदाधरः ।
रथाङ्गपाणिरक्षोभ्यः सर्वप्रहरणायुधः ॥ १०७ ॥

śaṅkhabhṛnnandakī cakrī śārṅgadhanvā gadādharaḥ |
rathāṅgapāṇirakṣobhyaḥ sarvapraharaṇāyudhaḥ || 107 ||

इति श्रीविष्णोर्दिव्यसहस्रनामस्तोत्रं सम्पूर्णम् ।

iti śrīviṣṇordivyasahasranāmastotraṁ sampūrṇam |

भीष्मस्तवराजः
bhīṣmastavarājaḥ

जनमेजय उवाच
janamejaya uvāca
Janamejaya said:

शरतल्पे शयानस्तु भरतानां पितामहः ।
कथमुत्सृष्टवान् देहं कं च योगमधारयत् ॥ १ ॥
śaratalpe śayānastu bharatānāṁ pitāmahaḥ |
kathamutsṛṣṭavān dehaṁ kaṁ ca yogamadhārayat || 1 ||
1. Tell how the Great Grandfather of all Bharat (the land where the light of wisdom always shines) left his body and entered in to union when he was laying on a bed of arrows.

वैशम्पायन उवाच
vaiśampāyana uvāca
Vaishampayana said:

शृणुष्वावहितो राजन् शुचिर्भूत्वा समाहितः ।
भीष्मस्य कुरुशार्दूल देहोत्सर्गं महात्मनः ॥ २ ॥
śṛṇuṣvāvahito rājan śucirbhūtvā samāhitaḥ |
bhīṣmasya kuruśārdūla dehotsargaṁ mahātmanaḥ || 2 ||
2. Listen to this story which will make you pure, Oh King, of how the great soul, Bhishma, the most eminent among the Kuru family, left his body and ascended to heaven.

निवृत्तमात्रे त्वयन उत्तरे वै दिवाकरे ।
समावेशयदात्मानमात्मन्येव समाहितः ॥ ३ ॥

nivṛttamātre tvayana uttare vai divākare |
samāveśayadātmānamātmanyeva samāhitaḥ || 3 ||

3. When the sun moved into the northern hemisphere, his time (course) of evolution was complete, he drew his soul into complete absorption only in the supreme soul.

विकीर्णांशुरिवादित्यो भीष्मः शरशतैश्चितः ।
शुशुभे परया लक्ष्म्या वृतो ब्राह्मणसत्तमैः ॥ ४ ॥

vikīrṇāṁśurivādityo bhīṣmaḥ śaraśataiścitaḥ |
śuśubhe parayā lakṣmyā vṛto brāhmaṇasattamaiḥ || 4 ||

4. The celebrated one of great strength, Bhishma, resting on a bed of arrows, shining brilliantly, defining the highest, surrounded by many true brahmins, began to speak.

व्यासेन वेदविदुषा नारदेन सुरर्षिणा ।
देवस्थानेन वात्स्येन तथाश्मकसुमन्तुना ॥ ५ ॥

vyāsena vedaviduṣā nāradena surarṣiṇā |
devasthānena vātsyena tathāśmakasumantunā || 5 ||

5. Present were Vyasa, expounder of the Vedas; Narada, the Seer among the gods; Devasthā, a great rishi; Vatsya, and then Maka, the son of a Vaishya; Sumantu, who is well known.

तथा जैमिनिना चैव पैलेन च महात्मना ।
शाण्डिल्यदेवलाभ्यां च मैत्रेयेण च धीमता ॥ ६ ॥

tathā jaimininā caiva pailena ca mahātmanā |
śāṇḍilyadevalābhyāṁ ca maitreyeṇa ca dhīmatā || 6 ||

6. Then there was Jaimini and Paila, both great souls; and Shandilya, Devala, and Maitreya all great thinkers.

असितेन वसिष्ठेन कौशिकेन महात्मना ।
हारीतलोमशाभ्यां च तथाऽऽत्रेयेण धीमता ॥ ७ ॥

asitena vasiṣṭhena kauśikena mahātmanā |
hārītalomaśābhyāṁ ca tathā--treyeṇa dhīmatā || 7 ||
7. Asita, Vasishtha, Kaushik great souls; Harit, Lamasha, and then Atri all great thinkers.

बृहस्पतिश्च शुक्रश्च च्यवनश्च महामुनिः ।
सनत्कुमारः कपिलो वाल्मीकिस्तुम्बुरुः कुरुः ॥ ८ ॥

bṛhaspatiśca śukraśca cyavanaśca mahāmuniḥ |
sanatkumāraḥ kapilo vālmīkistumburuḥ kuruḥ || 8 ||
8. Brihaspati and Shukra, Chyavana all great munis; Sanatkumar, Kapila, Valmiki, Tumburu, and Kuru.

मौद्गल्यो भार्गवो रामस्तृणबिन्दुर्महामुनिः
पिप्पलादोऽथ वायुश्च संवर्तः पुलहः कचः ॥ ९ ॥

maudgalyo bhārgavo rāmastṛṇabindurmahāmuniḥ
pippalādo-tha vāyuśca saṁvartaḥ pulahaḥ kacaḥ || 9 ||
9. Maudgalyo, Bhargava, Rama, Trianabindu, all great wise beings. Pipalad then Vayu, and Samvarta, Pulaha, Kaca;

काश्यपश्च पुलस्त्यश्च क्रतुर्दक्षः पराशरः ।
मरीचिरङ्गिराः काश्यो गौतमो गालवो मुनिः ॥ १० ॥

kāśyapaśca pulastyaśca kraturdakṣaḥ parāśaraḥ |
marīciraṅgirāḥ kāśyo gautamo gālavo muniḥ || 10 ||
10. Kashyapa and Pulastya and Kratu, Daksha, and Parasara; Marichi, Angirasa, Kashyo, Gautam, and Galava great munis.

धौम्यो विभाण्डो माण्डव्यो धौम्रः कृष्णानुभौतिकः ।
उलूकः परमो विप्रो मार्कण्डेयो महामुनिः ॥ ११ ॥

dhaumyo vibhāṇḍo māṇḍavyo
dhaumraḥ kṛṣṇānubhautikaḥ |
ulūkaḥ paramo vipro mārkaṇḍeyo mahāmuniḥ || 11 ||

11. Dhaumya, Vibhanda, Mandavya, Dhauma, Krishna-anubhotika, Uluka, and the supreme among the twice-born, the great soul Markendeya.

भास्करिः पूरणः कृष्णः सूतः परमधार्मिकः ।
एतैश्चान्यैर्मुनिगणैर्महाभागैर्महात्मभिः ॥ १२ ॥

bhāskariḥ pūraṇaḥ kṛṣṇaḥ sūtaḥ paramadhārmikaḥ |
etaiścānyairmunigaṇairmahābhāgairmahātmabhiḥ || 12 ||

12. Bhaskari, Purana, Krishna, Suta, all beings with supreme ideals. These and others of the multitude of wise and divine beings were fortunate to be with that great soul (Bhishma).

श्रद्धादमशमोपेतैर्वृतश्चन्द्र इव ग्रहैः ।
भीष्मस्तु पुरुषव्याघ्रः कर्मणा मनसा गिरा ॥ १३ ॥

śraddhādamaśamopetairvṛtaścandra iva grahaiḥ |
bhīṣmastu puruṣavyāghraḥ karmaṇā manasā girā || 13 ||

13. With faith, humility, peace, and tranquility, he appeared even like the Moon in the midst of the planets. Bhishma, supreme among men, with actions, thoughts, and words,

शरतल्पगतः कृष्णं प्रदध्यौ प्राञ्जलिः शुचिः ।
स्वरेण हृष्टपुष्टेन तुष्टाव मधुसूदनम् ॥ १४ ॥

śaratalpagataḥ kṛṣṇaṁ pradadhyau prāñjaliḥ śuciḥ |
svareṇa hṛṣṭapuṣṭena tuṣṭāva madhusūdanam || 14 ||

14. lying on a bed of arrows, praised Krishna with folded palms and purity. With great satisfaction, great nourishment, and great delight, he remembered the Slayer of Too Much (Madhusudan, who is always sweet),

योगेश्वरं पद्मनाभं विष्णुं जिष्णुं जगत्पतिम् ।
कृताञ्जलिपुटो भूत्वा वाग्विदां प्रवरः प्रभुः ।
भीष्मः परमधर्मात्मा वासुदेवमथास्तुवत् ॥ १५ ॥

yogeśvaraṁ padmanābhaṁ viṣṇuṁ jiṣṇuṁ jagatpatim |
kṛtāñjalipuṭo bhūtvā vāgvidāṁ pravaraḥ prabhuḥ |
bhīṣmaḥ paramadharmātmā vāsudevamathāstuvat || 15 ||
15. the supreme lord of union, who has a lotus-like naval, Vishnu, the lord of the perceivable world. Assuming the posture of respect with folded hands, the chief among men began to pronounce the invocation. Bhishma, supreme among ideal souls, then sang praise to Vasudeva, the lord of the earth.

भीष्म उवाच

bhīṣma uvāca
Bhishma said:

आरिराधयिषुः कृष्णं वाचं जिगदिषामि याम् ।
तया व्याससमासिन्या प्रीयतां पुरुषोत्तमः ॥ १६ ॥

ārirādhayiṣuḥ kṛṣṇaṁ vācaṁ jigadiṣāmi yām |
tayā vyāsasamāsinyā prīyatāṁ puruṣottamaḥ || 16 ||
16. Oh most excellent among men, Krishna, desiring to speak words of worship for you, I intend to practice self-restraint and to expound like Vyasa.

शिचिं शुचिपदं हंसं तत्पदं परमेष्ठिनम् ।
युक्त्वा सर्वात्मनाऽऽत्मानं तं प्रपद्ये प्रजापतिम् ॥ १७ ॥

śiciṁ śucipadaṁ haṁsaṁ tatpadaṁ parameṣṭhinam |
yuktvā sarvātmanā--tmānaṁ
taṁ prapadye prajāpatim || 17 ||
17. You are the swan of discrimination, the chosen form of the supreme deity, whose feet are most pure of the pure, steadfastly united with the soul of all souls, I fully surrender to you, to the lord of all beings born.

अनाद्यन्तं परं ब्रह्म न देवा नर्षयो विदुः ।
एको यं वेद भगवान्धाता नारायणो हरिः ॥ १८ ॥

anādyantaṁ paraṁ brahma na devā narṣayo viduḥ |
eko yaṁ veda bhagavāndhātā nārāyaṇo hariḥ || 18 ||

18. You are the highest supreme creator, without beginning or end, unknown by gods nor rishis nor intelligent wise people, spoken of in the Vedas as the One Supreme Divinity, the Creator, Narayan, Hari.

नारायणादृषिगणास्तथा सिद्धमहोरगाः ।
देवा देवर्षयश्चैव यं विदुः परमव्ययम् ॥ १९ ॥

nārāyaṇādṛṣigaṇāstathā siddhamahoragāḥ |
devā devarṣayaścaiva yaṁ viduḥ paramavyayam || 19 ||

19. From Narayan to the multitude of rishis, then to the attained ones down to the demons, the gods and the godly rishis, you are known as the supreme unchanging imperishable.

देवदानवगन्धर्वा यक्षराक्षसपन्नगाः ।
यं न जानन्ति को ह्येष कुतो वा भगवानिति ॥ २० ॥

devadānavagandharvā yakṣarākṣasapannagāḥ |
yaṁ na jānanti ko hyeṣa kuto vā bhagavāniti || 20 ||

20. Not the gods, demons, gandarvas, yakshas, demons, nor snakes know from where in what manner you came to be the supreme divinity thusly (like this).

यस्मिन् विश्वानि भूतानि तिष्ठन्ति च विशन्ति च ।
गुणभूतानि भूतेशे सूत्रे मणिगणा इव ॥ २१ ॥

yasmin viśvāni bhūtāni tiṣṭhanti ca viśanti ca |
guṇabhūtāni bhūteśe sūtre maṇigaṇā iva || 21 ||

21. You are the supreme of all existence in which the entire universe and all created beings enter and are situated, like a multitude of gems upon a string.

यस्मिन्निन्ये तते तन्तौ दृढे स्रगिव तिष्ठति ।
सदसद्ग्रथितं विश्वं विश्वाङ्गे विश्वकर्मणि ॥ २२ ॥

yasminninye tate tantau dṛḍhe sragiva tiṣṭhati |
sadasadgrathitaṁ viśvaṁ viśvāṅge viśvakarmaṇi || 22 ||

22. You bring together the universe, being and non-being, stringing together (uniting) all limbs of the universe and all actions in the universe, you firmly establish (all the parts) like a garland on a string.

हरिं सहस्रशिरसं सहस्रचरणेक्षणम् ।
सहस्रबाहुमुकुटं सहस्रवदनोज्ज्वलम् ॥ २३ ॥

hariṁ sahasraśirasaṁ sahasracaraṇekṣaṇam |
sahasrabāhumukuṭaṁ sahasravadanojjvalam || 23 ||

23. You are Hari, shining with a thousand heads, a thousand feet and eyes, a thousand arms, a thousand faces wearing a thousand crowns.

प्राहुर्नारायणं देवं यं विश्वस्य परायणम् ।
अणीयसामणीयांसं स्थविष्ठं च स्थवीयसाम् ॥ २४ ॥

prāhurnārāyaṇaṁ devaṁ yaṁ viśvasya parāyaṇam |
aṇīyasāmaṇīyāṁsaṁ sthaviṣṭhaṁ ca sthavīyasām || 24 ||

24. You are called Narayana, the divinity which manifests as the eternal universe, the most subtle of the subtle and the most gross of the gross.

गरीयसां गरिष्ठं च श्रेष्ठं च श्रेयसामपि ।
यं वाकेष्वनुवाकेषु निषत्सूपनिषत्सु च ॥ २५ ॥

garīyasāṁ gariṣṭhaṁ ca śreṣṭhaṁ ca śreyasāmapi |
yaṁ vākeṣvanuvākeṣu niṣatsūpaniṣatsu ca || 25 ||

25. You are the heaviest of the heavy and most excellent of the excellent; of all words or vibrations, you are the most excellent vibration; of all esoteric philosophies, you are sitting in worship.

गृणन्ति सत्यकर्माणं सत्यं सत्येषु सामसु ।
चतुर्भिश्चतुरात्मानं सत्त्वस्थं सात्वतां पतिम् ॥ २६ ॥

gṛṇanti satyakarmāṇaṁ satyaṁ satyeṣu sāmasu |
caturbhiścaturātmānaṁ
sattvasthaṁ sātvatāṁ patim || 26 ||

26. In the Sama Veda (in all songs) you are sung of as the truth of the lord of truth, performing truthful activities. In the four Vedas you are established as the soul of the four, as the true lord who is the cause of true being.

यं दिव्यैर्देवमर्चन्ति गुह्यैः परमनामभिः ।
यस्मिन्नित्यं तपस्तप्तं मदङ्गेष्वनुतिष्ठति ॥ २७ ॥

yaṁ divyairdevamarcanti guhyaiḥ paramanāmabhiḥ |
yasminnityaṁ tapastaptaṁ madaṅgeṣvanutiṣṭhati || 27 ||

27. In secret the gods and other divine ones offer to your supreme name. Thus (in this situation) you have been established as the eternal ruler of inspiration, performing great purifying austerities.

सर्वात्मा सर्ववित् सर्वः सर्वज्ञः सर्वभावनः ।
यं देवं देवकी देवी वसुदेवादजीजनत् ॥ २८ ॥

sarvātmā sarvavit sarvaḥ sarvajñaḥ sarvabhāvanaḥ |
yaṁ devaṁ devakī devī vasudevādajījanat || 28 ||

28. You are the soul of all, all that can be known, who is all, the knower of all, and all attitudes in existence. You are the God to whom birth was given by the Goddess Devaki and Vasudeva.

भौमस्य ब्रह्मणो गुप्त्यै दीप्तमग्निमिवारणिः ।
यमनन्यो व्यपेताशीरात्मानं वीतकल्मषम् ॥ २९ ॥

bhaumasya brahmaṇo guptyai dīptamagnimivāraṇiḥ |
yamananyo vyapetāśīrātmānaṁ vītakalmaṣam || 29 ||

29. You are the supreme divinity of the earth, secretly hidden within like fire is hidden in the sacrificial wood. You are the indestructible soul, who through self-control and others, separated the light and caused the darkness to vanish.

दृष्ट्यानन्त्याय गोविन्दं पश्यत्यात्मानमात्मनि ।
अतिवाय्विन्द्रकर्माणमतिसूर्यातितेजसम् ॥ ३० ॥

dṛṣṭyānantyāya govindaṁ paśyatyātmānamātmani |
ativāyvindrakarmāṇamatisūryātitejasam || 30 ||

30. To see the soul of all souls, Govinda (who is one pointed light) with infinite perception, the extremely strong ruler of all activities, the radiant Sun emits brilliant illumination.

अतिबुद्धीन्द्रियात्मानं तं प्रपद्ये प्रजापतिम् ।
पुराणे पुरुषं प्रोक्तं ब्रह्म प्रोक्तं युगादिषु ॥ ३१ ॥

atibuddhīndriyātmānaṁ taṁ prapadye prajāpatim |
purāṇe puruṣaṁ proktaṁ
brahma proktaṁ yugādiṣu || 31 ||

31. You are the extremely intelligent soul of the senses. I surrender to the lord of all beings born; the ancient, full, complete, and perfect being. In all activities in all time, you are addressed as the supreme divinity.

क्षये सङ्कर्षणं प्रोक्तं तमुपास्यमुपास्महे ।
यमेकं बहुधाऽऽत्मानं प्रादुर्भूतमधोक्षजम् ॥ ३२ ॥

kṣaye saṅkarṣaṇaṁ proktaṁ tamupāsyamupāsmahe |
yamekaṁ bahudhā--tmānaṁ
prādurbhūtamadhokṣajam || 32 ||

32. You are addressed as the end of cultivating conflict (a name of Balaram), worshiped sitting near me in my darkness; the one soul who bestows the diversity of existence, the supreme transcendental lord.

नान्यभक्ताः क्रियावन्तो यजन्ते सर्वकामदम् ।
यमाहुर्जगतः कोशं यस्मिन् संनिहिताः प्रजाः ॥ ३३ ॥

nānyabhaktāḥ kriyāvanto yajante sarvakāmadam |
yamāhurjagataḥ kośaṁ yasmin saṁnihitāḥ prajāḥ || 33 ||

33. All desires pursued or performed by all devotees ultimately unite in you. Controlling the entire perceivable universe, you are the sheath or covering in which all beings born are deposited or fixed together.

यस्मिन् लोकाः स्फुरन्तीमे जले शकुनयो यथा ।
ऋतमेकाक्षरं ब्रह्म यत्तत्सदसतोः परम् ॥ ३४ ॥

yasmin lokāḥ sphurantīme jale śakunayo yathā |
ṛtamekākṣaraṁ brahma yattatsadasatoḥ param || 34 ||

34. In which all the worlds shake or tremble, including the waters and birds; the one, undivided (eternal), imperishable, supreme divinity, that is the supreme truth of all truths (true being of all existence).

अनादिमध्यपर्यन्तं न देवा नर्षयो विदुः ।
यं सुरासुरगन्धर्वाः सिद्धा ऋषिमहोरगाः ॥ ३५ ॥

anādimadhyaparyantaṁ na devā narṣayo viduḥ |
yaṁ surāsuragandharvāḥ siddhā ṛṣimahoragāḥ || 35 ||

35. You are known as the origin, the middle, and the end by the gods and the rishis. The gods, asuras, gandarvas, siddhas (attained beings), rishis, and demons

प्रयता नित्यमर्चन्ति परमं दुःखभेषजम् ।
अनादिनिधनं देवमात्मयोनिं सनातनम् ॥ ३६ ॥

prayatā nityamarcanti paramaṁ duḥkhabheṣajam |
anādinidhanaṁ devamātmayoniṁ sanātanam || 36 ||

36. eternally strive in offering to you, the supreme who eradicates pain. At the conclusion of existence you are invariably the eternal womb of the soul of the gods.

अप्रेक्ष्यमनभिज्ञेयं हरिं नारायणं प्रभुम् ।
यं वै विश्वस्य कर्तारं जगतस्तस्थुषां पतिम् ।
वदन्ति जगतोऽध्यक्षमक्षरं परमं पदम् ॥ ३७ ॥

aprekṣyamanabhijñeyaṁ
hariṁ nārāyaṇaṁ prabhum |
yaṁ vai viśvasya kartāraṁ
jagatastasthuṣāṁ patim |
vadanti jagato-dhyakṣam
akṣaraṁ paramaṁ padam || 37 ||

37. You are known by the knowledgable as Hari (the gross, subtle and causal bodies; or who creates, protects, and transforms), Narayana (who sees all), Lord; Lord over all actions and actors in the perceivable universe.

हिरण्यवर्णं यं गर्भमदितेर्दैत्यनाशनम् ।
एकं द्वादशधा जज्ञे तस्मै सूर्यात्मने नमः ॥ ३८ ॥

hiraṇyavarṇaṁ yaṁ garbhamaditerdaityanāśanam |
ekaṁ dvādaśadhā jajñe tasmai sūryātmane namaḥ || 38 ||

38. In the womb of non-duality, you of golden color destroy duality. Being One, you appeared as twelve, and therefore, we bow to the soul of the Sun (the light of wisdom).

(The 12 sons of Aditi, aka Adaityas, are the first of the Vedic Gods.)

शुक्ले देवान् पितॄन् कृष्णे तर्पयत्यमृतेन यः ।
यश्च राजा द्विजातीनां तस्मै सोमात्मने नमः ॥ ३९ ॥

śukle devān pitṝn kṛṣṇe tarpayatyamṛtena yaḥ |
yaśca rājā dvijātīnāṁ tasmai somātmane namaḥ || 39 ||

39. Oh Krishna, you are bright (illuminated) among the gods and ancestors, you who are honored in worship with the nectar of immortal bliss. You are the king, who has taken birth twice (once from the womb of wisdom and once from his mother, Devaki), and therefore, we bow to the soul of the Moon (the emblem of devotion).

महतस्तमसः पारे पुरुषं ह्यतितेजसम् ।
यं ज्ञात्वा मृत्युमत्येति तस्मै ज्ञेयात्मने नमः ॥ ४० ॥

mahatastamasaḥ pāre puruṣaṁ hyatitejasam |
yaṁ jñātvā mṛtyumatyeti
tasmai jñeyātmane namaḥ || 40 ||

40. You are the supreme full, complete, and perfect consciousness, of extreme illumination, whose greatness shines in the darkness; those who have wisdom of you put an end to thoughts of death, and therefore, we bow to the soul of Wisdom.

यं बृहन्तं बृहत्युक्थे यमग्नौ यं महाध्वरे ।
यं विप्रसङ्घा गायन्ति तस्मै वेदात्मने नमः ॥ ४१ ॥

yaṁ bṛhantaṁ bṛhatyukthe yamagnau yaṁ mahādhvare |
yaṁ viprasaṅghā gāyanti
tasmai vedātmane namaḥ || 41 ||

41. You are great and strong, united with strength, the great destructive power of Yama (Death) and Agni (Fire). The assembly of twice-born (brahmins) sing about you, and therefore, we bow to the soul of the Vedas (the wisdom to be known).

ऋग्यजुःसामधामानं दशार्धहविरात्मकम् ।
यं सप्ततन्तुं तन्वन्ति तस्मै यज्ञात्मने नमः ॥ ४२ ॥

ṛgyajuḥsāmadhāmānaṁ daśārdhahavirātmakam |
yaṁ saptatantuṁ tanvanti
tasmai yajñātmane namaḥ || 42 ||

42. You support the Rig, Yajur, and Sama Vedas, the soul of the five kinds of offerings to the fire; seven preceded you in the line of your descendants, and therefore, we bow to the soul of Yajna (sacrifice in union).

चतुर्भिश्च चतुर्भिश्च द्वाभ्यां पञ्चभिरेव च ।
हूयते च पुनर्द्वाभ्यां तस्मै होमात्मने नमः ॥ ४३ ॥

caturbhiśca caturbhiśca dvābhyāṁ pañcabhireva ca |
hūyate ca punardvābhyāṁ
tasmai homātmane namaḥ || 43 ||

43. With four and with four and with two and even with five; and offer again with two (the various meters of Sanskrit), and therefore, we bow to the soul of Homa (the shorter fire sacrifice to maintain divine union).

यः सुपर्णा यजुर्नाम छन्दोगात्रस्त्रिवृच्छिराः ।
रथन्तरं बृहत्साम तस्मै स्तोत्रात्मने नमः ॥ ४४ ॥

yaḥ suparṇā yajurnāma chandogātrastrivṛcchirāḥ |
rathantaraṁ bṛhatsāma tasmai stotrātmane namaḥ || 44 ||

44. In your collections of hymns, like the Yajur Veda and the Sama Veda, you arrange meters like Gayatri in the great songs of praise, and therefore, we bow to the soul of Stotrams (songs in praise of divinity).

यं सहस्रसमे सत्रे जज्ञे विश्वसृजामृषिः ।
हिरण्यपक्षः शकुनिस्तस्मै हंसात्मने नमः ॥ ४५ ॥

yaṁ sahasrasame satre jajñe viśvasṛjāmṛṣiḥ |
hiraṇyapakṣaḥ śakunistasmai haṁsātmane namaḥ || 45 ||

45. By concentrating together thousands, you created this universe; as a rishi perceiving the birth of discrimination in the golden (bright) fortnight, and therefore, we bow to the soul of the swan (discrimination).

पदाङ्गं सन्धिपर्वाणं स्वरव्यञ्जनभूषणम् ।
यमाहुरक्षरं दिव्यं तस्मै वागात्मने नमः ॥ ४६ ॥

padāṅgaṁ sandhiparvāṇaṁ svaravyañjanabhūṣaṇam |
yamāhurakṣaraṁ divyaṁ
tasmai vāgātmane namaḥ || 46 ||

46. Individual syllables joined together in various ways, displaying a wealth of tunes and melodies; with self-control offered as oblations to the divine, and therefore, we bow to the soul of all vibrations.

यज्ञाङ्गो यो वराहो वै भूत्वा गामुज्जहार ह ।
लोकत्रयहितार्थाय तस्मै वीर्यात्मने नमः ॥ ४७ ॥

yajñāṅgo yo varāho vai bhūtvā gāmujjahāra ha |
lokatrayahitārthāya tasmai vīryātmane namaḥ || 47 ||

47. When the earth was being carried away, uniting the various limbs of sacrifice, in the form of the boar of sacrifice, and therefore, we bow to the soul of heroism and all heroes.

यः शेते योगमास्थाय पर्यङ्के नागभूषिते ।
फणासहस्ररचिते तस्मै निद्रात्मने नमः ॥ ४८ ॥

yaḥ śete yogamāsthāya paryaṅke nāgabhūṣite |
phaṇāsahasraracite tasmai nidrātmane namaḥ || 48 ||

48. You were situated in bliss, sleeping in mystical union, while sitting in a posture for meditation looking like a snake. The snake absorbed in consciousness in the sahasrara chakra (crown of the head), and therefore, we bow to the soul of sleep.

यस्तनोति सतां सेतुमृतेनामृतयोनिना ।
धर्मार्थव्यवहाराङ्गैस्तस्मै सत्यात्मने नमः ॥ ४९ ॥

yastanoti satāṁ setumṛtenāmṛtayoninā |
dharmārthavyavahārāṅgais
tasmai satyātmane namaḥ || 49 ||

49. You established all things in true existence as the bridge from death to the womb of eternal life; dharma, artha, the limbs of behavior, and therefore, we bow to the soul of truth.

यं पृथग्धर्मचरणाः पृथग्धर्मफलैषिणः ।
पृथग्धर्मैः समर्चन्ति तस्मै धर्मात्मने नमः ॥ ५० ॥

yaṁ pṛthagdharmacaraṇāḥ pṛthagdharmaphalaiṣiṇaḥ |
pṛthagdharmaiḥ samarcanti
tasmai dharmātmane namaḥ || 50 ||

50. You are the individual limbs of moving or behaving with dharma, the individual fruits of acting with dharma, the individual ways of offering with dharma, and therefore, we bow to the soul of dharma.

यतः सर्वे प्रसूयन्ते ह्यनङ्गात्माङ्गदेहिनः ।
उन्मादः सर्वभूतानां तस्मै कामात्मने नमः ॥ ५१ ॥

yataḥ sarve prasūyante hyanaṅgātmāṅgadehinaḥ |
unmādaḥ sarvabhūtānāṁ
tasmai kāmātmane namaḥ || 51 ||

51. The soul of the body became manifest in the embodiment of all children (creation) through restraint or self-control; making all manifested creation mad (with desire), and therefore, we bow to the soul of desire.

यं च व्यक्तस्थमव्यक्तं विचिन्वन्ति महर्षयः ।
क्षेत्रे क्षेत्रज्ञमासीनं तस्मै क्षेत्रात्मने नमः ॥ ५२ ॥

yaṁ ca vyaktasthamavyaktaṁ vicinvanti maharṣayaḥ |
kṣetre kṣetrajñamāsīnaṁ
tasmai kṣetrātmane namaḥ || 52 ||

52. The great rishis contemplate you as the being who is individual and universal; who is the field, who is the knower of the field without end, and therefore, we bow to the soul of the field.

यं त्रिधाऽऽत्मानमात्मस्थं वृतं षोडशभिर्गुणैः ।
प्राहुः सप्तदशं सांख्यास्तस्मै सांख्यात्मने नमः ॥ ५३ ॥

yaṁ tridhā--tmānamātmasthaṁ vṛtaṁ ṣoḍaśabhirguṇaiḥ |
prāhuḥ saptadaśaṁ sāṁkhyās
tasmai sāṁkhyātmane namaḥ || 53 ||

53. You are established with the three gunas as the soul of all souls existing, worshiped with sixteen articles; expressed in the enumeration of the seventeen (Stoma-17 parts of a Sanskrit Hymn), and therefore, we bow to the soul of the enumeration of the (twenty-four) principles.

यं विनिद्रा जितश्वासाः सत्त्वस्थाः संयतेन्द्रियाः ।
ज्योतिः पश्यन्ति युञ्जानास्तस्मै योगात्मने नमः ॥ ५४ ॥

yaṁ vinidrā jitaśvāsāḥ sattvasthāḥ saṁyatendriyāḥ |
jyotiḥ paśyanti yuñjānāstasmai yogātmane namaḥ || 54 ||

54. In wakefulness you are the breath of life established in truth, controlling the senses. You are successful at seeing the light, and therefore, we bow to the soul of yoga (the perfection of union).

अपुण्यपुण्योपरमे यं पुनर्भवनिर्भयाः ।
शान्ताः संन्यासिनो यान्ति तस्मै मोक्षात्मने नमः ॥ ५५ ॥

apuṇyapuṇyoparame yaṁ punarbhavanirbhayāḥ |
śāntāḥ saṁnyāsino yānti
tasmai mokṣātmane namaḥ || 55 ||

55. You are the supreme merit of all merits, again granting freedom from fear to all existence. Sannyasis (renunciates) attain to peace, and therefore, we bow to the soul of liberation.

योऽसौ युगसहस्रान्ते प्रदीप्तार्चिर्विभावसुः ।
सम्भक्षयति भूतानि तस्मै घोरात्मने नमः ॥ ५६ ॥

yo-sau yugasahasrānte pradīptārcirvibhāvasuḥ |
sambhakṣayati bhūtāni tasmai ghorātmane namaḥ || 56 ||

56. You offer light until the destruction of the worlds at the end of a thousand ages of time, and therefore, we bow to the soul of the frightful.

संभक्ष्य सर्वभूतानि कृत्वा चैकार्णवं जगत् ।
बालः स्वपिति यश्चैकस्तस्मै मायात्मने नमः ॥ ५७ ॥

saṁbhakṣya sarvabhūtāni kṛtvā caikārṇavaṁ jagat |
bālaḥ svapiti yaścaikastasmai māyātmane namaḥ || 57 ||

57. You devoured the perceivable world as one ocean of all existence. Children thus dream of you as the One, and therefore, we bow to the soul of Maya (the measurement of all that can be perceived).

तद्यस्य नाभ्यां सम्भूतं यस्मिन् विश्वं प्रतिष्ठितम् ।
पुष्करे पुष्कराक्षस्य तस्मै पद्मात्मने नमः ॥ ५८ ॥

tadyasya nābhyāṁ sambhūtaṁ
yasmin viśvaṁ pratiṣṭhitam |
puṣkare puṣkarākṣasya
tasmai padmātmane namaḥ || 58 ||

58. All existence and the entire universe is established within your naval, most excellent of all excellence, and therefore, we bow to the soul of the lotus (the wealth of peace).

सहस्रशिरसे चैव पुरुषायामितात्मने ।
चतुःसमुद्रपर्याययोगनिद्रात्मने नमः ॥ ५९ ॥

sahasraśirase caiva puruṣāyāmitātmane |
catuḥsamudraparyāyayoganidrātmane namaḥ || 59 ||

59. The full, complete, and perfect consciousness, the soul of that which cannot be measured, has a thousand heads, pervading the four (ages of time), the ocean of creation, and therefore, we bow to the soul of the sleep of mystical union.

यस्य केशेषु जीमूता नद्यः सर्वाङ्गसन्धिषु ।
कुक्षौ समुद्राश्चत्वारस्तस्मै तोयात्मने नमः ॥ ६० ॥

yasya keśeṣu jīmūtā nadyaḥ sarvāṅgasandhiṣu |
kukṣau samudrāścatvārastasmai toyātmane namaḥ || 60 ||

60. In the hair (on the summit) the sustainer of all is praised, and in the abdomen where all limbs are joined and the many oceans meet, and therefore, we bow to the soul of water.

यस्मात् सर्वाः प्रसूयन्ते सर्गप्रलयविक्रियाः ।
यस्मिंश्चैव प्रलीयन्ते तस्मै हेत्वात्मने नमः ॥ ६१ ॥

yasmāt sarvāḥ prasūyante sargapralayavikriyāḥ |
yasmiṁścaiva pralīyante
tasmai hetvātmane namaḥ || 61 ||

61. In which all of the children of existence, all created beings in manifestation, dissolved; and in which they even disappear, and therefore, we bow to the soul of motivation.

यो निषण्णो भवेद्रात्रौ दिवा भवति विष्ठितः ।
इष्टानिष्टस्य च द्रष्टा तस्मै द्रष्टात्मने नमः ॥ ६२ ॥

yo niṣaṇṇo bhavedrātrau divā bhavati viṣṭhitaḥ |
iṣṭāniṣṭasya ca draṣṭā tasmai draṣṭātmane namaḥ || 62 ||

62. While still or stationary night becomes day and the two become separated (distinguished), the judge or witness who discriminates (distinguishes) between the desirable and the not desired, and therefore, we bow to the soul of judgment.

अकुण्ठं सर्वकार्येषु धर्मकार्यार्थमुद्यतम् ।
वैकुण्ठस्य च तद्रूपं तस्मै कार्यात्मने नमः ॥ ६३ ॥

akuṇṭhaṁ sarvakāryeṣu dharmakāryārthamudyatam |
vaikuṇṭhasya ca tadrūpaṁ
tasmai kāryātmane namaḥ || 63 ||

63. Eternal in the performance of all appropriate actions, laboring diligently in causing the ideal of perfection and necessary resources, intrinsic to that form, and therefore, we bow to the soul of appropriate actions.

त्रिःसप्तकृत्वो यः क्षत्रं धर्मव्युत्क्रान्तगौरवम् ।
क्रुद्धो निजघ्ने समरे तस्मै क्रौर्यात्मने नमः ॥ ६४ ॥

triḥsaptakṛtvo yaḥ kṣatraṁ dharmavyutkrāntagauravam |
kruddho nijaghne samare
tasmai krauryātmane namaḥ || 64 ||

64. You fiercely destroyed the warrior and administrative class who transgressed dharma (the ideal of perfection) twenty-one times, striking down cruelty coming together in hostile encounter, and therefore, we bow to the soul of cruelty.

विभज्य पञ्चधाऽऽत्मानं वायुर्भूत्वा शरीरगः ।
यश्चेष्टयति भूतानि तस्मै वाय्वात्मने नमः ॥ ६५ ॥

vibhajya pañcadhā--tmānaṁ vāyurbhūtvā śarīragaḥ |
yaśceṣṭayati bhūtāni tasmai vāyvātmane namaḥ || 65 ||

65. Distinguishing the five elements of the supreme soul, like wind, existence became embodied; you make efforts for all existence, and therefore, we bow to the soul of the wind.

युगेष्वावर्तते योगैर्मासर्त्वयनहायनैः ।
सर्गप्रलययोः कर्ता तस्मै कालात्मने नमः ॥ ६६ ॥

yugeṣvāvartate yogairmāsartvayanahāyanaiḥ |
sargapralayayoḥ kartā tasmai kālātmane namaḥ || 66 ||

66. You are Lord in union, helper to revolve the months in the ages of time. You extinguish all created beings at the time of dissolution, and therefore, we bow to the soul of the Time.

ब्रह्म वक्त्रं भुजौ क्षत्रं कृत्स्नमूरूदरं विशः ।
पादौ यस्याश्रिताः शूद्रास्तस्मै वर्णात्मने नमः ॥ ६७ ॥

brahma vaktraṁ bhujau kṣatraṁ
kṛtsnamūrūdaraṁ viśaḥ |
pādau yasyāśritāḥ śūdrās
tasmai varṇātmane namaḥ || 67 ||

67. Brahmins were created as your head, your arms are kshatriya, vaishyas are in the thighs, and shudras take refuge in your feet, and therefore, we bow to the soul of all colors, creeds, and tribes.

यस्याग्निरास्यं द्यौर्मूर्द्धा खं नाभिश्चरणौ क्षितिः ।
सूर्यश्चक्षुर्दिशः श्रोत्रे तस्मै लोकात्मने नमः ॥ ६८ ॥

yasyāgnirāsyaṁ dyaurmūrddhā
khaṁ nābhiścaraṇau kṣitiḥ |
sūryaścakṣurdiśaḥ śrotre tasmai lokātmane namaḥ || 68 ||

68. You apportioned fire to the sun, the highest portion of the heavens and space to the naval, the earth to the feet, eyes and ears to all the directions, and therefore, we bow to the soul of the worlds.

परः कालात् परो यज्ञात् परात्परतरश्च यः ।
अनादिरादिर्विश्वस्य तस्मै विश्वात्मने नमः ॥ ६९ ॥

paraḥ kālāt paro yajñāt parātparataraśca yaḥ |
anādirādirviśvasya tasmai viśvātmane namaḥ || 69 ||

69. You are superior to time, superior to sacrifice, above and beyond and more superior still. You are one and the same among the multitude of variables of the universe, and therefore, we bow to the soul of the universe.

विषये वर्तमानानां यं तं वैशेषिकैर्गुणैः ।
प्राहुर्विषयगोप्तारं तस्मै गोप्त्रात्मने नमः ॥ ७० ॥

viṣaye vartamānānāṁ yaṁ taṁ vaiśeṣikairguṇaiḥ |
prāhurviṣayagoptāraṁ tasmai goptrātmane namaḥ || 70 ||

70. You are the qualities enumerated in the Vaisheshika Philosophy, the various ideas of the present time, expression of the concepts most secret, and therefore, we bow to the soul of He who is concealed within the universe (also protector of the universe).

अन्नपानेन्धनमयो रसप्राणविवर्धनः ।
यो धारयति भूतानि तस्मै प्राणात्मने नमः ॥ ७१ ॥

annapānendhanamayo rasaprāṇavivardhanaḥ |
yo dhārayati bhūtāni tasmai prāṇātmane namaḥ || 71 ||

71. Food, drink, manifestations of wealth increasing the nectar of life, you who support all beings, and therefore, we bow to the soul of the life force.

प्राणानां धारणार्थाय योऽन्नं भुङ्क्ते चतुर्विधम् ।
अन्तर्भूतः पचत्यग्निस्तस्मै पाकात्मने नमः ॥ ७२ ॥

prāṇānāṁ dhāraṇārthāya yo-nnaṁ bhuṅkte caturvidham |
antarbhūtaḥ pacatyagnistasmai pākātmane namaḥ || 72 ||

72. You are the meaning (objective) of all living beings who enjoy various kinds of foods in various ways. Fire devours the elements within, and therefore, we bow to the soul of fire.

पिङ्गेक्षणसटं यस्य रूपं दंष्ट्रानखायुधम् ।
दानवेन्द्रान्तकरणं तस्मै दृप्तात्मने नमः ॥ ७३ ॥

piṅgekṣaṇasaṭaṁ yasya rūpaṁ daṁṣṭrānakhāyudham |
dānavendrāntakaraṇaṁ tasmai dṛptātmane namaḥ || 73 ||

73. Your form with eyes red with anger fighting with tusks and nails (claws) (Varaha) is the cause of the end of the king of the Danavas (Hiranyaksha), and therefore, we bow to the soul of arrogance or pride.

यं न देवा न गन्धर्वा न दैत्या न च दानवाः ।
तत्त्वतो हि विजानन्ति तस्मै सूक्ष्मात्मने नमः ॥ ७४ ॥

yaṁ na devā na gandharvā na daityā na ca dānavāḥ |
tattvato hi vijānanti tasmai sūkṣmātmane namaḥ || 74 ||

74. Neither the gods, nor the gandarvas, nor the daityas (beings of duality), nor the danavas (enemies of the gods), none of them know you through the principles (of philosophy), and therefore, we bow to the soul of subtle body.

रसातलगतः श्रीमाननन्तो भगवान् विभुः ।
जगद्धारयते कृत्स्नं तस्मै वीर्यात्मने नमः ॥ ७५ ॥

rasātalagataḥ śrīmānananto bhagavān vibhuḥ |
jagaddhārayate kṛtsnaṁ tasmai vīryātmane namaḥ || 75 ||

75. The supreme sovereign, the respected supreme divinity, created the infinite and supports the perceivable universe extending from the lowest worlds, and therefore, we bow to the soul of the hero.

यो मोहयति भूतानि स्नेहपाशानुबन्धनैः ।
सर्गस्य रक्षणार्थाय तस्मै मोहात्मने नमः ॥ ७६ ॥

yo mohayati bhūtāni snehapāśānubandhanaiḥ |
sargasya rakṣaṇārthāya tasmai mohātmane namaḥ || 76 ||

76. You delude all beings born by binding them with the bonds of love. For the purpose of protecting all beings born, and therefore, we bow to the soul of the delusion.

आत्मज्ञानमिदं ज्ञानं ज्ञात्वा पञ्चस्ववस्थितम् ।
यं ज्ञानेनाभिगच्छन्ति तस्मै ज्ञानात्मने नमः ॥ ७७ ॥

ātmajñānamidaṁ jñānaṁ jñātvā pañcasvavasthitam |
yaṁ jñānenābhigacchanti
tasmai jñānātmane namaḥ || 77 ||

77. Remaining with the five senses steady and controlled, they know wisdom and this soul of wisdom, they attain you in the naval of wisdom, and therefore, we bow to the soul of the wisdom.

अप्रमेयशरीराय सर्वतोबुद्धिचक्षुषे ।
अनन्तपरिमेयाय तस्मै दिव्यात्मने नमः ॥ ७८ ॥

aprameyaśarīrāya sarvatobuddhicakṣuṣe |
anantaparimeyāya tasmai divyātmane namaḥ || 78 ||

78. Seeing all with the eyes of intelligence, your immeasurable body is infinite and supreme beyond all measurement, and therefore, we bow to the soul of divinity.

जटिने दण्डिने नित्यं लम्बोदरशरीरिणे ।
कमण्डलुनिषङ्गाय तस्मै ब्रह्मात्मने नमः ॥ ७९ ॥

jaṭine daṇḍine nityaṁ lambodaraśarīriṇe |
kamaṇḍaluniṣaṅgāya tasmai brahmātmane namaḥ || 79 ||

79. With matted locks of hair (a pious mendicant), bearing a staff, eternal, with a body with a big belly; with a water pot, a sword, and therefore, we bow to the soul of the supreme divinity (Brahma the creator).

शूलिने त्रिदशेशाय त्र्यम्बकाय महात्मने ।
भस्मदिग्धाङ्गलिङ्गाय तस्मै रुद्रात्मने नमः ॥ ८० ॥

śūline tridaśeśāya tryambakāya mahātmane |
bhasmadigdhāṅgaliṅgāya
tasmai rudrātmane namaḥ || 80 ||

80. The great soul with a spear, ruler of the three worlds, father of the three; wearing ashes, whose body fills all the directions as the subtle body, and therefore, we bow to the soul of the reliever from sufferings (Rudra).

चन्द्रार्धकृतशीर्षाय व्यालयज्ञोपवीतिने ।
पिनाकशूलहस्ताय तस्मा उग्रात्मने नमः ॥ ८१ ॥

candrārdhakṛtaśīrṣāya vyālayajñopavītine |
pinākaśūlahastāya tasmā ugrātmane namaḥ || 81 ||

81. Who wears the half moon upon his head, a tiger skin, and a sacred thread, in his hand he holds the trident spear named Pinak, and therefore, we bow to the soul of he who is terribly fierce (Shiva).

सर्वभूतात्मभूताय भूतादिनिधनाय च ।
अक्रोधद्रोहमोहाय तस्मै शान्तात्मने नमः ॥ ८२ ॥

sarvabhūtātmabhūtāya bhūtādinidhanāya ca |
akrodhadrohamohāya tasmai śāntātmane namaḥ || 82 ||

82. Who is all the elements, the soul of all existence, the conclusion of all existence as well; free from anger, he causes injury to those deluded by attachment, and therefore, we bow to the soul of peace.

यस्मिन् सर्वं यतः सर्वं यः सर्वं सर्वतश्च यः ।
यश्च सर्वमयो नित्यं तस्मै सर्वात्मने नमः ॥ ८३ ॥

yasmin sarvaṁ yataḥ sarvaṁ
yaḥ sarvaṁ sarvataśca yaḥ |
yaśca sarvamayo nityaṁ
tasmai sarvātmane namaḥ || 83 ||

83. You are all, in which all is controlled, you are totally all and everywhere, you are the eternal manifestation of all, and therefore, we bow to the soul of all.

विश्वकर्मन्नमस्तेऽस्तु विश्वात्मन् विश्वसम्भव ।
अपवर्गोऽसि भूतानां पञ्चानां परतः स्थित ॥ ८४ ॥

viśvakarmannamaste-stu viśvātman viśvasambhava |
apavargo-si bhūtānāṁ pañcānāṁ parataḥ sthita || 84 ||

84. We bow to you creator of the universe, soul of the universe, performer of all actions in the universe; you are the final beatitude of all existence, situated above all the fives.

नमस्ते त्रिषु लोकेषु नमस्ते परतस्त्रिषु ।
नमस्ते दिक्षु सर्वासु त्वं हि सर्वमयो निधिः ॥ ८५ ॥

namaste triṣu lokeṣu namaste paratastriṣu |
namaste dikṣu sarvāsu tvaṁ hi sarvamayo nidhiḥ || 85 ||

85. We bow to you who are the three worlds, we bow to you who are beyond the three worlds; we bow to you who are in every direction, you are the manifestation of the storehouse (ocean) of treasure.

नमस्ते भगवन् विष्णो लोकानां प्रभवाप्यय ।
त्वं हि कर्त्ता हृषीकेश संहर्ता चापराजितः ॥ ८६ ॥

namaste bhagavan viṣṇo lokānāṁ prabhavāpyaya |
tvaṁ hi karttā hṛṣīkeśa saṁhartā cāparājitaḥ || 86 ||
86. We bow to you supreme divinity, Vishnu, who disperses light upon the worlds. You are the creator, the ruler of the senses, into which all dissolves and unable to be defeated.

नहि पश्यामि ते भावं दिव्यं हि त्रिषु वर्त्मसु ।
त्वां तु पश्यामि तत्त्वेन यत्ते रूपं सनातनम् ॥ ८७ ॥

nahi paśyāmi te bhāvaṁ divyaṁ hi triṣu vartmasu |
tvāṁ tu paśyāmi tattvena yatte rūpaṁ sanātanam || 87 ||
87. No one in the three (worlds) can perceive your attitude of divinity according to the standard methods. Your form can only be perceived by means of the eternal principles (of philosophy).

दिवं ते शिरसा व्याप्तं पद्भ्यां देवी वसुन्धरा ।
विक्रमेण त्रयो लोकाः पुरुषोऽसि सनातनः ॥ ८८ ॥

divaṁ te śirasā vyāptaṁ padbhyāṁ devī vasundharā |
vikrameṇa trayo lokāḥ puruṣo-si sanātanaḥ || 88 ||
88. Each day the earth goddess places her head at your feet, to you who traverse the three worlds. You are distinguished as the full, complete, and perfect eternal.

दिशो भुजा रविश्चक्षुर्वीर्ये शुक्रः प्रतिष्ठितः ।
सप्त मार्गा निरुद्धास्ते वायोरमिततेजसः ॥ ८९ ॥

diśo bhujā raviścakṣurvīrye śukraḥ pratiṣṭhitaḥ |
sapta mārgā niruddhāste vāyoramitatejasaḥ || 89 ||
89. Your purity is established as the victorious hero, your arms fill all the directions, the sun is the unmeasured light in your eyes. Unobstructed are the seven paths through which the wind moves.

अतसीपुष्पसंकाशं पीतवाससमच्युतम् ।
ये नमस्यन्ति गोविन्दं न तेषां विद्यते भयम् ॥ ९० ॥

atasīpuṣpasaṁkāśaṁ pītavāsasamacyutam |
ye namasyanti govindaṁ
na teṣāṁ vidyate bhayam || 90 ||

90. You who are dressed in yellow cloth, appearing like a multitude of flowers permanently strung together, those who bow to you Govinda (who is one-pointed light) do not know any fear.

एकोऽपि कृष्णस्य कृतः प्रणामो
दशाश्वमेधावभृथेन तुल्यः ।
दशाश्वमेधी पुनरेति जन्म
कृष्णप्रणामी न पुनर्भवाय ॥ ९१ ॥

eko-pi kṛṣṇasya kṛtaḥ praṇāmo
daśāśvamedhāvabhṛthena tulyaḥ |
daśāśvamedhī punareti janma
kṛṣṇapraṇāmī na punarbhavāya || 91 ||

91. Bowing only to the one Krishna is equal to the performance of ten horse sacrifices. Who performs ten horse sacrifices will not be born again. Again there is no greater benefit than bowing to Krishna.

कृष्णव्रताः कृष्णमनुस्मरन्तो
रात्रौ च कृष्णं पुनरुत्थिता ये ।
ते कृष्णदेहाः प्रविशन्ति कृष्ण-
माज्यं यथा मन्त्रहुतं हुताशे ॥ ९२ ॥

kṛṣṇavratāḥ kṛṣṇamanusmaranto
rātrau ca kṛṣṇaṁ punarutthitā ye |
te kṛṣṇadehāḥ praviśanti kṛṣṇa-
mājyaṁ yathā mantrahutaṁ hutāśe || 92 ||

92. Krishna is the vow of worship, Krishna is the cherished recollection. Again Krishna took his birth in the night. Those who

take shelter in the body of Krishna, enter into Krishna, just like offerings of ghee enter into the divine fire (who eats oblations) with mantras.

नमो नरकसंत्राससरक्षामण्डलकारिणे ।
संसारनिम्नगावर्ततरिकाष्ठाय विष्णवे ॥ ९३ ॥

namo narakasaṁtrāsarakṣāmaṇḍalakāriṇe |
saṁsāranimnagāvartatarikāṣṭhāya viṣṇave || 93 ||

93. We bow to Vishnu, the cause of the circle which protects from the fears of hell, who is a boat which crosses the ocean of world in but an instant.

नमो ब्रह्मण्यदेवाय गोब्राह्मणहिताय च ।
जगद्धिताय कृष्णाय गोविन्दाय नमो नमः ॥ ९४ ॥

namo brahmaṇyadevāya gobrāhmaṇahitāya ca |
jagaddhitāya kṛṣṇāya govindāya namo namaḥ || 94 ||

94. We bow to to the supreme divinity, to god, to the benefactor and illuminator of brahmins, who is pleased by the perceivable universe, to Krishna, to Govinda we bow, we bow.

प्राणकान्तारपाथेयं संसारोच्छेदभेषजम् ।
दुःखशोकपरित्राणं हरिरित्यक्षरद्वयम् ॥ ९५ ॥

prāṇakāntārapātheyaṁ saṁsārocchedabheṣajam |
duḥkhaśokaparitrāṇaṁ haririty akṣaradvayam || 95 ||

95. The two letters, Hari, thus put an end to the journey of the life force through the ocean of worldliness, the remedy for curing or taking away pain and grief.

यथा विष्णुमयं सत्यं यथा विष्णुमयं जगत् ।
यथा विष्णुमयं सर्वं पाप्मा मे नश्यतां तथा ॥ ९६ ॥

yathā viṣṇumayaṁ satyaṁ
yathā viṣṇumayaṁ jagat |
yathā viṣṇumayaṁ sarvaṁ
pāpmā me naśyatāṁ tathā || 96 ||

96. It is this Vishnu that is my truth, and it is this Vishnu that is my world. It is this Vishnu that is my all. Please destroy all sin.

त्वां प्रपन्नाय भक्ताय गतिमिष्टां जिगीषवे ।
यच्छ्रेयः पुण्डरीकाक्ष तद्ध्यायस्व सुरोत्तम ॥ ९७ ॥

tvāṁ prapannāya bhaktāya gatimiṣṭāṁ jigīṣave |
yacchreyaḥ puṇḍarīkākṣa taddhyāyasva surottama || 97 ||
97. You are acknowledged by devotees desiring excellence as the chosen support. Oh one with lotus eyes, chief among the gods, in meditation you are the bliss of final emancipation.

इति विद्यातपोयोनिरयोनिर्विष्णुरीडितः ।
वाग्यज्ञेनार्चितो देवः प्रीयतां मे जनार्दनः ॥ ९८ ॥

iti vidyātapoyonirayonirviṣṇurīḍitaḥ |
vāgyajñenārcito devaḥ prīyatāṁ me janārdanaḥ || 98 ||
98. Thus the unborn Vishnu was praised as the womb of pure knowledge, offering vibrations in sacrifice to the god most beloved by me, Janardana (lord of beings).

नारायणः परं ब्रह्म नारायणपरं तपः ।
नारायणः परो देवः सर्वं नारायणः सदा ॥ ९९ ॥

nārāyaṇaḥ paraṁ brahma nārāyaṇaparaṁ tapaḥ |
nārāyaṇaḥ paro devaḥ sarvaṁ nārāyaṇaḥ sadā || 99 ||
99. The manifestation of consciousness is the supreme divinity, the manifestation of consciousness is the highest austerity, the manifestation of consciousness is the supreme god. Everything is the manifestation of consciousness.

वैशम्पायन उवाच

vaiśampāyana uvāca
Vaishampayana said:

एतावदुक्त्वा वचनं भीष्मस्तद्गतमानसः ।
नम इत्येव कृष्णाय प्रणाममकरोत्तदा ॥ १०० ॥

etāvaduktvā vacanaṁ bhīṣmastadgatamānasaḥ |
nama ityeva kṛṣṇāya praṇāmamakarottadā || 100 ||

100. Having spoken these words with a concentrated mind, Bhishma bowed to Krishna, offering his greatest respect.

अभिगम्य तु योगेन भक्तिं भीष्मस्य माधवः ।
त्रैलोक्यदर्शनं ज्ञानं दिव्यं दत्त्वा ययौ हरिः ॥ १०१ ॥

abhigamya tu yogena bhaktiṁ bhīṣmasya mādhavaḥ |
trailokyadarśanaṁ jñānaṁ
divyaṁ dattvā yayau hariḥ || 101 ||

101. Having been approached with Bhishma's devotion by means of Yoga, Madhava (who is always sweet), another name for Hari (who is the gross, subtle, and causal bodies) bestowed divine wisdom and the intuitive perception of the three worlds.

तस्मिन्नुपरते शब्दे ततस्ते ब्रह्मवादिनः ।
भीष्मं वाग्भिर्वाष्पकण्ठास्तमानर्चुर्महामतिम् ॥ १०२ ॥

tasminnuparate śabde tataste brahmavādinaḥ |
bhīṣmaṁ vāgbhirvāṣpakaṇṭhās
tamānarcurmahāmatim || 102 ||

102. In this way Bhishma shared these supremely divine words with tears in his eyes and his throat choked with the emotions of this great thinker.

ते स्तुवन्तश्च विप्राग्र्याः केशवं पुरुषोत्तमम् ।
भीष्मं च शनकैः सर्वे प्रशशंसुः पुनः पुनः ॥ १०३ ॥

te stuvantaśca viprāgryāḥ keśavaṁ puruṣottamam |
bhīṣmaṁ ca śanakaiḥ sarve
praśaśaṁsuḥ punaḥ punaḥ || 103 ||

103. Praise has been sung to you, Keshava, most excellent among men, by the well versed (proficient) twice born (brahmin). Bhishma and all increasingly offered praise again and again.

विदित्वा भक्तियोगं तु भीष्मस्य पुरुषोत्तमः ।
सहसोत्थाय संहृष्टो यानमेवान्वपद्यत ॥ १०४ ॥

viditvā bhaktiyogaṁ tu bhīṣmasya puruṣottamaḥ |
sahasotthāya saṁhṛṣṭo yānamevānvapadyata || 104 ||

104. You are known by the devotional yoga of Bhishma, most excellent among men, who gave birth to these syllables (verses), the vehicle which produces all delight.

केशवः सात्यकिश्चापि रथेनैकेन जग्मतुः ।
अपरेण महात्मानौ युधिष्ठिरधनञ्जयौ ॥ १०५ ॥

keśavaḥ sātyakiścāpi rathenaikena jagmatuḥ |
apareṇa mahātmānau yudhiṣṭhiradhanañjayau || 105 ||

105. Keshava and Satyaki rose upon one chariot and by its means set out (commenced their journey), followed by those two great souls, Yudhishthira and Dhananjaya (Arjuna - who is victorious over wealth).

भीमसेनो यमौ चोभौ रथमेकं समाश्रिताः ।
कृपो युयुत्सुः सूतश्च सञ्जयश्च परंतपः ॥ १०६ ॥

bhīmaseno yamau cobhau rathamekaṁ samāśritāḥ |
kṛpo yuyutsuḥ sūtaśca sañjayaśca paraṁtapaḥ || 106 ||

106. Bhimasen rode a chariot and the twins (Nakula and Sahadeva) took refuge in one chariot; Kripa, Yuyutsu, and the master charioteer Sanjay, purified through great austerities.

ते रथैर्नगराकारैः प्रयाताः पुरुषर्षभाः ।
नेमिघोषेण महता कम्पयन्तो वसुन्धराम् ॥ १०७ ॥

te rathairnagarākāraiḥ prayātāḥ puruṣarṣabhāḥ |
nemighoṣeṇa mahatā kampayanto vasundharām || 107 ||

107. In that appearance those eminent people arrived by their chariots in the city. The noise from the chariots of those great beings caused the earth to shake.

ततो गिरः पुरुषवरस्तवान्विता
द्विजेरिताः पथि सुमनाः स शुश्रुवे ।
कृताञ्जलिं प्रणतमथापरं जनं
स केशिहा मुदितमनाभ्यनन्दत ॥ १०८ ॥

tato giraḥ puruṣavarastavānvitā
dvijeritāḥ pathi sumanāḥ sa śuśruve |
kṛtāñjaliṁ praṇatamathāparaṁ janaṁ
sa keśihā muditamanābhyanandata || 108 ||

108. This is the speech sung about the full, complete, and perfect being by the excellent twice-born (brahmin) who knows the excellent way to have an excellent mind, which is excellent for all to hear. With hands folded in respect we bow to he who is certainly the supreme individual, who delighted minds and filled them with bliss by destroying the demon Keshi, who has long hair or a wild mane.

इति श्रीमहाभारते शान्तिपर्वणि राजधर्मानुशासनपर्वणि
भीष्मस्तवराजः समाप्तः ॥

iti śrīmahābhārate śāntiparvaṇi
rājadharmānuśāsanaparvaṇi
bhīṣmastavarājaḥ samāptaḥ ||

Thus ends the Bhishma Stava Raj (King of Songs of Bhishma) from the section on the dharma of kings in the Section on Peace within the Respected Mahabharata Scripture.

अथ अनुस्मृतिः

atha anusmṛtiḥ

And now, the Remembrance of the Most Subtle

शतानीक उवाच

śatānīka uvāca

Shatanik Said:

महामते महाप्राज्ञ सर्वशास्त्रविशारद ।
अक्षीणकर्मबन्धस्तु पुरुषो द्विजसत्तम ॥ १ ॥

mahāmate mahāprājña sarvaśāstraviśārada |
akṣīṇakarmabandhastu puruṣo dvijasattama || 1 ||

1. Oh great thinker, great knowledgeable being, having knowledge of all the scriptures, you are united in unfailing actions, full, complete, and perfect consciousness, most excellent among the twice-born.

सततं किं जपेज्जाप्यं विबुधः किमनुस्मरन् ।
मरणे यज्जपेज्जाप्यं यं च भावमनुस्मरन् ॥ २ ॥

satataṁ kiṁ japejjāpyaṁ vibudhaḥ kimanusmaran |
maraṇe yajjapejjāpyaṁ yaṁ ca bhāvamanusmaran || 2 ||

2. Whose mantra do you always recite and think about in the remembrance of the Most Subtle? At the time of death, which mantra do you recite, and with what attitude do you remember the Most Subtle?

यं च ध्यात्वा द्विजश्रेष्ठ पुरुषो मृत्युमागतः ।
परं पदमवाप्नोति तन्मे वद महामुने ॥ ३ ॥

yaṁ ca dhyātvā dvijaśreṣṭha puruṣo mṛtyumāgataḥ |
paraṁ padamavāpnoti tanme vada mahāmune || 3 ||

3. When death is approaching, upon whom do you meditate in order to reach the highest station, most excellent, full, complete, and perfect consciousness among the twice-born? Oh great wise being, please tell me.

शौनक उवाच

śaunaka uvāca
Shaunak said:

इदमेव महाप्राज्ञ पृष्टवांश्च पितामहम् ।
भीष्मं धर्मभृतां श्रेष्ठं धर्मपुत्रो युधिष्ठिरः ॥ ४ ॥

idameva mahāprājña pṛṣṭavāṁśca pitāmaham |
bhīṣmaṁ dharmabhṛtāṁ śreṣṭhaṁ
dharmaputro yudhiṣṭhiraḥ || 4 ||
4. This truly great knowledge was asked from the Great Grandfather, Bhishma, most excellent supporter of the Ideals of Perfection, by the son of Dharma, Yudhishthira.

युधिष्ठिर उवाच

yudhiṣṭhira uvāca
Yudhishthira said

पितामह महाप्राज्ञ सर्वशास्त्रविशारद ।
प्रयाणकाले किं जप्यं मोक्षिभिस्तत्त्वचिन्तकैः ॥ ५ ॥

pitāmaha mahāprājña sarvaśāstraviśārada |
prayāṇakāle kiṁ japyaṁ mokṣibhistattvacintakaiḥ || 5 ||
5. Oh Great Grandfather, great knowledgeable being, having knowledge of all the scriptures, at the time of death, what mantra should we recite, and which principles should we contemplate to attain liberation?

किमनुस्मरन् कुरुश्रेष्ठ मरणे पर्युपस्थिते ।
प्राप्नुयात्परमां सिद्धिं श्रोतुमिच्छामि तत्त्वतः ॥ ६ ॥

kimanusmaran kuruśreṣṭha maraṇe paryupasthite |
prāpnuyātparamāṁ siddhiṁ
śrotumicchāmi tattvataḥ || 6 ||
6. At the time of death how do we remember and honor the Most Subtle, oh most excellent of those who act? How do we attain the Supreme Perfection? I wish to listen to these principles.

भीष्म उवाच

bhīṣma uvāca
Bhishma said:

सद्युक्तिस्वहितः सूक्ष्म उक्तः प्रश्नस्त्वयानघ ।
शृणुष्वावहितो राजन्नारदेन पुरा श्रुतम् ॥ ७ ॥

sadyuktisvahitaḥ sūkṣma uktaḥ praśnastvayānagha |
śṛṇuṣvāvahito rājannāradena purā śrutam || 7 ||
7. Your question is about uniting with the subtle in communion. Listen, oh King, to the answer that Narad heard.

श्रीवत्साङ्कं जगद्बीजमनन्तं लोकसाक्षिणम् ।
पुरा नारायणं देवं नारदः परिपृष्टवान् ॥ ८ ॥

śrīvatsāṅkaṁ jagadbījamanantaṁ lokasākṣiṇam |
purā nārāyaṇaṁ devaṁ nāradaḥ paripṛṣṭavān || 8 ||
8. Vishnu (who embodies all creation), the infinite twice-born (knowledgeable one) of the perceivable universe, is the witness of all the worlds. Once before Narad asked this question of God Narayana.

नारद उवाच

nārada uvāca
Narad said:

त्वमक्षरं परं ब्रह्म निर्गुणं तमसः परम् ।
आहुर्वेद्यं परं धाम ब्रह्मादि कमलोद्भवम् ॥ ९ ॥

tvamakṣaraṁ paraṁ brahma nirguṇaṁ tamasaḥ param |
āhurvedyaṁ paraṁ dhāma
brahmādi kamalodbhavam || 9 ||
9. You are imperishable, the Supreme Creator, beyond all qualities, supreme above the darkness. You are the Supreme Residence of Knowledge for the creator and others who have their being in the lotus.

भगवन् भूतभव्येश श्रद्दधानैर्जितेन्द्रियैः ।
कथं भक्तैर्विचिन्त्योऽसि योगिभिर्मोक्षकाङ्क्षिभिः ॥ १० ॥

bhagavan bhūtabhavyeśa śraddadhānairjitendriyaiḥ |
kathaṁ bhaktairvicintyo-si
yogibhirmokṣakāṅkṣibhiḥ || 10 ||

10. One Supreme Divinity, Lord of All Existence, who has controlled His senses with faith, by thinking upon which words with devotion can we attain to union and liberation?

किं च जाप्यं जपेन्नित्यं कल्यमुत्थाय मानवः ।
कथं युञ्जन् सदा ध्यायेद् ब्रूहि तत्त्वं सनातनम् ॥ ११ ॥

kiṁ ca jāpyaṁ japennityaṁ kalyamutthāya mānavaḥ |
kathaṁ yuñjan sadā dhyāyed
brūhi tattvaṁ sanātanam || 11 ||

11. By which mantras and by which constant recitation can human beings increase in welfare? Continually meditating upon which words? Please tell me this eternal principle.

भीष्म उवाच

bhīṣma uvāca

Bhishma said:

श्रुत्वा तस्य तु देवर्षेर्वाक्यं वाचस्पतिः स्वयं ।
प्रोवाच भगवान्विष्णुर्नारदं वरदः प्रभुः ॥ १२ ॥

śrutvā tasya tu devarṣervākyaṁ vācaspatiḥ svayaṁ |
provāca bhagavānviṣṇurnāradaṁ varadaḥ prabhuḥ || 12 ||

12. Having heard the words from the Devarishi (seer among the Gods, Narad) the Lord of Vibrations himself, the Supreme Lord Vishnu blessed Narad with this answer.

श्रीभगवानुवाच

śrībhagavānuvāca

The Respected Supreme Divinity said:

हन्त ते कथयिष्यामि इमां दिव्यामनुस्मृतिम् ।
यामधीत्य प्रयाणे तु मद्भावायोपपद्यते ॥ १३ ॥

hanta te kathayiṣyāmi imāṁ divyāmanusmṛtim |
yāmadhītya prayāṇe tu madbhāvāyopapadyate || 13 ||
13. Pay attention as I tell you this divine remembrance of the Most Subtle. At the advance of departure (death) by restraining contemplations in my attitude, one becomes qualified.

ॐकारमग्रतः कृत्वा मां नमस्कृत्य नारद ।
एकाग्रः प्रयतो भूत्वा इमं मन्त्रमुदीरयेत् ॥ १४ ॥

oṁkāramagrataḥ kṛtvā māṁ namaskṛtya nārada |
ekāgraḥ prayato bhūtvā imaṁ mantramudīrayet || 14 ||
14. Narad, bowing to Me, while reciting the holy syllable Om, striving for unity with all existence, one should chant my mantra

ॐ नमो भगवते वासुदेवायेति ।
इत्युक्तो नारदः प्राह प्राञ्जलिः प्रणतः स्थितः ।
सर्वदेवेश्वरं विष्णुं सर्वात्मानं हरिं प्रभुम् ॥ १५ ॥

oṁ namo bhagavate vāsudevāyeti |
ityukto nāradaḥ prāha prāñjaliḥ praṇataḥ sthitaḥ |
sarvadeveśvaraṁ viṣṇuṁ
sarvātmānaṁ hariṁ prabhum || 15 ||
15. thusly: "Om Namo Bhagavate Vasudevaya."
Narad, one should remain bowing in union with the hands folded with respect before the Supreme Lord of all Gods, to He who pervades all, to the Soul of all, to Hari (who is the gross body, subtle body, causal body), to the Lord.

नारद उवाच

nārada uvāca
Narad said:

अव्यक्तं शाश्वतं देवं प्रभवं पुरुषोत्तमम् ।
प्रपद्ये प्राञ्जलिर्विष्णुमक्षरं परं पदम् ॥ १६ ॥

avyaktaṁ śāśvataṁ devaṁ prabhavaṁ puruṣottamam |
prapadye prāñjalirviṣṇumakṣaraṁ paraṁ padam || 16 ||
16. He is whole, eternal, God, Lord, the most excellent full, complete, and perfect consciousness. With folded hands I offer my full surrender to Vishnu, the imperishable Supreme Being.

पुराणं प्रभवं नित्यमक्षयं लोकसाक्षिणम् ।
प्रपद्ये पुण्डरीकाक्षमीशं भक्तानुकम्पिनम् ॥ १७ ॥

purāṇaṁ prabhavaṁ nityamakṣayaṁ lokasākṣiṇam |
prapadye puṇḍarīkākṣamīśaṁ bhaktānukampinam || 17 ||
17. Most ancient, Lord, un-decaying, eternal, witness of the worlds; I offer my full surrender to Lord Vishnu (who has lotus eyes), who is compassionate to devotees.

लोकनाथं सहस्राक्षमद्भुतं परमं पदम् ।
भगवन्तं प्रपन्नोऽस्मि भूतभव्यभवत्प्रभुम् ॥ १८ ॥

lokanāthaṁ sahasrākṣamadbhutaṁ paramaṁ padam |
bhagavantaṁ prapanno-smi
bhūtabhavyabhavatprabhum || 18 ||
18. Lord of the Worlds, who has a thousand parts, who is whole, the incredible Supreme Being. I acknowledge him as the Supreme Being, Lord of past, present, and future.

स्रष्टारं सर्वलोकानामनन्तं विश्वतोमुखम् ।
पद्मनाभं हृषीकेशं प्रपद्ये सत्यमच्युतम् ॥ १९ ॥

sraṣṭāraṁ sarvalokānāmanantaṁ viśvatomukham |
padmanābhaṁ hṛṣīkeśaṁ
prapadye satyamacyutam || 19 ||

19. Creator of all the worlds, without name, infinite, the mouth of the universe; with a lotus in his naval, ruler of the senses, I offer my full surrender to imperishable Truth.

हिरण्यगर्भममृतं भूगर्भं परतः परम् ।
प्रभोः प्रभुमनाद्यन्तं प्रपद्ये तं रविप्रभम् ॥ २० ॥

hiraṇyagarbhamamṛtaṁ bhūgarbhaṁ parataḥ param |
prabhoḥ prabhumanādyantaṁ
prapadye taṁ raviprabham || 20 ||

20. The nectar of eternal bliss in the golden womb, the womb of existence, the Supreme, and again superior; the Lord, Lord who is infinite, without beginning or end, I offer my full surrender to the source of the sun.

सहस्रशीर्षं पुरुषं महर्षिं तत्त्वभावनम् ।
प्रपद्ये सूक्ष्ममचलं वरेण्यमभयप्रदम् ॥ २१ ॥

sahasraśīrṣaṁ puruṣaṁ maharṣiṁ tattvabhāvanam |
prapadye sūkṣmamacalaṁ
vareṇyamabhayapradam || 21 ||

21. The great seers who contemplate the principles see Him as the full, complete, and perfect consciousness with a thousand heads. I offer my full surrender to the subtle beyond movement, to the highest, who grants freedom from fear.

नारायणं पुराणर्षिं योगात्मानं सनातनम् ।
संस्थानं सर्वतत्त्वानां प्रपद्ये ध्रुवमीश्वरम् ॥ २२ ॥

nārāyaṇaṁ purāṇarṣiṁ yogātmānaṁ sanātanam |
saṁsthānaṁ sarvatattvānāṁ
prapadye dhruvamīśvaram || 22 ||

22. Narayana, the ancient seer, the Soul of Union, who is eternal; established within all principles, I offer my full surrender to the supreme lord of Druva, the north star (who is full of devotion).

यः प्रभुः सर्वभूतानां येन सर्वमिदं ततम् ।
चराचरगुरुर्विष्णुः स मे देवः प्रसीदतु ॥ २३ ॥

yaḥ prabhuḥ sarvabhūtānāṁ yena sarvamidaṁ tatam |
carācaragururviṣṇuḥ sa me devaḥ prasīdatu || 23 ||

23. You are Lord of all existence by means of which all this and that exists. Vishnu, the Guru of all that moves and moves not, may that God be gracious to me.

यस्मादुत्पद्यते ब्रह्मा पद्मयोनिः पितामहः ।
ब्रह्मयोनिर्हि विश्वात्मा स मे विष्णुः प्रसीदतु ॥ २४ ॥

yasmādutpadyate brahmā padmayoniḥ pitāmahaḥ |
brahmayonirhi viśvātmā sa me viṣṇuḥ prasīdatu || 24 ||

24. From whence came forth the creator who was born in the lotus womb, the great-grandfather; the Womb of the Creator, the Soul of the Universe, may that Vishnu be gracious to me.

यः पुरा प्रलये प्राप्ते नष्टे स्थावरजङ्गमे ।
ब्रह्मादिषु प्रलिनेषु नष्टे लोके परावरे ॥ २५ ॥

yaḥ purā pralaye prāpte naṣṭe sthāvarajaṅgame |
brahmādiṣu pralineṣu naṣṭe loke parāvare || 25 ||

25. That most ancient Being, existing from the beginning as the cause of dissolution, whether gained or lost, that which is still or which changes; who is both divine consciousness and worldly unconsciousness, who is both cause and effect.

आभूतसंप्लवे चैव प्रलीने प्रकृतौ महान् ।
एकस्तिष्ठति विश्वात्मा स मे विष्णुः प्रसीदतु ॥ २६ ॥

ābhūtasaṁplave caiva pralīne prakṛtau mahān |
ekastiṣṭhati viśvātmā sa me viṣṇuḥ prasīdatu || 26 ||

26. Incredible is the submersion of unconsciousness in the greatness (vastness) of Nature; and also the Soul of the Universe established in the One, may that Vishnu be gracious to me.

चतुर्भिश्च चतुर्भिश्च द्वाभ्यां पञ्चभिरेव च ।
हूयते च पुनर्द्वाभ्यां स मे विष्णुः प्रसीदतु ॥ २७ ॥

caturbhiśca caturbhiśca dvābhyāṁ pañcabhireva ca |
hūyate ca punardvābhyāṁ sa me viṣṇuḥ prasīdatu || 27 ||

27. By four and by four, by two and even by five, offered again to the original two, may that Vishnu be gracious to me.

पर्जन्यः पृथिवी सस्यं कालो धर्मः क्रियाक्रिये ।
गुणाकरः स मे बभ्रुर्वासुदेवः प्रसीदतु ॥ २८ ॥

parjanyaḥ pṛthivī sasyaṁ kālo dharmaḥ kriyākriye |
guṇākaraḥ sa me babhrurvāsudevaḥ prasīdatu || 28 ||

28. Because of the merits of Dharma, the Ideal of Perfection, both what has been done and what has not been done, rain comes to earth; the fiery horse of sacrifice, manifesting its qualities, may that Vasudeva be gracious to me.

अग्निषोमार्कताराणां ब्रह्मरुद्रेन्द्रयोगिनाम् ।
यस्तेजयति तेजांसि स मे विष्णुः प्रसीदतु ॥ २९ ॥

agniṣomārkatārāṇāṁ brahmarudrendrayogināṁ |
yastejayati tejāṁsi sa me viṣṇuḥ prasīdatu || 29 ||

29. Fire, the moon, the sun, and the stars, Brahma the Creator, Rudra the Reliever of Suffering, Indra the Rule of the Pure, and the yogis; they illuminate That with their brilliant illumination, may that Vishnu be gracious to me.

योगावास नमस्तुभ्यं सर्वावास वरप्रद ।
यज्ञगर्भ हिरण्याङ्ग पञ्चयज्ञ नमोऽस्तु ते ॥ ३० ॥

yogāvāsa namastubhyaṁ sarvāvāsa varaprada |
yajñagarbha hiraṇyāṅga pañcayajña namo-stu te || 30 ||

30. I bow down to the practices of yoga, which grant the boon of all control; the womb of sacrifice, with golden limbs, I bow down to the five sacrifices.

चतुर्मूर्ते परं धाम लक्ष्म्यावास परार्चित ।
सर्ववास नमस्तेऽस्तु वासुदेव प्रधानकृत् ॥ ३१ ॥

caturmūrte paraṁ dhāma lakṣmyāvāsa parārcita |
sarvavāsa namaste-stu vāsudeva pradhānakṛt || 31 ||

31. The four images of divinity residing in the Supreme Residence are the goal of the Supreme Offering. I bow to you, Vasudeva, the Supreme Universal Soul, who controls all.

अजस्त्वमगमः पन्था ह्यमूर्तिर्विश्वमूर्तिधृक् ।
विकर्तः पञ्चकालज्ञ नमस्ते ज्ञानसागर ॥ ३२ ॥

ajastvamagamaḥ panthā hyamūrtirviśvamūrtidhṛk |
vikartaḥ pañcakālajña namaste jñānasāgara || 32 ||

32. You are the image of divinity, the leader, the universal image of divine support, who came by this ancient path; dividing the five seasons, I bow to the Ocean of Wisdom.

अव्यक्ताद्व्यक्तमुत्पन्नं व्यक्ताद्यस्तु परोऽक्षरः ।
यस्मात् परतरं नास्ति तमस्मि शरणं गतः ॥ ३३ ॥

avyaktādvyaktamutpannaṁ vyaktādyastu paro-kṣaraḥ |
yasmāt parataraṁ nāsti tamasmi śaraṇaṁ gataḥ || 33 ||

33. The Supreme Imperishable, which gives birth to both the individual and the universal, from which there is nothing greater than His Being, this is understood as taking refuge.

न प्रधानो न च महान् पुरुषश्चेतनो ह्यजः ।
अनयोर्यः परतरस्तमस्मि शरणं गतः ॥ ३४ ॥

na pradhāno na ca mahān puruṣaścetano hyajaḥ |
anayoryaḥ paratarastamasmi śaraṇaṁ gataḥ || 34 ||

34. There is no superior and no greater of which humans can be conscious; for both speakers and listeners there is nothing greater than His Being, this is understood as taking refuge.

चिन्तयन्तो हि यं नित्यं ब्रह्मेशानादयः प्रभुम् ।
निश्चयं नाधिगच्छन्ति तमस्मि शरणं गतः ॥ ३५ ॥

cintayanto hi yaṁ nityaṁ brahmeśānādayaḥ prabhum |
niścayaṁ nādhigacchanti tamasmi śaraṇaṁ gataḥ || 35 ||

35. Brahma and Shiva contemplate you eternally as the subtle body of sound, oh Lord; without a doubt they come into union, this is understood as taking refuge.

जितेन्द्रिया महात्मानो ज्ञानध्यानपरायणाः ।
यं प्राप्य न निवर्तन्ते तमस्मि शरणं गतः ॥ ३६ ॥

jitendriyā mahātmāno jñānadhyānaparāyaṇāḥ |
yaṁ prāpya na nivartante tamasmi śaraṇaṁ gataḥ || 36 ||

36. Who has conquered the senses, the Great Soul, whose only goal is wisdom and meditation; he achieves and in return he gives, this is understood as taking refuge.

एकांशेन जगत्सर्वमवष्ठभ्य विभुः स्थितः ।
अग्राह्यो निर्गुणो नित्यस्तमस्मि शरणं गतः ॥ ३७ ॥

ekāṁśena jagatsarvamavaṣṭhabhya vibhuḥ sthitaḥ |
agrāhyo nirguṇo nityastamasmi śaraṇaṁ gataḥ || 37 ||

37. Who is established in all circumstances, by means of which the perceivable universe is known, whose perception is eternally rejected (not to be perceived) because it is beyond all qualities, this is understood as taking refuge.

सोमार्काग्निमयं तेजो या च तारामयी द्युतिः ।
दिवि संजायते योऽयं स महात्मा प्रसीदतु ॥ ३८ ॥

somārkāgnimayaṁ tejo yā ca tārāmayī dyutiḥ |
divi saṁjāyate yo-yaṁ sa mahātmā prasīdatu || 38 ||

38. The brightness of the light of the moon, the sun, the fire, and the stars in the sky, is victorious when that Great Soul is pleased.

गुणादिर्निर्गुणश्चाद्यो लक्ष्मीवांश्चेतनो ह्यजः ।
सूक्ष्मः सर्वगतो योगी स महात्मा प्रसीदतु ॥ ३९ ॥

guṇādirnirguṇaścādyo lakṣmīvāṁścetano hyajaḥ |
sūkṣmaḥ sarvagato yogī sa mahātmā prasīdatu || 39 ||

39. Who is with qualities and beyond qualities, illuminates that ancient consciousness, is the wealth of the Goddess of Wealth. When a yogi completely merges in the subtle body, that great soul is pleased.

सांख्ययोगाश्च ये चान्ये सिद्धाश्च परमर्षयः ।
यं विदित्वा विमुच्यन्ते स महात्मा प्रसीदतु ॥ ४० ॥

sāṁkhyayogāśca ye cānye siddhāśca paramarṣayaḥ |
yaṁ viditvā vimucyante sa mahātmā prasīdatu || 40 ||

40. The union with the enumeration of the principles and other principles by the adepts who attained perfection, the supreme seers of eternal truth; with this knowledge they are liberated, that Great Soul is pleased.

अव्यक्तः समधिष्ठाता ह्यचिन्त्यः सदसत्परः ।
आस्थितिः प्रकृतिश्रेष्ठः स महात्मा प्रसीदतु ॥ ४२ ॥

avyaktaḥ samadhiṣṭhātā hyacintyaḥ sadasatparaḥ |
āsthitiḥ prakṛtiśreṣṭhaḥ sa mahātmā prasīdatu || 42 ||

41. Presiding over the undivided existence, always thinking of the highest truth; in constant motion, the ultimate of nature, that Great Soul is pleased.

क्षेत्रज्ञः पञ्चधा भुङ्क्ते प्रकृतिं पञ्चभिर्मुखैः ।
महान् गुणांश्च यो भुङ्क्ते स महात्मा प्रसीदतु ॥ ४२ ॥

kṣetrajñaḥ pañcadhā bhuṅkte
prakṛtiṁpañcabhirmukhaiḥ |
mahān guṇāṁśca yo bhuṅkte
sa mahātmā prasīdatu || 42 ||

42. Knower of the field, supporter and chief, who enjoys the five elements of nature; and who enjoys great qualities, that Great Soul is pleased.

सूर्यमध्ये स्थितः सोमस्तस्य मध्ये च या स्थिता ।
भूतबाह्या च या दीप्तिः स महात्मा प्रसीदतु ॥ ४३ ॥

sūryamadhye sthitaḥ somastasya madhye ca yā sthitā |
bhūtabāhyā ca yā dīptiḥ sa mahātmā prasīdatu || 43 ||

43. Stationed in the midst of the sun, and stationed in the middle of the moon; illuminating all existence with light, that Great Soul is pleased.

नमस्ते सर्वतः सर्व सर्वतोऽक्षिशिरोमुख ।
निर्विकार नमस्तेऽस्तु साक्षी क्षेत्रे व्यवस्थितः ॥ ४४ ॥

namaste sarvataḥ sarva sarvato-kṣiśiromukha |
nirvikāra namaste-stu sākṣī kṣetre vyavasthitaḥ || 44 ||

44. I bow to your All, the Totality, to You, whose head is above all; I bow to You who does not change, witness of the field of circumstances.

अतीन्द्रिय नमस्तुभ्यं लिङ्गैर्व्यक्तैर्न मीयसे ।
ये च त्वां नाभिजानन्ति संसारे संसरन्ति ते ॥ ४५ ॥

atīndriya namastubhyaṁ liṅgairvyaktairna mīyase |
ye ca tvāṁ nābhijānanti saṁsāre saṁsaranti te || 45 ||

45. I bow to You who is beyond the senses, whose subtle and individual forms will not perish. They know you as the chief, or center, in the ocean of objects and relationships, revolving through the cycles of birth and death.

कामक्रोधविनिर्मुक्ता रागद्वेषविवर्जिताः ।
नान्यभक्ता विजानन्ति न पुनर्नारका द्विजाः ॥ ४६ ॥

kāmakrodhavinirmuktā rāgadveṣavivarjitāḥ |
nānyabhaktā vijānanti na punarnārakā dvijāḥ || 46 ||

46. Becoming liberated from desire and anger, prohibiting enmity with the vicissitudes of life, You cannot be known by those who are not devotees, such as the twice-born who purify the inhabitants of hell.

एकान्तिनो हि निर्द्वन्द्वा निराशीः कर्मकारिणः ।
ज्ञानाग्निदग्धकर्माणस्त्वां विशन्ति विनिश्चिताः ॥ ४७ ॥

ekāntino hi nirdvandvā nirāśīḥ karmakāriṇaḥ |
jñānāgnidagdhakarmāṇastvāṁ viśanti viniścitāḥ || 47 ||

47. You are One, the Ultimate Being without conflict, without desires, the cause of all action; inauspicious actions have a decided meaning as they enter the fire of Your Wisdom.

अशरीरं शरीरस्थं समं सर्वेषु देहिषु ।
पुण्यपापविनिर्मुक्ता भक्तास्त्वां प्रविशन्त्युत ॥ ४८ ॥

aśarīraṁ śarīrasthaṁ samaṁ sarveṣu dehiṣu |
puṇyapāpavinirmuktā bhaktāstvāṁ praviśantyuta || 48 ||

48. You are the same wearer of the body in all, whether situated in a body or without. Liberated from both merit and sin, Your devotees enter into You or take shelter in You.

अव्यक्तं बुद्ध्यहंकारमनोभूतेन्द्रियाणि च ।
त्वयि तानि च तेषु त्वं न तेषु त्वं न ते त्वयि ॥ ४९ ॥

avyaktaṁ buddhyahaṁkāramanobhūtendriyāṇi ca |
tvayi tāni ca teṣu tvaṁ na teṣu tvaṁ na te tvayi || 49 ||

49. Beyond individuality, intellect, ego, mind, and the senses of all beings; all of them, all living entities are in You, and You are in all living entities, all of them.

एकत्वान्यत्वनानात्वं ये विदुर्यान्ति ते परम् ।
समोऽसि सर्वभूतेषु न ते द्वेष्योऽस्ति न प्रियः ॥ ५० ॥

ekatvānyatvanānatvaṁ ye viduryānti te param |
samo-si sarvabhūteṣu na te dveṣyo-sti na priyaḥ || 50 ||

50. You are understood as the Supreme by those who love You as the one beloved; the same in all existence with no duality or enmity.

समत्वमभिकाङ्क्षेऽहं भक्त्या वै नान्यचेतसा ।
चराचरमिदं सर्वं भूतग्रामं चतुर्विधम् ॥ ५१ ॥

samatvamabhikāṅkṣe-haṁ bhaktyā vai nānyacetasā |
carācaramidaṁ sarvaṁ bhūtagrāmaṁ caturvidham || 51 ||

51. Longing for You exclusively in four ways (dhyan, jnan, bhakti, karma), with no other thoughts, like other devotees, I (perceive) this all, moving and unmoving, as the village of existence.

त्वया त्वय्येव तत्प्रोतं सूत्रे मणिगणा इव ।
स्रष्टा भोक्तासि कूटस्थो ह्यतत्त्वस्तत्त्वसंज्ञितः ॥ ५२ ॥

tvayā tvayyeva tatprotaṁ sūtre maṇigaṇā iva |
sraṣṭā bhoktāsi kūṭastho hyatattvastattvasaṁjñitaḥ || 52 ||

52. By You and You alone all is strung together like a number of gems on a thread. In the beginning, the creator established the multitude of principles and knowledge of the principles for His enjoyment.

अकर्महेतुरचलः पृथगात्मन्यवस्थितः ।
न मे भूतेषु संयोगो भूततत्त्वगुनातिगः ॥ ५३ ॥

akarmaheturacalaḥ pṛthagātmanyavasthitaḥ |
na me bhūteṣu saṁyogo bhūtatattvagunātigaḥ || 53 ||

53. The circumstances of the individual soul are motivated by non-action and non-movement. You are in all existence completely united with all, as the principle beyond all qualities.

अहंकारेण बुद्ध्या वा न ते योगस्त्रिभिर्गुणैः ।
न ते धर्मोऽस्त्यधर्मो वा नारम्भो जन्म वा पुनः ॥ ५४ ॥

ahaṁkāreṇa buddhyā vā na te yogastribhirguṇaiḥ |
na te dharmo-styadharmo vā
nārambho janma vā punaḥ || 54 ||

54. You are the cause of the ego "I", the intellect, and in union with the three qualities (satya, raja, tamas). You are the Ideal of Perfection, and human beings who understand You as the Ideal of Perfection, will not take birth again.

जरामरणमोक्षार्थं त्वां प्रपन्नोऽस्मि सर्वशः ।
ईश्वरोऽसि जगन्नाथ ततः परम उच्यसे ॥ ५५ ॥

jarāmaraṇamokṣārthaṁ tvāṁ prapanno-smi sarvaśaḥ |
īśvaro-si jagannātha tataḥ parama ucyase || 55 ||

55. Oh all powerful, for the purpose of (achieving) liberation from old age and death, I am propitiating you! You are the Supreme Consciousness, Lord of the Perceivable World, from whence you rise to the highest extreme limit.

भक्तानां यद्धितं देव तद्ध्याहि त्रिदशेश्वर ।
विषयैरिन्द्रियैर्वापि न मे भूयः समागमः ॥ ५६ ॥

bhaktānāṁ yaddhitaṁ deva taddhyāhi tridaśeśvara |
viṣayairindriyairvāpi na me bhūyaḥ samāgamaḥ || 56 ||

56. The thirty Vedic Gods (Indra, Agni, etc.) meditate on the God with Devotion and Knowledge. The senses provide an abundance for my well of thoughts, you assemble together in unity.

पृथिवीं यातु मे घ्राणं यातु मे रसना जलम् ।
रूपं हुताशनं यातु स्पर्शो यातु च मारुतम् ॥ ५७ ॥

pṛthivīṁ yātu me ghrāṇaṁ yātu me rasanā jalam |
rūpaṁ hutāśanaṁ yātu sparśo yātu ca mārutam || 57 ||

57. Earth incites my sense of smell, water incites my sense of taste; fire incites my sense of form (sight), wind incites my sense of touch.

श्रोत्रमाकाशमप्येतु मनो वैकारिकं पुनः ।
इन्द्रियाण्यपि संयान्तु स्वासु स्वासु च योनिषु ॥ ५८ ॥

śrotramākāśamapyetu mano vaikārikaṁ punaḥ |
indriyāṇyapi saṁyāntu svāsu svāsu ca yoniṣu || 58 ||

58. Hearing comes from the ether, the mind from intuitive feeling again; all the senses come together, and one's own being is in the womb.

पृथिवी यातु सलिलमापोऽग्निमनलोऽनिलम् ।
वायुराकाशमप्येतु मनश्चाकाश एव च ॥ ५९ ॥

pṛthivī yātu salilamāpo-gnimanalo-nilam |
vāyurākāśamapyetu manaścākāśa eva ca || 59 ||

59. Earth incites rain from the waters, the fire from fire, and the wind from the wind; the ether is connected with the ether, and the ether is connected with thought.

अहंकारं मनो यातु मोहनं सर्वदेहिनाम् ।
अहंकारस्ततो बुद्धिं बुद्धिरव्यक्तमच्युत ॥ ६० ॥

ahaṁkāraṁ mano yātu mohanaṁ sarvadehinām |
ahaṁkārastato buddhiṁ buddhiravyaktamacyuta || 60 ||

60. The sense of ego "I" compels all to manifest in individual bodies, which incites the delusion of the mind. Then the sense of ego "I" brings forth intelligence, and from the intellect arises understanding of individual separation.

प्रधाने प्रकृतिं याते गुणसाम्ये व्यवस्थिते ।
वियोगः सर्वकरणैर्गुणभूतैश्च मे भवेत् ॥ ६१ ॥

pradhāne prakṛtiṁ yāte guṇasāmye vyavasthite |
viyogaḥ sarvakaraṇairguṇabhūtaiśca me bhavet || 61 ||

61. Foremost is Nature which controls the circumstances and conditions of the qualities. For the one who is in union, all the causes of all qualities of existence become me.

निष्कैवल्यपदं तात काङ्क्षेऽहं परमं तव ।
एकीभावस्त्वया मेऽस्तु न मे जन्म भवेत् पुनः ॥ ६२ ॥

niṣkaivalyapadaṁ tāta kāṅkṣe-haṁ paramaṁ tava |
ekībhāvastvayā me-stu na me janma bhavet punaḥ || 62 ||

62. In that condition of absolute unity I only desire the Highest Supreme. Only one attitude of me being in You, and for me there will not be birth again.

त्वद्बुद्धिस्त्वद्गतप्राणस्त्वद्भक्तस्त्वत्परायणः ।
त्वामेवाहं स्मरिष्यामि मरणे पर्युपस्थिते ॥ ६३ ॥

tvadbuddhistvadgataprāṇastvadbhaktastvatparāyaṇaḥ |
tvāmevāhaṁ smariṣyāmi maraṇe paryupasthite || 63 ||

63. That understanding, that movement, that life force, that devotion, that is the highest goal. I am actually You! I wish to remember THAT at the time when death is imminent.

पूर्वदेहकृता ये मे व्याधयः प्रविशन्तु माम् ।
अर्दयन्तु च दुःखानि ऋणं मे प्रतिमुञ्चतु ॥ ६४ ॥

pūrvadehakṛtā ye me vyādhayaḥ praviśantu mām |
ardayantu ca duḥkhāni ṛṇaṁ me pratimuñcatu || 64 ||

64. Father allowed disease to take shelter in me, which distresses me with pains, and debts which must be repaid.

अनुध्यातोऽसि देवेश न मे जन्म भवेत्पुनः ।
तस्माद् ब्रवीमि कर्माणि ऋणं मे न भवेदिति ॥ ६५ ॥

anudhyāto-si deveśa na me janma bhavetpunaḥ |
tasmād bravīmi karmāṇi ṛṇaṁ me na bhavediti || 65 ||

65. I meditate upon the Subtle Lord of Gods, and for me there will not be birth again. Therefore, I am speaking about karma, and in this way debts will not be incurred.

उपतिष्ठन्तु मां सर्वे व्याधयः पूर्वसंचिताः ।
अनृणो गन्तुमिच्छामि तद्विष्णोः परमं पदम् ॥ ६६ ॥

upatiṣṭhantu māṁ sarve vyādhayaḥ pūrvasaṁcitāḥ |
anṛṇo gantumicchāmi tadviṣṇoḥ paramaṁ padam || 66 ||

66. All maladies and old thoughts honor and follow me. I desire to be a traveler free from debt, with Vishnu as the attainment.

श्रीभगवानुवाच

śrībhagavānuvāca

The Respected Supreme Divinity said:

अहं भगवतस्तस्य मम चासौ सनातनः ।
तस्याहं न प्रणश्यामि स च मे न प्रणश्यति ॥ ६७ ॥

ahaṁ bhagavatastasya mama cāsau sanātanaḥ |
tasyāhaṁ na praṇaśyāmi sa ca me na praṇaśyati || 67 ||

67. I am the Supreme Divinity that is eternal. I am not lost to him, and he is not lost to me.

कर्मेन्द्रियाणि संयम्य पञ्च बुद्धिन्द्रियाणि च ।
दशेन्द्रियाणि मनसि अहंकारे तथा मनः ॥ ६८ ॥

karmendriyāṇi saṁyamya pañca buddhindriyāṇi ca |
daśendriyāṇi manasi ahaṁkāre tathā manaḥ || 68 ||

68. Controlling the five organs of action and the five organs of knowledge as well; bring the ten senses into the mind, then the intellect, mind, and ego "I".

अहंकारं तथा बुद्धौ बुद्धिमात्मनि योजयेत् ।
यतबुद्धीन्द्रियः पश्यन् बुद्धया बुद्धयेत् परात्परम् ॥ ६९ ॥

ahaṁkāraṁ tathā buddhau buddhimātmani yojayet |
yatabuddhīndriyaḥ paśyan
buddhyā buddhyet parātparam || 69 ||

69. Uniting the ego "I" with the intellect, reveals the soul of intelligence. Controlling the organs of knowledge with intelligent perception, the knower unites with knowledge supreme and again superior.

ममायमिति यस्याहं येन सर्वमिदं ततम् ।
आत्मनाऽऽत्मनि संयोज्य परमात्मन्यनुस्मरेत् ॥ ७० ॥

mamāyamiti yasyāhaṁ yena sarvamidaṁ tatam |
ātmanā--tmani saṁyojya paramātmanyanusmaret || 70 ||

70. Thus, by means of such control, all of this manifests as That. The supreme soul unites with the individual soul, the remembrance of which is the Most Subtle Supreme Universal Soul.

ततो बुद्धेः परं बुद्ध्वा लभते न पुनर्भवम् ।
मरणे समनुप्राप्ते यश्चैवं मामनुस्मरेत् ॥ ७१ ॥

tato buddheḥ paraṁ buddhvā labhate na punarbhavam |
maraṇe samanuprāpte yaścaivaṁ māmanusmaret || 71 ||

71. Then those who know gain the highest intelligence, and they need not take birth again. In death he assumes only That, my remembrance which is Most Subtle.

अपि पापसमाचारः स याति परमां गतिम् ।
ॐ नमो भगवते तस्मै देहिनां परमात्मने ॥ ७२ ॥

api pāpasamācāraḥ sa yāti paramāṁ gatim |
oṁ namo bhagavate tasmai
dehināṁ paramātmane || 72 ||

72. Even if he had been guilty of bad conduct, he goes to the supreme refuge. I bow to the manifestation of Supreme Divinity, to the Infinite Beyond Conception, Om, to Him, the Supreme Soul of Consciousness, who wears a body;

नारायणाय भक्तानामेकनिष्ठाय शाश्वते ।
इमामनुस्मृतिं दिव्यां वैष्णवीं सुसमाहितः ॥ ७३ ॥

nārāyaṇāya bhaktānāmekaniṣṭhāya śāśvate |
imāmanusmṛtiṁ divyāṁ vaiṣṇavīṁ susamāhitaḥ || 73 ||

73. to Narayana, to the one name to which devotees offer loyalty and allegiance, who is eternal. This remembrance of the Most Subtle Divinity is the excellent grantor of welfare for followers of the Supreme Lord who pervades all, Vishnu.

स्वपन्विबुध्यंश्च पठन् यत्र तत्र समभ्यसेत् ।
पौर्णमास्याममायां च द्वादश्यां च विशेषतः ॥ ७४ ॥

svapanvibudhyaṁśca paṭhan yatra tatra samabhyaset |
paurṇamāsyāmamāyāṁ ca
dvādaśyāṁ ca viśeṣataḥ || 74 ||

74. Wherever someone recites this with understanding, there one should carefully practice this. On the full moon, on the new moon, and especially on the twelfth day,

श्रावयेच्छ्रद्दधानांश्च मद्भक्तांश्च विशेषतः ।
यद्यहंकारमाश्रित्य यज्ञदानतपःक्रियाः ॥ ७५ ॥

śrāvayecchraddadhānāṁśca madbhaktāṁśca viśeṣataḥ |
yadyahaṁkāramāśritya yajñadānatapaḥkriyāḥ || 75 ||

75. listening to this creates the greatest wealth, especially for those who are devoted to Me by surrendering the ego "I". He takes shelter in the performance of sacrifice, philanthropy, and purifying austerities,

कुर्वंस्तत्फलमाप्नोति पुनरावर्तनं तु तत् ।
अभ्यर्चयन् पितॄन् देवान् पठन् जुह्वन् बलिं ददत् ॥ ७६ ॥

kurvaṁstatphalamāpnoti punarāvartanaṁ tu tat |
abhyarcayan pitṝn devān
paṭhan juhvan baliṁ dadat || 76 ||

76. obtaining the fruits of repetitive actions, making offerings to the ancestors, to the Gods, offerings in sacrifice, and recitation of mantras.

ज्वलन्नग्निं स्मरेद्यो मां स याति परमां गतिम् ।
यज्ञो दानं तपश्चैव पावनानि मनीषिणाम् ॥ ७७ ॥

jvalannagniṁ smaredyo māṁ sa yāti paramāṁ gatim |
yajño dānaṁ tapaścaiva pāvanāni manīṣiṇām || 77 ||

77. Remembering Me in the radiant fire, he goes to the supreme refuge. Sacrifice, charity, purifying austerities make all pure, oh most excellent among men.

यज्ञं दानं तपस्तस्मात्कुर्यादाशीर्विवर्जितः ।
नम इत्येव यो ब्रूयान्मद्भक्तः श्रद्धयान्वितः ॥ ७८ ॥

yajñaṁ dānaṁ tapastasmātkuryādāśīrvivarjitaḥ |
nama ityeva yo brūyān
madbhaktaḥ śraddhayānvitaḥ || 78 ||

78. By sacrifice, charity, and purifying austerities he and his family receive all blessings. In this way My devotees bow with full faith.

तस्याक्षयो भवेल्लोकः श्वपाकस्यापि नारद ।
किं पुनर्ये यजन्ते मां साधका विधिपूर्वकम् ॥ ७९ ॥

tasyākṣayo bhavellokaḥ śvapākasyāpi nārada |
kiṁ punarye yajante māṁ sādhakā vidhipūrvakam || 79 ||

79. This un-decaying, imperishable, being of all the worlds, is true for all, from the lowest of men to Narad Muni, a seer among the Gods. This is how the efficient spiritual aspirants (sadhus) sacrifice to me again and again according to the ancient discipline.

श्रद्धावन्तो यतात्मानस्ते मां यान्ति मदाश्रिताः ।
कर्माण्याद्यन्तवन्तीह मद्भक्तो नान्तमश्नुते ॥ ८० ॥

śraddhāvanto yatātmānaste māṁ yānti madāśritāḥ |
karmāṇyādyantavantīha madbhakto nāntamaśnute || 80 ||

80. Because of his faith, he controls his soul and mind, becoming intoxicated with Me. The actions by My devotees are not destroyed and are never ending.

मामेव तस्माद्देवर्षे ध्याहि नित्यमतन्द्रितः ।

अवाप्स्यसि ततः सिद्धिं द्रक्ष्यस्येव पदं मम ॥ ८१ ॥

māmeva tasmāddevarṣe dhyāhi nityamatandritaḥ |
avāpsyasi tataḥ siddhiṁ
drakṣyasyeva padaṁ mama || 81 ||

81. That seer among the Gods meditates eternally on me without any laziness. Attaining that perfection, my divine position shall surely be perceived.

अज्ञानाय च यो ज्ञानं दद्याद्धर्मोपदेशतः ।

कृत्स्नां वा पृथिवीं दद्यात्तेन तुल्यं न तत् फलम् ॥ ८२ ॥

ajñānāya ca yo jñānaṁ dadyāddharmopadeśataḥ |
kṛtsnāṁ vā pṛthivīṁ dadyāt
tena tulyaṁ na tat phalam || 82 ||

82. He gives instructions on the Ideals of Perfection so that wisdom will illuminate ignorance. He offers the fruits of that offering to the earth as a father.

तस्मात्प्रदेयं साधुभ्यो जन्मबन्धभयापहम् ।

एवं दत्त्वा नरश्रेष्ठ श्रेयो वीर्यं च विन्दति ॥ ८३ ॥

tasmātpradeyaṁ sādhubhyo janmabandhabhayāpaham |
evaṁ dattvā naraśreṣṭha śreyo vīryaṁ ca vindati || 83 ||

83. By means of these instructions (these knowledge) efficient spiritual aspirants (sadhus) remove the fear of attachment to birth. And whoever gives knowledge is a respected hero, excellent among men.

अश्वमेधसहस्राणां सहस्रं यः समाचरेत् ।
नासौ पदमवाप्नोति मद्भक्तैर्यदवाप्यते ॥ ८४ ॥

aśvamedhasahasrāṇāṁ sahasraṁ yaḥ samācaret |
nāsau padamavāpnoti madbhaktairyadavāpyate || 84 ||

84. Achieving that station is equal to performing one thousand horse sacrifices, sounding a thousand syllables for those who achieve.

भीष्म उवाच

bhīṣma uvāca

Bhishma said:

एवं पृष्टः पुरा तेन नारदेन सुरर्षिणा ।
यदुवाच तदा शम्भुस्तदुक्तं तव सुव्रत ॥ ८५ ॥

evaṁ pṛṣṭaḥ purā tena nāradena surarṣiṇā |
yaduvāca tadā śambhustaduktaṁ tava suvrata || 85 ||

85. Thus was the ancient inquiry posed by Narad, Seer Among the Gods. From that time forward the performers of excellent vows are in union with Shambhu, who manifests peace.

त्वमप्येकमना भूत्वा ध्याहि ध्येयं गुणातिगम् ।
भजस्व सर्वभावेन परमात्मानमव्ययम् ॥ ८६ ॥

tvamapyekamanā bhūtvā dhyāhi dhyeyaṁ guṇātigam |
bhajasva sarvabhāvena paramātmānamavyayam || 86 ||

86. Meditate upon the one mind of all existence, beyond all qualities. Meditate by extolling this all with an attitude of the eternal Supreme Soul.

श्रुत्वैतन्नारदो वाक्यं दिव्यं नारायणेरितम् ।
अत्यन्तभक्तिमान् देव एकान्तत्वमुपेयिवान् ॥ ८७ ॥

śrutvaitannārado vākyaṁ divyaṁ nārāyaṇeritam |
atyantabhaktimān deva ekāntatvamupeyivān || 87 ||

87. By listening to these divine words of Narayana, Narad became filled with extreme devotion, and approached God alone in solitude.

नारायणमृषिं देवं दशवर्षाण्यनन्यभाक् ।
इमं जपिन् वै प्राप्नोति तद्विष्णोः परमं पदम् ॥ ८८ ॥

nārāyaṇamṛṣiṁ devaṁ daśavarṣāṇyananyabhāk |
imaṁ japin vai prāpnoti
tadviṣṇoḥ paramaṁ padam || 88 ||

88. The seer worshiped the god Narayana for ten years without distraction or deviation, and through this recitation achieved that supreme realization of Vishnu.

किं तस्य बहुभिर्मन्त्रैर्भक्तिर्यस्य जनार्दने ।
नमो नारायणायेति मन्त्रः सर्वार्थसाधकः ॥ ८९ ॥

kiṁ tasya bahubhirmantrairbhaktiryasya janārdane |
namo nārāyaṇāyeti mantraḥ sarvārthasādhakaḥ || 89 ||

89. With great frequency which mantras did he recite with devotion to Janardana? "Namo Narayanāya - I bow to Narayana" is the mantra to accomplish all the purposes of an efficient spiritual aspirant.

इमां रहस्यां परमामनुस्मृति
मधीत्य बुद्धिं लभते च नैष्ठिकीम् ।
विहाय दुःखान्यपमुच्य सङ्कटात्
स वीतरागो विचरेन्महीमिमाम् ॥ ९० ॥

imāṁ rahasyāṁ paramāmanusmṛti-
madhītya buddhiṁ labhate ca naiṣṭhikīm |
vihāya duḥkhānyapamucya saṅkaṭāt
sa vītarāgo vicarenmahīmimām || 90 ||

90. This is the secret of the supreme remembrance of the Subtle. When contemplated, intelligence is gained, and the highest, perfect, complete definition. Disregarding all pains and erasing all conflict, free from passion, calm and tranquil, one will wander the great earth.

इति श्रीमन्महाभारते सान्तिपुर्वनि मोक्षधर्मपर्वनि
श्रीविष्णोर्दिव्यमनुस्मृतिस्तोत्रं संपूर्णम् ॥

iti śrīmanmahābhārate sāntipurvani mokṣadharmaparvani śrīviṣṇordivyamanusmṛtistotraṁ saṁpūrṇam ||

Thus completes the Divine Song of Praise of the Respected Viṣṇu, Anusmṛti, from the Respected Mahābhārat, from the section on Peace, Liberation and the Ideals of Perfection.

अथ गजेन्द्र मोक्ष

atha gajendra mokṣa
And Now, the Liberation of the King of Elephants

नारद उवाच

nārada uvāca
Narad said:

यान् जप्यान् भगवद् भक्त्या प्रह्लादो दानवोऽजपत् ।
गजेन्द्रमोक्षणादींस्तु चतुरस्तान् वदस्व मे ॥ १ ॥

yān japyān bhagavad bhaktyā prahlādo dānavo-japat |
gajendramokṣaṇādīṁstu caturastān vadasva me || 1 ||

1. Please kindly describe for me the recitation about the liberation of the King of Elephants, which gives the four aims of life (dharma, artha, kama, moksha), made by Prahlad, the devotee of the Supreme Divinity, King of the enemies of the gods.

पुलस्त्य उवाच

pulastya uvāca
Pulastya said:

शृणुष्व कथयिष्यामि जप्यानेतांस्तपोधन ।
दुःस्वप्ननाशो भवति यैरुक्तैः संश्रुतैः स्मृतैः ॥ २ ॥

śṛṇuṣva kathayiṣyāmi japyānetāṁstapodhana |
duḥsvapnanāśo bhavati
yairuktaiḥ saṁśrutaiḥ smṛtaiḥ || 2 ||

2. Please listen as I speak to you about the recitation which bears the wealth of purifying austerities. When remembered or listened to by souls in union, it destroys bad dreams.

गजेन्द्रमोक्षणं त्वादौ शृणुष्व तदनन्तरम् ।
सारस्वतं ततः पुण्यौ पापप्रशमनौ स्तवौ ॥ ३ ॥

gajendramokṣaṇaṁ tvādau śṛṇuṣva tadanantaram |
sārasvataṁ tataḥ puṇyau pāpapraśamanau stavau || 3 ||

3. Immediately upon listening to this hymn about the liberation of the King of Elephants, all sin (confusion) will be destroyed and those who are eloquent will receive all merits.

सर्वरत्नमयः श्रीमांस्त्रिकूटो नाम पर्वतः ।
सुतः पर्वतराजस्य सुमेरोर्भास्करद्युतेः ॥ ४ ॥

sarvaratnamayaḥ śrīmāṁstrikūṭo nāma parvataḥ |
sutaḥ parvatarājasya sumerorbhāskaradyuteḥ || 4 ||

4. The respected Trikut is the name of the mountain, which is the manifestation of all jewels, the child of the King of mountains, Sumeru, with the illumination of the sun shining upon it.

क्षीरोदजलवीच्यग्रैर्धौतामलशिलातलः ।
उत्थितः सागरं भित्त्वा देवर्षिगणसेवितः ॥ ५ ॥

kṣīrodajalavīcyagrairdhautāmalaśilātalaḥ |
utthitaḥ sāgaraṁ bhittvā devarṣigaṇasevitaḥ || 5 ||

5. The waves of the ocean of milk rise in the ocean and break on the surface of the rocky shores, shining in the darkness like a seer among the gods performing loving service to the multitudes.

अप्सरोभिः परिवृतः श्रीमान्प्रस्रवणाकुलः ।
गन्धर्वैः किन्नरैर्यक्षैः सिद्धचारणपन्नगैः ॥ ६ ॥

apsarobhiḥ parivṛtaḥ śrīmānprasravaṇākulaḥ |
gandharvaiḥ kinnarairyakṣaiḥ
siddhacāraṇapannagaiḥ || 6 ||

6. Streams and waterfalls within that range of mountains conceal a community of heavenly maidens, celestial singers, desirable beings, lords of wealth, attained ones, wandering singers, and snakes.

विद्याधरैः सपत्नीकैः संयतैश्च तपस्विभिः ।
वृकद्वीपिगजेन्द्रैश्च वृतगात्रो विराजते ॥ ७ ॥

vidyādharaiḥ sapatnīkaiḥ saṁyataiśca tapasvibhiḥ |
vṛkadvīpigajendraiśca vṛtagātro virājate || 7 ||

7. The supporters of knowledge with their wives, those who practice self control, and those who perform purifying austerities; the King of elephants majestically advanced towards the river with his body beautifully shining.

पुन्नागैः कर्णिकारैश्च बिल्वामलकपाटलैः ।
चूतनीपकदम्बैश्च चन्दनागुरुचम्पकैः ॥ ८ ॥

punnāgaiḥ karṇikāraiśca bilvāmalakapāṭalaiḥ |
cūtanīpakadambaiśca candanāgurucampakaiḥ || 8 ||

8. There were many kinds of trees, like punnag, karnikar, bilva, and malika; mango, ashok, kadamba (turmeric, white mustard), sandal, wood-apple, bread-fruit;

शालैस्तालैस्तमालैश्च सरलार्जुनपर्पटैः ।
तथान्यैर्विविधैर्वृक्षैः सर्वतः समलंकृतः ॥ ९ ॥

śālaistālaistamālaiśca saralārjunaparpaṭaiḥ |
tathānyairvividhairvṛkṣaiḥ sarvataḥ samalaṁkṛtaḥ || 9 ||

9. shal trees, palmyra palm trees, trees with dark bark (tobacco), pine trees, and trees with white bark; trees were on display in many various ways.

नानाधात्वङ्कितैः शृङ्गैः प्रस्रवद्भिः समन्ततः ।
शोभितो रुचिरप्रख्यैस्त्रिभिर्विस्तीर्णसानुभिः ॥ १० ॥

nānādhātvaṅkitaiḥ śṛṅgaiḥ prasravadbhiḥ samantataḥ |
śobhito ruciraprakhyaistribhirvistīrṇasānubhiḥ || 10 ||

10. There were innumerable rocks and minerals with streams on every side of those expansive mountain ridges, and three mountain peaks were displayed, the perception of which was very pleasing.

मृगैः शाखामृगैः सिंहैर्मातङ्गैश्च सदामदैः ।
जीवंजीवकसंघुष्टैश्चकोरशिखिनादितैः ॥ ११ ॥

mṛgaiḥ śākhāmṛgaiḥ siṁhairmātaṅgaiśca sadāmadaiḥ |
jīvaṁjīvakasaṁghuṣṭaiścakoraśikhināditaiḥ || 11 ||
11. Present were deer, monkeys, lions, and elephants, who were always delighted. The live sounds of peacocks and other birds combined with the sounds of various forms of life.

तस्यैकं काञ्चनं शृङ्गं सेवते यं दिवाकरः ।
नानापुष्पसमाकीर्णं नानागन्धाधिवासितम् ॥ १२ ॥

tasyaikaṁ kāñcanaṁ śṛṅgaṁ sevate yaṁ divākaraḥ |
nānāpuṣpasamākīrṇaṁ nānāgandhādhivāsitam || 12 ||
12. The first peak was of a golden color, which reflected the light of the sun, reflecting rays of light like various flowers exuding many and various scents.

द्वितीयं राजतं शृङ्गं सेवते यं निशाकरः ।
पाण्डुराम्बुदसंकाशं तुषारचयसंनिभम् ॥ १३ ॥

dvitīyaṁ rājataṁ śṛṅgaṁ sevate yaṁ niśākaraḥ |
pāṇḍurāmbudasaṁkāśaṁ tuṣāracayasaṁnibham || 13 ||
13. The second peak was of a silver color, which reflected the light of the moon, having the appearance of a lotus emanating bright light, similar to camphor,

वज्रेन्द्रनीलवैडूर्यतेजोभिर्भासयन् दिशः ।
तृतीयं ब्रह्मसदनं प्रकृष्टं शृङ्गमुत्तमम् ॥ १४ ॥

vajrendranīlavaiḍūryatejobhirbhāsayan diśaḥ |
tṛtīyaṁ brahmasadanaṁ
prakṛṣṭaṁ śṛṅgamuttamam || 14 ||
14. shining like Indra's thunderbolt with the radiance of excellent gold, gems, or sapphires illuminating the directions. The third peak was most superior and excellent being the abode of the Creator.

न तत्कृतघ्नाः पश्यन्ति न नृशंसा न नास्तिकाः ।
नातप्ततपसो लोके ये च पापकृतो जनाः ॥ १५ ॥

na tatkṛtaghnāḥ paśyanti na nṛśaṁsā na nāstikāḥ |
nātaptatapaso loke ye ca pāpakṛto janāḥ || 15 ||

15. The mischievous and the non-believers, those without appreciation, those who perform un-illuminated purifying austerities in the worlds, and those people who perform sin cannot see it.

तस्य सानुमतः पृष्ठे सरः काञ्चनपङ्कजम् ।
कारण्डवसमाकीर्णं राजहंसोपशोभितम् ॥ १६ ॥

tasya sānumataḥ pṛṣṭhe saraḥ kāñcanapaṅkajam |
kāraṇḍavasamākīrṇaṁ rājahaṁsopaśobhitam || 16 ||

16. There was a lake completely covered with golden lotuses on the back side of the summit of this mountain peak. A flock of ducks were shining along with royal swans.

कुमुदोत्पलकह्लारैः पुण्डरीकैश्च मण्डितम् ।
कमलैः शतपत्रैश्च काञ्चनैः समलङ्कृतम् ॥ १७ ॥

kumudotpalakahlāraiḥ puṇḍarīkaiśca maṇḍitam |
kamalaiḥ śatapatraiśca kāñcanaiḥ samalaṅkṛtam || 17 ||

17. There were red lotuses, blue lotuses, lotuses of various kinds, with hundreds of petals and golden adornments;

पत्रैर्मरकतप्रख्यैः पुष्पैः काञ्चनसंनिभैः ।
गुल्मैः कीचकवेणूनां समन्तात् परिवेष्टितम् ॥ १८ ॥

patrairmarakataprakhyaiḥ puṣpaiḥ kāñcanasaṁnibhaiḥ |
gulmaiḥ kīcakaveṇūnāṁ samantāt pariveṣṭitam || 18 ||

18. with leaves appearing like emeralds and flowers resembling gold. The commander of the herd of elephants was surrounded on every side by bamboo.

तस्मिन् सरसि दुष्टात्मा विरूपोऽन्तर्जलेशयः ।
आसीद् ग्राहो गजेन्द्राणां रिपुराकेकरेक्षणः ॥ १९ ॥

tasmin sarasi duṣṭātmā virūpo-ntarjaleśayaḥ |
āsīd grāho gajendrāṇāṁ ripurākekarekṣaṇaḥ || 19 ||

19. In this lake there was seated an ugly, evil soul, in the form of a crocodile with squinted eyes, lurking beneath the waters, waiting to grasp Gajendra (the King of elephants) as an enemy.

अथ दन्तोज्ज्वलमुखः कदाचिद् गजयूथपः ।
मदस्रावी जलाकाङ्क्षी पादचारीव पर्वतः ॥ २० ॥

atha dantojjvalamukhaḥ kadācid gajayūthapaḥ |
madasrāvī jalākāṅkṣī pādacārīva parvataḥ || 20 ||

20. And then on this one occasion, the one with shining tusks on his face, the chief protector of the herd of elephants, was filled with delight and had the desire for water, walking on his feet like a mountain.

वासयन्मदगन्धेन गिरिमैरावतोपमः ।
गजो ह्यञ्जनसंकाशो मदाच्चलितलोचनः ॥ २१ ॥

vāsayanmadagandhena girimairāvatopamaḥ |
gajo hyañjanasaṁkāśo madāccalitalocanaḥ || 21 ||

21. There in the mountains the excellent Airavat (the King of elephants), dwelling in the intoxication of that circumstance, now appeared amongst his subjects with darting eyes from that intoxication.

तृषितः पातुकामोऽसौ अवतीर्णश्च तज्जलम् ।
सलीलः पङ्कजवने यूथमध्यगतश्चरन् ॥ २२ ॥

tṛṣitaḥ pātukāmo-sau avatīrṇaśca tajjalam |
salīlaḥ paṅkajavane yūthamadhyagataścaran || 22 ||

22. Being thirsty, desiring to protect his female (companions), he came down to the water to play in sport in the forest of lotuses, and he went to the middle of the herd,

गृहीतस्तेन रौद्रेण ग्राहेणाव्यक्तमूर्तिना ।
पश्यन्तीनां करेणूनां क्रोशन्तीनां च दारुणम् ॥ २३ ॥

gṛhītastena raudreṇa grāheṇāvyaktamūrtinā |
paśyantīnāṁ kareṇūnāṁ krośantīnāṁ ca dāruṇam || 23 ||

23. where he was grasped (taken, seized) fiercely by the imperceptible (hidden) form of the crocodile, as the female elephants watched and cried in horror.

ह्रियते पङ्कजवने ग्राहेणातिबलीयसा ।
वारुणैः संयतः पाशैर्निष्प्रयत्नगतिः कृतः ॥ २४ ॥

hriyate paṅkajavane grāheṇātibalīyasā |
vāruṇaiḥ saṁyataḥ pāśairniṣprayatnagatiḥ kṛtaḥ || 24 ||

24. Seized (taken) in the forest of lotuses by the very strong crocodile, he was bound (fettered, imprisoned) by the web (net) of that water animal, which created the condition of an inability to act (move).

वेष्ट्यमानः सुघोरैस्तु पाशैर्नागो दृढैस्तथा ।
विस्फूर्य च यथाशक्ति विक्रोसंश्च महारवान् ॥ २५ ॥

veṣṭyamānaḥ sughoraistu pāśairnāgo dṛḍhaistathā |
visphūrya ca yathāśakti vikrosaṁśca mahāravān || 25 ||

25. Surrounded (bound) by those dreadful (fearful) bonds, the elephant was firmly fastened in that way. Roaring and losing all his energy, he was crying in alarm for help with a great tumultuous sound.

व्यथितः स निरुत्साहो गृहीतो घोरकर्मणा ।
परमापदमापन्नो मनसाऽचिन्तयद्धरिम् ॥ २६ ॥

vyathitaḥ sa nirutsāho gṛhīto ghorakarmaṇā |
paramāpadamāpanno manasā-cintayaddharim || 26 ||

26. He was in pain and perturbation, without energy or courage, seized by the performer of terrible deeds. Afflicted by this supreme calamity, he began to consider the following thoughts:

स तु नागवरः श्रीमन् नारायणपरायणः ।
तमेव शरणं देवं गतः सर्वात्मना तदा ॥ २७ ॥

sa tu nāgavaraḥ śrīman nārāyaṇaparāyaṇaḥ |
tameva śaraṇaṁ devaṁ gataḥ sarvātmanā tadā || 27 ||

27. He, the best of elephants, (thought) the respected Narayana (the consciousness of human beings), is the highest goal. You are the only refuge, oh God, you are situated in all, as the soul of all,

एकात्मा निगृहीतात्मा विशुद्धेनान्तरात्मना ।
जन्मजन्मान्तराभ्यासाद्भक्तिमान्गारुडध्वजे ॥ २८ ॥

ekātmā nigṛhītātmā viśuddhenāntarātmanā |
janmajanmāntarābhyāsādbhaktimāngaruḍadhvaje || 28 ||

28. the one soul which cannot be seized (grasped), the immaculate (completely) pure soul within all souls. From repeated spiritual practices in birth after birth, one attains to Your devotion, oh You who have Garuda (the eagle) on Your flag (Vishnu).

नान्यं देवं महादेवात् पूजयामास केशवात् ।
मथितामृतफेनाभं शङ्खचक्रगदाधरम् ॥ २९ ॥

nānyaṁ devaṁ mahādevāt pūjayāmāsa keśavāt |
mathitāmṛtaphenābhaṁ śaṅkhacakragadādharam || 29 ||

29. He worshiped no other god, only the Great God, Keshava (one with beautiful hair; the beginning, middle, and end of all). Being afflicted, he roared forth with the nectar of immortal bliss to He who holds the conch, discuss, and club.

सहस्रशुभनामानमादिदेवमजं विभुम् ।
प्रगृह्य पुष्करागेण काञ्चनं कमलोत्तमम् ।
आपद्विमोक्षमन्विच्छन् गजः स्तोत्रमुदीरयत् ॥ ३० ॥

sahasraśubhanāmānamādidevamajaṁ vibhum |
pragṛhya puṣkarāgreṇa kāñcanaṁ kamalottamam |
āpadvimokṣamanvicchan gajaḥ stotramudīrayat || 30 ||

30. I bow to He with a thousand pure names, who pervades all other gods. Having been seized (grabbed) in this lake in front of these excellent golden lotuses, (pursuing) liberation from difficulties and to render homage, the elephant began to chant this hymn.

गजेन्द्र उवाच ।

gajendra uvāca |
The King of the Elephants said:

ॐ नमो मूलप्रकृतये अजिताय महात्मने ।
अनाश्रिताय देवाय निःस्पृहाय नमोऽस्तु ते ॥ ३१ ॥

oṁ namo mūlaprakṛtaye ajitāya mahātmane |
anāśritāya devāya niḥspṛhāya namo-stu te || 31 ||
31. Om I bow to the Primordial Nature, who is unable to be defeated, to the Great Soul; who has no other support, to the God, who is without desire, I bow to You.

नम आद्याय बीजाय आर्षेयाय प्रवर्तिने ।
अनन्तराय चैकाय अव्यक्ताय नमो नमः ॥ ३२ ॥

nama ādyāya bījāya ārṣeyāya pravartine |
anantarāya caikāya avyaktāya namo namaḥ || 32 ||
32. I bow to the Foremost, to the seed of all, to the venerable (respected) Cause of all; to He who is Infinite, and embodies the One, to the Universal Spirit, I bow, I bow.

नमो गुह्याय गूढाय गुणाय गुणवर्तिने ।
अप्रतर्क्याप्रमेयाय अतुलाय नमो नमः ॥ ३३ ॥

namo guhyāya gūḍhāya guṇāya guṇavartine |
apratarkyāprameyāya atulāya namo namaḥ || 33 ||
33. I bow to the Secret, to the place where the secret is hidden, to the qualities, to He who is unimpeded by the qualities; to He who is unable to be known through conjecture or reasoning, unable to be measured, who is incomparable, I bow, I bow.

नमः शिवाय शान्ताय निश्चिन्ताय यशस्विने ।
सनातनाय पूर्वाय पुराणाय नमो नमः ॥ ३४ ॥

namaḥ śivāya śāntāya niścintāya yaśasvine |
sanātanāya pūrvāya purāṇāya namo namaḥ || 34 ||
34. I bow to the Consciousness of Infinite Goodness, to Peace, beyond thought, who gives fame and welfare; to He who is eternal, most old, to the ancient One, I bow, I bow.

नमो देवाधिदेवाय स्वभावाय नमो नमः ।
नमो जगत्प्रतिष्ठाय गोविन्दाय नमो नमः ॥ ३५ ॥

namo devādhidevāya svabhāvāya namo namaḥ |
namo jagatpratiṣṭhāya govindāya namo namaḥ || 35 ||
35. I bow to the God of all gods, to the Intrinsic Nature of all, I bow, I bow. I bow to He who establishes the perceivable world, to He who is one pointed light, I bow, I bow.

नमोऽस्तु पद्मनाभाय नमो योगोद्भवाय च ।
विश्वेश्वराय देवाय शिवाय हरये नमः ॥ ३६ ॥

namo-stu padmanābhāya namo yogodbhavāya ca |
viśveśvarāya devāya śivāya haraye namaḥ || 36 ||
36. I bow to you who has a lotus in His naval, and I bow to the Attitude of Yogis; to the Lord of the universe, to the God, to the Consciousness of Infinite Goodness, to He who is the embodiment of the gross body, the subtle body, and the causal body, I bow.

नमोऽस्तु तस्मै देवाय निर्गुणाय गुणात्मने ।
नारायणाय विश्वाय देवानां परमात्मने ॥ ३७ ॥

namo-stu tasmai devāya nirguṇāya guṇātmane |
nārāyaṇāya viśvāya devānāṁ paramātmane || 37 ||
37. I bow to He who is God, beyond all qualities, the soul of all qualities; to Narayana (the consciousness of human beings), to He who is the universe, to God, to the Supreme Soul.

नमो नमः कारणवामनाय
नारायणायामितविक्रमाय ।
श्रीशार्ङ्गचक्रासिगदाधराय
नमोऽस्तु तस्मै पुरुषोत्तमाय ॥ ३८ ॥

namo namaḥ kāraṇavāmanāya
nārāyaṇāyāmitavikramāya |
śrīśārṅgacakrāsigadādharāya
namo-stu tasmai puruṣottamāya || 38 ||

38. I bow, I bow to the Cause, who came as a dwarf, to Narayana (the consciousness of human beings), who is all movement beyond limitations; to the respected One, who holds a conch, a discus, a sword, and a club. I bow to He who is the most excellent, full, complete, and perfect consciousness.

गुह्याय वेदनिलयाय महोदराय
सिंहाय दैत्यनिधनाय चतुर्भुजाय ।
ब्रह्मेन्द्ररुद्रमुनिचारणसंस्तुताय
देवोत्तमाय वरदाय नमोऽच्युताय ॥ ३९ ॥

guhyāya vedanilayāya mahodarāya
siṁhāya daityanidhanāya caturbhujāya |
brahmendrarudramunicāraṇasaṁstutāya
devottamāya varadāya namo-cyutāya || 39 ||

39. I bow to the repository of secrets, the dwelling place of wisdom (vedas), who is mighty and powerful, who is most eminent, who has four arms and causes the destruction of duality. Brahma (the Creator), Indra (the Rule of the Pure), Rudra (the Reliever of Sufferings), the munis (the wise beings) sing praises (worship) to His feet, most excellent among the gods, grantor of boons, I bow to He who is Imperishable.

नागेन्द्रदेहशयनासनसुप्रियाय
गोक्षीरहेमशुकनीलघनोपमाय ।
पीताम्बराय मधुकैटभनाशनाय
विश्वाय चारुमुकुटाय नमोऽजराय ॥ ४० ॥

nāgendradehaśayanāsanasupriyāya
gokṣīrahemaśukanīlaghanopamāya |
pītāmbarāya madhukaiṭabhanāśanāya
viśvāya cārumukuṭāya namo-jarāya || 40 ||

40. He loves to rest on the body of the king of snakes, enjoys cow's milk, wears a blue turban with gold upon it; wears a yellow cloth, destroys Too Much and Too Little, who is the universe, who has a beautiful crown, I bow to He who is immortal.

नाभिप्रजातकमलस्थचतुर्मुखाय
क्षीरोदकार्णवनिकेतयशोधराय ।
नानाविचित्रमुकुटाङ्गदभूषणाय
सर्वेश्वराय वरदाय नमो वराय ॥ ४१ ॥

nābhiprajātakamalasthacaturmukhāya
kṣīrodakārṇavaniketayaśodharāya |
nānāvicitramukuṭāṅgadabhūṣaṇāya
sarveśvarāya varadāya namo varāya || 41 ||

41. The One with four faces, who gives birth to all, is situated in the lotus of His naval. He supports fame and welfare from his habitation on the waves of the milk ocean. He displays various and assorted jewels on His body and crown. I bow to the Lord of All, to the Giver of boons, who manifests the boon.

भक्तिप्रियाय वरदीप्तसुदर्शनाय
फुल्लारविन्दविपुलायतलोचनाय ।
देवेन्द्रविघ्नशमनोद्यतपौरुषाय
योगेश्वराय विरजाय नमो वराय ॥ ४२ ॥

bhaktipriyāya varadīptasudarśanāya
phullāravindavipulāyatalocanāya |
devendravighnaśamanodyatapauruṣāya
yogeśvarāya virajāya namo varāya || 42 ||

42. To the Lover of devotion, who gives the boon of the excellent intuitive vision of light, whose eyes are extensive like a lotus in blossom; who is the cause of the full, complete, and perfect consciousness, who brings peace to the obstacles encountered by the Ruler of the gods, I bow to He who resides as the Supreme Lord of Union, who manifests the boon.

ब्रह्मायनाय त्रिदशायनाय
लोकाधिनाथाय भवापनाय ।
नारायणायात्महितायनाय
महावराहाय नमस्करोमि ॥ ४३ ॥

brahmāyanāya tridaśāyanāya
lokādhināthāya bhavāpanāya |
nārāyaṇāyātmahitāyanāya
mahāvarāhāya namaskaromi || 43 ||

43. To He who causes Brahma (the Creator) and the thirty (Vedic gods) to come, to He who is the Lord of the worlds, who has obtained creation; to Narayana (the consciousness of human beings) who has obtained the benefit of the soul, to the greatest of boons, I bow with respect.

कूटस्थमव्यक्तमचिन्त्यरूपं
नारायणं कारणमादिदेवम् ।
युगान्तशेषं पुरुषं पुराणं
तं देवदेवं शरणं प्रपद्ये ॥ ४४ ॥

kūṭasthamavyaktamacintyarūpaṁ
nārāyaṇaṁ kāraṇamādidevam |
yugāntaśeṣaṁ puruṣaṁ purāṇaṁ
taṁ devadevaṁ śaraṇaṁ prapadye || 44 ||

44. Whose unthinkable infinite form does not change, Narayana (the consciousness of human beings), the God who is the first Cause; who is the full, complete, and perfect consciousness most ancient from the end of time, I surrender and take refuge in Him, the God of gods.

योगेश्वरं चारुविचित्रमौलि-
मज्ञेयमग्र्यं प्रकृतेः परस्थम् ।
क्षेत्रज्ञमात्मप्रभवं वरेण्यं
तं वासुदेवं शरणं प्रपद्य ॥ ४५ ॥

yogeśvaraṁ cāruvicitramauli-
majñeyamagryaṁ prakṛteḥ parastham |
kṣetrajñamātmaprabhavaṁ vareṇyaṁ
taṁ vāsudevaṁ śaraṇaṁ prapadya || 45 ||

45. He is the Supreme Lord of Union, who is known as the foremost, best, and most beautiful, Supreme above Nature. He is the highest, who gives birth to the knowledge of the field (creation). I surrender and take refuge in Him, the Supreme Soul of the universe.

अदृश्यमव्यक्तमचिन्त्यमव्ययं
महर्षयो ब्रह्ममयं सनातनम् ।
वदन्ति यं वै पुरुषं सनातनं
तं देवगुह्यं शरणं प्रपद्ये ॥ ४६ ॥

adṛśyamavyaktamacintyamavyayaṁ
maharṣayo brahmayaṁ sanātanam |
vadanti yaṁ vai puruṣaṁ sanātanaṁ
taṁ devaguhyaṁ śaraṇaṁ prapadye || 46 ||

46. He is imperishable, unthinkable, infinite, imperceptible, the great seers call Him the manifestation of the Supreme, who is Eternal; the full, complete, and perfect eternal consciousness, I surrender and take refuge in Him, the God most hidden or secret.

यदक्षरं ब्रह्म वदन्ति सर्वगं
निशम्य यं मृत्युमुखात् प्रमुच्यते ।
तमीश्वरं तृप्तमनुत्तमैर्गुणैः
परायणं विष्णुमुपैमि साश्वतम् ॥ ४७ ॥

yadakṣaraṁ brahma vadanti sarvagaṁ
niśamya yaṁ mṛtyumukhāt pramucyate |
tamīśvaraṁ tṛptamanuttamairguṇaiḥ
parāyaṇaṁ viṣṇumupaimi sāśvatam || 47 ||

47. Who is called the imperishable soul of the Supreme Divinity, the foremost; those who perceive Him become completely liberated from death. He is the Supreme Lord whose excellent qualities bring satisfaction, achieving the eternal Vishnu is the chief objective or goal.

कार्यं क्रिया कारणमप्रमेयं
हिरण्यबाहुं वरपद्मनाभम् ।
महाबलं वेदनिधिं सुरेशं
व्रजामि विष्णुं शरणं जनार्दनम् ॥ ४८ ॥

kāryaṁ kriyā kāraṇamaprameyaṁ
hiraṇyabāhuṁ varapadmanābham |
mahābalaṁ vedanidhiṁ sureśaṁ
vrajāmi viṣṇuṁ śaraṇaṁ janārdanam || 48 ||

48. He is the unmeasurable Cause of all causes and effects, who gives boons, and has a lotus in His naval and golden arms. He is the Lord of the gods, has great strength, and the discipline of the Vedas. I prostrate myself before Vishnu (He who pervades the universe), taking refuge in the Lord of all beings.

किरीटकेयूरमहार्हनिष्कै-
र्मण्युत्तमालंकृतसर्वगात्रम् ।
पीताम्बरं काञ्चनभक्तिचित्रं
मालाधरं केशवमभ्युपैमि ॥ ४९ ॥

kirīṭakeyūramahārhaniṣkai-
rmaṇyuttamālaṁkṛtasarvagātram |
pītāmbaraṁ kāñcanabhakticitraṁ
mālādharaṁ keśavamabhyupaimi || 49 ||

49. Displaying a crown and ornaments on His arms, excellent gems as ornaments on all the parts of his body; wearing a yellow cloth, whose wealth is the variety of devotion, who wears a garland, I shall achieve that Keshava (One with beautiful hair; the beginning, middle, and end of all).

भवोद्भवं वेदविदां वरिष्ठं
योगात्मनां सांख्यविदां वरिष्ठम् ।
आदित्यरुद्राश्विवसुप्रभावं
प्रभुं प्रपद्येऽच्युतमात्मवन्तम् ॥ ५० ॥

bhavodbhavaṁ vedavidāṁ variṣṭhaṁ
yogātmanāṁ sāṁkhyavidāṁ variṣṭham |
ādityarudrāśvivasuprabhāvaṁ
prabhuṁ prapadye-cyutamātmavantam || 50 ||

50. I surrender with perfect consciousness to the Lord, to the infinite soul in all manifestations of all existence, in knowledge and wisdom, to the highest, the soul of union, known as the highest enumeration of the principles; who is the strength and power of the sons of non-duality (gods), the Reliever of Sufferings (Rudra), the Consciousness of Infinite Goodness (Shiva), the lords of wealth with supernatural powers and beauty.

श्रीवत्साङ्कं महादेवं देवगुह्यमनौपमम् ।
प्रपद्ये सूक्ष्ममचलं वरेण्यमभयप्रदम् ॥ ५१ ॥

śrīvatsāṅkaṁ mahādevaṁ devaguhyamanaupamam |
prapadye sūkṣmamacalaṁ
vareṇyamabhayapradam || 51 ||

51. I surrender to the respected Vishnu, the Great God, who hides the most excellent thoughts of God, to the highest, most subtle, which does not move, which bestows freedom from fear.

प्रभवं सर्वभूतानां निर्गुणं परमेश्वरम् ।
प्रपद्ये मुक्तसंगानां यतीनां परमां गतिम् ॥ ५२ ॥

prabhavaṁ sarvabhūtānāṁ nirguṇaṁ parameśvaram |
prapadye muktasaṁgānāṁ
yatīnāṁ paramāṁ gatim || 52 ||

52. Those who make efforts with the desire for liberation, who move towards the Supreme, surrender to the Supreme Lord who is beyond all qualities, who is the cause of the existence of all the elements.

भगवन्तं गुणाध्यक्षमक्षरं पुष्करेक्षणम् ।
शरण्यं शरणं भक्त्या प्रपद्ये भक्तवत्सलम् ॥ ५३ ॥

bhagavantaṁ guṇādhyakṣamakṣaraṁ puṣkarekṣaṇam |
śaraṇyaṁ śaraṇaṁ bhaktyā
prapadye bhaktavatsalam || 53 ||

53. With perfect consciousness devotees take refuge and surrender to the imperishable leader of all qualities, who has lotus-like eyes, and who is kind to those who worship.

त्रिविक्रमं त्रिलोकेशं सर्वेषां प्रपितामहम् ।
योगात्मानं महात्मानं प्रपद्येऽहं जनार्दनम् ॥ ५४ ॥

trivikramaṁ trilokeśaṁ sarveṣāṁ prapitāmaham |
yogātmānaṁ mahātmānaṁ
prapadye-haṁ janārdanam || 54 ||

54. The Supreme Lord of the three worlds, who moves in the three, who is in all, who is the great-grandfather (Supreme Spirit); the soul of union, the great soul, I take refuge in the Lord of all beings born.

आदिदेवमजं शभुं व्यक्ताव्यक्तं सनातनम् ।
नारायणमणीयांसं प्रपद्ये ब्राह्मणप्रियम् ॥ ५५ ॥

ādidevamajaṁ śabhuṁ vyaktāvyaktaṁ sanātanam |
nārāyaṇamaṇīyāṁsaṁ prapadye brāhmaṇapriyam || 55 ||

55. Who is foremost of all the Gods, whose existence is Peace, who is both manifest and un-manifest, eternal; I surrender to Narayana (the consciousness of human beings), who is smaller than the smallest, and although existing everywhere, remains invisible to material eyes.

नमो वराय देवाय नमः सर्वसहाय च ।
प्रपद्ये देवदेवेशमणीयांसमणोः सदा ॥ ५६ ॥

namo varāya devāya namaḥ sarvasahāya ca |
prapadye devadeveśamaṇīyāṁsamaṇoḥ sadā || 56 ||

56. I bow to the Helper of All, I bow to God, I bow to His boon; I surrender to the Lord, God of all gods, who is always equal to the Supreme Jewel.

एकाय लोकतत्त्वाय परतः परमात्मने ।
नमः सहस्रशिरसे अनन्ताय महात्मने ॥ ५७ ॥

ekāya lokatattvāya parataḥ paramātmane |
namaḥ sahasraśirase anantāya mahātmane || 57 ||

57. To the Supreme Soul, and again superior, to the One Principle of the worlds, I bow to He who has a thousand heads, who is infinite, to the Great Soul.

त्वामेव परमं देवमृषयो वेदपारगाः ।
कीर्तयन्ति च यं सर्वे ब्रह्मादीनां परायणम् ॥ ५८ ॥

tvāmeva paramaṁ devamṛṣayo vedapāragāḥ |
kīrtayanti ca yaṁ sarve brahmādīnāṁ parāyaṇam || 58 ||

58. The gods and rishis sing the praises of He who alone is the Master of the Vedas (all wisdom), the Supreme of all, the highest goal of the creator and others.

नमस्ते पुण्डरीकाक्ष भक्तानामभयप्रद ।
सुब्रह्मण्य नमस्तेऽस्तु त्राहि मां शरणागतम् ॥ ५९ ॥

namaste puṇḍarīkākṣa bhaktānāmabhayaprada |
subrahmaṇya namaste-stu trāhi māṁ śaraṇāgatam || 59 ||

59. I bow before the One with lotus eyes, whose name gives devotees freedom from fear. With this excellent recitation which protects me, I bow, I who have taken His refuge.

पुलस्त्य उवाच

pulastya uvāca

Pulastya said:

भक्तिं तस्यानुसञ्चिन्त्य नागस्यामोघसंभवः ।
प्रीतिमानभवद् विष्णुः शङ्खचक्रगदाधरः ॥ ६० ॥

bhaktiṁ tasyānusañcintya nāgasyāmoghasaṁbhavaḥ |
prītimānabhavad viṣṇuḥ śaṅkhacakragadādharaḥ || 60 ||

60. Thus searching in thoughts of devotion, the most excellent gave birth to the infallible. Vishnu, who holds the conch, discuss, and club is the Beloved.

सांनिध्यं कल्पयामास तस्मिन् सरसि केशवः ।
गरुडस्थो जगत्स्वामी लोकाधारस्तपोधनः ॥ ६१ ॥

sāṁnidhyaṁ kalpayāmāsa tasmin sarasi keśavaḥ |
garuḍastho jagatsvāmī lokādhārastapodhanaḥ || 61 ||

61. Keshava (who is creation, preservation, and transformation), seated upon Garuda (His divine eagle), is within the thoughts of the mind, the Master of the perceivable universe, who supports the worlds with the generosity of His purifying austerities.

ग्राहग्रस्तं गजेन्द्रं तं तं च ग्राहं जलाशयात् ।
उज्जहाराप्रमेयात्मा तरसा मधुसूदनः ॥ ६२ ॥

grāhagrastaṁ gajendraṁ taṁ taṁ ca grāhaṁ jalāśayāt |
ujjahārāprameyātmā tarasā madhusūdanaḥ || 62 ||

62. The crocodile had seized Gajendra, and the crocodile pulled him below the water. Then that Immeasurable Soul, the Destroyer of Too Much, speedily delivered Him (Gajendra).

स्थलस्थं दारयामास ग्राहं चक्रेण माधवः ।
मोक्षयामास नागेन्द्रं पाशेभ्यः शरणागतम् ॥ ६३ ॥

sthalasthaṁ dārayāmāsa grāhaṁ cakreṇa mādhavaḥ |
mokṣayāmāsa nāgendraṁ pāśebhyaḥ śaraṇāgatam || 63 ||

63. Situated in that place, Madhava (who is always sweet), killed the crocodile with His discuss, and liberated from bondage the King of elephants, who had taken refuge in Him.

स हि देवलशापेन हूहूर्गन्धर्वसत्तमः ।
ग्राहत्वमगमत् कृष्णाद् वधं प्राप्य दिवं गतः ॥ ६४ ॥

sa hi devalaśāpena hūhūrgandharvasattamaḥ |
grāhatvamagamat kṛṣṇād
vadhaṁ prāpya divaṁ gataḥ || 64 ||

64. The (Gandarva) Celestial Singer Hu Hu was most virtuous and respectable. The curse of the pious man (Deval Rishi) made him into a crocodile, from which he gave up this darkness and attained the light.

गजोऽपि विष्णुना स्पृष्टो जातो दिव्यवपुः पुमान् ।
आपद्विक्तौ युगपद् गजगन्धर्वसत्तमौ ॥ ६५ ॥

gajo-pi viṣṇunā spṛṣṭo jāto divyavapuḥ pumān |
āpadviktau yugapad gajagandharvasattamau || 65 ||

65. Even an elephant touched by Vishnu gave birth to divinity embodied in a living entity. Liberated from his difficulties, the elephant immediately became a most venerable and respectable Gandarva (again).

प्रीतिमान् पुण्डरीकाक्षः शरणागतवत्सलः ।
अभवत्त्वथ देवेशस्ताभ्यां चैव प्रपूजितः ॥ ६६ ॥

prītimān puṇḍarīkākṣaḥ śaraṇāgatavatsalaḥ |
abhavattvatha deveśastābhyāṁ caiva prapūjitaḥ || 66 ||

66. The beloved with lotus eyes who gives only kindness to those who take refuge; at the time of non-existence, He alone is worshiped by the gods.

इदं च भगवान् योगी गजेन्द्रं शरणागतम् ।
प्रोवाच मुनिशार्दूल मधुरं मधुसूदनः ॥ ६७ ॥

idaṁ ca bhagavān yogī gajendraṁ śaraṇāgatam |
provāca muniśārdūla madhuraṁ madhusūdanaḥ || 67 ||

67. People in union (yogis) take refuge in the King of elephants. Thus the wise muni Shardula (most eminent) described the Supreme Divinity and the sweetness of He who slays Too Much.

श्रीभगवानुवाच

śrībhagavānuvāca
The Supreme Divinity said:

ये मां त्वां च सरश्चैव ग्राहस्य च विदारणम् ।
गुल्मकीचकरेणूनां रूपं मेरोः सुतस्य च ॥ ६८ ॥

ye māṁ tvāṁ ca saraścaiva grāhasya ca vidāraṇam |
gulmakīcakareṇūnāṁ rūpaṁ meroḥ sutasya ca || 68 ||
68. Killing the crocodile in the lake saved the commander of the herd of female elephants (Gajendra), who appeared like the form of the astrological houses revolving around the (central axis) of Mount Meru (like the planets revolving around the Sun).

अश्वत्थं भास्करं गङ्गां नैमिषारण्यमेव च ।
संस्मरिष्यन्ति मनुजाः प्रयताः स्थिरबुद्धयः ॥ ६९ ॥

aśvatthaṁ bhāskaraṁ gaṅgāṁ naimiṣāraṇyameva ca |
saṁsmariṣyanti manujāḥ
prayatāḥ sthirabuddhayaḥ || 69 ||
69. Beside a fig tree, looking at the sun, on the bank of the Ganges, or also in a sacred grove or forest; humans who remember and make efforts with a controlled intellect,

कीर्तयिष्यन्ति भक्त्या च श्रोष्यन्ति च शुचिव्रताः ।
दुःस्वप्नो नश्यते तेषां सुस्वप्नश्च भविष्यति ॥ ७० ॥

kīrtayiṣyanti bhaktyā ca śroṣyanti ca śucivratāḥ |
duḥsvapno naśyate teṣāṁ susvapnaśca bhaviṣyati || 70 ||
70. will sing and listen to this pure worship with devotion, and destroy bad dreams, and the bad dreams will become good dreams.

मात्स्यं कौर्मं च वाराहं वामनं ताक्ष्र्यमेव च ।
नारसिंहं च नागेन्द्रं सृष्टिप्रलयकारकम् ॥ ७१ ॥

mātsyaṁ kaurmaṁ ca vārāhaṁ
vāmanaṁ tārkṣyameva ca |
nārasiṁhaṁ ca nāgendraṁ sṛṣṭipralayakārakam || 71 ||
71. He incarnated as a fish, a tortoise, a boar, a dwarf, and even as a bird; half-man/half-lion, and the king of snakes, and He is the Cause of creation and dissolution too.

एतानि प्रातरुत्थाय संस्मरिष्यन्ति ये नराः ।
सर्वपापैः प्रमुच्यन्ते पुण्यं लोकमवाप्नुयुः ॥ ७२ ॥

etāni prātarutthāya saṁsmariṣyanti ye narāḥ |
sarvapāpaiḥ pramucyante
puṇyaṁ lokamavāpnuyuḥ || 72 ||
72. Those humans who remember this (story) in the early morning, erase (expunge) all sin (confusion) and spread merit (goodness) in the world.

पुलस्त्य उवाच

pulastya uvāca
Pulastya said:

एवमुक्त्वा हृषीकेशो गजेन्द्रं गरुडध्वजः ।
स्पर्शयामास हस्तेन गजं गन्धर्वमेव च ॥ ७३ ॥

evamuktvā hṛṣīkeśo gajendraṁ garuḍadhvajaḥ |
sparśayāmāsa hastena gajaṁ gandharvameva ca || 73 ||
73. In this way the King of elephants united with the Controller of the senses, who has Garuda (the eagle) on his banner. From the mere touch of His hand, the elephant even became a Gandarva (celestial singer).

ततो दिव्यवपुर्भत्वा गजेन्द्रो मधुसूदनम् ।
जगाम शरणं विप्र नारायणपरायणः ॥ ७४ ॥

tato divyavapurbhatvā gajendro madhusūdanam |
jagāma śaraṇaṁ vipra nārāyaṇaparāyaṇaḥ || 74 ||

74. Then the King of elephants appeared in a divine beautiful body and approached the Slayer of Too Much. The twice-born (man of wisdom) took refuge in Narayana (the consciousness of human beings), the highest goal.

ततो नारायणः श्रीमान् मोक्षयित्वा गजोत्तमम् ।
पापबन्धाच्च शापाच्च ग्राहं चाद्भुतकर्मकृत् ॥ ७५ ॥

tato nārāyaṇaḥ śrīmān mokṣayitvā gajottamam |
pāpabandhācca śāpācca grāhaṁ cādbhutakarmakṛt || 75 ||

75. Then the respected Narayana (the consciousness of human beings) bestowed liberation upon the most excellent of elephants, and the crocodile was freed from his curse and from his bondage to sin (confusion), and from the amazing actions he had performed.

ऋषिभिः स्तूयमानश्च देवगुह्यपरायणैः ।
गतः स भगवान् विष्णुर्दुर्विज्ञेयगतिः प्रभुः ॥ ७६ ॥

ṛṣibhiḥ stūyamānaśca devaguhyaparāyaṇaiḥ |
gataḥ sa bhagavān viṣṇurdurvijñeyagatiḥ prabhuḥ || 76 ||

76. The rishis sing with their complete minds about this secret (hidden) goal of the gods; moving towards and going to the Lord, the Supreme Divinity, Vishnu, who is difficult to know.

गजेन्द्रमोक्षणं दृष्ट्वा देवाः शक्रपुरोगमाः ।
ववन्दिरे महात्मानं प्रभुं नारायणं हरिम् ॥ ७७ ॥

gajendramokṣaṇaṁ dṛṣṭvā devāḥ śakrapurogamāḥ |
vavandire mahātmānaṁ
prabhuṁ nārāyaṇaṁ harim || 77 ||

77. The gods perceive the power of the liberation of the King of elephants, who goes before all, and the great souls offer their prayers to Lord Narayana (the consciousness of human beings), Hari (gross, subtle, and causal bodies).

महर्षयश्चारणाश्च दृष्ट्वा गजविमोक्षणम् ।
विस्मयोत्फूल्लनयनाः संस्तुवन्ति जनार्दनम् ॥ ७८ ॥

maharṣayaścāraṇāśca dṛṣṭvā gajavimokṣaṇam |
vismayotphūllanayanāḥ saṁstuvanti janārdanam || 78 ||

78. The great rishis perceive the feet of the elephant who had been liberated. Their eyes blossom with wonder, when they sing the praises of the Lord of all beings born.

प्रजापतिपतिर्ब्रह्मा चक्रपाणिविचेष्टितम् ।
गजेन्द्रमोक्षणं दृष्ट्वा इदं वचनमब्रवीत् ॥ ७९ ॥

prajāpatipatirbrahmā cakrapāṇiviceṣṭitam |
gajendramokṣaṇaṁ dṛṣṭvā idaṁ vacanamabravīt || 79 ||

79. The Lord of the Lord of all beings born, the Creator, who has a discuss in His hand, makes efforts for those who perceive (listen, grok) these words I have spoken about the liberation of the King of elephants.

य इदं श‍ृणुयान्नित्यं प्रातरुत्थाय मानवः ।
प्राप्नुयात् परमां सिद्धिं दुःस्वप्नस्तस्य नश्यति ॥ ८० ॥

ya idaṁ śṛṇuyānntityaṁ prātarutthāya mānavaḥ |
prāpnuyāt paramāṁ siddhiṁ
duḥsvapnastasya naśyati || 80 ||

80. Whichever human being will continually repeat this story or listen to it in the early morning, will attain the highest perfection, and destroy all bad dreams.

गजेन्द्र मोक्षणं पुण्यं सर्वपापप्रणाशनम् ।
कथितेन स्मृतेनाथ श्रुतेन च तपोधनः ।
गजेन्द्रमोक्षणेनेह सद्यः पापात् प्रमुच्यते ॥ ८१ ॥

**gajendra mokṣaṇaṁ puṇyaṁ sarvapāpapraṇāśanam |
kathitena smṛtenātha śrutena ca tapodhanaḥ |
gajendramokṣaṇeneha sadyaḥ pāpāt pramucyate || 81 ||**

81. This story of the liberation of the King of elephants has such merits that it destroys all sin. Remembering the Lord by means of listening to this story, one attains the wealth of spiritual austerities. By means of this story of the liberation of the King of elephants, one will become liberated from all sin (confusion).

एतत् पवित्रं परमं सुपुण्यं
संकीर्तनीयं चरितं मुरारेः ।
यस्मिन् किलोक्ते बहुपापबन्धना-
ल्लभ्येत मोक्षो द्विरदेन यद्वत् ॥ ८२ ॥

**etat pavitraṁ paramaṁ supuṇyaṁ
saṁkīrtanīyaṁ caritaṁ murāreḥ |
yasmin kilokte bahupāpabandhanā-
llabhyeta mokṣo dviradena yadvat || 82 ||**

82. One gains pure, supreme, excellent merits by singing this saga of Murari (Krishna as the slayer of the demon Mura, who encompasses, surrounds us). From there, verily it is said that one gains liberation from the bondage to many sins, just as (in the same way as) did the elephant.

अजं वरेण्यं वरपद्मनाभं
नारायणं ब्रह्मनिधिं सुरेशम् ।
तं देवगुह्यं पुरुषं पुराणं
वन्दाम्यहं लोकपतिं वरेण्यम् ॥ ८३ ॥

ajaṁ vareṇyaṁ varapadmanābhaṁ
nārāyaṇaṁ brahmanidhiṁ sureśam |
taṁ devaguhyaṁ puruṣaṁ purāṇaṁ
vandāmyahaṁ lokapatiṁ vareṇyam || 83 ||

83. I laud in praise the Highest, Unborn, who has a lotus in His naval, Giver of Boons, Narayana (the consciousness of human beings), the discipline of the Creator, Lord of the gods. He is the secret of the gods, the full, complete, and perfect consciousness, most Ancient, the Highest Lord of the Worlds.

पुलस्त्य उवाच

pulastya uvāca

Pulastya said:

एतत् तवोक्तं प्रवरं स्तवानां
स्तवं मुरारेर्वरनागकीर्तनम् ।
यं कीर्त्य संश्रुत्य तथा विचिन्त्य
पापापनोदं पुरुषो लभेत ॥ ८४ ॥

etat tavoktaṁ pravaraṁ stavānāṁ
stavaṁ murārervaranāgakīrtanam |
yaṁ kīrtya saṁśrutya tathā vicintya
pāpāpanodaṁ puruṣo labheta || 84 ||

84. In this way the invocation of this hymn of praise was made. Singing this brings the benefits of Murari (Krishna, slayer of the demon Mura, who encompasses, surrounds us). Whoever will sing or listen to this without other thoughts, that individual will gain freedom from all sin (confusion).

इति श्रीवामनपुराणे वामनप्रादुर्भावे गजेन्द्रमोक्षः समाप्तः

iti śrīvāmanapurāṇe vāmanaprādurbhāve gajendramokṣaḥ samāptaḥ

Thus ends the story about the Liberation of the King of Elephants from the Respected Vaman Purana.

जय जगदीश हरे

Jaya Jagadīśa Hare

Victory to Hari, the Lord of the Universe!

\- 1 -

जय जगदीश हरे, भक्त जनन के सङ्कट
क्षणमें दूर करे, ॐ जय जगदीश हरे

**jaya jagadīśa hare, bhakta janana ke saṅkaṭa
kṣaṇameṁ dūra kare, oṁ jaya jagadīśa hare**

Victory to Hari, the Lord of the Universe, who in but a moment removes all the difficulties of devotees. Victory to Hari, the Lord of the Universe.

\- 2 -

जो ध्यावे फल पावे, दुःख बिनसे मनका
सुख सम्पति घर आवे, कष्ट मिटे तनका
ॐ जय जगदीश हरे

**jo dhyāve phala pāve, duḥkha binase manakā
sukha sampati ghara āve, kaṣṭa miṭe tanakā
oṁ jaya jagadīśa hare**

Whoever will meditate will receive fruit, all pain will be removed from the mind. Comfort and wealth will come to your home, and all problems will be removed from your body. Victory to Hari, the Lord of the Universe.

\- 3 -

माता पिता तुम मेरे, शरणा गहूँ किसकी
तुम बिना और न दूजा, आस करूँ जिसकी
ॐ जय जगदीश हरे

mātā pitā tuma mere, śaraṇā gahūṁ kisakī
tuma binā aura na dūjā, āsa karuṁ jisakī
oṁ jaya jagadīśa hare

You are my Mother and Father, whoever takes refuge in you like this; beyond you there is no other. Fulfill my longing. Victory to Hari, the Lord of the Universe.

\- 4 -

तुम पूरण परमात्मा, तुम अन्तर्यामी
पारब्रह्म परमेश्वर, तुम सबके स्वामी
ॐ जय जगदीश हरे

tuma pūraṇa paramātmā, tuma antaryāmī
pārabrahma parameśvara, tuma sabake svāmī
oṁ jaya jagadīśa hare

You are the Supreme Soul from ancient times, you are the Soul within as well. You are the Supreme Divinity and the Lord Supreme. You are everything, oh Master. Victory to Hari, the Lord of the Universe.

- 5 -

तुम करुणा के सागर, तुम पालन कर्ता
मैं सेवक तुम स्वामी, कृपा करो भर्ता
ॐ जय जगदीश हरे

tuma karuṇā ke sāgara, tuma pālana kartā
maiṁ sevaka tuma svāmī, kṛpā karo bhartā
oṁ jaya jagadīśa hare

You are the ocean of compassion. You are the Protector as well. I am your servant, oh Master. Please give me your grace, oh Beloved. Victory to Hari, the Lord of the Universe.

- 6 -

तुम हो एक अगोचर, सबके प्राणापति
किस विधि मीलहुँ दयामय, तुमको मैं कुमति
ॐ जय जगदीश हरे

tuma ho eka agocara, sabake prāṇāpati
kisa vidhi mīlahum̐ dayāmaya, tumako maim̐ kumati
oṁ jaya jagadīśa hare

You are the One Imperceivable, the Lord of all life. How shall I receive your compassion, because I manifest bad behavior. Victory to Hari, the Lord of the Universe.

- 7 -

दीन बन्धु दुःख हर्ता, तुम रक्षक मेरे
आपने हात उठाओ, द्वार परा तेरे
ॐ जय जगदीश हरे

dīna bandhu duḥkha hartā, tuma rakṣaka mere
āpane hāta uṭhāo, dvāra parā tere
oṁ jaya jagadīśa hare

You take away the pain from the afflicted, you are my Protector. Please raise your hands, and open the door to your perception. Victory to Hari, the Lord of the Universe.

- 8 -

विषय विकार मिटाओ, पाप हरो देवा
श्रद्धा भक्ति बढाओ, सन्तन की सेवा
ॐ जय जगदीश हरे

viṣaya vikāra miṭāo, pāpa haro devā
śraddhā bhakti baḍhāo, santana kī sevā
oṁ jaya jagadīśa hare

Take away all other thoughts, oh Lord who takes away sin. Increase my faith and devotion as a loving service to your children. Victory to Hari, the Lord of the Universe.

प्रणाम्

praṇām

शान्ताकारं भुजग-शयनं पद्मनाभं सुरेशम् ।
विश्वाधारं गगन-सदृशं मेघवर्णं शुभाङ्गम् ॥

śāntākāraṁ bhujaga-śayanaṁ
padmanābhaṁ sureśam
viśvādhāraṁ gagana-sadṛśaṁ
meghavarṇaṁ śubhāṅgam

The Cause of Peace is lying on a snake, from whose navel sprang the lotus. He is the Lord of Gods, who supports the universe, appearing as the sky, and is dark as a cloud, with a beautiful body.

लक्ष्मीकान्तं कमलनयनं योगिभिर्ध्यान-गम्यम् ।
वन्दे विष्णुं भव-भय-हरं सर्वलोकैकनाथम् ॥

lakṣmīkāntaṁ kamalanayanaṁ
yogibhirdhyāna-gamyam
vande viṣṇuṁ bhava-bhaya-haraṁ sarvalokaikanātham

The Lord of Lakṣmī, with lotus eyes, is realized by Yogis in meditation. We worship Viṣṇu, who removes the fear of existence and who is Master of the all of the worlds.

त्वमेव माता च पिता त्वमेव त्वमेव बन्धुश्च सखा त्वमेव ।
त्वमेव विद्या द्रविणं त्वमेव त्वमेव सर्वम् मम देवदेव ॥

tvameva mātā ca pitā tvameva
tvameva bandhuśca sakhā tvameva
tvameva vidyā draviṇaṁ tvameva
tvameva sarvam mama deva deva

You alone are Mother and Father, you alone are friend and relative. You alone are knowledge and wealth, Oh my God of Gods, you alone are everything.

कायेन वाचा मनसेन्द्रियैर्वा बुद्ध्यात्मानवप्रकृतस्वभावत् ।
करोमि यद्यत् सकलम् परस्मै नारायणायेति समर्पयामि ॥

kāyena vācā manasendriyairvā
buddhyātmā nava prakṛta svabhavat
karomi yadyat sakalam parasmai
nārāyaṇāyeti samarpayāmi

Body, speech, mind, the five organs of knowledge (five senses) and the intellect; these nine are the natural condition of human existence. In their highest evolution, I move beyond them all, as I surrender completely to the Supreme Consciousness.

ॐ पापोऽहं पापकर्माहं पापात्मा पापसम्भव ।
त्राहि मां पुण्डरीकाक्षं सर्वपापहरो हरिः ॥

oṁ pāpo-haṁ pāpakarmāhaṁ
pāpātmā pāpasambhava
trāhi māṁ puṇḍarīkākṣaṁ sarvapāpa haro hariḥ

oṁ I am of sin, confusion, duality; my actions are of duality; this entire existence is of duality. Oh Savior and Protector, Oh Great Consciousness, take away all sin, confusion, duality.

ॐ मन्त्रहीनं क्रियाहीनं भक्तिहीनं सुरेश्वरि ।
यत्पूजितं मया देवि परिपूर्णं तदस्तु मे ॥

oṁ mantrahīnaṁ kriyāhīnaṁ
bhaktihīnaṁ sureśvari
yatpūjitaṁ mayā devi paripūrnaṁ tadastu me

oṁ I know nothing of mantras. I do not perform good conduct. I have no devotion, Oh Supreme Goddess. But Oh my God, please accept the worship that I offer.

त्वमेव प्रत्यक्षम् ब्रह्माऽसि ।
त्वामेव प्रत्यक्षम् ब्रह्म वदिष्यामि ।
ऋतम् वदिष्यामि, सत्यम् वदिष्यामि ।
तन मामवतु, तद वक्तारमवतु ।
अवतु माम्, अवतु वक्तारम् ॥

tvameva pratyakṣam brahmā-si
tvāmeva pratyakṣam brahma vadiṣyāmi
ṛtam vadiṣyāmi, satyam vadiṣyāmi
tana māmavatu, tada vaktāramavatu
avatu mām, avatu vaktāram

You alone are the Perceivable Supreme Divinity. You alone are the Perceivable Supreme Divinity, so I shall declare. I shall speak the nectar of immortality. I shall speak Truth. May this body be your instrument. May this mouth be your instrument. May the Divine always be with us. May it be thus.

ॐ सह नाववतु सह नौ भुनक्तु । सह वीर्यं करवावहै ।
तेजस्विनावधीतमस्तु । मा विद्विषावहै ॥

oṁ saha nāvavatu, saha nau bhunaktu
saha vīryam karavāvahai tejasvināvadhītamastu
mā vidviṣāvahai

oṁ May the Lord protect us. May the Lord grant us enjoyment of all actions. May we be granted strength to work together. May our studies be thorough and faithful. May all disagreement cease.

ॐ असतो मा सद् गमय । तमसो मा ज्योतिर्गमय ।
मृत्योर्मा अमृतं गमय ॥

oṁ asatomā sad gamaya tamasomā jyotirgamaya
mṛtyormā amṛtaṁ gamaya

oṁ From untruth lead us to Truth. From darkness lead us to the Light. From death lead us to Immortality.

ॐ सर्वेषां स्वस्तिर्भवतु । सर्वेषां शान्तिर्भवतु । सर्वेषां पूर्णं भवतु । सर्वेषां मङ्गलं भवतु सर्वे भवन्तु सुखिनः । सर्वे सन्तु निरामयाः । सर्वे भद्राणि पश्यन्तु । मा कश्चिद् दुःख भाग्भवेत् ॥

oṁ sarveṣāṁ svastir bhavatu sarveṣāṁ śāntir bhavatu sarveṣāṁ pūrṇaṁ bhavatu sarveṣaṁ maṅgalaṁ bhavatu sarve bhavantu sukhinaḥ
sarve santu nirāmayāḥ sarve bhadrāṇi paśyantu mā kaścid duḥkha bhāgbhavet

oṁ May all be blessed with the highest realization. May all be blessed with Peace. May all be blessed with Perfection. May all be blessed with Welfare. May all be blessed with comfort and happiness. May all be free from misery. May all perceive auspiciousness. May all be free from infirmities.

गुरुर्ब्रह्मा गुरुर्विष्णुः गुरुर्देवो महेश्वरः ।
गुरुः साक्षात् परं ब्रह्म तस्मै श्रीगुरवे नमः ॥

gurur brahmā gururviṣṇuḥ gururdevo maheśvaraḥ
guruḥ sākṣāt paraṁ brahma tasmai śrīgurave namaḥ

The Guru is Brahmā, Guru is Viṣṇu, Guru is the Lord Maheśvara. The Guru is actually the Supreme Divinity, and therefore we bow down to the Guru.

ॐ ब्रह्मार्पणं ब्रह्म हविर्ब्रह्माग्नौ ब्रह्मणा हुतम् ।
ब्रह्मैव तेन गन्तव्यं ब्रह्मकर्मसमाधिना ॥

oṁ brahmārpaṇaṁ brahma havir
brahmāgnau brahmaṇā hutam
brahmaiva tena gantavyaṁ
brahmakarma samādhinā

oṁ The Supreme Divinity makes the offering; the Supreme Divinity is the offering; offered by the Supreme Divinity, in the fire of the Supreme Divinity. By seeing the Supreme Divinity in all actions, one realizes that Supreme Divinity.

ॐ पूर्णमदः पूर्णमिदं पूर्णात् पूर्णमुदच्यते ।
पूर्णस्य पूर्णमादाय पूर्णमेवावशिष्यते ॥

oṁ pūrṇamadaḥ pūrṇamidaṁ
pūrṇāt pūrṇamudacyate
pūrṇasya pūrṇamādāya pūrṇamevāva śiṣyate
oṁ That is whole and perfect; this is whole and perfect. From the whole and perfect, the whole and perfect becomes manifest. If the whole and perfect issue forth from the whole and perfect, even still only the whole and perfect will remain.

ॐ शान्तिः शान्तिः शान्तिः

oṁ śāntiḥ śāntiḥ śāntiḥ
oṁ Peace, Peace, Peace

अथ विष्णुसहस्रनामावल्याः स्वाहाकारविधिः
Atha Viṣṇusahasranāmāvalyāḥ Svāhākāravidhiḥ

अस्य श्रीविष्णोर्दिव्यसहस्रनामस्तोत्रमन्त्रस्य भगवान् वेदव्यास ऋषिः अनुष्टुप् छन्दः श्रीकृष्णः परमात्मा देवता अमृतांशुद्भवो भानुरिति बीजम् देवकीनन्दनः स्रष्टेति शक्तिः त्रिसामा-मामगः सामेति हृदयम् शङ्खभृन्नन्दकी चक्रीति कीलकम् शार्ङ्गधन्वागदाधर इत्यस्त्रम् रथाङ्गपाणिरक्षोभ्य इति कवचम् उद्भवः क्षोभणो देव इति परमो मन्त्रः श्रीविष्णुप्रीत्यर्थे जपे (होमे) (सहस्रतुलसीदलसमर्पणे) (च) विनियोगः ।

asya śrīviṣṇordivyasahasranāmastotramantrasya bhagavān vedavyāsa ṛṣiḥ anuṣṭup chandaḥ śrīkṛṣṇaḥ paramātmā devatā amṛtāṁśudbhavo bhānuriti bījam devakīnandanaḥ sraṣṭeti śaktiḥ trisāmā-māmagaḥ sāmeti hṛdayamśaṅkhabhṛnnandakī cakrīti kīlakam śārṅgadhanvāgadādhara ityastram rathāṅgapāṇirakṣobhya iti kavacam udbhavaḥ kṣobhaṇo deva iti paramo mantraḥ śrīviṣṇuprītyarthe jape (home) (sahasratulasīdalasamarparṇe) (ca) viniyogaḥ |

And now, the mantras of the song of the thousand divine names of the respected Viṣṇu, the seer is the supreme divinity Veda Vyāsa, the meter is anuṣṭup (32 syllables to the verse), the supreme soul the respected Kṛṣṇa is the deity, the seed is the pure nectar of the immortal bliss of being, the energy is the most excellent offspring of Devakī, in the heart are the three songs of the Sāma Veda, the pin is the conch shell containing delight and the discus of revolving time, the weapons are the bow and the club, the armor that protects is He who has a discus in his hand, the deity that gives birth to purity manifests through the supreme mantras, for the purpose of satisfying the respected Viṣṇu, the recitation of these mantras (and) (fire ceremony) (and) (offering of one thousand leaves of tulasī) is being applied.

- 1 -

ॐ विश्वस्मै स्वाहा

oṁ viśvasmai svāhā
To He who is the universe

- 2 -

ॐ विष्णवे स्वाहा

oṁ viṣṇave svāhā
To He who pervades the universe

- 3 -

ॐ वषट्काराय स्वाहा

oṁ vaṣaṭkārāya svāhā
To He who purifies

- 4 -

ॐ भूतभव्यभवत्प्रभवे स्वाहा

oṁ bhūtabhavyabhavatprabhave svāhā
To He who is the lord of the past, present, and future

- 5 -

ॐ भूतकृते स्वाहा

oṁ bhūtakṛte svāhā
To He who creates all beings

- 6 -

ॐ भूतभृते स्वाहा

oṁ bhūtabhṛte svāhā
To He who protects all beings

- 7 -

ॐ भावाय स्वाहा

oṁ bhāvāya svāhā
To He who is the attitude of existence

- 8 -

ॐ भूतात्मने स्वाहा

oṁ bhūtātmane svāhā
To He who is the soul of existence

- 9 -

ॐ भूतभावनाय स्वाहा

oṁ bhūtabhāvanāya svāhā
To He who is the attitude that pervades existence

- 10 -

ॐ पूतात्मने स्वाहा

oṁ pūtātmane svāhā
To He who is the pure soul

- 11 -

ॐ परमात्मने स्वाहा

oṁ paramātmane svāhā
To He who is the supreme soul

- 12 -

ॐ मुक्तानां परमागतये स्वाहा

oṁ muktānāṁ paramāgataye svāhā
To He who is the supreme goal of liberation

- 13 -

ॐ अव्ययाय स्वाहा

oṁ avyayāya svāhā
To He who is unchanging

- 14 -

ॐ पुरुषाय स्वाहा

oṁ puruṣāya svāhā
To He who is full, complete, perfect consciousness

- 15 -

ॐ साक्षिणे स्वाहा

oṁ sākṣiṇe svāhā
To He who is the witness

- 16 -

ॐ क्षेत्रज्ञाय स्वाहा

oṁ kṣetrajñāya svāhā
To He who is the knower of the field

- 17 -

ॐ अक्षराय स्वाहा

oṁ akṣarāya svāhā
To He who is without change

- 18 -

ॐ योगाय स्वाहा

oṁ yogāya svāhā
To He who is union

- 19 -

ॐ योगविदां नेत्रे स्वाहा

oṁ yogavidāṁ netre svāhā
To He who is the leader of knowers of union

- 20 -

ॐ प्रधानपुरुषेश्वराय स्वाहा

oṁ pradhānapuruṣeśvarāya svāhā
To He who is the foremost, complete consciousness of God

- 21 -

ॐ नारसिंहवपुषे स्वाहा

oṁ nārasiṁhavapuṣe svāhā
To He who is half-man, half-lion

- 22 -

ॐ श्रीमते स्वाहा

oṁ śrīmate svāhā
To He who is respect

- 23 -

ॐ केशवाय स्वाहा

oṁ keśavāya svāhā
To He who has beautiful hair, who creates, protects, and transforms existence

- 24 -

ॐ पुरुषोत्तमाय स्वाहा

oṁ puruṣottamāya svāhā
To He who is excellent, perfect consciousness

- 25 -

ॐ सर्वस्मै स्वाहा

oṁ sarvasmai svāhā
To He who is all

- 26 -

ॐ शर्वाय स्वाहा

oṁ śarvāya svāhā
To He who is beyond qualities

- 27 -

ॐ शिवाय स्वाहा

oṁ śivāya svāhā
To He who is the consciousness of infinite goodness

- 28 -

ॐ स्थाणवे स्वाहा

oṁ sthāṇave svāhā
To He who is the residence of all

- 29 -

ॐ भुतादये स्वाहा

oṁ bhutādaye svāhā
To He who creates all the elements

- 30 -

ॐ अव्ययनिधये स्वाहा

oṁ avyayanidhaye svāhā
To He who is the system that does not change

- 31 -

ॐ सम्भवाय स्वाहा

oṁ sambhavāya svāhā
To He who has the attitude of peace

- 32 -

ॐ भावनाय स्वाहा

oṁ bhāvanāya svāhā
To He who is the supreme attitude

- 33 -

ॐ भर्त्रे स्वाहा

oṁ bhartre svāhā
To He who is the husband

- 34 -

ॐ प्रभवाय स्वाहा

oṁ prabhavāya svāhā
To He who is luminous

- 35 -

ॐ प्रभवे स्वाहा

oṁ prabhave svāhā
To He who is illumination

- 36 -

ॐ ईश्वराय स्वाहा

oṁ īśvarāya svāhā
To He who is the supreme lord

- 37 -

ॐ स्वयम्भुवे स्वाहा

oṁ svayambhuve svāhā
To He who is born by himself

- 38 -

ॐ शम्भवे स्वाहा

oṁ śambhave svāhā
To He who dwells in peace

- 39 -

ॐ आदित्याय स्वाहा

oṁ ādityāya svāhā
To He who is beyond dualism

- 40 -

ॐ पुष्कराक्षाय स्वाहा

oṁ puṣkarākṣāya svāhā
To He who is the protector of the cause of nourishment

- 41 -

ॐ महास्वनाय स्वाहा

oṁ mahāsvanāya svāhā
To He who himself is good

- 42 -

ॐ अनादिनिधनाय स्वाहा

oṁ anādinidhanāya svāhā
To He who is attained through various methods

- 43 -

ॐ धात्रे स्वाहा

oṁ dhātre svāhā
To He who is the giver

- 44 -

ॐ विधात्रे स्वाहा

oṁ vidhātre svāhā
To He who is the creator

- 45 -

ॐ धातुरुत्तमाय स्वाहा

oṁ dhāturuttamāya svāhā
To He who is the most excellent essence

- 46 -

ॐ अप्रमेयाय स्वाहा

oṁ aprameyāya svāhā
To He who is undefinable

- 47 -

ॐ हृषीकेशाय स्वाहा

oṁ hṛṣīkeśāya svāhā
To He who controls the senses

- 48 -

ॐ पद्मनाभाय स्वाहा

oṁ padmanābhāya svāhā
To He who has a lotus in his navel

- 49 -

ॐ अमरप्रभवे स्वाहा

oṁ amaraprabhave svāhā
To He who illuminates immortality

- 50 -

ॐ विश्वकर्मणे स्वाहा

oṁ viśvakramaṇe svāhā
To He who performs all actions in the universe

- 51 -

ॐ मनवे स्वाहा

oṁ manave svāhā
To He who is the thinker

- 52 -

ॐ त्वष्ट्रे स्वाहा

oṁ tvaṣṭre svāhā
To He who creates divine designs

- 53 -

ॐ स्थविष्ठाय स्वाहा

oṁ sthaviṣṭhāya svāhā
To He who is large

- 54 -

ॐ स्थविरोध्रुवाय स्वाहा

oṁ sthavirodhruvāya svāhā
To He who is fixed in immensity

- 55 -

ॐ अग्राह्याय स्वाहा

oṁ agrāhyāya svāhā
To He who is unable to be perceived

- 56-

ॐ शाश्वताय स्वाहा

oṁ śāśvatāya svāhā
To He who is eternal

- 57 -

ॐ कृष्णाय स्वाहा

oṁ kṛṣṇāya svāhā
To He who is the doer of all

- 58 -

ॐ लोहिताक्षाय स्वाहा

oṁ lohitākṣāya svāhā
To He who is the light in the eyes

- 59 -

ॐ प्रतर्दनाय स्वाहा

oṁ pratardanāya svāhā
To He who is the dissolver of all

- 60 -

ॐ प्रभूताय स्वाहा

oṁ prabhūtāya svāhā
To He who is lord

- 61 -

ॐ त्रिककुब्धाम्ने स्वाहा

oṁ trikakubdhāmne svāhā
To He who supports the three worlds

- 62 -

ॐ पवित्राय स्वाहा

oṁ pavitrāya svāhā
To He who is pure

- 63 -

ॐ मङ्गलपराय स्वाहा

oṁ maṅgalaparāya svāhā
To He who is the supreme welfare

- 64 -

ॐ ईशानाय स्वाहा

oṁ īśānāya svāhā
To He who is the ruler

- 65 -

ॐ प्राणदाय स्वाहा

oṁ prāṇadāya svāhā
To He who is the giver of life

- 66 -

ॐ प्राणाय स्वाहा

oṁ prāṇāya svāhā
To He who is life

- 67 -

ॐ ज्येष्ठाय स्वाहा

oṁ jyeṣṭāya svāhā
To He who is the oldest

- 68 -

ॐ श्रेष्ठाय स्वाहा

oṁ śreṣṭāya svāhā
To He who is the best

- 69 -

ॐ प्रजापतये स्वाहा

oṁ prajāpataye svāhā
To He who is the lord of all beings born

- 70 -

ॐ हिरण्यगर्भाय स्वाहा

oṁ hiraṇyagarbhāya svāhā
To He who is the golden womb

- 71 -

ॐ भूगर्भाय स्वाहा

oṁ bhūgarbhāya svāhā
To He who is the womb of the earth

- 72 -

ॐ माधवाय स्वाहा

oṁ mādhavāya svāhā
To He who is sweet

- 73 -

ॐ मधुसूदनाय स्वाहा

oṁ madhusūdanāya svāhā
To He who is the slayer of the demon Too Much

- 74 -

ॐ ईश्वराय स्वाहा

oṁ īśvarāya svāhā
To He who is the seer of all

- 75 -

ॐ विक्रमिणे स्वाहा

oṁ vikramiṇe svāhā
To He who organizes the creation

- 76 -

ॐ धन्विने स्वाहा

oṁ dhanvine svāhā
To He who is the ideal of perfection

- 77 -

ॐ मेधाविने स्वाहा

oṁ medhāvine svāhā
To He who is the intellect of love

- 78 -

ॐ विक्रमाय स्वाहा

oṁ vikramāya svāhā
To He who is the organization of creation

- 79 -

ॐ क्रमाय स्वाहा

oṁ kramāya svāhā
To He who is order

- 80 -

ॐ अनुत्तमाय स्वाहा

oṁ anuttamāya svāhā
To He who has none superior

- 81 -

ॐ दुराधर्षाय स्वाहा

oṁ durādharṣāya svāhā

To He who is difficult to perceive

- 82 -

ॐ कृतज्ञाय स्वाहा

oṁ kṛtajñāya svāhā

To He who knows all effects

- 83 -

ॐ कृतये स्वाहा

oṁ kṛtaye svāhā

To He who is all effects

- 84 -

ॐ आत्मवते स्वाहा

oṁ ātmavate svāhā

To He who is in the souls of all

- 85 -

ॐ सुरेशाय स्वाहा

oṁ sureśāya svāhā

To He who is the lord of the gods

- 86 -

ॐ शरणाय स्वाहा

oṁ śaraṇāya svāhā

To He who is the refuge of all

- 87 -

ॐ शर्मणे स्वाहा

oṁ śarmaṇe svāhā

To He who is always delighted

- 88 -

ॐ विश्वरेतसे स्वाहा

oṁ viśvaretase svāhā

To He who is the seed of the universe

- 89 -

ॐ प्रजाभवाय स्वाहा

oṁ prajābhavāya svāhā
To He who is the source of the people

- 90 -

ॐ अह्नये स्वाहा

oṁ ahnaye svāhā
To He who is the eternal day

- 91 -

ॐ संवत्सराय स्वाहा

oṁ saṁvatsarāya svāhā
To He who is the years

- 92 -

ॐ व्यालाय स्वाहा

oṁ vyālāya svāhā
To He who is difficult to grasp

- 93 -

ॐ प्रत्ययाय स्वाहा

oṁ pratyayāya svāhā
To He who is the subtle body of consciousness

- 94 -

ॐ सर्वदर्शनाय स्वाहा

oṁ sarvadarśanāya svāhā
To He who perceives all

- 95 -

ॐ अजाय स्वाहा

oṁ ajāya svāhā
To He who is unborn

- 96 -

ॐ सर्वेश्वराय स्वाहा

oṁ sarveśvarāya svāhā
To He who is the supreme lord of all

- 97 -

ॐ सिद्धाय स्वाहा

oṁ siddhāya svāhā
To He who is attainment

- 98 -

ॐ सिद्धये स्वाहा

oṁ siddhaye svāhā
To He who has attained

- 99 -

ॐ सर्वादये स्वाहा

oṁ sarvādaye svāhā
To He who gives all

- 100 -

ॐ अच्युताय स्वाहा

oṁ acyutāya svāhā
To He who is infinite

- 101 -

ॐ वृषाकपये स्वाहा

oṁ vṛṣākapaye svāhā
To He who travels with a bull or a monkey

- 102 -

ॐ अमेयात्मने स्वाहा

oṁ ameyātmane svāhā
To He who has an immeasurable soul

- 103 -

ॐ सर्वयोगविनिःसृताय स्वाहा

oṁ sarvayogaviniḥsṛtāya svāhā
To He who gives birth to all union

- 104 -

ॐ वसवे स्वाहा

oṁ vasave svāhā
To He who is all wealth

\- 105 -

ॐ वसुमनसे स्वाहा

oṁ vasumanase svāhā
To He whose mind is filled with wealth

\- 106 -

ॐ सत्याय स्वाहा

oṁ satyāya svāhā
To He who is truth

\- 107 -

ॐ समात्मने स्वाहा

oṁ samātmane svāhā
To He whose soul is always in equilibrium

\- 108 -

ॐ सम्मिताय स्वाहा

oṁ sammitāya svāhā
To He who has balance

\- 109 -

ॐ समाय स्वाहा

oṁ samāya svāhā
To He who is equal

\- 110 -

ॐ अमोघाय स्वाहा

oṁ amoghāya svāhā
To He who is unfailing

\- 111 -

ॐ पुण्डरीकाक्षाय स्वाहा

oṁ puṇḍarīkākṣāya svāhā
To He who is the lotus-eyed one

\- 112 -

ॐ वृषाकर्मणे स्वाहा

oṁ vṛṣākarmaṇe svāhā
To He who acts with determination

- 113 -

ॐ वृषाकृतये स्वाहा

oṁ vṛṣākṛtaye svāhā

To He who is the effect of determination

- 114 -

ॐ रुद्राय स्वाहा

oṁ rudrāya svāhā

To He who relieves suffering

- 115 -

ॐ बहुशिरसे स्वाहा

oṁ bahuśirase svāhā

To He who has many heads

- 116 -

ॐ बभ्रवे स्वाहा

oṁ babhrave svāhā

To He who is the support of the world

- 117 -

ॐ विश्वयोनये स्वाहा

oṁ viśvayonaye svāhā

To He who is the womb of the universe

- 118 -

ॐ शुचिश्रवसे स्वाहा

oṁ śuciśravase svāhā

To He who listens to purity

- 119 -

ॐ अमृताय स्वाहा

oṁ amṛtāya svāhā

To He who is the nectar of immortal bliss

- 120 -

ॐ शाश्वतस्थाणवे स्वाहा

oṁ śāśvatasthāṇave svāhā

To He who resides in the eternal residence

- 121 -

ॐ वरारोहाय स्वाहा

oṁ varārohāya svāhā
To He who gives the boon of light

- 122 -

ॐ महातपसे स्वाहा

oṁ mahātapase svāhā
To He who performs great austerities

- 123 -

ॐ सर्वगाय स्वाहा

oṁ sarvagāya svāhā
To He who moves all

- 124 -

ॐ सर्वविद्भानवे स्वाहा

oṁ sarvavidbhānave svāhā
To He who resides in all knowledge

- 125 -

ॐ विष्वक्सेनाय स्वाहा

oṁ viṣvaksenāya svāhā
To He who scatters armies

- 126 -

ॐ जनार्दनाय स्वाहा

oṁ janārdanāya svāhā
To He who resides in all beings born

- 127 -

ॐ वेदाय स्वाहा

oṁ vedāya svāhā
To He who is the wisdom to be known

- 128 -

ॐ वेदविदे स्वाहा

oṁ vedavide svāhā
To He who is the knower of wisdom

- 129 -

ॐ अव्यङ्गाय स्वाहा

oṁ avyaṇgāya svāhā
To He who has various limbs

- 130 -

ॐ वेदाङ्गाय स्वाहा

oṁ vedāṇgāya svāhā
To He who is the body of wisdom

- 131 -

ॐ वेदविदे स्वाहा

oṁ vedavide svāhā
To He who is the knower of wisdom

- 132 -

ॐ कवये स्वाहा

oṁ kavaye svāhā
To He who is an inspired poet

- 133 -

ॐ लोकाध्यक्षाय स्वाहा

oṁ lokādhyakṣāya svāhā
To He who is the leader of the worlds

- 134 -

ॐ सुराध्यक्षाय स्वाहा

oṁ surādhyakṣāya svāhā
To He who is the leader of the Gods

- 135 -

ॐ धर्माध्यक्षाय स्वाहा

oṁ dharmadhyakṣāya svāhā
To He who is the leader of the ideals of perfection

- 136 -

ॐ कृताकृताय स्वाहा

oṁ kṛtākṛtāya svāhā
To He who is the cause and effect

- 137 -

ॐ चतुरात्मने स्वाहा

oṁ caturātmane svāhā
To He who is the soul of the four (Vedas)

- 138 -

ॐ चतुर्व्युहाय स्वाहा

oṁ caturvyuhāya svāhā
To He who is the four formations of power

- 139 -

ॐ चतुर्दंष्ट्राय स्वाहा

oṁ caturdaṁṣṭrāya svāhā
To He who has four tusks

- 140 -

ॐ चतुर्भुजाय स्वाहा

oṁ caturbhujāya svāhā
To He who has four arms

- 141 -

ॐ भ्राजिष्णवे स्वाहा

oṁ bhrājiṣṇave svāhā
To He who is the essence of light

- 142 -

ॐ भोजनाय स्वाहा

oṁ bhojanāya svāhā
To He who is food

- 143 -

ॐ भोक्त्रे स्वाहा

oṁ bhoktre svāhā
To He who enjoys

- 144 -

ॐ सहिष्णवे स्वाहा

oṁ sahiṣṇave svāhā
To He who is with enjoyment

- 145 -

ॐ जगदादिजाय स्वाहा

oṁ jagadādijāya svāhā
To He who gives birth to the perceivable universe

- 146 -

ॐ जनघाय स्वाहा

oṁ janaghāya svāhā
To He who gives to the people

- 147 -

ॐ विजयाय स्वाहा

oṁ vijayāya svāhā
To He who is undefeatable

- 148 -

ॐ जेत्रे स्वाहा

oṁ jetre svāhā
To He who is the conqueror

- 149 -

ॐ विश्वयोनये स्वाहा

oṁ viśvayonaye svāhā
To He who is the womb of the universe

- 150 -

ॐ पुनर्वसवे स्वाहा

oṁ punarvasave svāhā
To He who lives again and again

- 151 -

ॐ उपेन्द्राय स्वाहा

oṁ upendrāya svāhā
To He who is near to Indra

- 152 -

ॐ वामनाय स्वाहा

oṁ vāmanāya svāhā
To He who is a dwarf

- 153 -

ॐ प्रांशवे स्वाहा

oṁ prāṁśave svāhā
To He who is tall

- 154 -

ॐ अमोघाय स्वाहा

oṁ amoghāya svāhā
To He who is unfailing

- 155 -

ॐ सुचये स्वाहा

oṁ sucaye svāhā
To He who causes purity

- 156 -

ॐ ऊर्जिताय स्वाहा

oṁ ūrjitāya svāhā
To He who conquers all circumstances

- 157 -

ॐ अतीन्द्राय स्वाहा

oṁ atīndrāya svāhā
To He who is the highest lord of heaven

- 158 -

ॐ सङ्ग्रहाय स्वाहा

oṁ saṅgrahāya svāhā
To He who absorbs all into Himself

- 159 -

ॐ सर्गाय स्वाहा

oṁ sargāya svāhā
To He who is matter

- 160 -

ॐ धृतात्मने स्वाहा

oṁ dhṛtātmane svāhā
To He whose soul is consistent

- 161 -

ॐ नियमाय स्वाहा

oṁ niyamāya svāhā
To He who is all discipline

- 162 -

ॐ यमाय स्वाहा

oṁ yamāya svāhā
To He who controls

- 163 -

ॐ वेद्याय स्वाहा

oṁ vedyāya svāhā
To He who dwells in wisdom

- 164 -

ॐ वैद्याय स्वाहा

oṁ vaidyāya svāhā
To He who dwells in the application of wisdom

- 165 -

ॐ सदायोगिने स्वाहा

oṁ sadāyogine svāhā
To He who is always in union

- 166 -

ॐ वीरघ्ने स्वाहा

oṁ vīraghne svāhā
To He who slays heroic warriors

- 167 -

ॐ माधवाय स्वाहा

oṁ mādhavāya svāhā
To He who is sweetest

- 168 -

ॐ मधवे स्वाहा

oṁ madhave svāhā
To He who is sweet

- 169 -

ॐ अतीन्द्रियाय स्वाहा

oṁ atīndriyāya svāhā

To He who is beyond the knowledge of the senses

- 170 -

ॐ महामायाय स्वाहा

oṁ mahāmāyāya svāhā

To He who is the great measurement of consciousness

- 171 -

ॐ महोत्साहाय स्वाहा

oṁ mahotsāhāya svāhā

To He who gives great enthusiasm

- 172 -

ॐ महाबलाय स्वाहा

oṁ mahābalāya svāhā

To He who is great strength

- 173 -

ॐ महाबुद्धये स्वाहा

oṁ mahābuddhaye svāhā

To He who is great intelligence

- 174 -

ॐ महावीर्याय स्वाहा

oṁ mahāvīryāya svāhā

To He who is great heroism

- 175 -

ॐ महाशक्तये स्वाहा

oṁ mahāśaktaye svāhā

To He who is great energy

- 176 -

ॐ महाद्युतये स्वाहा

oṁ mahādyutaye svāhā

To He who is great light

- 177 -

ॐ अनिर्देश्यवपुषे स्वाहा

oṁ anirdeśyavapuṣe svāhā
To He who is undefinable

- 178 -

ॐ श्रीमते स्वाहा

oṁ śrīmate svāhā
To He who is respected

- 179 -

ॐ अमेयात्मने स्वाहा

oṁ ameyātmane svāhā
To He who is the immeasurable soul

- 180 -

ॐ महाद्रिधृषे स्वाहा

oṁ mahādridhṛṣe svāhā
To He who is the great perceiver of consistency

- 181 -

ॐ महेष्वासाय स्वाहा

oṁ maheṣvāsāya svāhā
To He who resides in great perception

- 182 -

ॐ महीभर्त्रे स्वाहा

oṁ mahībhatre svāhā
To He who is the spouse of the earth

- 183 -

ॐ श्रीनिवासाय स्वाहा

oṁ śrīnivāsāya svāhā
To He who dwells in respect

- 184 -

ॐ सताङ्गतये स्वाहा

oṁ satāṅgataye svāhā
To He who has one hundred bodies

\- 185 -

ॐ अनिरुद्धाय स्वाहा

oṁ aniruddhāya svāhā
To He who expands limitations

\- 186 -

ॐ सुरानन्दाय स्वाहा

oṁ surānandāya svāhā
To He who is the bliss of the Gods

\- 187 -

ॐ गोविन्दाय स्वाहा

oṁ govindāya svāhā
To He who is one-pointed light

\- 188 -

ॐ गोविदाम्पतये स्वाहा

oṁ govidāmpataye svāhā
To He who is the lord of one-pointed light

\- 189 -

ॐ मरीचये स्वाहा

oṁ marīcaye svāhā
To He who is luminous

\- 190 -

ॐ दमनाय स्वाहा

oṁ damanāya svāhā
To He who controls

\- 191 -

ॐ हंसाय स्वाहा

oṁ haṁsāya svāhā
To He who is a swan

\- 192 -

ॐ सुपर्णाय स्वाहा

oṁ suparṇāya svāhā
To He who has excellent parts

- 193 -

ॐ भुजगोत्तमाय स्वाहा

oṁ bhujagottamāya svāhā
To He who is an excellent snake

- 194 -

ॐ हिरण्यनाभाय स्वाहा

oṁ hiraṇyanābhāya svāhā
To He who has a golden navel

- 195 -

ॐ सुतपसे स्वाहा

oṁ sutapase svāhā
To He who performs excellent austerities

- 196 -

ॐ पद्मनाभाय स्वाहा

oṁ padmanābhāya svāhā
To He who possesses the lotus navel

- 197 -

ॐ प्रजापतये स्वाहा

oṁ prajāpataye svāhā
To He who is the lord of all beings born

- 198 -

ॐ अमृत्यवे स्वाहा

oṁ amṛtyave svāhā
To He who is without death

- 199 -

ॐ सर्वदृशे स्वाहा

oṁ sarvadṛśe svāhā
To He who sees all

- 200 -

ॐ सिंहाय स्वाहा

oṁ siṁhāya svāhā
To He who is a lion

- 201 -

ॐ सन्धात्रे स्वाहा

oṁ sandhātre svāhā
To He who is the creator of true existence

- 202 -

ॐ सन्धिमते स्वाहा

oṁ sandhimate svāhā
To He who contemplates truth

- 203 -

ॐ स्थिराय स्वाहा

oṁ sthirāya svāhā
To He who is still, unchanging

- 204 -

ॐ अजाय स्वाहा

oṁ ajāya svāhā
To He who is unborn

- 205 -

ॐ दुर्मर्षणाय स्वाहा

oṁ durmarṣaṇāya svāhā
To He who is difficult to attain

- 206 -

ॐ शास्त्रे स्वाहा

oṁ śāstre svāhā
To He who is scripture

- 207 -

ॐ विश्रुतात्मने स्वाहा

oṁ viśrutātmane svāhā
To He who is the imperceptible soul

- 208 -

ॐ सुरारिघ्ने स्वाहा

oṁ surārighne svāhā
To He who is the destroyer of the enemies of the Gods

- 209 -

ॐ गुरवे स्वाहा

oṁ gurave svāhā
To He who is the guru

- 210 -

ॐ गुरुतमाय स्वाहा

oṁ gurutamāya svāhā
To He who is the excellent guru

- 211 -

ॐ धाम्ने स्वाहा

oṁ dhāmne svāhā
To He who is the greatest places of pilgrimage

- 212 -

ॐ सत्याय स्वाहा

oṁ satyāya svāhā
To He who is truth

- 213 -

ॐ सत्यपराक्रमाय स्वाहा

oṁ satyaparākramāya svāhā
To He who is invincible truth

- 214 -

ॐ निमिषाय स्वाहा

oṁ nimiṣāya svāhā
To He who causes the eyes to blink

- 215 -

ॐ अनिमिषाय स्वाहा

oṁ animiṣāya svāhā
To He who cannot be made to blink

- 216 -

ॐ स्रग्विणे स्वाहा

oṁ sragviṇe svāhā
To He who is a garland of mantras

- 217 -

ॐ वाचस्पतिरुदारधियें स्वाहा

oṁ vācaspatirudāradhiye svāhā

To He who contemplates the rise of the lord of vibrations

- 218 -

ॐ अग्रण्ये स्वाहा

oṁ agraṇye svāhā

To He who bestows liberation

- 219 -

ॐ ग्रामण्ये स्वाहा

oṁ grāmaṇye svāhā

To He who radiates unsurpassing beauty

- 220 -

ॐ श्रीमते स्वाहा

oṁ śrīmate svāhā

To He who is respected

- 221 -

ॐ न्यायाय स्वाहा

oṁ nyāyāya svāhā

To He who uses logic

- 222 -

ॐ नेत्रे स्वाहा

oṁ netre svāhā

To He who dwells in the eyes

- 223 -

ॐ समीरणाय स्वाहा

oṁ samīraṇāya svāhā

To He who is the cause of all movement

- 224 -

ॐ सहस्रमूर्ध्ने स्वाहा

oṁ sahasramūrdne svāhā

To He who has a thousand heads

- 225 -

ॐ विश्वात्मने स्वाहा

oṁ viśvātmane svāhā
To He who is the soul of the universe

- 226 -

ॐ सहस्राक्षाय स्वाहा

oṁ sahasrākṣāya svāhā
To He who has a thousand eyes

- 227 -

ॐ सहस्रपदे स्वाहा

oṁ sahasrapade svāhā
To He who has a thousand feet

- 228 -

ॐ आवर्त्तनाय स्वाहा

oṁ āvarttanāya svāhā
To He who is continual change

- 229 -

ॐ निवृत्तात्मने स्वाहा

oṁ nivṛttātmane svāhā
To He who is the soul of all change

- 230 -

ॐ संवृताय स्वाहा

oṁ saṁvṛtāya svāhā
To He who is all change

- 231 -

ॐ सम्प्रमर्दनाय स्वाहा

oṁ sampramardanāya svāhā
To He who is the essence of all proof

- 232 -

ॐ अहःसंवर्तकाय स्वाहा

oṁ ahaḥsaṁvartakāya svāhā
To He who is the light of the day

- 233 -

ॐ वह्ने स्वाहा

oṁ vahne svāhā
To He who is fire

- 234 -

ॐ अनिलाय स्वाहा

oṁ anilāya svāhā
To He who has no residence

- 235 -

ॐ धरणीधराय स्वाहा

oṁ dharaṇīdharāya svāhā
To He who is the support of all supports

- 236 -

ॐ सुप्रसादाय स्वाहा

oṁ suprasādāya svāhā
To He who is the excellent, consecrated offering

- 237 -

ॐ प्रसन्नात्मने स्वाहा

oṁ prasannātmane svāhā
To He whose soul is delighted

- 238 -

ॐ विश्वभृषे स्वाहा

oṁ viśvabhṛṣe svāhā
To He who is the delight of the universe

- 239 -

ॐ विश्वभुजे स्वाहा

oṁ viśvabhuje svāhā
To He who is the arms of the universe

- 240 -

ॐ विभवे स्वाहा

oṁ vibhave svāhā
To He who is beyond all existence

- 241 -

ॐ सत्कर्त्रे स्वाहा

oṁ satkartre svāhā
To He who acts with truth

- 242 -

ॐ सत्कृताय स्वाहा

oṁ satkṛtāya svāhā
To He who is the action of truth

- 243 -

ॐ साधवे स्वाहा

oṁ sādhave svāhā
To He who is efficient

- 244 -

ॐ जह्नवे स्वाहा

oṁ jahnave svāhā
To He who is the Ganges River

- 245 -

ॐ नारायणाय स्वाहा

oṁ nārāyaṇāya svāhā
To He who is the manifestation of consciousness

- 246 -

ॐ नराय स्वाहा

oṁ narāya svāhā
To He who is the embodiment of humanity

- 247 -

ॐ असंख्येयाय स्वाहा

oṁ asaṁkhyeyāya svāhā
To He who is innumerable

- 248 -

ॐ अप्रमेयात्मने स्वाहा

oṁ aprameyātmane svāhā
To He whose soul is immeasurable

- 249 -

ॐ विशिष्टाय स्वाहा

oṁ viśiṣṭāya svāhā
To He who is unique

- 250 -

ॐ शिष्टकृते स्वाहा

oṁ śiṣṭakṛte svāhā
To He who creates the ultimate

- 251 -

ॐ शुचये स्वाहा

oṁ śucaye svāhā
To He who is pure

- 252 -

ॐ सिद्धार्थाय स्वाहा

oṁ siddhārthāya svāhā
To He who is the object of attainment

- 253 -

ॐ शिद्धसङ्कल्पाय स्वाहा

oṁ śiddhasaṅkalpāya svāhā
To He who is the vow of discipline to attain perfection

- 254 -

ॐ सिद्धिदाय स्वाहा

oṁ siddhidāya svāhā
To He who grants perfection

- 255 -

ॐ सिद्धिसाधनाय स्वाहा

oṁ siddhisādhanāya svāhā
To He who is the discipline of perfection

- 256 -

ॐ वृषाहिने स्वाहा

oṁ vṛṣāhine svāhā
To He who fulfills all desires

- 257 -

ॐ वृषभाय स्वाहा

oṁ vṛṣabhāya svāhā
To He who grants power

- 258 -

ॐ विष्णवे स्वाहा

oṁ viṣṇave svāhā
To He who pervades all

- 259 -

ॐ वृषपर्वणे स्वाहा

oṁ vṛṣaparvaṇe svāhā
To He who rises to the ultimate

- 260 -

ॐ वृषोद्‌राय स्वाहा

oṁ vṛṣodarāya svāhā
To He who contains all

- 261 -

ॐ वर्द्धनाय स्वाहा

oṁ varddhanāya svāhā
To He who is evolution

- 262 -

ॐ वर्द्धमानाय स्वाहा

oṁ varddhamānāya svāhā
To He who is change with evolution

- 263 -

ॐ विविक्ताय स्वाहा

oṁ viviktāya svāhā
To He who is unaffected by change

- 264 -

ॐ स्तुतिसागराय स्वाहा

oṁ stutisāgarāya svāhā
To He who is the ocean of praise

- 265 -

ॐ सुभुजाय स्वाहा

oṁ subhujāya svāhā
To He who has excellent arms

- 266 -

ॐ दुर्धराय स्वाहा

oṁ durdharāya svāhā
To He who is difficult to contemplate

- 267 -

ॐ वाग्मिने स्वाहा

oṁ vāgmine svāhā
To He who is in all vibrations

- 268 -

ॐ महेन्द्राय स्वाहा

oṁ mahendrāya svāhā
To He who is the great ruler

- 269 -

ॐ वसुदाय स्वाहा

oṁ vasudāya svāhā
To He who is the giver of wealth

- 270 -

ॐ वसवे स्वाहा

oṁ vasave svāhā
To He who is wealth

- 271 -

ॐ नैकरूपाय स्वाहा

oṁ naikarūpāya svāhā
To He who is many forms

- 272 -

ॐ बृहद्रूपाय स्वाहा

oṁ bṛhadrūpāya svāhā
To He who is the form of the great

- 273 -

ॐ शिपिविष्टाय स्वाहा

oṁ śipiviṣṭaya svāhā
To He who is the source of luminous rays

- 274 -

ॐ प्रकाशनाय स्वाहा

oṁ prakāśanāya svāhā
To He who illuminates all

- 275 -

ॐ ओजस्तेजोद्युतिधराय स्वाहा

oṁ ojastejodyutidharāya svāhā
To He who supports divine light, both subtle and gross

- 276 -

ॐ प्रकाशात्मने स्वाहा

oṁ prakāśātmane svāhā
To He who is the soul of illumination

- 277 -

ॐ प्रतापनाय स्वाहा

oṁ pratāpanāya svāhā
To He who is courageous

- 278 -

ॐ ऋद्धाय स्वाहा

oṁ ṛddhāya svāhā
To He who is full of knowledge

- 279 -

ॐ स्पष्टाक्षराय स्वाहा

oṁ spaṣṭākṣarāya svāhā
To He who is clear letters

- 280 -

ॐ मन्त्राय स्वाहा

oṁ mantrāya svāhā
To He who is the mantra, words of divine inspiration

- 281 -

ॐ चन्द्रांशवे स्वाहा

oṁ candrāṁśave svāhā
To He who is the rays of the moon

- 282 -

ॐ भास्करद्युतये स्वाहा

oṁ bhāskaradyutaye svāhā
To He who is the light of the sun

- 283 -

ॐ अमृतांशूद्भवाय स्वाहा

oṁ amṛtāṁśūdbhavāya svāhā
To He who creates the portion of nectar

- 284 -

ॐ भानवे स्वाहा

oṁ bhānave svāhā
To He who is shining gloriously

- 285 -

ॐ शशिविन्दवे स्वाहा

oṁ śaśivindave svāhā
To He who is the bindu above the moon

- 286 -

ॐ सुरेश्वराय स्वाहा

oṁ sureśvarāya svāhā
To He who is the lord of the gods

- 287 -

ॐ औषधाय स्वाहा

oṁ auṣadhāya svāhā
To He who is the medicines, the healing plants

- 288 -

ॐ जगतःसेतवे स्वाहा

oṁ jagataḥsetave svāhā
To He who is the bridge across worldliness

- 289 -

ॐ सत्धर्मपराक्रमाय स्वाहा

oṁ satdharmaparākramāya svāhā
To He who protects the dharma

- 290 -

ॐ भूतभव्यभवन्नाथाय स्वाहा

oṁ bhūtabhavyabhavannāthāya svāhā
To He who is the lord of all time

- 291 -

ॐ पवनाय स्वाहा

oṁ pavanāya svāhā
To He who is pure

- 292 -

ॐ पावनाय स्वाहा

oṁ pāvanāya svāhā
To He who gives life to the wind

- 293 -

ॐ अनलाय स्वाहा

oṁ analāya svāhā
To He who is fire

- 294 -

ॐ कामघ्ने स्वाहा

oṁ kāmaghne svāhā
To He who destroys desire

- 295 -

ॐ कामकृते स्वाहा

oṁ kāmakṛte svāhā
To He who fulfills desire

- 296 -

ॐ कान्ताय स्वाहा

oṁ kāntāya svāhā
To He who is beauty enhanced by love

- 297 -

ॐ कामाय स्वाहा

oṁ kāmāya svāhā
To He who is all desire

- 298 -

ॐ कामप्रदाय स्वाहा

oṁ kāmapradāya svāhā
To He who bestows objects of desire

- 299 -

ॐ प्रभवे स्वाहा

oṁ prabhave svāhā
To He who is lord

- 300 -

ॐ युगादिकृते स्वाहा

oṁ yugādikṛte svāhā
To He who divides time

- 301 -

ॐ युगावर्त्ताय स्वाहा

oṁ yugāvarttāya svāhā
To He who creates time

- 302 -

ॐ नैकमायाय स्वाहा

oṁ naikamāyāya svāhā
To He who has various forms of māyā

- 303 -

ॐ महाशनाय स्वाहा

oṁ mahāśanāya svāhā
To He who eats all

- 304 -

ॐ अदृश्याय स्वाहा

oṁ adṛśyāya svāhā
To He who is imperceivable

- 305 -

ॐ अव्यक्तरूपाय स्वाहा

oṁ avyaktarūpāya svāhā
To He whose form is imperceivable

- 306 -

ॐ सहस्रजिते स्वाहा

oṁ sahasrajite svāhā
To He who defeats thousands of enemies

- 307 -

ॐ अनन्तजिते स्वाहा

oṁ anantajite svāhā
To He who defeats all

- 308 -

ॐ इष्टाय स्वाहा

oṁ iṣṭāya svāhā
To He who is desired

- 309 -

ॐ विशिष्टाय स्वाहा

oṁ viśiṣṭāya svāhā
To He who has special love for all

- 310 -

ॐ शिष्टेष्टाय स्वाहा

oṁ śiṣṭeṣṭāya svāhā
To He who is specially loved by all

- 311 -

ॐ शिखण्डिने स्वाहा

oṁ śikhaṇḍine svāhā
To He who is the peacock feather in the crown

- 312 -

ॐ नहुषाय स्वाहा

oṁ nahuṣāya svāhā
To He who is bound by illusion

- 313 -

ॐ वृषाय स्वाहा

oṁ vṛṣāya svāhā
To He who is the bull of discipline

- 314 -

ॐ क्रोधघ्ने स्वाहा

oṁ krodhaghne svāhā
To He who destroys anger

- 315 -

ॐ क्रोधकृत्कर्त्रे स्वाहा

oṁ krodhakṛtkartre svāhā
To He who becomes angry with the angered

- 316 -

ॐ विश्वबाहवे स्वाहा

oṁ viśvabāhave svāhā
To He whose arms pervade the universe

- 317 -

ॐ महीधराय स्वाहा

oṁ mahīdharāya svāhā
To He who supports the earth

- 318 -

ॐ अच्युताय स्वाहा

oṁ acyutāya svāhā
To He who is without change

- 319 -

ॐ प्रथिताय स्वाहा

oṁ prathitāya svāhā
To He who is foremost

- 320 -

ॐ प्राणाय स्वाहा

oṁ prāṇāya svāhā
To He who is life

\- 321 -

ॐ प्राणदाय स्वाहा

oṁ prāṇadāya svāhā
To He who is the giver of life

\- 322 -

ॐ वासवानुजाय स्वाहा

oṁ vāsavānujāya svāhā
To He who gives birth to wealth

\- 323 -

ॐ अपांनिधये स्वाहा

oṁ apāṁnidhaye svāhā
To He who is the great ocean

\- 324 -

ॐ अधिष्ठानाय स्वाहा

oṁ adhiṣṭhānāya svāhā
To He who is the substratum of existence

\- 325 -

ॐ अप्रमत्ताय स्वाहा

oṁ apramattāya svāhā
To He who is without error

\- 326 -

ॐ प्रतिष्ठिताय स्वाहा

oṁ pratiṣṭhitāya svāhā
To He who is established

\- 327 -

ॐ स्कन्दाय स्वाहा

oṁ skandāya svāhā
To He who is the commander of the armies of divinity

\- 328 -

ॐ स्कन्दधराय स्वाहा

oṁ skanddharāya svāhā
To He who supports the commander of the armies of divinity

- 329 -

ॐ धुर्याय स्वाहा

oṁ dhuryāya svāhā
To He who is difficult to support

- 330 -

ॐ वरदाय स्वाहा

oṁ varadāya svāhā
To He who is the giver of boons

- 331 -

ॐ वायुवाहनाय स्वाहा

oṁ vāyuvāhanāya svāhā
To He who is the winds

- 332 -

ॐ वासुदेवाय स्वाहा

oṁ vāsudevāya svāhā
To He who is the lord of the wealth of existence

- 333 -

ॐ बृहद्भानवे स्वाहा

oṁ bṛhadbhānave svāhā
To He whose rays of light are immense

- 334 -

ॐ आदिदेवाय स्वाहा

oṁ ādidevāya svāhā
To He who is the foremost deity

- 335 -

ॐ पुरन्दराय स्वाहा

oṁ purandarāya svāhā
To He who destroys demons

- 336 -

ॐ अशोकाय स्वाहा

oṁ aśokāya svāhā
To He who is devoid of grief

- 337 -

ॐ तारणाय स्वाहा

oṁ tāraṇāya svāhā
To He who takes others across the ocean of worldliness

- 338 -

ॐ ताराय स्वाहा

oṁ tārāya svāhā
To He who takes away fear

- 339 -

ॐ शूराय स्वाहा

oṁ śūrāya svāhā
To He who has great strength

- 340 -

ॐ शौरये स्वाहा

oṁ śauraye svāhā
To He who is son of the divine

- 341 -

ॐ जनेश्वराय स्वाहा

oṁ janeśvarāya svāhā
To He who is the supreme lord of the form of all beings

- 342 -

ॐ अनुकूलाय स्वाहा

oṁ anukūlāya svāhā
To He who is friend of the family of all

- 343 -

ॐ शतावर्त्ताय स्वाहा

oṁ śatāvarttāya svāhā
To He who comes a hundred times

- 344 -

ॐ पद्मिने स्वाहा

oṁ padmine svāhā
To He who is the bearer of a lotus

- 345 -

ॐ पद्मनिभेक्षणाय स्वाहा

oṁ padmanibhekṣaṇāya svāhā
To He who has lotus eyes

- 346 -

ॐ पद्मनाभाय स्वाहा

oṁ padmanābhāya svāhā
To He who has a lotus navel

- 347 -

ॐ अरविन्दाक्षाय स्वाहा

oṁ aravindākṣāya svāhā
To He who has lotus eyes

- 348 -

ॐ पद्मगर्भाय स्वाहा

oṁ padmagarbhāya svāhā
To He who is the womb of the lotus

- 349 -

ॐ शरीरभृते स्वाहा

oṁ śarīrabhṛte svāhā
To He who dwells within the body

- 350 -

ॐ महर्द्धये स्वाहा

oṁ maharddhaye svāhā
To He who possesses unquestionable sovereignty

- 351 -

ॐ ऋद्धाय स्वाहा

oṁ ṛddhāya svāhā
To He who is expansive

- 352 -

ॐ वृद्धात्मने स्वाहा

oṁ vṛddhātmane svāhā
To He who is the oldest soul

- 353 -

ॐ महाक्षाय स्वाहा

oṁ mahākṣāya svāhā
To He who has great eyes

- 354 -

ॐ गरुडध्वजाय स्वाहा

oṁ garuḍadhvajāya svāhā
To He who bears the king of birds on his flag

- 355 -

ॐ अतुलाय स्वाहा

oṁ atulāya svāhā
To He with whom none can be compared

- 356 -

ॐ शरभाय स्वाहा

oṁ śarabhāya svāhā
To He who is the luminous self

- 357 -

ॐ भीमाय स्वाहा

oṁ bhīmāya svāhā
To He who is terrible

- 358 -

ॐ समयज्ञाय स्वाहा

oṁ samayajñāya svāhā
To He who is the knower of time

- 359 -

ॐ हविर्हरये स्वाहा

oṁ havirharaye svāhā
To He who takes away oblations

- 360 -

ॐ सर्वलक्षणलक्षण्याय स्वाहा

oṁ sarvalakṣaṇalakṣaṇyāya svāhā
To He who is the definition of all definitions

- 361 -

ॐ लक्ष्मीवते स्वाहा

oṁ lakṣmīvate svāhā
To He who lives with Lakṣmī

- 362 -

ॐ समितिञ्जयाय स्वाहा

oṁ samitiñjayāya svāhā
To He who is always victorious

- 363 -

ॐ विक्षराय स्वाहा

oṁ vikṣarāya svāhā
To He who does not decay

- 364 -

ॐ रोहिताय स्वाहा

oṁ rohitāya svāhā
To He who is of reddish hue

- 365 -

ॐ मार्गाय स्वाहा

oṁ mārgāya svāhā
To He who is the way

- 366 -

ॐ हेतवे स्वाहा

oṁ hetave svāhā
To He who is motivation

- 367 -

ॐ दामोदराय स्वाहा

oṁ dāmodarāya svāhā
To He who is the generous giver

- 368 -

ॐ सहाय स्वाहा

oṁ sahāya svāhā
To He who endures all

- 369 -

ॐ महीधराय स्वाहा

oṁ mahīdharāya svāhā
To He who supports the earth

- 370 -

ॐ महाभागाय स्वाहा

oṁ mahābhāgāya svāhā
To He who is great fortune

- 371 -

ॐ वेगवते स्वाहा

oṁ vegavate svāhā
To He who is great speed

- 372 -

ॐ अमिताशनाय स्वाहा

oṁ amitāśanāya svāhā
To He who has an insatiable appetite

- 373 -

ॐ उद्भवाय स्वाहा

oṁ udbhavāya svāhā
To He from whom all are born

- 374 -

ॐ क्षोभणाय स्वाहा

oṁ kṣobhaṇāya svāhā
To He who shines

- 375 -

ॐ देवाय स्वाहा

oṁ devāya svāhā
To He who is God

- 376 -

ॐ श्रीगर्भाय स्वाहा

oṁ śrīgarbhāya svāhā
To He who is the womb of respect

- 377 -

ॐ परमेश्वराय स्वाहा

oṁ parameśvarāya svāhā
To He who is the supreme lord

- 378 -

ॐ करणाय स्वाहा

oṁ karaṇāya svāhā
To He who is the instrumental cause

- 379 -

ॐ कारणाय स्वाहा

oṁ kāraṇāya svāhā
To He who is the material cause

- 380 -

ॐ कर्त्रे स्वाहा

oṁ kartre svāhā
To He who is the actor

- 381 -

ॐ विकर्त्रे स्वाहा

oṁ vikartre svāhā
To He who is the recipient of action

- 382 -

ॐ गहनाय स्वाहा

oṁ gahanāya svāhā
To He who is hidden from view

- 383 -

ॐ गुहाय स्वाहा

oṁ guhāya svāhā
To He who is secret or hidden

- 384 -

ॐ व्यवसाय स्वाहा

oṁ vyavasāya svāhā
To He who is determined

- 385 -

ॐ व्यवस्थानाय स्वाहा

oṁ vyavasthānāya svāhā
To He who is situated in circumstances

- 386 -

ॐ संस्थानाय स्वाहा

oṁ saṁsthānāya svāhā
To He who is in all situations

- 387 -

ॐ स्थानदाय स्वाहा

oṁ sthānadāya svāhā
To He who is the giver of situations

- 388 -

ॐ ध्रुवाय स्वाहा

oṁ dhruvāya svāhā
To He who is fixed

- 389 -

ॐ परर्द्धये स्वाहा

oṁ pararddhaye svāhā
To He who is of the greatest majesty

- 390-

ॐ परमस्पष्टाय स्वाहा

oṁ paramaspaṣṭāya svāhā
To He who is the highest clarity

- 391 -

ॐ तुष्टाय स्वाहा

oṁ tuṣṭāya svāhā
To He who is satisfied

- 392 -

ॐ पुष्टाय स्वाहा

oṁ puṣṭāya svāhā
To He who is nourishment

- 393 -

ॐ शुभेक्षणाय स्वाहा

oṁ śubhekṣaṇāya svāhā
To He whose glance is auspicious

- 394 -

ॐ रामाय स्वाहा

oṁ rāmāya svāhā
To He who is the manifestation of the subtle body of consciousness

- 395 -

ॐ विरामाय स्वाहा

oṁ virāmāya svāhā
To He within whom all take rest

- 396 -

ॐ विरजसे स्वाहा

oṁ virajase svāhā
To He who is free from desire

- 397 -

ॐ मार्गाय स्वाहा

oṁ mārgāya svāhā
To He who is the way

- 398 -

ॐ नेयाय स्वाहा

oṁ neyāya svāhā
To He who shows the way

- 399 -

ॐ नयाय स्वाहा

oṁ nayāya svāhā
To He who moves all along the way

- 400 -

ॐ अनयाय स्वाहा

oṁ anayāya svāhā
To He who is not moved

- 401 -

ॐ वीराय स्वाहा

oṁ vīrāya svāhā
To He who is a hero

- 402 -

ॐ शक्तिमतां श्रेष्ठाय स्वाहा

oṁ śaktimatāṁ śreṣṭāya svāhā
To He who is supreme energy

- 403 -

ॐ धर्माय स्वाहा

oṁ dharmāya svāhā
To He who is the ideal of perfection

- 404 -

ॐ धर्मविदुत्तमाय स्वाहा

oṁ dharmaviduttamāya svāhā
To He who is the ambassador of dharma

- 405 -

ॐ वैकुण्ठाय स्वाहा

oṁ vaikuṇṭhāya svāhā
To He who is the supreme abode of Viṣṇu

- 406 -

ॐ पुरुषाय स्वाहा

oṁ puruṣāya svāhā
To He who is full, complete, perfect consciousness

- 407 -

ॐ प्राणाय स्वाहा

oṁ prāṇāya svāhā
To He who is life

- 408 -

ॐ प्राणदाय स्वाहा

oṁ prāṇadāya svāhā
To He who is the giver of life

- 409 -

ॐ प्रणवाय स्वाहा

oṁ praṇavāya svāhā
To He who is Oṁ

- 410 -

ॐ पृथवे स्वाहा

oṁ pṛthave svāhā
To He who is king of the earth

- 411 -

ॐ हिरण्यगर्भाय स्वाहा

oṁ hirṇyagarbhāya svāhā
To He who is the golden womb

- 412 -

ॐ शत्रुघ्नाय स्वाहा

oṁ śatrughnāya svāhā
To He who is the destroyer of enemies

- 413 -

ॐ व्याप्ताय स्वाहा

oṁ vyāptāya svāhā
To He who individualizes creation

- 414 -

ॐ वायवे स्वाहा

oṁ vāyave svāhā
To He who is the wind

- 415 -

ॐ अधोक्षजाय स्वाहा

oṁ adhokṣajāya svāhā
To He who is not bound by the senses

- 416 -

ॐ ऋतवे स्वाहा

oṁ ṛtave svāhā
To He who is beyond the seasons

- 417 -

ॐ सुदर्शनाय स्वाहा

oṁ sudarśanāya svāhā
To He who has excellent vision

- 418 -

ॐ कालाय स्वाहा

oṁ kālāya svāhā
To He who is time

- 419 -

ॐ परमेष्ठिने स्वाहा

oṁ parameṣṭhine svāhā
To He who is supreme desire

- 420 -

ॐ परिग्रहाय स्वाहा

oṁ parigrahāya svāhā
To He who is the receiver of all action

- 421 -

ॐ उग्राय स्वाहा

oṁ ugrāya svāhā
To He who is fierce

- 422 -

ॐ संवत्सराय स्वाहा

oṁ saṁvatsarāya svāhā
To He who is years

- 423 -

ॐ दक्षाय स्वाहा

oṁ dakṣāya svāhā
To He who is ability

- 424 -

ॐ विश्रामाय स्वाहा

oṁ viśrāmāya svāhā
To He who is rest

- 425 -

ॐ विश्वदक्षिणाय स्वाहा

oṁ viśvadakṣiṇāya svāhā
To He who is the gift of respect in the universe

- 426 -

ॐ विस्ताराय स्वाहा

oṁ vistārāya svāhā
To He who extends infinity

- 427 -

ॐ स्थावरस्थाणवे स्वाहा

oṁ sthāvarasthāṇave svāhā
To He who resides in hymns of praise

- 428 -

ॐ प्रमाणाय स्वाहा

oṁ pramāṇāya svāhā
To He who is proof

- 429 -

ॐ बीजमव्ययाय स्वाहा

oṁ bījamavyayāya svāhā
To He who is the unchanging seed

- 430 -

ॐ अर्थाय स्वाहा

oṁ arthāya svāhā
To He who is meaning

- 431 -

ॐ अनर्थाय स्वाहा

oṁ anarthāya svāhā
To He who is beyond definition

- 432 -

ॐ महाकोशाय स्वाहा

oṁ mahākośāya svāhā
To He who is the great covering

- 433 -

ॐ महाभोगाय स्वाहा

oṁ mahābhogāya svāhā
To He who is great enjoyment

- 434 -

ॐ महाधनाय स्वाहा

oṁ mahādhanāya svāhā
To He who is great wealth

- 435 -

ॐ अनिर्विण्णाय स्वाहा

oṁ anirviṇṇāya svāhā
To He who never tires

- 436 -

ॐ स्थविष्ठाय स्वाहा

oṁ sthaviṣṭhāya svāhā
To He who is established in perceivable existence

- 437 -

ॐ अभुवे स्वाहा

oṁ abhuve avāhā
To He who has not been born

- 438 -

ॐ धर्मयूपाय स्वाहा

oṁ dharmayūpāya svāhā
To He who is the sacrificial pillar

- 439 -

ॐ महामखाय स्वाहा

oṁ mahāmakhāya svāhā
To He who performs great sacrifices

- 440 -

ॐ नक्षत्रनेमिने स्वाहा

oṁ nakṣatranemine svāhā
To He who is the center of the light of the stars

- 441 -

ॐ नक्षत्रिणे स्वाहा

oṁ nakṣatriṇe svāhā
To He who is the lord of the stars

- 442 -

ॐ क्षमाय स्वाहा

oṁ kṣamāya svāhā
To He who demonstrates ability in all action

- 443 -

ॐ क्षामाय स्वाहा

oṁ kṣāmāya svāhā
To He who is resides in infinity

- 444 -

ॐ समीहनाय स्वाहा

oṁ samīhanāya svāhā
To He who only desires pure souls

- 445 -

ॐ यज्ञाय स्वाहा

oṁ yajñāya svāhā
To He who is the sacrifice of union

- 446 -

ॐ ईज्याय स्वाहा

oṁ ījyāya svāhā
To He who is the goal of the sacrifice of union

- 447 -

ॐ महेज्याय स्वाहा

oṁ mahejyāya svāhā
To He who is the most excellent who is worshipped

- 448 -

ॐ क्रतवे स्वाहा

oṁ kratave svāhā
To He who is the sacrificial post

- 449 -

ॐ सत्राय स्वाहा

oṁ satrāya svāhā
To He who protects the dharma of all

- 450 -

ॐ सताङ्गतये स्वाहा

oṁ satāṅgataye svāhā
To He who moves a hundred bodies

- 451 -

ॐ सर्वदर्शिने स्वाहा

oṁ sarvadarśine svāhā
To He who sees all

- 452 -

ॐ विमुक्तात्मने स्वाहा

oṁ vimuktātmane svāhā
To He who is the liberated soul

- 453 -

ॐ सर्वज्ञाय स्वाहा

oṁ sarvajñāya svāhā
To He who is the knower of all

- 454 -

ॐ ज्ञानमुत्तमाय स्वाहा

oṁ jñānamuttamāya svāhā
To He who is the highest wisdom

- 455 -

ॐ सुव्रताय स्वाहा

oṁ suvratāya svāhā
To He who is excellent vows

- 456 -

ॐ सुमुखाय स्वाहा

oṁ sumukhāya svāhā
To He who has an excellent face

- 457 -

ॐ सूक्ष्माय स्वाहा

oṁ sūkṣmāya svāhā
To He who is subtle

- 458 -

ॐ सुघोषाय स्वाहा

oṁ sughoṣāya svāhā
To He who is the excellent sound of God

- 459 -

ॐ सुखदाय स्वाहा

oṁ sukhadāya svāhā
To He who is the giver of happiness

- 460 -

ॐ सुहृदे स्वाहा

oṁ suhṛde svāhā
To He who is excellent delight

- 461 -

ॐ मनोहराय स्वाहा

oṁ manoharāya svāhā
To He who is beautiful

- 462 -

ॐ जितक्रोधाय स्वाहा

oṁ jitakrodhāya svāhā
To He who conquers anger

- 463 -

ॐ वीरबाहवे स्वाहा

oṁ vīrabāhave svāhā
To He who has heroic arms

- 464 -

ॐ विदारणाय स्वाहा

oṁ vidāraṇāya svāhā
To He who is the destroyer of evil

- 465 -

ॐ स्वापनाय स्वाहा

oṁ svāpanāya svāhā
To He who deludes all by māyā

- 466 -

ॐ स्ववशाय स्वाहा

oṁ svavaśāya svāhā
To He who is independent

- 467 -

ॐ व्यापिने स्वाहा

oṁ vyāpine svāhā
To He who pervades all

- 468 -

ॐ नैकात्मने स्वाहा

oṁ naikātmane svāhā
To He who is many souls

- 469 -

ॐ नैककर्मकृते स्वाहा

oṁ naikakarmakṛte svāhā
To He who performs many actions

- 470 -

ॐ वत्सराय स्वाहा

oṁ vatsarāya svāhā
To He who is the abode of all

- 471 -

ॐ वत्सलाय स्वाहा

oṁ vatsalāya svāhā
To He who is the lover of all

- 472 -

ॐ वत्सिने स्वाहा

oṁ vatsine svāhā
To He who is the father of all

- 473 -

ॐ रत्नागर्भाय स्वाहा

oṁ ratnāgarbhāya svāhā
To He who is the womb of jewels

- 474 -

ॐ धनेश्वराय स्वाहा

oṁ dhaneśvarāya svāhā
To He who is the supreme lord of wealth

- 475 -

ॐ धर्मगुप्तये स्वाहा

oṁ dharmaguptaye svāhā
To He who is the protector of the ideals of perfection

- 476 -

ॐ धर्मकृते स्वाहा

oṁ dharmakṛte svāhā
To He who is the performer of the ideals of perfection

- 477 -

ॐ धर्मिणे स्वाहा

oṁ dharmiṇe svāhā
To He who is the seer of the ideals of perfection

- 478 -

ॐ सते स्वाहा

oṁ sate svāhā
To He who is manifest in true existence

- 479 -

ॐ असते स्वाहा

oṁ asate svāhā
To He who is manifest in the perishable

- 480 -

ॐ क्षराय स्वाहा

oṁ kṣarāya svāhā
To He who is limited

- 481 -

ॐ अक्षराय स्वाहा

oṁ akṣarāya svāhā
To He who is unlimited

- 482 -

ॐ अविज्ञात्रे स्वाहा

oṁ avijñātre svāhā
To He who is in those who do not know

- 483 -

ॐ सहस्रांशवे स्वाहा

oṁ sahasrāṁśave svāhā
To He who has a thousand parts

- 484 -

ॐ विधात्रे स्वाहा

oṁ vidhātre svāhā
To He who is the creator

- 485 -

ॐ कृतलक्षणाय स्वाहा

oṁ kṛtalakṣaṇāya svāhā
To He who is the author of all criteria

- 486 -

ॐ गभस्तिनेमये स्वाहा

oṁ gabhastinemaye svāhā
To He who is the light of all lights

- 487 -

ॐ सत्त्वस्थाय स्वाहा

oṁ sattvasthāya svāhā
To He who is situated in truth

- 488 -

ॐ सिंहाय स्वाहा

oṁ siṁhāya svāhā
To He who has the courage of a lion

- 489 -

ॐ भूतमहेश्वराय स्वाहा

oṁ bhūtamaheśvarāya svāhā
To He who is the supreme lord of all existence

- 490 -

ॐ आदिदेवाय स्वाहा

oṁ ādidevāya svāhā
To He who is the foremost divinity

- 491 -

ॐ महादेवाय स्वाहा

oṁ mahādevāya svāhā
To He who is the great God

- 492 -

ॐ देवेशाय स्वाहा

oṁ deveśāya svāhā
To He who is supreme among Gods

- 493 -

ॐ देवभृद्गुरवे स्वाहा

oṁ devabhṛdgurave svāhā
To He who is the great Guru of the Gods

- 494 -

ॐ उत्तराय स्वाहा

oṁ uttarāya svāhā
To He who is in the north

- 495 -

ॐ गोपतये स्वाहा

oṁ gopataye svāhā
To He who is the lord of light

- 496 -

ॐ गोप्त्रे स्वाहा

oṁ goptre svāhā
To He who is hidden

- 497 -

ॐ ज्ञानगम्याय स्वाहा

oṁ jñānagamyāya svāhā
To He who moves with wisdom

- 498 -

ॐ पुरातनाय स्वाहा

oṁ purātanāya svāhā
To He who is most old

- 499 -

ॐ शरीरभूतभृते स्वाहा

oṁ śarirabhūtabhṛte svāhā
To He who is the creator of the elements of the body

- 500 -

ॐ भोक्त्रे स्वाहा

oṁ bhoktre svāhā
To He who is the enjoyer

- 501 -

ॐ कपीन्द्राय स्वाहा

oṁ kapīndrāya svāhā
To He who is the lord of monkeys

- 502 -

ॐ भूरिदक्षिणाय स्वाहा

oṁ bhūridakṣiṇāya svāhā
To He who gives offerings of respect graciously

- 503 -

ॐ सोमपाय स्वाहा

oṁ somapāya svāhā
To He who drinks the nectar of devotion

- 504 -

ॐ अमृतपाय स्वाहा

oṁ amṛtapāya svāhā
To He who drinks immortal nectar

- 505 -

ॐ सोमाय स्वाहा

oṁ somāya svāhā
To He who is the moon of devotion

- 506 -

ॐ पुरुजिते स्वाहा

oṁ purujite svāhā
To He who is completely victorious

- 507 -

ॐ पुरुषोत्तमाय स्वाहा

oṁ puruṣottamāya svāhā
To He who is full, complete, excellent consciousness

- 508 -

ॐ विनयाय स्वाहा

oṁ vinayāya svāhā
To He who has great humility

- 509 -

ॐ जयाय स्वाहा

oṁ jayāya svāhā
To He who is victorious

- 510 -

ॐ सत्यसन्धाय स्वाहा

oṁ satyasandhāya svāhā
To He who is the search for truth

- 511 -

ॐ दाशार्हाय स्वाहा

oṁ dāśārhāya svāhā
To He who is the recipient of all offerings

- 512 -

ॐ सात्वताम्पतये स्वाहा

oṁ sātvatāmpataye svāhā
To He who is the lord of all true beings

- 513 -

ॐ जीवाय स्वाहा

oṁ jīvāya svāhā
To He who is life

- 514 -

ॐ विनयितासाक्षिणे स्वाहा

oṁ vinayitāsākṣiṇe svāhā
To He who is the witness of the humble

- 515 -

ॐ मुकुन्दाय स्वाहा

oṁ mukundāya svāhā
To He who gives liberation

- 516 -

ॐ अमितविक्रमाय स्वाहा

oṁ amitavikramāya svāhā
To He who is immeasurable organization

- 517 -

ॐ अम्भोनिधये स्वाहा

oṁ ambhonidhaye svāhā
To He who is the root of devotion

- 518 -

ॐ अनन्तात्मने स्वाहा

oṁ anantātmane svāhā
To He who is the infinite soul

- 519 -

ॐ महोदधिशयाय स्वाहा

oṁ mahodadhiśayāya svāhā
To He who rests on the ocean of being

- 520 -

ॐ अन्तकाय स्वाहा

oṁ antakāya svāhā
To He who dissolves all creation

- 521 -

ॐ अजाय स्वाहा

oṁ ajāya svāhā
To He who is without birth or death

- 522 -

ॐ महार्हाय स्वाहा

oṁ mahārhāya svāhā
To He who is worthy of pūjā

- 523 -

ॐ स्वाभाव्याय स्वाहा

oṁ svābhāvyāya svāhā
To He who is established in his own attitude

- 524 -

ॐ जितामित्राय स्वाहा

oṁ jitāmitrāya svāhā
To He in whom friendship prevails

- 525 -

ॐ प्रमोदनाय स्वाहा

oṁ pramodanāya svāhā
To He who is always delighted

- 526 -

ॐ आनन्दाय स्वाहा

oṁ ānandāya svāhā
To He who is bliss

- 527 -

ॐ नन्दनाय स्वाहा

oṁ nandanāya svāhā
To He who is joy

- 528 -

ॐ नन्दाय स्वाहा

oṁ nandāya svāhā
To He who is delight

- 529 -

ॐ सत्यधर्मिणे स्वाहा

oṁ satyadharmiṇe svāhā
To He who is the true ideals of perfection

- 530 -

ॐ त्रिविक्रमाय स्वाहा

oṁ trivikramāya svāhā
To He who organizes the three worlds

- 531 -

ॐ महर्षिकपिलाचार्याय स्वाहा

oṁ maharṣkapilācāryāya svāhā
To He who is the great ṛṣi Kapilā

- 532 -

ॐ कृतज्ञाय स्वाहा

oṁ kṛtajñāya svāhā
To He who is the knower of action

- 533 -

ॐ मेदिनीपतये स्वाहा

oṁ medinīpataye svāhā
To He who is lord of the earth

- 534 -

ॐ त्रिपदाय स्वाहा

oṁ tripadāya svāhā
To He who took three steps

- 535 -

ॐ त्रिदशाध्यक्षाय स्वाहा

oṁ tridaśādhyakṣāya svāhā
To He who is the leader of all the threes

- 536 -

ॐ महाशृङ्गाय स्वाहा

oṁ mahāśṛṅgāya svāhā
To He who is with great horn

- 537 -

ॐ कृतान्तकृते स्वाहा

oṁ kṛtāntakṛte svāhā

To He who is the destroyer of creations

- 538 -

ॐ महावराहाय स्वाहा

oṁ mahāvarāhāya svāhā

To He who is the great boar of sacrifice

- 539 -

ॐ गोविन्दाय स्वाहा

oṁ govindāya svāhā

To He who is one-pointed light

- 540 -

ॐ सुषेणाय स्वाहा

oṁ suṣeṇāya svāhā

To He who is an excellent doctor

- 541 -

ॐ कनकाङ्गदिने स्वाहा

oṁ kanakāṅgadine svāhā

To He who wears golden ornaments on his arms

- 542 -

ॐ गुह्याय स्वाहा

oṁ guhyāya svāhā

To He who is the cave

- 543 -

ॐ गम्भीराय स्वाहा

oṁ gambhīrāya svāhā

To He who is serious

- 544 -

ॐ गहनाय स्वाहा

oṁ gahanāya svāhā

To He who cannot be penetrated

- 545 -

ॐ गुप्ताय स्वाहा

oṁ guptāya svāhā
To He who is hidden

- 546 -

ॐ चक्रगदाधराय स्वाहा

oṁ cakragadādharāya svāhā
To He who holds the discus and club

- 547 -

ॐ वेधसे स्वाहा

oṁ vedhase svāhā
To He who is the ultimate in the universe

- 548 -

ॐ स्वाङ्गाय स्वाहा

oṁ svāṅgāya svāhā
To He who is the embodiment of his self

- 549 -

ॐ अजिताय स्वाहा

oṁ ajitāya svāhā
To He who is undefeatable

- 550 -

ॐ कृष्णाय स्वाहा

oṁ kṛṣṇāya svāhā
To He who is dark

- 551 -

ॐ दृढाय स्वाहा

oṁ dṛḍhāya svāhā
To He who is of firm resolve

- 552 -

ॐ सङ्कर्षणाय स्वाहा

oṁ saṅkarṣaṇāya svāhā
To He who dissolves creation into his own self

- 553 -

ॐ वरुणाय स्वाहा

oṁ varuṇāya svāhā
To He who is the rays of the setting sun

- 554 -

ॐ वारुणाय स्वाहा

oṁ vāruṇāya svāhā
To He who is the son of Varuṇa, either Vaśiṣṭha or Agastya

- 555 -

ॐ वृक्षाय स्वाहा

oṁ vṛkṣāya svāhā
To He who is a tree

- 556 -

ॐ पुष्कराक्षाय स्वाहा

oṁ puṣkarākṣāya svāhā
To He who is protector of the cause of nourishment

- 557 -

ॐ महामनसे स्वाहा

oṁ mahāmanase svāhā
To He who is the great mind

- 558 -

ॐ भगवते स्वाहा

oṁ bhagavate svāhā
To He who is the supreme lord

- 559 -

ॐ भगघ्ने स्वाहा

oṁ bhagaghne svāhā
To He who dissolves creation

- 560 -

ॐ आनन्दिने स्वाहा

oṁ ānandine svāhā
To He who apportions bliss

- 561 -

ॐ वनमालिने स्वाहा

oṁ vanamāline svāhā
To He who cultivates the forest

- 562 -

ॐ हलायुधाय स्वाहा

oṁ halāyudhāya svāhā
To He who pulls the plow

- 563 -

ॐ आदित्याय स्वाहा

oṁ ādityāya svāhā
To He who is light without a second

- 564 -

ॐ ज्योतिरादित्याय स्वाहा

oṁ jyotirādityāya svāhā
To He who is indivisible light

- 565 -

ॐ सहिष्णवे स्वाहा

oṁ sahiṣṇave svāhā
To He who is with delight

- 566 -

ॐ गतिसत्तमाय स्वाहा

oṁ gatisattamāya svāhā
To He who moves with truth

- 567 -

ॐ सुधन्वने स्वाहा

oṁ sudhanvane svāhā
To He who is excellent wealth

- 568 -

ॐ खण्डपरशवे स्वाहा

oṁ khaṇḍaparaśave svāhā
To He who has many parts

- 569 -

ॐ दारुणाय स्वाहा

oṁ dāruṇāya svāhā
To He who is excellent

- 570 -

ॐ द्रविणप्रदाय स्वाहा

oṁ draviṇapradāya svāhā
To He who grants liberation to devotees

- 571 -

ॐ दिवस्पृशे स्वाहा

oṁ divaspṛśe svāhā
To He who imparts divine light

- 572 -

ॐ सर्वदृग्व्यासाय स्वाहा

oṁ sarvadṛgvyāsāya svāhā
To He who is most wise among the wise

- 573 -

ॐ वाचस्पतये स्वाहा

oṁ vācaspataye svāhā
To He who is the lord of vibrations

- 574 -

ॐ त्रिसाम्ने स्वाहा

oṁ trisāmne svāhā
To He who is the song of the three Vedas

- 575 -

ॐ सामगाय स्वाहा

oṁ sāmagāya svāhā
To He who is the singer of songs

- 576 -

ॐ साम्ने स्वाहा

oṁ sāmne svāhā
To He who is the Sāma Veda

- 577 -

ॐ निर्वाणाय स्वाहा

oṁ nirvārṇāya svāhā
To He who is the supreme unity

- 578 -

ॐ भेषजाय स्वाहा

oṁ bheṣajāya svāhā
To He who is the cure for all maladies

- 579 -

ॐ भिषजे स्वाहा

oṁ bhiṣaje svāhā
To He who is the best doctor

- 580 -

ॐ सन्यासकृते स्वाहा

oṁ sanyāsakṛte svāhā
To He who is the maker of sannyāsis

- 581 -

ॐ शमाय स्वाहा

oṁ śamāya svāhā
To He who is in equilibrium

- 582 -

ॐ शान्ताय स्वाहा

oṁ śāntāya svāhā
To He who is peaceful

- 583 -

ॐ निष्ठायै स्वाहा

oṁ niṣṭhāyai svāhā
To He who is disciplined

- 584 -

ॐ शान्त्यै स्वाहा

oṁ śāntyai svāhā
To He who exudes peace

\- 585 -

ॐ परायणाय स्वाहा

oṁ parāyaṇāya svāhā
To He who is the ultimate goal

\- 586 -

ॐ शुभाङ्गाय स्वाहा

oṁ śubhāṅgāya svāhā
To He whose body is extremely beautiful

\- 587 -

ॐ शान्तिदाय स्वाहा

oṁ śāntidāya svāhā
To He who is the giver of peace

\- 588 -

ॐ स्रष्टे स्वाहा

oṁ sraṣṭe svāhā
To He who gives birth to creation

\- 589 -

ॐ कुमुदाय स्वाहा

oṁ kumudāya svāhā
To He who is like the full moon

\- 590 -

ॐ कुवलेशयाय स्वाहा

oṁ kuvaleśayāya svāhā
To He who rests on the ocean of consciousness

\- 591 -

ॐ गोहिताय स्वाहा

oṁ gohitāya svāhā
To He who is the benefactor or delighter of delight

\- 592 -

ॐ गोपतये स्वाहा

oṁ gopataye svāhā
To He who is the lord of light

- 593 -

ॐ गोप्त्रे स्वाहा

oṁ goptre svāhā

To He who protects the perceivable universe hidden within

- 594 -

ॐ वृषभाक्षाय स्वाहा

oṁ vṛṣabhākṣāya svāhā

To He who sees through the eyes of dharma

- 595 -

ॐ वृषप्रियाय स्वाहा

oṁ vṛṣapriyāya svāhā

To He who delights in dharma

- 596 -

ॐ अनिवर्तिने स्वाहा

oṁ anivartine svāhā

To He who does not retreat

- 597 -

ॐ निवृत्तात्मने स्वाहा

oṁ nivṛttātmane svāhā

To He whose soul does not change

- 598 -

ॐ संक्षेप्त्रे स्वाहा

oṁ saṁkṣeptre svāhā

To He who dissolves existence into his being

- 599 -

ॐ क्षेमकृते स्वाहा

oṁ kṣemakṛte svāhā

To He who provides welfare to all

- 600 -

ॐ शिवाय स्वाहा

oṁ śivāya svāhā

To He who is the consciousness of infinite goodness

- 601 -

ॐ श्रीवत्सवक्षसे स्वाहा

oṁ śrīvatsavakṣase svāhā
To He who has the mark of respect on his chest

- 602 -

ॐ श्रीवासाय स्वाहा

oṁ śrīvāsāya svāhā
To He who resides in respect

- 603 -

ॐ श्रीपतये स्वाहा

oṁ śrīpataye svāhā
To He who is the lord of respect

- 604 -

ॐ श्रीमतां वराय स्वाहा

oṁ śrīmatāṁ varāya svāhā
To He who gives the boon of respect

- 605 -

ॐ श्रीदाय स्वाहा

oṁ śrīdāya svāhā
To He who gives respect

- 606 -

ॐ श्रीशाय स्वाहा

oṁ śrīśāya svāhā
To He who reposes in respect

- 607 -

ॐ श्रीनिवासाय स्वाहा

oṁ śrīnivāsāya svāhā
To He who dwells in respect

- 608 -

ॐ श्रीनिधये स्वाहा

oṁ śrīnidhaye svāhā
To He who is the discipline of respect

- 609 -

ॐ श्रीविभावनाय स्वाहा

oṁ śrīvibhāvanāya svāhā

To He who has the attitude of respect

- 610 -

ॐ श्रीधराय स्वाहा

oṁ śrīdharāya svāhā

To He who is the support of respect

- 611 -

ॐ श्रीकराय स्वाहा

oṁ śrīkarāya svāhā

To He who is the cause of respect

- 612 -

ॐ श्रेयसे स्वाहा

oṁ śreyase svāhā

To He who is the wisdom of respect

- 613 -

ॐ श्रीमते स्वाहा

oṁ śrīmate svāhā

To He who is respected

- 614 -

ॐ लोकत्रयाश्रयाय स्वाहा

oṁ lokatrayāśrayāya svāhā

To He who is the refuge of the three worlds

- 615 -

ॐ स्वाक्षाय स्वाहा

oṁ svākṣāya svāhā

To He who sees himself

- 616 -

ॐ स्वाङ्गाय स्वाहा

oṁ svāṅgāya svāhā

To He who embodies all

- 617 -

ॐ शतानन्दाय स्वाहा

oṁ śatānanadāya svāhā
To He who is one hundred times bliss

- 618 -

ॐ नन्दिने स्वाहा

oṁ nandine svāhā
To He who exudes bliss

- 619 -

ॐ ज्योतिर्गणेश्वराय स्वाहा

oṁ jyotirgaṇeśvarāya svāhā
To He who is the lord of the multitudes of light

- 620 -

ॐ विजितात्मने स्वाहा

oṁ vijitātmane svāhā
To He who is the undefeatable soul

- 621 -

ॐ विधेयात्मने स्वाहा

oṁ vidheyātmane svāhā
To He who is the disciplined soul

- 622 -

ॐ सत्कीर्तये स्वाहा

oṁ satkīrtaye svāhā
To He who is the performer of truth

- 623 -

ॐ छिन्नसंशयाय स्वाहा

oṁ chinnasaṁśayāya svāhā
To He who cuts apart doubts

- 624 -

ॐ उदीर्णाय स्वाहा

oṁ udīrṇāya svāhā
To He who holds aloft the universe

- 625 -

ॐ सर्वतश्चक्षुषे स्वाहा

oṁ sarvataścakṣuṣe svāhā

To He whose eyes see everywhere

- 626 -

ॐ अनीशाय स्वाहा

oṁ anīśāya svāhā

To He who is with none superior

- 627 -

ॐ शाश्वतस्थिराय स्वाहा

oṁ śāśvatasthirāya svāhā

To He who is fixed in the infinite

- 628 -

ॐ भूशयाय स्वाहा

oṁ bhūśayāya svāhā

To He who rests upon the earth

- 629 -

ॐ भूषणाय स्वाहा

oṁ bhūṣaṇāya svāhā

To He who is adorned with shining ornaments

- 630 -

ॐ भूतये स्वाहा

oṁ bhūtaye svāhā

To He who is all elements

- 631 -

ॐ विशोकाय स्वाहा

oṁ viśokāya svāhā

To He who is without grief

- 632 -

ॐ शोकनाशनाय स्वाहा

oṁ śokanāśanāya svāhā

To He who destroys grief

- 633 -

ॐ अर्चिष्मते स्वाहा

oṁ arciṣmate svāhā
To He who radiates light

- 634 -

ॐ अर्चिताय स्वाहा

oṁ arcitāya svāhā
To He who is worshipped

- 635 -

ॐ कुम्भाय स्वाहा

oṁ kumbhāya svāhā
To He who is the divine container

- 636 -

ॐ विशुद्धात्मने स्वाहा

oṁ viśuddhātmane svāhā
To He who is the pure soul

- 637 -

ॐ विशोधनाय स्वाहा

oṁ viśodhanāya svāhā
To He who is completely pure

- 638 -

ॐ अनिरुद्धाय स्वाहा

oṁ aniruddhāya svāhā
To He who cannot be defeated by enemies

- 639 -

ॐ अप्रतिरथाय स्वाहा

oṁ apratirathāya svāhā
To He who is without an opponent

- 640 -

ॐ प्रद्युम्नाय स्वाहा

oṁ pradhyumnāya svāhā
To He who possesses great strength and energy

- 641 -

ॐ अमितविक्रमाय स्वाहा

oṁ amitavikramāya svāhā
To He whose prowess cannot be measured

- 642 -

ॐ कालनेमिनिघ्ने स्वाहा

oṁ kālaneminighne svāhā
To He who destroys the time of darkness

- 643 -

ॐ वीराय स्वाहा

oṁ vīrāya svāhā
To He who is a hero

- 644 -

ॐ शौरये स्वाहा

oṁ śauraye svāhā
To He who has great heroism

- 645 -

ॐ शूरजनेश्वराय स्वाहा

oṁ śūrajaneśvarāya svāhā
To He who is the lord of beings human and divine

- 646 -

ॐ त्रिलोकात्मने स्वाहा

oṁ trilokātmane svāhā
To He who is the soul of the three worlds

- 647 -

ॐ त्रिलोकेशाय स्वाहा

oṁ trilokeśāya svāhā
To He who is the lord of the three worlds

- 648 -

ॐ केशवाय स्वाहा

oṁ keśavāya svāhā
To He who creates, protects, transforms

- 649 -

ॐ केशिघ्ने स्वाहा

oṁ keśighne svāhā
To He who destroys the enemies of the supreme

- 650 -

ॐ हरये स्वाहा

oṁ haraye svāhā
To He who takes away

- 651 -

ॐ कामदेवाय स्वाहा

oṁ kāmadevāya svāhā
To He who is the God of love, desire

- 652 -

ॐ कामपालाय स्वाहा

oṁ kāmapālāya svāhā
To He who is the protector of desire

- 653 -

ॐ कामिने स्वाहा

oṁ kāmine svāhā
To He who is this desire

- 654 -

ॐ कान्ताय स्वाहा

oṁ kāntāya svāhā
To He who is beauty enhanced by love

- 655 -

ॐ कृतागमाय स्वाहा

oṁ kṛtāgamāya svāhā
To He who is the bringer of action

- 656 -

ॐ अनिर्देश्यवपुषे स्वाहा

oṁ anirdeśyavapuṣe svāhā
To He who cannot be explained in words

- 657 -

ॐ विष्णवे स्वाहा

oṁ viṣṇave svāhā
To He who pervades the universe

- 658 -

ॐ वीराय स्वाहा

oṁ vīrāya svāhā
To He who is a hero

- 659 -

ॐ अनन्ताय स्वाहा

oṁ anantāya svāhā
To He who is infinite

- 660 -

ॐ धनञ्जयाय स्वाहा

oṁ dhanañjayāya svāhā
To He who is the victor over wealth

- 661 -

ॐ ब्रह्मन्याय स्वाहा

oṁ brahmanyāya svāhā
To He who belongs to the supreme

- 662 -

ॐ ब्रह्मकृते स्वाहा

oṁ brahmakṛte svāhā
To He who creates the supreme

- 663 -

ॐ ब्रह्माणे स्वाहा

oṁ brahmāṇe svāhā
To He who knows the supreme

- 664 -

ॐ ब्रह्मणे स्वाहा

oṁ brahmaṇe svāhā
To He who knows supreme knowledge

\- 665 -

ॐ ब्रह्मविवर्द्धनाय स्वाहा

oṁ brahmavivarddhanāya svāhā
To He who is the unchanging supreme

\- 666 -

ॐ ब्रह्मविदे स्वाहा

oṁ brahmavide svāhā
To He who is the supreme divinity

\- 667 -

ॐ ब्राह्मणाय स्वाहा

oṁ brāhmaṇāya svāhā
To He who is the knower of the ultimate divinity

\- 668 -

ॐ ब्रह्मिणे स्वाहा

oṁ brahmiṇe svāhā
To He who has the intrinsic nature of the supreme

\- 669 -

ॐ ब्रह्मज्ञाय स्वाहा

oṁ brahmajñāya svāhā
To He who lives in the supreme

\- 670 -

ॐ ब्राह्मणप्रियाय स्वाहा

oṁ brāhmaṇapriyāya svāhā
To He who is loved by knowers of the supreme

\- 671 -

ॐ महाक्रमाय स्वाहा

oṁ mahākramāya svāhā
To He whose steps are very great

\- 672 -

ॐ महाकर्मने स्वाहा

oṁ mahākarmane svāhā
To He who performs great works

- 673 -

ॐ महातेजसे स्वाहा

oṁ mahātejase svāhā
To He who emits great light

- 674 -

ॐ महोरगाय स्वाहा

oṁ mahoragāya svāhā
To He who is the great snake, Ananta

- 675 -

ॐ महाक्रतवे स्वाहा

oṁ mahākratave svāhā
To He who is the great yajña

- 676 -

ॐ महायज्वने स्वाहा

oṁ mahāyajvane svāhā
To He who performs great yajñas

- 677 -

ॐ महायज्ञाय स्वाहा

oṁ mahāyajñāya svāhā
To He whose intrinsic nature is a great yajña

- 678 -

ॐ महाहविषे स्वाहा

oṁ mahāhaviṣe svāhā
To He whose life is a great offering

- 679 -

ॐ स्तव्याय स्वाहा

oṁ stavyāya svāhā
To He who is worthy of praise in hymns

- 680 -

ॐ स्तवप्रियाय स्वाहा

oṁ stavapriyāya svāhā
To He whose love is expressed in hymns

\- 681 -

ॐ स्तोत्राय स्वाहा

oṁ stotrāya svāhā
To He who is the essence of divine song

\- 682 -

ॐ स्तुतये स्वाहा

oṁ stutaye svāhā
To He who is one with divine songs

\- 683 -

ॐ स्तोत्रे स्वाहा

oṁ stotre svāhā
To He who praises with divine songs

\- 684 -

ॐ रणप्रियाय स्वाहा

oṁ raṇapriyāya avāhā
To He who is ready for battle

\- 685 -

ॐ पूर्णाय स्वाहा

oṁ pūrṇāya svāhā
To He who is full, complete, perfect

\- 686 -

ॐ पूरायत्रे स्वाहा

oṁ pūrāyatre svāhā
To He who fulfills the desires of the mind

\- 687 -

ॐ पुण्याय स्वाहा

oṁ puṇyāya svāhā
To He who is pure

\- 688 -

ॐ पुण्यकीर्तये स्वाहा

oṁ puṇyakīrtaye svāhā
To He whose purity is famous

- 689 -

ॐ अनामयाय स्वाहा

oṁ anāmayāya svāhā
To He who has no disease

- 690 -

ॐ मनोजवाय स्वाहा

oṁ manojavāya svāhā
To He who comes with the speed of thought

- 691 -

ॐ तीथकराय स्वाहा

oṁ tīthakarāya svāhā
To He who is the great teacher of knowledge

- 692 -

ॐ वसुरेतसे स्वाहा

oṁ vasuretase svāhā
To He who is the seed of all things

- 693 -

ॐ वसुप्रदाय स्वाहा

oṁ vasupradāya svāhā
To He who gives imperishable wealth

- 694 -

ॐ वसुप्रदाय स्वाहा

oṁ vasupradāya svāhā
To He who gives imperishable wealth

- 695 -

ॐ वासुदेवाय स्वाहा

oṁ vāsudevāya svāhā
To He who is the God that dwells within all

- 696 -

ॐ वसवे स्वाहा

oṁ vasave svāhā
To He within whom all take refuge

- 697 -

ॐ वसुमनसे स्वाहा

oṁ vasumanase svāhā
To He who dwells within the thoughts of all

-698 -

ॐ हविषे स्वाहा

oṁ haviṣe svāhā
To He who is the sacred offering in sacrifice

- 699 -

ॐ सद्गतये स्वाहा

oṁ sadgataye svāhā
To He who is the goal of the truthful

- 700 -

ॐ सत्कृतये स्वाहा

oṁ satkṛtaye svāhā
To He whose every action is truth

- 701 -

ॐ सत्तायै स्वाहा

oṁ sattāyai svāhā
To He who is the one true existence

- 702 -

ॐ सद्भूतये स्वाहा

oṁ sadbhūtaye svāhā
To He who has extensive greatness

- 703 -

ॐ सत्परायणाय स्वाहा

oṁ satprāyaṇāya svāhā
To He who is the path and goal of the truthful

- 704 -

ॐ शूरसेनाय स्वाहा

oṁ śūrasenāya svāhā
To He who has a strong army

- 705 -

ॐ यदुश्रेष्ठाय स्वाहा

oṁ yaduśreṣṭhāya svāhā
To He who is most the excellent among cow herders

- 706 -

ॐ सन्निवासाय स्वाहा

oṁ sannivāsāya svāhā
To He who dwells with pure souls

- 707 -

ॐ सुयामुनाय स्वाहा

oṁ suyāmunāya svāhā
To He who is the excellent inhabitants along the Yamunā River

- 708 -

ॐ भूतावासाय स्वाहा

oṁ bhūtāvāsāya svāhā
To He who dwells in the great elements

- 709 -

ॐ वासुदेवाय स्वाहा

oṁ vāsudevāya svāhā
To He who is the God who dwells within all

- 710 -

ॐ सर्वासुनिलयाय स्वाहा

oṁ sarvāsunilayāya svāhā
To He who is the indestructible energy of life

- 711 -

ॐ अनलाय स्वाहा

oṁ analāya svāhā
To He whose energy has no limit

- 712 -

ॐ दर्पघ्ने स्वाहा

oṁ darpaghne svāhā
To He who destroys pride

- 713 -

ॐ दर्पदाय स्वाहा

oṁ darpadāya svāhā
To He who grants respect to those who move with God

- 714 -

ॐ दृप्ताय स्वाहा

oṁ dṛptāya svāhā
To He who gives bliss to the truthful

- 715 -

ॐ दुर्धराय स्वाहा

oṁ durdharāya svāhā
To He who is attained through difficult austerities

- 716 -

ॐ अपराजिताय स्वाहा

oṁ aparājitāya svāhā
To He who is undefeatable

- 717 -

ॐ विश्वमुर्तये स्वाहा

oṁ viśvamurtaye svāhā
To He who is the worshipful embodiment of the universe

- 718 -

ॐ महामूर्तये स्वाहा

oṁ mahāmūrtaye svāhā
To He who is the great form of worship

- 719 -

ॐ दीप्तमूर्तये स्वाहा

oṁ dīptamūrtaye svāhā
To He who is the worshipped embodiment of light

- 720 -

ॐ अमूर्तिमते स्वाहा

oṁ amūrtimate svāhā
To He who is beyond form

- 721 -

ॐ अनेकमूर्तये स्वाहा

oṁ anekamūrtaye svāhā
To He who has many forms

- 722 -

ॐ अव्यक्ताय स्वाहा

oṁ avyaktāya svāhā
To He who cannot be illuminated

- 723 -

ॐ शतमूर्तये स्वाहा

oṁ śatamūrtaye svāhā
To He who has innumerable forms

- 724 -

ॐ शताननाय स्वाहा

oṁ śatānanāya svāhā
To He who has innumerable heads

- 725 -

ॐ एकाय स्वाहा

oṁ ekāya svāhā
To He who is one

- 726 -

ॐ नैकाय स्वाहा

oṁ naikāya svāhā
To He who is many

- 727 -

ॐ सवाय स्वाहा

oṁ savāya svāhā
To He who is offered the soma with devotion

- 728 -

ॐ काय स्वाहा

oṁ kāya svāhā
To He whose intrinsic nature is bliss

- 729 -

ॐ कस्मै स्वाहा

oṁ kasmai svāhā
To He who is the unknown goal of life

- 730 -

ॐ यस्मै स्वाहा

oṁ yasmai svāhā
To He who is that which is self-existent

- 731 -

ॐ तस्मै स्वाहा

oṁ tasmai svāhā
To He who is that

- 732 -

ॐ पदमनुत्तमाय स्वाहा

oṁ padamanuttamāya svāhā
To He who has unequaled perfection

- 733 -

ॐ लोकबन्धवे स्वाहा

oṁ lokabandhave svāhā
To He who is the friend of the universe

- 734 -

ॐ लोकनाथाय स्वाहा

oṁ lokanāthāya svāhā
To He who is the lord of the universe

- 735 -

ॐ माधवाय स्वाहा

oṁ mādhavāya svāhā
To He who is sweet

- 736 -

ॐ भक्तवत्सलाय स्वाहा

oṁ bhaktavatsalāya svāhā
To He who is the most beloved by devotees

- 737 -

ॐ सुवर्णवर्णाय स्वाहा

oṁ suvarṇavarṇāya svāhā
To He who is of the color of excellent gold

- 738 -

ॐ हेमाङ्गाय स्वाहा

oṁ hemāṅgāya svāhā
To He whose body is golden

- 739 -

ॐ वराङ्गाय स्वाहा

oṁ varāṅgāya svāhā
To He whose body is extremely beautiful

- 740 -

ॐ चन्दनाङ्गदिने स्वाहा

oṁ candanāṅgadine svāhā
To He who wears beautiful armlets

- 741 -

ॐ वीरघ्ने स्वाहा

oṁ vīraghne svāhā
To He who destroys heroes

- 742 -

ॐ विषमाय स्वाहा

oṁ viṣamāya svāhā
To He who has no equal

- 743 -

ॐ शून्याय स्वाहा

oṁ śūnyāya svāhā
To He who is void

- 744 -

ॐ घृताशिषे स्वाहा

oṁ ghṛtāśiṣe svāhā
To He who is free from desire

- 745 -

ॐ अचलाय स्वाहा

oṁ acalāya svāhā
To He who does not move

- 746 -

ॐ चलाय स्वाहा

oṁ calāya svāhā
To He who always moves

- 747 -

ॐ अमानिने स्वाहा

oṁ amānine svāhā
To He who has no false pride

- 748 -

ॐ मानदाय स्वाहा

oṁ mānadāya svāhā
To He who confers respect upon devotees

- 749 -

ॐ मान्याय स्वाहा

oṁ mānyāya svāhā
To He who is the object of respect

- 750 -

ॐ लोकस्वामिने स्वाहा

oṁ lokasvāmine svāhā
To He who is the lord of the worlds

- 751 -

ॐ त्रिलोकधृषे स्वाहा

oṁ trilokadhṛṣe svāhā
To He who is the support of the three worlds

- 752 -

ॐ सुमेधसे स्वाहा

oṁ sumedhase svāhā
To He who has an excellent intellect filled with love

- 753 -

ॐ मेधजाय स्वाहा

oṁ medhajāya svāhā
To He who is born from the yajña

- 754 -

ॐ धन्याय स्वाहा

oṁ dhanyāya svāhā
To He to whom we are grateful

- 755 -

ॐ सत्यमेधसे स्वाहा

oṁ satyamedhase svāhā
To He who is the intellect of loving truth

- 756 -

ॐ धराधराय स्वाहा

oṁ dharādharāya svāhā
To He who is the support of all supports

- 757 -

ॐ तेजोवृषाय स्वाहा

oṁ tejovṛṣāya svāhā
To He who illuminates all souls

- 758 -

ॐ द्युतिधराय स्वाहा

oṁ dyutidharāya svāhā
To He who expresses the various natures of creation

- 759 -

ॐ सर्वशस्त्रभृतांवराय स्वाहा

oṁ sarvaśastrabhṛtāṁvarāya svāhā
To He who holds the most excellent weapons

- 760 -

ॐ प्रग्रहाय स्वाहा

oṁ pragrahāya svāhā
To He who accepts the worship of all

- 761 -

ॐ निग्रहाय स्वाहा

oṁ nigrahāya svāhā
To He who has disciplined the senses

- 762 -

ॐ व्यग्रहाय स्वाहा

oṁ vyagrahāya svāhā
To He who is free from desire

- 763 -

ॐ नैकशृङ्गाय स्वाहा

oṁ naikaśṛṅgāya svāhā
To He whose consciousness is always aware

- 764 -

ॐ गदाग्रजाय स्वाहा

oṁ gadāgrajāya svāhā
To He who is called with mantras

- 765 -

ॐ चतुर्मूर्त्तये स्वाहा

oṁ caturmūrttaye svāhā
To He who is worshipped in four forms

- 766 -

ॐ चतुर्बाहवे स्वाहा

oṁ caturbāhave svāhā
To He who has four arms

- 767 -

ॐ चतुर्व्यूहाय स्वाहा

oṁ caturvyūhāya svāhā
To He who has four formations

- 768 -

ॐ चतुर्गतये स्वाहा

oṁ caturgataye svāhā
To He who is the goal of the four castes

- 769 -

ॐ चतुरात्मने स्वाहा

oṁ caturātmane svāhā

To He who is free from desires and ego

- 770 -

ॐ चतुर्भावाय स्वाहा

oṁ caturbhāvāya svāhā

To He who has four attitudes

- 771 -

ॐ चतुर्वेदविदे स्वाहा

oṁ caturvedavide svāhā

To He who knows the four Vedas

- 772 -

ॐ एकपदे स्वाहा

oṁ ekapade svāhā

To He of whom only a small part can be perceived

- 773 -

ॐ समावर्ताय स्वाहा

oṁ samāvartāya svāhā

To He who turns the wheel of life

- 774 -

ॐ निवृत्तात्मने स्वाहा

oṁ nivṛttātmane svāhā

To He whose soul never changes

- 775 -

ॐ दुर्जयाय स्वाहा

oṁ durjayāya svāhā

To He who is impossible to defeat

- 776 -

ॐ दुरतिक्रमाय स्वाहा

oṁ duratikramāya svāhā

To He whose orders are obeyed

- 777 -

ॐ दुर्लभाय स्वाहा

oṁ durlabhāya svāhā

To He who is difficult to attain

- 778 -

ॐ दुर्गमाय स्वाहा

oṁ durgamāya svāhā

To He who is understood with difficulty

- 779 -

ॐ दुर्गाय स्वाहा

oṁ durgāya svāhā

To He who can only be reached with difficulty

- 780 -

ॐ दुरावासाय स्वाहा

oṁ durāvāsāya svāhā

To He who is found by those with great self-control

- 781 -

ॐ दुरारिघ्ने स्वाहा

oṁ durārighne svāhā

To He who destroys the performers of evil

- 782 -

ॐ शुभाङ्गाय स्वाहा

oṁ śubhāṅgāya svāhā

To He whose body is beautiful

- 783 -

ॐ लोकसारङ्गाय स्वाहा

oṁ lokasāraṅgāya svāhā

To He who knows all individual phenomena

- 784 -

ॐ सुतन्तवे स्वाहा

oṁ sutantave svāhā

To He who has an excellent body

- 785 -

ॐ तन्तुवर्धनाय स्वाहा

oṁ tantuvardhanāya svāhā
To He who protects all his children

- 786 -

ॐ इन्द्रकर्मणे स्वाहा

oṁ indrakarmaṇe svāhā
To He who rules over all action

- 787 -

ॐ महाकर्मणे स्वाहा

oṁ mahākarmaṇe svāhā
To He who performs all great action

- 788 -

ॐ कृतकर्मणे स्वाहा

oṁ kṛtakarmaṇe svāhā
To He whose every action is fulfilled

- 789 -

ॐ कृतागमाय स्वाहा

oṁ kṛtāgamāya svāhā
To He who has elucidated the Vedas

- 790 -

ॐ ऊद्भवाय स्वाहा

oṁ ūdbhavāya svāhā
To He who is the essence of all creation

- 791 -

ॐ सुन्दराय स्वाहा

oṁ sundarāya svāhā
To He who is beautiful

- 792 -

ॐ सुन्दाय स्वाहा

oṁ sundāya svāhā
To He who is compassionate

- 793 -

ॐ रत्ननाभाय स्वाहा

oṁ ratnanābhāya svāhā
To He who has a jewel in his navel

- 794 -

ॐ सुलोचनाय स्वाहा

oṁ sulocanāya svāhā
To He who has excellent eyes

- 795 -

ॐ अर्काय स्वाहा

oṁ arkāya svāhā
To He who illuminates the sun

- 796 -

ॐ वाजसनाय स्वाहा

oṁ vājasanāya svāhā
To He who grows all food

- 797 -

ॐ शृङ्गिणे स्वाहा

oṁ śṛiṅgiṇe svāhā
To He who has a horn

- 798 -

ॐ जयन्ताय स्वाहा

oṁ jayantāya svāhā
To He who is victorious over enemies

- 799 -

ॐ सर्वविज्ञयिने स्वाहा

oṁ sarvavijjayine svāhā
To He whose knowledge conquers all

- 800 -

ॐ सुवर्णबिन्दवे स्वाहा

oṁ suvarṇabindave svāhā
To He who is the excellent golden origin of existence

- 801 -

ॐ अक्षोभ्याय स्वाहा

oṁ akṣobhyāya svāhā
To He who is fixed in the infinite

- 802 -

ॐ सर्ववागीश्वरेश्वराय स्वाहा

oṁ sarvavāgīśvareśvarāya svāhā
To He who is the supreme lord of the goddess of all vibrations

- 803 -

ॐ महाह्रदाय स्वाहा

oṁ mahāhradāya svāhā
To He who gives great delight

- 804 -

ॐ महागर्त्ताय स्वाहा

oṁ mahāgarttāya svāhā
To He whose māyā is unknowable

- 805 -

ॐ महाभूताय स्वाहा

oṁ mahābhūtāya svāhā
To He who is the great existence

- 806 -

ॐ महानिधये स्वाहा

oṁ mahānidhaye svāhā
To He who is the great refuge

- 807 -

ॐ कुमुदाय स्वाहा

oṁ kumudāya svāhā
To He who gives bliss to the earth

- 808 -

ॐ कुन्दराय स्वाहा

oṁ kundarāya svāhā
To He who wore the form of a boar to raise the earth

\- 809 -

ॐ कुन्दाय स्वाहा

oṁ kundāya svāhā
To He who is like a beautiful flower

\- 810 -

ॐ पर्जन्याय स्वाहा

oṁ parjanyāya svāhā
To He who showers his grace

\- 811 -

ॐ पावनाय स्वाहा

oṁ pāvanāya svāhā
To He who makes all pure

\- 812 -

ॐ अनिलाय स्वाहा

oṁ anilāya svāhā
To He who is the breath of all life

\- 813 -

ॐ अमृताशाय स्वाहा

oṁ amṛitāśāya svāhā
To He whose desire is immortal bliss

\- 814 -

ॐ अमृतवपुषे स्वाहा

oṁ amṛtavapuṣe svāhā
To He who embodies immortal bliss

\- 815 -

ॐ सर्वज्ञाय स्वाहा

oṁ sarvajñāya svāhā
To He who knows all

\- 816 -

ॐ सर्वतोमुखाय स्वाहा

oṁ sarvatomukhāya svāhā
To He who is the face of all

- 817 -

ॐ सुलभाय स्वाहा

oṁ sulabhāya svāhā
To He who is easily attained

- 818 -

ॐ सुव्रताय स्वाहा

oṁ suvratāya svāhā
To He who has excellent vows

- 819 -

ॐ सिद्धाय स्वाहा

oṁ siddhāya svāhā
To He who has attained

- 820 -

ॐ शत्रुजिते स्वाहा

oṁ śatrujite svāhā
To He who destroys enemies

- 821 -

ॐ शत्रुतापनाय स्वाहा

oṁ śatrutāpanāya svāhā
To He who destroys enemies through austerities

- 822 -

ॐ न्यग्रोधाय स्वाहा

oṁ nyagrodhāya svāhā
To He who deludes all with his māyā

- 823 -

ॐ उदुम्बराय स्वाहा

oṁ udumbarāya svāhā
To He who nourishes all according to their needs

- 824 -

ॐ अश्वत्थाय स्वाहा

oṁ aśvatthāya svāhā
To He who takes the form of a tree

- 825 -

ॐ चाणूरान्ध्रनिषूदनाय स्वाहा

oṁ cāṇūrāndhraniṣūdanāya svāhā
To He who defeated the wrestler Chānūr

- 826 -

ॐ सहस्रार्चिषे स्वाहा

oṁ sahasrācirṣe svāhā
To He who emits a thousand rays

- 827 -

ॐ सप्तजिह्वाय स्वाहा

oṁ saptajihvāya svāhā
To He who is the seven tongues of fire

- 828 -

ॐ सप्तैधसे स्वाहा

oṁ saptaidhase svāhā
To He who bears the seven tongues of fire

- 829 -

ॐ सप्तवाहनाय स्वाहा

oṁ saptavāhanāya svāhā
To He who is carried by seven horses (the sun)

- 830 -

ॐ अमूर्तये स्वाहा

oṁ amūrtaye svāhā
To He who is beyond form

- 831 -

ॐ अनघाय स्वाहा

oṁ anaghāya svāhā
To He who has no fault or sin

- 832 -

ॐ अचिन्त्याय स्वाहा

oṁ acintyāya svāhā
To He who cannot be conceived

- 833 -

ॐ भयकृते स्वाहा

oṁ bhayakṛte svāhā
To He who instills fear

- 834 -

ॐ भयनाशनाय स्वाहा

oṁ bhayanāśanāya svāhā
To He who destroys fear

- 835 -

ॐ अणवे स्वाहा

oṁ aṇave svāhā
To He who is as small as an atom

- 836 -

ॐ वृहते स्वाहा

oṁ vṛhate svāhā
To He who is immense

- 837 -

ॐ कृशाय स्वाहा

oṁ kṛśāya svāhā
To He who is subtle

- 838 -

ॐ स्थूलाय स्वाहा

oṁ sthūlāya svāhā
To He who is gross

- 839 -

ॐ गुणभृते स्वाहा

oṁ guṇabhṛte svāhā
To He who is illuminated within qualities

- 840 -

ॐ निर्गुणाय स्वाहा

oṁ nigurṇāya svāhā
To He who is beyond all qualities

- 841 -

ॐ महते स्वाहा

oṁ mahate svāhā
To He who is great

- 842 -

ॐ अधृताय स्वाहा

oṁ adhṛtāya svāhā
To He who cannot be supported but is the support of all

- 843 -

ॐ स्वधृताय स्वाहा

oṁ svadhṛtāya svāhā
To He who supports himself

- 844 -

ॐ स्वास्याय स्वाहा

oṁ svāsyāya svāhā
To He whose face emits light

- 845 -

ॐ प्राग्वंशाय स्वाहा

oṁ prāgvaṁśāya svāhā
To He whose ancestors are ancient

- 846 -

ॐ वंशवर्द्धनाय स्वाहा

oṁ vaṁśavarddhanāya svāhā
To He whose relatives extend everywhere

- 847 -

ॐ भारभृते स्वाहा

oṁ bhārabhṛte svāhā
To He who carries the entire responsibility

- 848 -

ॐ कथिताय स्वाहा

oṁ kathitāya svāhā
To He whose story is continuously told

- 849 -

ॐ योगिने स्वाहा

oṁ yogine svāhā
To He who is known through yoga

- 850 -

ॐ योगीशाय स्वाहा

oṁ yogīśāya svāhā
To He who is the lord of all yogis

- 851 -

ॐ सर्वकामदाय स्वाहा

oṁ sarvakāmadāya svāhā
To He fulfills all desires

- 852 -

ॐ आश्रमाय स्वाहा

oṁ āśramāya svāhā
To He who gives refuge to all

- 853 -

ॐ श्रमणाय स्वाहा

oṁ śramaṇāya svāh
To He who performs all hard work

- 854 -

ॐ क्षामाय स्वाहा

oṁ kṣāmāya svāhā
To He who is the end for all beings

- 855 -

ॐ सुपर्णाय स्वाहा

oṁ suparṇāya svāhā
To He who is of excellent gold

- 856 -

ॐ वायुवाहनाय स्वाहा

oṁ vāyuvāhanāya svāhā
To He who is the carrier of the wind

\- 857 -

ॐ धनुर्धराय स्वाहा

oṁ dhanurdharāya svāhā
To He who is the most excellent of those who carry a bow

\- 858 -

ॐ धनुर्वेदाय स्वाहा

oṁ dhanurvedāya svāhā
To He who has the wisdom of weaponry

\- 859 -

ॐ दण्डाय स्वाहा

oṁ daṇḍāya svāhā
To He who disciplines the evil

\- 860 -

ॐ दमयित्रे स्वाहा

oṁ damayitre svāhā
To He who gives peace to the wicked

\- 861 -

ॐ दमाय स्वाहा

oṁ damāya avāhā
To He who controls the senses

\- 862 -

ॐ अपराजिताय स्वाहा

oṁ aparājitāya svāhā
To He who cannot be defeated

\- 863 -

ॐ सर्वसहाय स्वाहा

oṁ sarvasahāya svāhā
To He who helps all

\- 864 -

ॐ नियन्त्रे स्वाहा

oṁ niyantre svāhā
To He who controls the cosmos

- 865 -

ॐ नियमाय स्वाहा

oṁ niyamāya svāhā
To He who cannot be controlled

- 866 -

ॐ यमाय स्वाहा

oṁ yamāya svāhā
To He who is the ultimate controller

- 867 -

ॐ सत्त्ववते स्वाहा

oṁ sattvavate svāhā
To He who is the repository of truth

- 868 -

ॐ सात्त्विकाय स्वाहा

oṁ sāttvikāya svāhā
To He whose ornament is truth

- 869 -

ॐ सत्याय स्वाहा

oṁ satyāya svāhā
To He whose intrinsic nature is truth

- 870 -

ॐ सत्यधर्मपरायणाय स्वाहा

oṁ satyadharmaparāyaṇāya svāhā
To He who always acts in the ideal of perfection of truth

- 871 -

ॐ अभिप्रायाय स्वाहा

oṁ abhiprāyāya svāhā
To He who supports spiritual seekers from within the creation

- 872 -

ॐ प्रियार्हाय स्वाहा

oṁ priyārhāya svāhā
To He who is worthy of receiving love from all

- 873 -

ॐ अर्हाय स्वाहा

oṁ arhāya svāhā
To He who is worthy of worship from all

- 874 -

ॐ प्रियकृते स्वाहा

oṁ priyakṛte svāhā
To He who fulfills all that is dear to devotees

- 875 -

ॐ प्रीतिवर्धनाय स्वाहा

oṁ prītivardhanāya svāhā
To He whose love continually grows in devotee's hearts

- 876 -

ॐ विहायसगतये स्वाहा

oṁ vihāyasagataye svāhā
To He who dwells in the sky

- 877 -

ॐ ज्योतिषे स्वाहा

oṁ jyotiṣe svāhā
To He who is light

- 878 -

ॐ सुरुचये स्वाहा

oṁ surucaye svāhā
To He who has excellent illumination

- 879 -

ॐ हुतभुजे स्वाहा

oṁ hutabhuje svāhā
To He who enjoys all oblations

- 880 -

ॐ विभवे स्वाहा

oṁ vibhave svāhā
To He who is omnipresent

- 881 -

ॐ रवये स्वाहा

oṁ ravaye svāhā
To He who is the sun

- 882 -

ॐ विरोचनाय स्वाहा

oṁ virocanāya svāhā
To He who shines in various forms

- 883 -

ॐ सूर्याय स्वाहा

oṁ sūryāya svāhā
To He who is the sun

- 884 -

ॐ सवित्रे स्वाहा

oṁ savitre svāhā
To He who is the source of light

- 885 -

ॐ रविर्लोचनाय स्वाहा

oṁ ravirlocanāya svāhā
To He whose eyes are the sun

- 886 -

ॐ अनन्ताय स्वाहा

oṁ anantāya svāhā
To He who has no end

- 887 -

ॐ हुतभुजे स्वाहा

oṁ hutabhuje svāhā
To He who enjoys all offerings

- 888 -

ॐ भोक्त्रे स्वाहा

oṁ bhoktre svāhā
To He who is the enjoyer

- 889 -

ॐ सुखदाय स्वाहा

oṁ sukhadāya svāhā
To He who gives comfort

- 890 -

ॐ नैकजाय स्वाहा

oṁ naikajāya svāhā
To He who is unborn

- 891 -

ॐ अग्रजाय स्वाहा

oṁ agrajāya svāhā
To He who is before all who are born

- 892 -

ॐ अनिर्विण्णाय स्वाहा

oṁ anirviṇṇāya svāhā
To He who is full of hope

- 893 -

ॐ सदामर्षिणे स्वाहा

oṁ sadāmarṣiṇe svāhā
To He who always gives forgiveness

- 894 -

ॐ लोकाधिष्ठानाय स्वाहा

oṁ lokādhiṣṭhānāya svāhā
To He who worships for all beings

- 895 -

ॐ अद्भुताय स्वाहा

oṁ adbhutāya svāhā
To He who is wonderful and fantastic

- 896 -

ॐ सनाताय स्वाहा

oṁ sanātāya svāhā
To He who is primary existence from beginning to end

- 897 -

ॐ सनातनतमाय स्वाहा

oṁ sanātanatamāya svāhā
To He who is as old as eternity

- 898 -

ॐ कपिलाय स्वाहा

oṁ kapilāya svāhā
To He who came as Kapilā muni

- 899 -

ॐ कपये स्वाहा

oṁ kapaye svāhā
To He who came as a monkey

- 900 -

ॐ अपययाय स्वाहा

oṁ apyayāya svāhā
To He who is infinite

- 901 -

ॐ स्वस्तिदाय स्वाहा

oṁ svastidāya svāhā
To He who gives imperishable blessings

- 902 -

ॐ स्वस्तिकृते स्वाहा

oṁ svastikṛte svāhā
To He who makes imperishable blessings

- 903 -

ॐ स्वस्तिने स्वाहा

oṁ svastine svāhā
To He who loves imperishable blessings

- 904 -

ॐ स्वस्तिभुजे स्वाहा

oṁ svastibhuje svāhā
To He who enjoys imperishable blessings

- 905 -

ॐ स्वस्तिदक्षिणाय स्वाहा

oṁ svastidakṣiṇāya svāhā
To He who has the ability to give imperishable blessings

- 906 -

ॐ अरौद्राय स्वाहा

oṁ araudrāya svāhā
To He who has no anger

- 907 -

ॐ कुण्डलिने स्वाहा

oṁ kuṇḍaline svāhā
To He who has beautiful earrings

- 908 -

ॐ चक्रिणे स्वाहा

oṁ cakriṇe svāhā
To He who holds a discus

- 909 -

ॐ विक्रमिने स्वाहा

oṁ vikramine svāhā
To He who is most heroic

- 910 -

ॐ ऊर्जितशासनाय स्वाहा

oṁ ūjitaśāsanāya svāhā
To He whose orders must be followed

- 911-

ॐ सब्दातिगाय स्वाहा

oṁ sabdātigāya svāhā
To He whose meaning is beyond words

- 912 -

ॐ शब्दसहाय स्वाहा

oṁ śabdasahāya svāhā
To He who is propitiated by words

- 913 -

ॐ शिशिराय स्वाहा

oṁ śiśirāya svāhā
To He who is propitiated in cold and silent places

- 914 -

ॐ सर्वरीकराय स्वाहा

oṁ sarvarīkarāya svāhā
To He who creates darkness

- 915 -

ॐ अक्रूराय स्वाहा

oṁ akrūrāya svāhā
To He within whom there is no cruelty

- 916 -

ॐ पेशलाय स्वाहा

oṁ peśalāya svāhā
To He whose compassion has no end

- 917 -

ॐ दक्षाय स्वाहा

oṁ dakṣāya svāhā
To He who has ability

- 918 -

ॐ दक्षिणाय स्वाहा

oṁ dakṣiṇāya svāhā
To He who is the respectful offering to the guru or priest

- 919 -

ॐ क्षमिणांवराय स्वाहा

oṁ kṣamiṇāṁvarāya svāhā
To He who gives blessings of forgiveness

- 920 -

ॐ विद्वत्तमाय स्वाहा

oṁ vidvattamāya svāhā
To He who has excellent wisdom

- 921 -

ॐ वीतभयाय स्वाहा

oṁ vītabhayāya svāhā
To He who is free from fear

- 922 -

ॐ पुण्यश्रवणकीर्तनाय स्वाहा

oṁ puṇyaśravaṇakīrtanāya svāhā
To He who gives merit to devotees who hear or sing his songs of praise

- 923 -

ॐ उत्तारणाय स्वाहा

oṁ uttāraṇāya svāhā
To He who saves all from the ocean of attachment

- 924 -

ॐ दुष्कृतिघ्ने स्वाहा

oṁ duṣkṛtighne svāhā
To He who destroys impure actions

- 925 -

ॐ पुण्याय स्वाहा

oṁ puṇyāya svāhā
To He who is extremely pure

- 926 -

ॐ दुःस्वप्ननाशनाय स्वाहा

oṁ duḥsvapnanāśanāya svāhā
To He who destroys bad dreams

- 927 -

ॐ वीरघ्ने स्वाहा

oṁ vīraghne svāhā
To He who destroys the cycle of birth and death

- 928 -

ॐ रक्षणाय स्वाहा

oṁ rakṣaṇāya svāhā
To He who protects all beings

- 929 -

ॐ सद्भ्यो स्वाहा

oṁ sadbhyo svāhā
To He who dwells with great souls

- 930 -

ॐ जीवनाय स्वाहा

oṁ jīvanāya svāhā
To He who dwells with all life

- 931 -

ॐ पर्यवस्थिताय स्वाहा

oṁ paryavasthitāya svāhā
To He who dwells with all life in all places

- 932 -

ॐ अनन्तरूपाय स्वाहा

oṁ anantarūpāya svāhā
To He who has infinite form

- 933 -

ॐ अनन्तश्रिये स्वाहा

oṁ anantaśriye svāhā
To He who has infinite respect

- 934 -

ॐ जितमन्यवे स्वाहा

oṁ jitamanyave svāhā
To He who has conquered anger

- 935 -

ॐ भयापहाय स्वाहा

oṁ bhayāpahāya svāhā
To He who destroys fear

- 936 -

ॐ चतुरस्राय स्वाहा

oṁ caturasrāya svāhā
To He who treats all equally

- 937 -

ॐ गभीरात्मने स्वाहा

oṁ gabhīrātmane svāhā
To He whose soul is unfanthomable

- 938 -

ॐ विदिशाय स्वाहा

oṁ vidiśāya svāhā
To He who has great generosity

- 939 -

ॐ व्यादिशाय स्वाहा

oṁ vyādiśāya svāhā
To He who rules with both the capacity to order and to forgive

- 940 -

ॐ दिशाय स्वाहा

oṁ diśāya svāhā
To He who gives wisdom freely

- 941 -

ॐ अनादये स्वाहा

oṁ anādaye svāhā
To He who is the first cause of creation

- 942 -

ॐ भूर्भुवाय स्वाहा

oṁ bhūrbhuvāya svāhā
To He who is the gross body and the subtle body

- 943 -

ॐ लक्ष्म्यै स्वाहा

oṁ lakṣmyai svāhā
To He who is the goal of all

- 944 -

ॐ सुवीराय स्वाहा

oṁ suvīrāya svāhā
To He who incarnates to save the world

- 945 -

ॐ रुचिराङ्गदाय स्वाहा

oṁ rucirāṅgadāya svāhā
To He who has beautiful armlets

- 946 -

ॐ जननाय स्वाहा

oṁ jananāya svāhā
To He who is the father of creation

- 947 -

ॐ जनजन्मादये स्वाहा

oṁ janajanmādaye svāhā
To He who is the cause of the mother of all

- 948 -

ॐ भीमाय स्वाहा

oṁ bhīmāya svāhā
To He who appears fearful to the selfish

- 949 -

ॐ भीमपराक्रमाय स्वाहा

oṁ bhīmaparākramāya svāhā
To He whose prowess is terrifying to enemies

- 950 -

ॐ आधारनिलयाय स्वाहा

oṁ ādhāranilayāya svāhā
To He who is the fundamental support of all beings

- 951 -

ॐ धात्रे स्वाहा

oṁ dhātre svāhā
To He who is the creator

- 952 -

ॐ पुष्पहासाय स्वाहा

oṁ puṣpahāsāya svāhā
To He who shines like a flower

\- 953 -

ॐ प्रजागराय स्वाहा

oṁ prajāgarāya svāhā
To He who is free from I and mine

\- 954 -

ॐ ऊर्ध्वगाय स्वाहा

oṁ ūrdhvagāya svāhā
To He who adheres to the highest truth

\- 955 -

ॐ सत्पथाचाराय स्वाहा

oṁ satpathācārāya svāhā
To He who moves along the path of truth

\- 956 -

ॐ प्राणदाय स्वाहा

oṁ prāṇadāya svāhā
To He who is the giver of life

\- 957 -

ॐ प्रणवाय स्वाहा

oṁ praṇavāya svāhā
To He who is expressed by Oṁ

\- 958 -

ॐ पणाय स्वाहा

oṁ paṇāya svāhā
To He who gives names to all forms

\- 959 -

ॐ प्रमाणाय स्वाहा

oṁ pramāṇāya svāhā
To He who is the proof of truth

\- 960 -

ॐ प्राणनिलयाय स्वाहा

oṁ prāṇanilayāya svāhā
To He within whom resides all life

- 961 -

ॐ प्राणभृते स्वाहा

oṁ prāṇabhṛte svāhā
To He who supports all life

- 962 -

ॐ प्राणजीवनाय स्वाहा

oṁ prāṇajīvanāya svāhā
To He who is the life force of all that lives

- 963 -

ॐ तत्त्वाय स्वाहा

oṁ tattvāya svāhā
To He who is the principles of truth

- 964 -

ॐ तत्त्वविदे स्वाहा

oṁ tattvavide svāhā
To He who knows the principles

- 965 -

ॐ एकात्मने स्वाहा

oṁ ekātmane svāhā
To He who is the one universal soul

- 966 -

ॐ जन्ममृत्युजरातिगाय स्वाहा

oṁ janmamṛtyujarātigāya svāhā
To He who is beyond birth and death

- 967 -

ॐ भूर्भुवः स्वस्तरवे स्वाहा

oṁ bhūrbhuvaḥ svastarave svāhā
To He who is the nectar of life in the beings of the three worlds

- 968 -

ॐ ताराय स्वाहा

oṁ tārāya svāhā
To He who takes us all across the ocean of worldliness

- 969 -

ॐ सवित्रे स्वाहा

oṁ savitre svāhā
To He who is the light of all

- 970 -

ॐ प्रपितामहाय स्वाहा

oṁ prapitāmahāya svāhā
To He who is the grandfather of all

- 971 -

ॐ यज्ञाय स्वाहा

oṁ yajñāya svāhā
To He who is the essence of all sacrifice

- 972 -

ॐ यज्ञपतये स्वाहा

oṁ yajñapataye svāh
To He who is the lord of sacrifice

- 973 -

ॐ यज्वने स्वाहा

oṁ yajvane svāhā
To He who performs sacrifice

- 974 -

ॐ यज्ञाङ्गाय स्वाहा

oṁ yajñāṅgāya svāhā
To He who is the embodiment of sacrifice

- 975 -

ॐ यज्ञवाहनाय स्वाहा

oṁ yajñavāhanāya svāhā
To He who is the conveyance of sacrifice

- 976 -

ॐ यज्ञभृते स्वाहा

oṁ yajñabhṛte svāhā
To He who makes sacrifice happen

- 977 -

ॐ यज्ञकृते स्वाहा

oṁ yajñakṛte svāhā
To He who perform sacrifice

- 978 -

ॐ यज्ञिने स्वाहा

oṁ yajñine svāhā
To He who enjoys sacrifice

- 979 -

ॐ यज्ञभुजे स्वाहा

oṁ yajñabhuje svāhā
To He who is the supreme enjoyer of all sacrifice

- 980 -

ॐ यज्ञसाधनाय स्वाहा

oṁ yajñasādhanāya svāhā
To He who performs the sādhana of the fire sacrifice

- 981 -

ॐ यज्ञान्तकृते स्वाहा

oṁ yajñāntakṛte svāhā
To He who completes all sacrifices

- 982 -

ॐ यज्ञगुह्याय स्वाहा

oṁ yajñaguhyāya svāhā
To He who is the secret of all sacrifices

- 983 -

ॐ अन्नाय स्वाहा

oṁ annāya svāhā
To He who is the food of all

- 984 -

ॐ अन्नदाय स्वाहा

oṁ annadāya svāhā
To He who is the eater of all food

- 985 -

ॐ आत्मयोनये स्वाहा

oṁ ātmayonaye svāhā
To He who is the womb of the soul

- 986 -

ॐ स्वयञ्जाताय स्वाहा

oṁ svayañjātāya svāhā
To He who gives birth to himself

- 987 -

ॐ वैखानाय स्वाहा

oṁ vaikhānāya svāhā
To He who frees us from gross bondage

- 988 -

ॐ सामगायनाय स्वाहा

oṁ sāmagāyanāya svāhā
To He who sings songs of wisdom

- 989 -

ॐ देवकीनन्दनाय स्वाहा

oṁ devakīnandanāya svāhā
To He who is the son of Devakī, Kṛṣṇa

- 990 -

ॐ स्रष्ट्रे स्वाहा

oṁ sraṣṭre svāhā
To He who creates

- 991 -

ॐ क्षितीशाय स्वाहा

oṁ kṣitīśāya svāhā
To He who is the lord of the earth

- 992 -

ॐ पापनाशनाय स्वाहा

oṁ pāpanāśanāya svāhā
To He who destroys sin

- 993 -

ॐ शङ्खभृते स्वाहा

oṁ śaṅkhabhṛte svāhā
To He who holds the conch

- 994 -

ॐ नन्दकिने स्वाहा

oṁ nandakine svāhā
To He who bestows great bliss

- 995 -

ॐ चक्रिणे स्वाहा

oṁ cakriṇe svāhā
To He who holds the discuss

- 996 -

ॐ शार्ङ्गधन्वने स्वाहा

oṁ śārṅgadhanvane svāhā
To He who holds the bow

- 997 -

ॐ गदाधराय स्वाहा

oṁ gadādharāya svāhā
To He who holds the club

- 998 -

ॐ रथाङ्गपाणये स्वाहा

oṁ rathāṅgapāṇaye svāhā
To He who sings the praise of God

- 999 -

ॐ अक्षोभ्याय स्वाहा

oṁ akṣobhyāya svāhā
To He who never loses his peace

- 1000 -

ॐ सर्वप्रहरणायुधाय स्वाहा

oṁ sarvapraharaṇāyudhāya svāhā
To He who is always armed for battle

ॐ नमः इति

oṁ namaḥ iti
Oṁ we bow to the completion

इति विष्णुसहस्रनामावल्याः स्वाहाकारः समाप्तः

iti viṣṇusahasranāmāvalyāḥ svāhākāraḥ samāptaḥ
Thus ends the thousand names of Viṣṇu

The Pronunciation of Saṁskṛta Transliteration

a organ, sum
ā father
ai ai sle
au sauerkraut
b but
bh abhor
c church
ḍ dough
d dough (slightly toward the th sound of though)
ḍh adh ere
dh adhere
e prey
g go
gh doghouse
ḥ slight aspiration of preceding vowel
h hot
i it
ī police
j jump
jh lodgehouse
k kid
kh workhorse
l lug
ṁ resonant nasalization of preceding vowe
m mud
ṅ sing
ṇ under
ñ piñata
n no
o no
p pub
ph uphill
ṛ no English equivalent; a simple vowel r , such as appears in many Slavonic languages
r room
ś shawl (pronounced with a slight whistle; German sprechen)
ṣ shun
s sun
ṭ tomato
t water
ṭh Thailand
u push

ū	rude
v	vodka (midway between w and v)
y	yes

www.ingramcontent.com/pod-product-compliance
Lightning Source LLC
Chambersburg PA
CBHW021050080526
44587CB00010B/195
* 9 7 8 1 8 7 7 7 9 5 0 7 7 *